# WHY LAW ENFORCEMENT
# ORGANIZATIONS FAIL

# Why Law Enforcement Organizations Fail

*Mapping the Organizational Fault Lines in Policing*

SECOND EDITION

Patrick O'Hara

John Jay College of Criminal Justice
The City University of New York

Carolina Academic Press
Durham, North Carolina

Library of Congress Cataloging-in-Publication Data

O'Hara, Patrick, 1946-
Why law enforcement organizations fail : mapping the organizational fault
lines in policing / Patrick O'Hara. -- 2nd ed.
     p. cm.
Includes bibliographical references and index.
ISBN 978-1-59460-911-4 (alk. paper)
1. Law enforcement--United States. 2. Police administration--United
States. 3. Organizational effectiveness. I. Title.

HV8141.O53 2012
363.2'30973--dc23

                          2012021332

Carolina Academic Press
700 Kent Street
Durham, NC 27701
Telephone (919) 489-7486
Fax (919) 493-5668
www.cap-press.com

Printed in the United States of America

*To my wife, Kim, and my sons Christopher and Michael.*
*To my daughter-in-law Kristin, my mother-in-law Lyn*
*and my grandchildren Hudson, Rowan and Harper.*
*Nothing is more important than family and the love amongst us.*

*Bless you all.*

# CONTENTS

# Preface to the Second Edition

This book has enjoyed success.

Professors who adopted the book have let me know they consider it a valuable teaching tool.

Emails and surveys from students as far away as Australia have made plain that they get what the book is about and value what it has taught them.

Police agencies have used this book for executive training, a professional recognition that this book captures the realities of police management and organization.

Police officers have communicated with the author praising the book as accurately conveying the world in which they work.

What does everyone like?

The cases: Each is real, most are high profile. Each case is presented with minimal editorial interruption—the analytical bits follow. The cases engage students and readers in general. The analyses provoke thought and discussion and, in the college classroom, allow for other perspectives that students or faculty members choose to inject.

The writing—it is direct, jargon-free and dedicated above all to communicating clearly with the reader, whether it is Professor X, Student Y or Officer Z.

The conceptual clarity—the framework used by this book may not be the periodic table but does provide a way to sort diverse cases of dysfunction into categories that make sense to most readers.

So I haven't changed the book's basic approach.

The cases from the first edition are still here, so are the associated analyses and the overall framework. If you are a faculty member with lesson plans built around the first edition, those lessons will work just fine with this one. Same goes if you are a police trainer who has been using this book.

So what's new?

A new case has been added in each chapter, along with analyses that zero in on issues arising from each new case.

Most of the new cases occurred, or came to a climax, after the first edition went to press.

Bernard Kerik, once NYPD Commissioner and poised to become Homeland Security Secretary in late 2004, sits in federal prison as I write this. His exploitation of public office for his own enrichment makes his a marquee case for the chapter on "Resource Diversion."

In Hurricane Katrina's aftermath in 2005, a group of New Orleans police officers gunned down unarmed civilians doing nothing wrong, investigating officers conspired to cover it up, and jeering officers swarmed the halls at the subsequent state murder trial that was aborted by a technicality. The problematic New Orleans police culture revealed in the five years it took to bring the officers to justice in federal court makes this the capstone case in the chapter on "Cultural Deviation." Documentary material regarding this case, from Frontline and other sources, is available online as a powerful supplement to what's in this book.

In Luzerne County, Pennsylvania, the two judges who ran the Court of Common Pleas with an iron hand were railroading juvenile defendants to fill a detention facility whose principals were funneling money to the judges even as ground was broken for construction. This went on through early 2009, nearly a decade in all, and was abetted by an organization staffed via patronage and nepotism, run by favoritism and infected with a see/hear/speak no evil mindset. Those familiar with the first edition will recognize this as "Institutionalization" writ large, and that's the chapter where this case lands.

In 2011, a ticket-fixing scandal engulfed the NYPD after blindsiding Internal Affairs investigators who were looking into allegations about a drug dealing cop when the wiretaps lit up with union delegate officers arranging to "disappear" tickets issued to particular individuals. Despite police union leaders' unselfconscious claims that this was a widespread "professional courtesy," more than a dozen officers were indicted, including an Internal Affairs lieutenant accused of tipping off fellow cops. The allegations against the Internal Affairs lieutenant, plus the fact that Internal Affairs needed to stumble over a practice that was supposedly so common, earned this case a place in the "Oversight Failure" chapter.

Two older, but quite high profile and very teachable, cases have also been added.

The case of John O'Neill, who ran national security programs for the FBI right up until 9/11, has been added. O'Neill was the FBI's brain for all things Al Qaeda but got caught up in headquarters versus field office struggles and other issues that left him marginalized. His case has been added to the "Structural Failure" chapter. This case dovetails with, and adds to, the case in that chapter concerning border enforcement in the run-up to 9/11. The presence online of a dramatic Frontline documentary about O'Neill, *The Man Who Knew*, also makes this a very teachable case.

The Amadou Diallo case is iconic, memorialized by Bruce Springsteen's *41 Shots*. I chose not to put it in the first edition, but reading Malcolm Gladwell's *Blink* recently caused me to reconsider. *Blink* is about how we misperceive when information is coming at us fast and is very relevant to what happened that night in the Bronx, as Gladwell so well explains in his own analysis of the case. Those familiar with this book's first edition will know that the Eleanor Bumpurs shooting was analyzed in terms of the velocity of the situation and how other actors shaped the misperceptions that police then acted on. The Diallo case, therefore, has been coupled with the Bumpurs case in the "Normal Accident" chapter to further dissect these perception issues and also to illuminate NYPD policy and operational choices that had street crime officers chasing too hard after crime reductions that, mathematically, were becoming more and more elusive.

And, finally, there is Trayvon Martin.

This edition had basically been put to bed when the Martin case broke. But the more I pondered what happened, which at times I did in Florida during the uproar, the more I was convinced the case belonged in this book, even if the publisher had to wait. So, at the very end of this book the Trayvon Martin case has been added as a parting lesson on how public policy, as opposed to organizational dysfunction, can handcuff the police, camouflage crimes and put the public more at risk. My hope is that, in criminal justice programs where this book is used, students will have come from, or will be going on to, courses that deal with criminal justice-related policy. Let this case, so stark and so tragic, be a post-script or an entrée to the reader's understanding that sometimes policy, not policing, is the problem.

So, whether you are a student, a police officer, a professor or just an interested reader, I hope you enjoy this book. And, if you have a mind to, let me know what you think: patohara@jjay.cuny.edu.

Patrick O'Hara
April 2012

# ACKNOWLEDGMENTS

No author's labor comes to fruition without the help of many, and this is even truer of scholarly work. I have been blessed to be able to rely on so many friends, colleagues and family members.

Thanks, first and foremost, to my wife, Kim, whom I love for bearing with me as, insane and isolated, I wrapped up this edition. My gratitude also goes to Lyn Kenyon, whose home was my office for this book's final edits.

My friends and colleagues at John Jay College of Criminal Justice have given me unstinting support. This edition was made possible by a sabbatical that was just one way John Jay's President Jeremy Travis and Provost Jane Bowers encouraged my work. And this continues the college's support of my research for this book dating back to 2004, when another sabbatical and a small grant helped me along thanks to President Emeritus Gerald W. Lynch and Dr. Basil Wilson who was then provost.

Professor Maki Haberfeld and Dean Jannette Domingo, my partners in building the NYPD Certificate Program more than a decade ago, have remained go-to sources for testing my thinking about police and community. This book would never have been written were it not for our joint commitment to providing a credit-bearing opportunity for NYPD officers and commanders to engage with the realities of community and organization in a college-centered learning environment.

My thanks go as well to colleagues who helped review what I wrote. A professional eye was cast by retired Paterson, New Jersey, Police Director Michael Walker, long an NYPD Program mainstay as well as a faculty member at Passaic County Community College in New Jersey. The legacy material in this volume owes much to Dr. Harald Otto Schweizer of California State University Fresno, a primary reviewer for the first edition, which he convinced me to write. Eugene O'Donnell of John Jay's Law and Police Science Department shared his expertise on this go-around. Dr. Enzo Sainato, of Loyola University New Orleans, was also a reviewer, as was Caroline McMahon, Adjunct Professor of Public Management at John Jay, a proofreader for the first edition, who did that and more for this one.

I would also like to thank my long-time faculty colleagues at John Jay's Department of Public Management. Marilyn Rubin, my friend who directs John Jay's Master of Public Administration, goads me into writing. Someday I may achieve a reputation in organizational analysis equal to hers in public finance. Ned Benton, the Chair of the Department of Public Management did nothing, and everything. He has insulated our faculty from administrative distractions so well for so long that I have no frame of reference when colleagues at other universities complain about bureaucratic distractions from their teaching and research.

I'll not name every faculty member in my department, but I will thank them all. We are a family, and a pretty happy one at that, which helps all of us get more done. That said, a few specific recognitions are in order.

The feedback years ago of Professors Peter Mameli and Bob Sermier on what was little more than a series of concept papers shaped the book you see today, particularly the case study approach that Bob so champions. Professor Andy Rudyk—attorney, long-time federal executive and Renaissance man—has long been a go-to person for all manner of questions that stump me. Professor Adam Wandt is my guide for cutting edge online instruction and the creation of web-based supplements for this book. Lisa Rodriguez, our departmental administrator as well as an adjunct lecturer, always has my back

And everyone should have a friend and colleague like Dr. Judy-Lynne Peters. She also reviewed this volume, but her support goes far beyond that. She is always there to keep me honest, to tolerate my lunacy, and to catch my mistakes. I appreciate her more than she could ever know.

I also owe a debt to former colleagues now elsewhere, retired or, sadly, passed on, as is the case with Dr. Lotte Feinberg, who helped shape my thinking for this book back in 2004. Dr. Lydia Segal, now at Suffolk University, influenced my thinking when she was on faculty at John Jay and her book, *Battling Corruption in America's Public Schools*, was ahead of its time in identifying the critical fault lines in public education that are now such a policy focus.

Professors Jae Kim, Ellen Rosen and Flora Rothman, all now retired from my department, were major influences on what you are about to read. Dr. Kim, the MPA Program's organization and management expert when I arrived at John Jay, was always incisive, especially with his comparative skills. Ellen Rosen's legacy to me was the "Bureaupathology" course that is very much a foundation for this book. She remains, in her eighties, a person I hope to keep up with. Flora Rothman, when she retired last year, gave me yet more books about backfiring public policies and imploding public organizations. Those gifts shaped this edition much as her thinking helped shape the first.

Sharon Tanenhaus, a friend and confidante since my program director days at John Jay, is always ready with her support, even from faraway Florida. John Jay Professor Bob Fox, who recently retired but will not so easily escape being my friend, is always there for me whether the issue is academic—he knows more about stress in policing than I could ever learn—or personal. I am grateful to Bob and Sharon for everything.

I also must thank two individuals I count on for mental exercise: Fannette Druz Kaiser, my progressive friend who rages at folly, and Bill Fraher, who does the same, but more conservatively. Fannette has been politically active forever, and time hasn't dulled her edge. Bill Fraher, Police Chief (acting, as I write) of Paterson, New Jersey, regularly sends me organizational dysfunction articles, on higher education even! He is also a colleague, combining his political science graduate degree with full-spectrum law enforcement experience to teach organizational leadership to NYPD Program officers.

Jacob Marini, Director of Sponsored Programs at John Jay, provided critical support for the first edition of this book, as well as kind, supportive words for my work always. If his oft-threatened retirement ever happens, I owe him a game of golf.

Publisher Keith Sipe was kind enough to buy into the idea for this book years ago, and leads a Carolina Academic Press team that sold enough copies to warrant a second edition. Beth Hall, Tim Colton and Karen Clayton have also put up with me in the rush to deadline, and I also thank everyone else at the press for doing the heavy lifting to get this in print.

Finally, I am indebted to all the police officers and commanders who have sat in my classes educating me about policing. What I have learned from them has made this book immeasurably better.

And to anyone I forget, please forgive, for I owe you as much as anyone else.

# WHY LAW ENFORCEMENT ORGANIZATIONS FAIL

# Prologue

# Ordinary Disorder

The Federal Bureau of Investigation—what better icon for United States law enforcement could there be?

The FBI has been in the forefront of federal law enforcement since the early 1930s when it battled gangsters with colorful names like Machine Gun Kelley. That campaign was mounted by FBI Director J. Edgar Hoover, who had been appointed in 1924 with a mandate to reform what had been the lightly regarded Bureau of Investigation of the Department of Justice. Hoover reinvented the organization, which was renamed the Federal Bureau of Investigation in 1935, and he campaigned relentlessly to increase the FBI's power and autonomy until his death in 1972.[1]

Under Hoover, the FBI pursued missions linked to shifting public passions and fears. Hoover dedicated FBI units to counter-intelligence work against Nazi infiltration in the U.S. before and during the Second World War,[2] and similarly positioned the Bureau relative to Communism in the 1950s.[3] In the 1960s, he marshaled the FBI against die-hard segregationists violently resisting integration in the South,[4] even though Hoover's obsession with "communist influences" also led to surveillance of civil rights workers and leaders such as Martin Luther King.[5] As opposition to the Viet Nam war grew on college campuses in the 1960s, Hoover added student activists and progressive professors to the FBI watch list and made speeches that played on the anxieties of parents of college-age students.

Hoover constantly burnished the FBI's image. The 1959 movie *The FBI Story* featured a voice-over cameo by Hoover.[6] In 1965, *The FBI* began a nine-year run as a Sunday night TV staple in U.S. living rooms.[7] Washington visitors toured the agency, including the vaunted FBI Lab, which pioneered the scientific analysis of evidence. FBI profilers were zeroing in on serial killers years before fictional agent Clarice Starling matched wits with Hannibal "The Cannibal" Lecter in *Silence of the Lambs*.[8] Since 1930 the FBI has published the Uniform Crime Reports (UCR), the annual register of US crimes. The marquee "FBI Ten Most Wanted" list has been around since 1950. As symbolized by the red "deceased" banner the FBI attached to Osama Bin Laden's "most wanted" photo in 2011, the Bureau doesn't have to make the arrest to share the glory in a major case.

The FBI was not without critics, including Eleanor Roosevelt, a towering figure long after the 1945 death of her husband, Franklin, the 32nd President of the United States. Mrs. Roosevelt was the subject of voluminous FBI files and, because of her pointed critiques of the FBI, earned Hoover's barely disguised antipathy.[9] Congressional investigations later concluded that the FBI's counterintelligence surveillances of the 1960s and 1970s ensnared many more citizens exercising their rights than individuals engaged in criminally subversive behavior.[10]

Other embarrassments for the FBI followed upon Hoover's death. Sexual indiscretions and personal peccadilloes had been catalogued in raw FBI files that Hoover maintained in order to neutralize various public officials and influential citizens. Hoover's immediate successor, L. Patrick Gray, urged on by White House staff, destroyed files related to the Watergate burglary that ultimately led to the resignation of President Richard M. Nixon.[11] In 1993, FBI Director William Sessions was fired by President Clinton after the Justice Department's Office of Professional Responsibility questioned reimbursements and tax write-offs Sessions sought for trips to and from his home and other properties owned by family members.[12]

Despite these occasional critiques and stumbles, the FBI remained solid in the eyes of the media, the general public and, most importantly, Washington policy makers. Even critics were complimentary in a backhanded way, attributing to the FBI a tremendous capacity to suppress dissent. To most Americans, however, the FBI remained the exemplar of what a law enforcement agency should be.

The FBI's stock only rose when President Bill Clinton, in 1993, appointed Federal Judge Louis B. Freeh as Director. Led by Freeh, a former FBI field agent and federal prosecutor, the FBI seemed poised to reach new heights.

Instead the FBI imploded.

The fuse was the 1992 Ruby Ridge case that Freeh inherited from Sessions. Things went wrong from the start at Ruby Ridge in rural Idaho, home to Randy Weaver, a white separatist, and his family. Because Weaver had failed to appear for a court date on a weapons charge, a team of U.S. Marshals was staking out the family cabin when a gunfight erupted between the marshals, Weaver's fourteen-year-old son and Kevin Harris, a friend of the Weavers. When the smoke cleared, a U.S. Marshal was dead, as was Weaver's son and the family dog. The next day the FBI entered the fray with controversial "fire at will" rules of engagement, under which an FBI sniper inadvertently killed Weaver's wife while she was holding their infant child. Weaver and Harris, charged with murdering a federal agent, ultimately were acquitted on all but minor charges. The trial, and its extended aftermath, turned into an indictment of the FBI's tactics, forensic work and veracity that eventually led to obstruction of justice charges against one FBI agent, and administrative action against several Bureau officials.[13]

As the 1993 Ruby Ridge trial loomed, the FBI stumbled again, this time at the Waco, Texas compound of the Branch Davidian religious sect.[14] At Waco, the FBI took over after the Bureau of Alcohol, Tobacco and Firearms (ATF) had suffered twenty casualties, including four agents dead, while storming the compound in order to serve a weapons violations warrant. A siege ensued but, after six weeks of stalled negotiations, FBI officials who favored an assault gained the upper hand in the Bureau and in the Department of Justice, where Attorney General Janet Reno had just taken office. Concerned about allegations of child abuse and relying on understated FBI descriptions of the planned assault, Reno gave the go-ahead. Shortly after the assault began, flames consumed the compound, leaving over seventy Branch Davidians dead. Years of investigations followed and, as late as 2000, Congressional reports continued to dissect the FBI's decision-making and tactical choices at Waco.[15]

The FBI Lab's stellar reputation also took a dive in the 1990s. The qualifications of the lab's analysts, the validity of its testing procedures and its conclusions about evidence were all successfully challenged in case after case.[16] Federal prosecutors at times resorted to outside forensic experts instead of putting FBI lab personnel on the stand.[17]

The FBI seemed no better at spotting a rogue agent in its midst. On and off from 1985 to 2001 Robert Hanssen, an FBI agent working in counterintelligence, had given the Russians vital U.S. secrets, including the identity of Russian officials working for the U.S. Hanssen was an arrogant loner whose peculiar behavior did not escape the attention of his co-workers, or his FBI agent brother-in-law who alerted superiors that Hanssen might present a security risk. Nonetheless, Robert Hanssen progressed steadily to ever more responsible positions in the FBI that further enabled his deadly spying.[18]

Then there was 9/11. By August 2001, FBI field agents in Arizona and Minnesota had evidence pointing to a terrorist plot to hijack U.S. airliners. In Arizona, an FBI agent had documented flight training by several young males from the Middle East in the U.S. on visas. Agents in the Minneapolis field office were holding Zacarias Moussouai on immigration charges but their real concern was his recent jumbo jet flight training, French intelligence reports indicating terrorist ties and his adamant refusal to allow a search of his computer. But FBI headquarters failed to connect the dots. A search warrant request for Moussouai's computer was denied by headquarters in a process as much concerned with maintaining the FBI's internal and external boundaries as with the capture of terrorists. And, to compound the poor interagency coordination, FBI headquarters staff was not privy to CIA information that would have fleshed out the skeletal pattern of terrorist threat uncovered by the two FBI field offices.[19] When the twin towers of the World Trade Center fell, so too did the stock of the FBI.

The FBI's administrative operations have also been plagued. Entering the new millennium with multiple, antiquated and incompatible computer systems, the FBI began developing the Virtual Case File, which promised state of the art digital case management, at least until the plug was pulled after five years and $170 million dollars.[20] Sentinel, the FBI's next attempt at 21st century case management, was also beset by delays and cost overruns and had a May 2012 launch date as this book went to press.[21]

How could the vaunted FBI encounter this succession of debacles? And why did the FBI share the sorry stage with other federal agencies whose strategic and tactical blunders helped raise the curtain? Why did these failures so surprise administration officials and legislators who had long expressed confidence in the FBI, as well as in the CIA, even as the competitive codependency of the two agencies helped mask Hanssen's spying and shield the 9/11 terrorists?

One part of the answer is that we generally have a positive image of our organizations. That we put a lot of stock in the organizations that serve us is understandable. We buy from them, work in them and read about this or that organization brought to new heights by one or another dynamic executive. It's not that we are blind when a company like Lehman Brothers collapses, or management struggles destabilize premier companies like Disney or Morgan Stanley. We do notice, but that doesn't shatter our faith. We have too much invested in the success of all of our organizations to dwell very long on their failures.

We are similarly invested in our public organizations and particularly our law enforcement agencies, whose functions are so critical. But, paradoxically, we expect less of them. Our lowered expectations are shaped by a drumbeat of "bureaucracy bashing" from the media, from free market champions, and also from political candidates and office holders who shamelessly decry agency structures and processes they may have helped create. But bureaucracy, per se, is not pathological, though some elements peculiar to some government agencies, such as contradictory mandates, can pave the way for failure.

If bureaucracy is not to blame then what is? Organizational failures, public or private, are often blamed on inept executives, wrongheaded policies, or the errors of individual employees or particular work groups. The common theme of all of these "explanations" is that the cause of failure is localized, identifiable and can be surgically removed, leaving a healthy organization behind.

So, for instance, if you remove William Sessions, a less than inspiring leader who did not mesh smoothly with the FBI culture, all will be well. If your big city police agency is torn by a malignant corruption scandal, just identify and prosecute the corrupt cops, make some administrative reforms and pronounce the department cancer-free. These quick cures usually "work"—until the department continues off course under new leadership or a new group of renegade officers sets out to beat the system.

The fact of the matter, and the primary focus of this book, is that law enforcement agencies fail because of deeply rooted and largely hidden defects of structure, culture and collective behavior. These defects, far from being anomalies in law enforcement agencies or in organizations generally, are embedded in the everyday life of any organization. The FBI did not simply have a run of bad luck that produced discrete failures involving poor assessments of terrorist threats, breakdowns in the FBI Lab, or the presence of an agent-mole spying for Russia. Quite the contrary: Each of these FBI failures was deeply rooted in an agent-centric culture, structures focused on criminal investigation, a history of bureaucratic infighting and a continuing drive for dominance in federal law enforcement. Because common and enduring characteristics of organizations so often set the stage for failure, we ought to fully understand what those characteristics are and how they operate and interact.

So this book will endeavor to make sense of the factors that cause law enforcement organizations to fail. We will do this without cant or righteousness, mainly because organizations are neither inherently bad nor inhumane. In fact, organizations often fail because they provide such a supportive culture for humans to be humans, flaws and all. All organizations, law enforcement agencies included, provide fertile grounds for struggles over hierarchical ascent, the shunning of whistleblowers, policy sabotage by renegade workgroups, and abuse of the organization's resources by executives and rank-and-file alike.

Law enforcement organizations fail, and fail way more often than we think or even know, because all organizations are inherently fragile and error-prone. Particular organizations, moreover, cannot easily escape their essential natures. We should not be surprised when 21st century FBI operational problems feature "agents in charge" approaches and bureaucratic infighting—significant factors in the FBI's ten-year quest for a working integrated case management system. Nor should we be surprised when the next big city police scandal features a renegade group of cops administering street justice, planting evidence or using perjury to gain convictions.

We are going to walk the "dark side" of law enforcement organizations because it is there, always. The law enforcement agency in crisis ought to be carefully illuminated and thoroughly understood, not just demonized as a tool of class oppression or simplistically diagnosed as bungling bureaucracy. Understood, the "dark side" of any organization becomes at once less threatening and more manageable. Policy inertia can be recognized more quickly. Malignant individuals can be more easily spotted. Perverse incentives can be highlighted. Deviant cultures within the organization can be identified. Bankrupt philosophies can be confronted. Solutions can be targeted to address both the symptoms and the underlying conditions.

For those who study organizations, we hope to provide meaningful categories of organizational pathology that help make better sense of the many ways organizations fail. Pathology, per se, is a little utilized approach to organizational analysis but it shouldn't be. Most observers of police organization and management are fundamentally concerned with the health of the law enforcement enterprise. Without a strong understanding of the pathologies that threaten the well being of law enforcement agencies, policy makers, law enforcement executives and academics may well prescribe the wrong medicine.

The real-life cases that populate the categories will engage readers, students included. Some cases remain extremely high-profile and dealt major blows to the agencies involved—the New Orleans Police Department is still in recovery from its epic breakdowns during 2005's Hurricane Katrina. Other cases were more of an embarrassment to police departments forced to explain brainless policies, clueless management or slapstick employee behavior. Whether a disaster or an embarrassment, each case becomes an entrée to learning about how law enforcement organizations work and how they can work better. This book should be an accessible and effective learning tool in the criminal justice classroom and beyond.

This book is also intended for the men and women working on the front lines of law enforcement. I have taught both aspiring and in-career law enforcement officers at John Jay College of Criminal Justice of The City University of New York for over thirty years. The organizational dynamics course that led to this book was custom-built for New York City Police Department (NYPD) officers and commanders as part of a four-course sequence designed to heighten their awareness of how community and organizational factors impact the effectiveness and legitimacy of law enforcement. I have learned so much over the years from the law enforcement officers in my classes that this book is, in many ways, a repayment.

Law enforcement supervisors deserve the tools, which this book provides, for making sense of things gone wrong. When law enforcement organizations face crises or make high-profile mistakes, the maelstrom of criticism that erupts tempts executives to escape the storm by pinning blame on individual officers and commanders who are no more than the symptoms of a larger organizational disease. This book is about treating the diseases, not the symptoms; and discusses measured and judicious approaches that keep individual error in proper perspective. All things considered, the public safety agency is simply more manageable when supervisors and commanders understand the structural, cultural and behavioral factors that make their organizations vulnerable to crisis, turmoil and forced change.

For rank-and-file officers, I hope this book makes their agency less of an inscrutable "black box." Officers who better understand the perspectives, incentives and duties that guide managerial behavior are less likely to reflexively oppose initiatives from above. Satisfaction at work and long-term career success are also more likely for public safety personnel who really understand their agency's organizational dynamics, even and especially the potential for those dynamics to cause "crazy situations."

This book also speaks to the citizenry at large, including the student-citizens. All of us, sooner or later, have our wellbeing tightly coupled with one or another organization and, especially in this age of terror, we all must rely on the effectiveness of our law enforcement agencies. Each of us ought to be a discerning reviewer of reports concerning problems in our public safety services. More generally, we all ought to understand, and do what we can to strengthen, the essential fragility of the organizations that serve us, employ us and upon which so much of modern life depends.

# Endnotes

1. Bryan Burrough, *Public Enemies: America's Greatest Crime Wave and the Birth of the FBI, 1933–34* (New York: Penguin, 2004).

2. G. Gregg Webb, "New Insights into J. Edgar Hoover's Role," *Studies in Intelligence* 48, no. 1 (2004), http://www.cia.gov/csi/studies/vol48no1/index.html (Accessed April 1, 2005). See also Rob Evans and David Hencke, "Wallis Simpson, The Nazi Minister, The Telltale Monk and An FBI Plot," *The Guardian*, June 29, 2002. http://www.guardian.co.uk/uk_news/story/0,3604,746297,00.html (Accessed April 15, 2005)

3. Ellen W. Schrecker, *The Age of McCarthyism: A Brief History with Documents,* (Boston: Bedford, 1994).

4. Federal Bureau of Investigation, *History of the FBI, Postwar America: 1945—1960s.* Federal Bureau of Investigation, http://www.fbi.gov/libref/historic/history/postwar.htm (Accessed April 15, 2005).

5. Athan G. Theoharis, "The FBI and the Politics of Surveillance, 1908–1985," *Criminal Justice Review* 15, no. 2 (1990): 226.

6. L. Wayne Hicks, "J. Edgar Hoover and the FBI," *TV Party*, http://www.tvparty.com/tvp-AC/actfbi.html (Accessed February 27, 2005).

7. Ibid.

8. Thomas Harris, The Silence of the Lambs (New York: St. Martin's Press, 1988).

9. *American Experience: Eleanor Roosevelt.* Prod. WGBH/PBS, http://www.pbs.org/wgbh/amex/eleanor/filmmore/transcript/transcript2.html (Accessed February 28, 2005).

10. U.S. Senate Select Committee to Study Governmental Operations with Respect to Intelligence Operations (Church Committee), *Final Report—Book II, Intelligence Activities and the Rights of Americans*, 94th Cong., 2d sess, 1976, S. Rep. 94-755.

11. Ronald Kessler, *The Bureau: The Secret History of the FBI* (New York: St. Martin's Press, 2002): 181.

12. Henry J. Reske, "FBI Head Rebuts Report," *ABA Journal* 79 (Mar 1993): 29.

13. U.S. Department of Justice, *Report Regarding Internal Investigation of Shootings at Ruby Ridge, Idaho during the Arrest of Randy Weaver, Court TV Online*, http://www.courttv.com/archive/legaldocs/government/rubyridge.html (Accessed April 1, 2005).

14. Dick J. Reavis, *The Ashes of Waco: An Investigation,* (Syracuse, New York: Syracuse University Press, 1998).

15. U.S. House of Representatives, Committee on Government Reform, *The Tragedy at Waco: New Evidence Examined,* 106th Cong., 2nd Sess., 2000, H. Rep. 106–1037

16. John F. Kelly and Phillip K. Wearne, *Tainting Evidence: Inside the Scandals at the FBI Crime Lab* (New York: The Free Press, 1998).

17. Ibid., 142.

18. David Wise, *Spy: The Inside Story of How the FBI's Robert Hanssen Betrayed America* (New York: Random House, 2002).

19. National Commission on Terrorist Attacks Upon the United States, *The 9/11 Commission Report: Final Report of the National Commission on Terrorist Attacks Upon the United States* (New York: W.W. Norton, 2003).

20. Harry Goldstein, "Who Killed the Virtual Case File," IEEE Spectrum 42, no. 3 (September 2005), 24–35.

21. Alice Lipowicz, "Latest Sentinel Delay Sparks Spat with IG." *Federal Computer Week,* January 3, 2012.

# CHAPTER ONE

# DIAGNOSING ORGANIZATIONAL DYSFUNCTION IN POLICING

This purpose of this book is to develop a more applied understanding of why law enforcement organizations fail. Plenty is written about law enforcement failures. Numerous books and articles address prominent cases, such as the 1985 confrontation involving the Philadelphia Police Department and the MOVE group, in which eleven of the group's members died and two city blocks were burned to the ground. Much of the analysis is deductive, flowing from wider perspectives on race and class,[1] discourse analysis[2] or conflict management.[3] Official reports, on the other hand, are inductive by nature, building from facts towards conclusions, but strong-willed and opinionated fact-finders often shape those conclusions. Two members of the Philadelphia Special Investigation Commission, impaneled in the aftermath of the MOVE incident, filed separate strongly worded opinions taking issue with the equally powerful conclusions of the majority of the commissioners.[4]

Having numerous, varied and frequently passionate critiques of a particular law enforcement failure tends to generate as much, if not more, heat than light. At best, the reports and critical analyses lead to the adoption of positive reforms in a specific law enforcement agency and/or specific police operations. At worst, explanation and suggested remedies emerge from the clash of strongly voiced interpretations mediated on a public stage, which allows the targeted law enforcement agency and its members to dismiss and resist these "radical" or "political" prescriptions.

## Discerning Management Failure

Two law enforcement debacles underscore how a variety of explanations can emerge from similar failures in police strategy and tactics. One is the final FBI assault on the Branch Davidians of Waco, Texas in 1993. The other is the assault of the Philadelphia Police Department on the MOVE organization in 1985.

The similarities were many. In each case:

- Armed clashes between law enforcement officers and the group had occurred earlier.
- Law enforcement officers had died in those clashes.
- Each group was cult-like, with members blindly devoted to their leader.
- Each leader preached the inevitability of an apocalyptic clash with law enforcement.
- A "hostage" element existed—women and children were in the besieged quarters.
- Attempts to get the women and/or children out prior to the assault were mostly (Waco) or completely (Philadelphia) a failure.
- Extended, fruitless negotiations with unwavering group members put proponents of a tactical assault by law enforcement in the driver's seat.
- The sudden shift to an assault option led to hastily developed plans and overkill tactics.
- The assaults had disastrous outcomes, each residence burned to the ground, killing men, women and children.[5]

These similarities, however, need to be teased out of the divergent critiques leveled in the two cases. Activists in Philadelphia and around the world saw racism in the disastrous assault by a mostly white police department against the African Americans of MOVE. The Special Investigation Commission blamed the inept handling of MOVE by three successive city administrations, but saved some of its sharpest criticisms for Mayor Wilson Goode. Goode, once he had ordered the assault, reverted to the hands off posture that he had assumed for more than a year as tensions escalated between MOVE and the surrounding, largely African-American, neighborhood. The commission saw this as an abdication of leadership by Goode who, as Philadelphia's first African-American mayor, had good reason to be actively engaged both before and during the police action. But the commission also concluded that the police commissioner was grossly negligent in planning and carrying out the assault,[6] and one of the commissioners strongly believed the police had acted criminally.[7]

The Waco siege lacked a racial element, but did begin with a dubious firearms charge and ended in a holocaust. This energized libertarian and pro-gun groups who blamed the ATF, the FBI and the Department of Justice for criminalizing weapons possession and persecuting the practice of particular religions. The Internet was awash for years with speculation about the ulterior and/or sinister motives behind the actions of newly appointed Attorney General Janet Reno, her Justice Department subordinates, the FBI and the military with respect to the Waco assault. One individual mobilized by these dark interpretations was Timothy McVeigh, who in 1995 blew up the federal office building in Oklahoma City, killing 168, on the second anniversary of the Waco fire.[8] What happened at Waco remained in dispute into the new millennium when a 2000 Congressional Report, not surprisingly featuring majority and dissenting opinions, was delving into new revelations.[9]

Beyond mobilized activists, few believed at the time that racism was at the heart of the MOVE assault, or that a conspiracy to destroy the First and Second Amendments set the Waco siege in motion. Most Philadelphians, including MOVE's African American neighbors who for years prodded the city to act, viewed the group as inflammatory, threatening and disruptive.[10] At Waco, the FBI raid, tragic as it was, ended a crime scene siege of a group caught on tape killing ATF agents. Most Americans, who had seen these tapes over and over, did not see the FBI as an agent of a gun suppression conspiracy. Yet these agenda-linked charges of racism and fascist conspiracy, leveled fervently for years on end, have taken on a validity born of endurance as much as anything else. Obscured by this cacophony were the failures of organization and management that provided the proximate sparks that ignited the conflagrations in Waco and Philadelphia.

Little improvement in policing, per se, derives from analyses of law enforcement failures premised on embedded organizational racism or an abiding institutional disdain for the Constitution. Racism does at times manifest itself in law enforcement failures, as does playing fast and loose with the Constitution, and we will consider cases of both types in this book. But as blanket statements, these assertions are false. Most police professionals express respect for both diversity and the Constitution.[11] And, even to the extent that some do not, blanket charges indict innocent and guilty alike, thus instigating a collective defensiveness that only impedes officers from better understanding the communities they patrol and the rights of citizens with whom they interact.

There is another problem with applying overarching motivations as summary diagnoses of organizational failure. Mindset and motivation are elusive concepts in general, and specific worldviews are hard to pin down, easy to deny, difficult to reverse and not necessarily linked to action. If some cops are biased towards one or another group, few will admit it. Furthermore, any bigots in our police agencies are the least likely to be moved by training or exhortation, which they may nonetheless dutifully salute and even may faithfully implement. Still, there is great value in teaching police personnel to better understand diverse communities, and to appreciate why tolerance makes for better policing than stereotyping. That value is maximized when officers are approached like partners in the search for improved police effectiveness across diverse communities, not like the perpetrators of poor police-community relations whose thoughts and habits need correcting.

The truth is we don't have to delve into the psyches of law enforcement officers to explain most law enforcement failures. Law enforcement failures are, by and large, organizational. Much more is to be learned about the FBI's tragic Waco assault by examining the organizational factors involved than by deducing any individual's state of mind or by searching for a grand, hidden agenda. Similarly, though Philadelphia cops had angry memories about a fellow officer killed in a 1978 confrontation with MOVE, we can best learn how not to burn down two city blocks and kill eleven people by looking at what the Philadelphia police department did wrong in the rapid run-up to the 1985 MOVE assault.

The strengths of an "organizational" analysis of failure are many. Organizational components are identifiable and concrete. Records usually exist of decisions, actions, and directives. Law enforcement failures play out in an organizational context and involve authoritatively prescribed roles, supervisory and command level oversight, and cultural practices that commonly emerge in law enforcement agencies. These elements are concrete and knowable, and one or more of them are inevitably symptomatic in the failures of law enforcement.

Not only does an organizational analysis lead us more readily to symptoms underlying failure, it also leads us more readily to cures. A high-profile murder investigation may run aground as an inflexible, isolationist, "my way or the highway" supervisor of detectives rejects outside help and alienates key subordinates and potential allies. If this is the case, several straightforward organizational fixes are available to prevent a recurrence, including removal of the supervisor, mandating interagency cooperation and keeping departmental channels of communication open. All of these are more likely to improve the effectiveness of the detective bureau than trying to make an inflexible commander believe in collaboration, cooperation and the brotherhood of man.

So we are going to look at law enforcement failure through an organizational lens. This book will present, apply and justify a typology of organizational failure by examining high-profile instances of police corruption, mismanagement, and operational debacle. The purpose is two-fold. The first is to develop a framework that generally helps make better sense of a range of law enforcement failures. The second purpose is to provide police managers and students of police organization with a set of conceptual tools to better diagnose and address organizational conditions in which disaster may lurk.

# Defining Failure

"Failure" occurs in an organization when some operation, employee, policy or process produces results that deviate from expectations in substantial and disruptive ways. Failure encompasses accident, non-performance, corrupt performance and deviant behavior. The Space Shuttle Columbia accident was a NASA failure.[12] The collapse of Enron, which stood on Byzantine financial structures that hid huge losses from investors, was a failure.[13] Firehouse drinking parties that end in on-duty brawls are failures of management and oversight.[14]

Failure frequently, but not necessarily, exposes the organization to criminal charges, civil liability, media firestorm, loss of public confidence and punishment by the marketplace or by elected executives and legislators. Failure can become chronic, preventing organizations from carrying out their missions. Many urban public schools wrestle with chronic failure of mission, with well over half their charges reading and writing below grade level.[15] Police agencies in countries with powerful drug cartels have had their crime-fighting missions severely compromised by pervasive, deadly lawlessness.[16]

Failure is not simply error. All organizations err in the normal course of business. In law enforcement, suspects slip away, procedures sloppily done imperil investigations, patrol officers wander off post, and supervisors fail to keep their charges on track. Errors, when expected and examined as opposed to decried and demonized, are events that alert management in a timely way that things may be getting off track. In fact, we will devote a chapter to "normal accidents" that erupt more from obscure technical flaws, human error and fallible perceptions than from ill-motivated employees or inept management.

The bulk of this book, however, will be devoted to failures arising from employee and management miscues that are neither obscure nor innocent. These failures are of a magnitude that calls into question the fundamental ability of the organization to craft effective operations, select and control personnel, monitor its own activities, and formulate policies that pass legal and ethical muster.

Law enforcement in the United States is no stranger to organizational failure. When a hastily crafted Philadelphia police assault upon a fortified, armed group resulted in multiple fatalities—including women and children—and burned down two city blocks, that was an organizational failure.[17] When eccentric, discontented and problematic cops that the New York City Police Department had consigned to Brooklyn's 77th precinct coalesced into a criminal enterprise preying on the neighborhood, their organization had failed as much as they had.[18] Organizational failure was at work when the New Orleans Police Department, for two years in a row, gave its crime reduction award to a captain who had been cooking the statistical books the whole time.[19] When the New Jersey State Police failed to modify racial profiling practices in the face of critical court rulings and rising public protest, the stage was set for the highway stop in which unarmed minority passengers were wounded, launching a firestorm of criticism and forced reform that roiled the agency for years.[20]

Failure, as opposed to error, reflects fundamentally on the ability of the law enforcement agency to conduct its business effectively and/or with integrity. Failure sets off scrutiny by powerful overseers and/or funding sources, causes upheaval within the agency and usually imposes changes that the organization neither seeks nor welcomes. Failure, in the short term, damages the ability of the organization to do its job and, in the long term, may diminish its resources, autonomy and legitimacy.

## The Analysis of Failure: Searching for Suspects

Failures are of such a magnitude that there is plenty of blame to go around, as attested to by the internal investigations, commission reports, personnel actions, executive resignations, agency restructurings, criminal indictments and civil suits that follow upon failure. In the ill-fated Philadelphia police assault against MOVE, one might blame the lone police officer that developed much of the plan. If not him, then perhaps the officer who improvised a too powerful bomb with secret ingredients few knew he had. Or one could blame the headquarters brass who remained aloof or nodded perfunctorily as the plan developed. Or blame could be laid at the feet of the police commissioner who delegated the complex, highly charged MOVE assault planning to lower-ranking personnel because he knew them and seemed to trust few others in the department. One could also blame—as the Philadelphia Special Investigative Commission did—the mayor, who left the police to handle a situation charged with racial, political and community tension exacerbated by years of mayoral indecision.[21]

Failure has, indeed, many suspects. But parsing out key organizational causes is not only complicated by the variety of suspects but also by the number of investigators that can end up on the case. Police chiefs and commissioners are often first out of the box in judging culpability and recommending remedies, even if they helped author the failed operations, processes or policies. These executives, not surprisingly, often blame failure on "a few rotten apples," or on the processes and procedures inherited from their predecessors. Reporters covering a failed operation tend to catalog the gamut of causes, with pro and con views relative to each, which can sow as much confusion as clarity. Activists zero in on organizational failure with belief systems that have pre-identified culprits and causes, and often arrive at their conclusions within hours of a failure event.

Legislative hearings do not necessarily clarify fundamental causes of organizational failure. These hearings often involve clashing political agendas and inquisitions by committees of partisans. The resulting reports often tell us more about which partisans prevailed than about which policies, practices and individuals most contributed to the law enforcement failure.[22]

"Blue ribbon" commissions appointed by presidents, governors and mayors are hardly more neutral. Political executives define the investigative body's purpose and membership, which directs attention toward some causes and away from others. The presidential commission investigating the false weapons of mass destruction intelligence used to justify the Iraq war was mandated to focus on what went wrong in the US intelligence community. The commission was not empowered to examine how intelligence agencies may have been influenced from above, even though senior administration officials frequently and forcefully made crystal clear their belief that weapons of mass destruction were in Iraq.[23]

Courts, which weigh facts and parcel out culpability, hold out more promise for getting to the bottom of major organizational failures. However, court cases often go on for years before concluding with confidential and/or "no fault" settlements in civil suits; and criminal cases, narrowly drawn to begin with, often result in pleas to even narrower violations that shed little light on what went wrong organizationally.

With the biases and limitations of various failure investigations, it is often years before someone, most often a first-rate investigative reporter, sifts through source documents, official reports, court transcripts and interviews to paint a comprehensive and balanced picture of a specific organizational failure.[24] By the time such definitive analyses emerge, few may remember and fewer still may care.

And so, not surprisingly, failures repeat themselves, giving rise to laments about the cycle of corruption or the irrepressible dark side of human nature. This conveniently attributes chronic organizational failures to immutable characteristics of individuals and groups. Though therapeutic and absolving, these laments minimize the organizational characteristics that precipitate and sustain failure. Employees—high and low—are very much a product of the organizations in which they are embedded. "Bad" employees are nurtured by cultures that accept them, organizational structures that enable them, territoriality that insulates them and overseers blinded to their offenses. Perverse

processes and disastrous plans are conceived organizationally, are championed by executives and work groups, and can operate with the blessing of nearly every employee right up until disaster occurs.

The remainder of this book will view the police organization as a medium in which the germ of failure is cultured. We will consider how various structural elements of police organizations enable behaviors that pave the way for failure. We will consider how law enforcement supervision and oversight fails to detect or address budding pathologies that subsequently grow to ominous, and ultimately destructive, proportions. We will look at how cultures within organizations encourage and then normalize deviant behaviors that can lead to disaster. Finally, we will consider how cascading pathologies can transform police organizations into introspective, self-serving enterprises that alienate the citizens and communities upon whom their legitimacy depends.

# Categories of Failure

The framework developed in this book establishes six broad categories of organizational failure. Each category is briefly explained below, followed by a thumbnail description of the cases that will help illuminate each category.

**Normal accidents:** Occur when complex technological elements malfunction and human operators misjudge what's happening, responding with actions that can accelerate the deterioration of the situation. This concept has been most often applied to disasters in high technology organizational settings[25] but, as we shall see in Chapter 2, it also applies to more prosaic technology/employee interactions in law enforcement settings.

The cases analyzed from a normal accident perspective will show:

- How police cruisers with obscure glitches needed only the slightest of officer missteps to veer fatally off course.
- How ill-advised tactics and ineffective equipment conspired with incorrect intelligence to put an officer on trial for the tragic killing of an elderly, emotionally disturbed woman.
- How initial misperceptions in rapidly arising situations set a tone for further misreads fueling incorrect police responses that led to failure.
- How high speed pursuits can lethally test the motor skill limits of police officers, suspects and the vehicles they drive.

**Structural failures:** Occur when operations, procedures and processes that are functioning according to design lead to failure. Organizations are arrangements of tasks and coordinating mechanisms designed to get particular jobs done. Organizational design is continuous and iterative, which creates susceptibility to error under the best of circumstances. But, as we shall see in Chapter 3, organizational construction is less an engineering process than a negotiated one, less science than art. Pressures of time and resources, as well as competing interests within and outside the organization, lead to the creation of structures that are unwieldy, flimsy and quite capable of failing when certain, usually foreseeable, conditions arise.

The cases analyzed from a structural failure perspective will show:

- How hierarchical friction and territorial combat paralyzed a major homicide investigation, ended careers and debilitated the involved criminal justice agencies.
- How contradictory agency mandates compromised immigration enforcement efforts, giving safe passage to terrorists planning monstrous acts.
- How inconsistent decisions and policy confusion emerge from struggles for dominance between headquarters and field offices, and between different organizational functions.
- How agency structures frustrated officials trying to craft plans for dealing with a racially and politically charged enforcement situation.

**Oversight failures:** Occur when operational supervision and oversight staff fail to detect and/or address organizational conditions that depart significantly from the norm. Organizations depend on oversight by external boards, internal auditors, and quality control units to guard against mistakes that crop up routinely. But, as Chapter 4 illustrates, oversight bodies also experience structural failure due to insufficient resources or inadequate mandates, and staff units as well as supervisors may have to mute their oversight in the face of powerful superiors and muscular employee groups.

The cases analyzed from an oversight failure perspective will show:

- How inadequate oversight structures and insufficient resources immunized a thoroughly corrupt officer for years.
- How lack of clear guidelines and misplaced solidarity enabled a ranking officer to spiral into a death dive.
- How the crucial role modeling required of internal affairs personnel broke down at the highest levels.
- How oversight personnel can sabotage investigations into corrupt practices viewed as everyday business by the rank and file.

**Cultural deviation:** Occurs when elements of the organization increasingly operate according to their own standards, with little regard for the larger organization and its rules. Organization members will always affiliate with each other in ways that go beyond the groupings and purposes intended by management. Managers can't prevent this and, in fact, often are complicit as they merge and break apart units for operational reasons with little thought to the emergent and/or clashing cultures that result. The lesson of Chapter 5 is that, when a deviant culture takes hold, rule-defying behavior can become a matter of daily process and moral value as members edge the organization ever closer to disaster.

The cases analyzed from a cultural deviation perspective will show:

- How a renegade police subculture took root and prospered in an isolated command.
- How minimal supervision of problem personnel helped a group of officers degrade into a criminal enterprise.
- How a state law enforcement agency became increasingly at risk as pockets of personnel exhibited attitudes and behaviors that exploited women, at times in violation of law.
- How a culture that enabled and protected lawless acts pervaded a department, enduring for decades while fending off repeated attempts at reform.

**Institutionalization:** Occurs when an organization increasingly bases its approach to customers or clients on what best serves the comfort or preferences of the employees. The organizations we will look at in Chapter 6 strove for dominance and certainty and often achieved a substantial measure of both. But this creates a paradoxical trap. With self-congratulation and hubris born of success and comfort in the "tried and true" processes and roles that made them dominant, organization members can increasingly see priority number one as maintaining their processes, their ways and each other. The organization thus loses touch with the customers, markets and other external elements upon which its survival depends.

The cases analyzed from an institutionalization perspective will show:

- How performance in a crime lab degraded dramatically without denting member self-esteem or their wholehearted commitment to existing practices.
- How an institutionalized agency actively resisted legal and political mandates to end unacceptable racial profiling practices.
- How the substitution of "member in good standing" for careful performance evaluation enabled egregious behavior by employees who boasted about how insulated they were from organizational scrutiny.

- How a criminal conspiracy involving the leadership of an institutionalized, politicized county court enriched the leaders, perverted justice and treated juvenile offenders as currency.

**Resource diversion:** Occurs when organizational resources end up being used for other than intended purposes through illicit schemes or legal but exploitative manipulations by employee beneficiaries. Exposure of resource diversions, especially if they are substantial and/or widespread, brings disrepute upon a law enforcement organization and may initiate investigations and personnel shake-ups. Issues of equity and morale also come to the fore, especially if a small group of employee beneficiaries has managed to legitimate some special claim to diverted resources.

The cases analyzed from a resource diversion perspective will show:

- How law enforcement officers took advantage of systems designed to compensate them for extra work and disabling on-the-job injuries.
- How lucrative overtime tied to special details came to be seen as entitlement by officers who sought to perpetuate their claims and punish those who resisted.
- How resource diversions by an executive dealt a subversive blow to agency morale and employees' sense of commitment.
- How getting away with high-level malfeasance is no assurance that those who know won't spill the beans just as the perpetrator reaches a career pinnacle years later.

# Applying the Categories

The structure of this book consists of "fitting" actual law enforcement cases into these six categories, with a chapter devoted to each. The explanatory power of a given category will be tested by its "goodness of fit" with prominent cases where law enforcement or criminal justice agencies failed. This approach is descriptive and inductive—the cases help build, validate and even modify the categories.

Organizations are highly complex, multi-faceted phenomena. The danger in any organizational analysis is that the simplification involved in description distorts the reality of the organization under review. The elemental facts of a given case are a function of available information and how that information was constructed by various sources, and is further a function of this author's choices in weaving together "the stories" used as cases in this book. I have chosen the elements that have gone into this book's principal case examples after extensive research and careful analysis but also with an appreciation of the limitations of "reality construction."

I also appreciate that the organizational focus mostly excludes larger social and economic structures but this is a conscious epistemological choice. But it is also a practical choice, since these issues are largely peripheral to law enforcement management. Nor do I think that much learning is lost by the exclusion. The organizational form takes on immense social mass and gravity and is highly resistant to surrounding social, political and economic structures. I expect that police officers in China, Scotland, Venezuela, or Nigeria who read this book will find much that relates to the organizations in which they work.

To some extent, the marriage of case to single category is a forced one. Few, if any, organizational crises are the exclusive result of a single category failure. When organizations fail, multiple causes generally come into play, as Chapter 8 recognizes. So the reader may well see an element of cultural deviation in what I have categorized as structural failure, or an element of any of the other categories in a case that I have placed in the resource diversion category. The aim of this book is not to put that fine a point on things but to test roughly the ability of the categories to subsume a variety of organizational failures based on the predominant profile of a given case.

This approach also seeks to serve a crucial aim of this book—to provide working police personnel with a framework that can aid in the early detection of, and intervention in, situations with the potential to seriously damage their organizations and/or their careers. If the framework succeeds on that most practical of levels, then the energy devoted to its development and explication will have been well spent indeed.

# Going Forward

The final chapter is titled "Managing Imperfection," which is the major subtext throughout the book. One case considered in the final chapter tries to make organizational sense of the appalling loss of public safety officers in the 9/11 atrocities. These officers were victims, to be sure, of terrorist crimes against the law of nations, acts of war targeting non-combatants, and capital crimes under state law.

But their organizations also exhibited failings that kept many public safety personnel too long in harm's way on 9/11. This was due to a failure to fully correct organizational imperfections that had been thrown into stark relief by the 1993 World Trade Center bombing.

We will end this book with a case at the intersection of public policy and law enforcement organization—the death of Trayvon Martin. It is easy to point a finger at police when urban shootouts claim innocent lives, or when the shooter of Trayvon Martin walks out the station house door hours later. But these are not police failures, they are policy failures, and we want to leave the reader with this understanding.

From here on we will catalog the various imperfections with which law enforcement organizations wrestle constantly. Organizational imperfections, for the most part, can only be partially corrected, not eliminated. However, we can identify actions and attitudes that help combat imperfections, and suggest structural and process changes that can go a long way towards correcting them. And this we will do, to a modest extent, in each chapter.

We will not get to perfect, but we will doggedly pursue the better.

# Endnotes

1. Margot Harry, *Attention, MOVE! This is America* (Chicago: Banner Press, 1987).

2. Robin Wagner-Pacifici, *Discourse and Destruction: The City of Philadelphia versus MOVE* (Chicago: University of Chicago Press, 1994).

3. Hizkias Assefa and Paul Wahrhaftig, *The MOVE Crisis in Philadelphia: Extremist Groups and Conflict Resolution* (Pittsburgh: University of Pittsburgh Press, 1990).

4. City of Philadelphia, *Report of the Philadelphia Special Investigation Commission,* (Philadelphia, 1986).

5. The sources for these comparisons are: John Anderson and Hilary Hevenor, *Burning Down the House: Move and the Tragedy of Philadelphia* (New York: W.W. Norton, 1990); Dick Reavis, *The Ashes of Waco: An Investigation* (Syracuse, New York: Syracuse University Press, 1998).

6. Anderson and Hevenor, *Burning Down the House,* 389.

7. Charles W. Bowser, *Let the Bunker Burn: The Final Battle with MOVE* (Philadelphia: Camino Press, 1989): 120, 174.

8. Tricia Escobedo, "What Is It about Mid-April and Violence in America?" *CNN.com,* April 19, 2011 http://articles.cnn.com/2011-04-19/us/april.attacks.conspiracy_1_waco-compound-branch-davidian-conspiracy-theories?_s=PM:US (Accessed April 1, 2012).

9. U.S. House of Representatives, Committee on Government Reform, *The Tragedy of Waco: New Evidence Examined,* 106th Cong., 2nd Sess., 2000, H. Rep. 106-1037.

10. Anderson and Hevenor, *Burning Down the House,* 79–80.

11. James R. Lasley and Michael K Hooper, "On Racism and the LAPD: Was the Christopher Commission Wrong?" *Social Science Quarterly* 79 no. 2 (June 1998): 378–89; David Weisburd, Rosann Greenspan and Edwin E. Hamilton, *Police Attitudes Toward Abuse Of Authority: Findings From A National Study* (Washington, DC: U.S. National Institute of Justice, 2000).

12. Columbia Accident Investigation Board, *Report of the Columbia Accident Investigation Board* (U.S. Government Printing Office: Washington, DC, 2003).

13.Bethany McLean and Peter Elkind, *Smartest Guys in the Room: The Amazing Rise and Scandalous Fall of Enron* (New York: Portfolio, 2003).

14. New York City Department of Investigation, *A Report to Mayor Michael R. Bloomberg and Commissioner Nicholas Scoppetta: The Department of Investigation's Examination of the Circumstances Surrounding the Assault of a Firefighter and Subsequent Cover-up at the New York City Fire Department Engine Company 151/Ladder Company 76 on Staten Island* (New York, 2004).

15. U.S. Department of Education Institute of Education Sciences, *The Nation's Report Card: Trial Urban District Assessment 2003* (Washington, DC: 2004).

16. William Cartwright, ed., *Mexico: Facing the Challenges of Human Rights and Crime* (Ardsley, NY: Transnational Publishers, 2000).

17. Most emphatic on this score is Bowser, *Let the Bunker Burn.*

18. Mike McAlary, *Buddy Boys: When Good Cops Turn Bad* (New York: Putnam & Sons, 1987).

19. "Compstat Consequences: Five axed over bad stats." *Law Enforcement News*, January 2004.

20. Associated Press, "Report: New Jersey State Police Knew of Racial Profiling in 1996," CNN.com: U.S. News, October 12, 2000 PERLINK"http://cnnstudentnews.cnn.com/2000/US/10/12/njstate.police.ap/"http://cnnstudentnews.cnn.com/2000/US/10/12/njstate.police.ap/(Accessed March 8, 2004).

21. Anderson and Hevenor, *Burning Down the House*, 389.

22. House Committee on Government Reform, *The Tragedy of Waco.*

23. Commission on the Intelligence Capabilities of the United States Regarding Weapons of Mass Destruction, *Report of the Commission on the Intelligence Capabilities of the United States Regarding Weapons of Mass Destruction* (Washington, D.C.: 2005).

24. See, for instance, Lou Cannon. *Official Negligence: How Rodney King and the Riots Changed Los Angeles and the LAPD* (Boulder, CO: Westview, 1999).

25. Charles Perrow, *Normal Accidents: Living with High Risk Technologies* (Princeton: Princeton University Press, 1999)

# CHAPTER TWO

# NORMAL ACCIDENTS IN LAW ENFORCEMENT: MAKING SENSE OF THINGS GONE WRONG

Well-designed and carefully implemented structures, policies and processes will produce errors as a matter of course in any organization. When a police department recruits more than 2000 candidates a year, which the New York City Police Department (NYPD) has done, a few misfits will inevitably survive the rigorous and highly reliable process of screening, training and probation. That this happens is hardly an indictment of the organization, or of its recruiting and training structure. Let's say, for instance, that 19 behaviorally ill-equipped officers emerge from a police academy graduating class of 2,000. The recruitment and training reliability exceeds 99%, a figure that would make any private firm envious. Yet, in police departments all across the country, this still puts uniforms on individuals primed for problematic behavior on the job.

Once in uniform, some of these officers behave in ways that lead to their separation from the force during the probationary period. Other marginal rookies survive but later missteps get them exiled to posts that minimize the consequences of their problematic tendencies. Still, a few cops with serious, simmering issues stay on the front lines. The NYPD's Justin Volpe was one such cop in 1997. Volpe's explosive temper fueled his brutal station house assault on Abner Louima that we will discuss further along in this chapter.

Volpe failed, criminally, and went to prison as a result. The NYPD failed because Volpe wreaked such havoc while operating under its auspices. And New York City paid a price—just under $9 million in a settlement with Abner Louima.[1] Although the NYPD was responsible and the city was accountable for the failures in the Louima case, such failures can't be completely eliminated. A high-risk employee can occasionally slip through the cracks in any law enforcement organization. And, indeed, such employees are but a few of the hidden, unrecognized defects that, in all organizations, stand ready to precipitate failures given the right combination of circumstances.

The cars cops drive, the guns they carry, the computers they consult are all susceptible to breakdown—and officers and civilians can die as a consequence. Gaps lurk in the procedures and tactics that law enforcement agencies design to control intractable individuals or agitated groups. Since these plans can't be foolproof to begin with, nor can they account for all behaviors, law enforcement officers will inevitably be placed in the position of deciding—often within seconds in dangerous, rapidly developing situations—just how to modify tactics that are suddenly useless. And, of course, officers are only human, prone on occasion to be fallible in their perceptions, judgments, and actions—especially when their machinery and equipment fails, procedures that are supposed to work don't, and the situation is fraught with danger and time pressure.

# Normal Accidents

When Charles Perrow wrote the book *Normal Accidents* in 1984,[2] he was addressing events such as the 1979 nuclear reactor meltdown at Three Mile Island, chemical plant explosions and airline crashes. In a later edition,[3] Perrow included in his analysis the crash of the space shuttle Challenger and the explosion at the Chernobyl nuclear plant in Ukraine (then part of the USSR), each of which took place in 1986. These events had short-term adverse effects on the organizations directly involved, longer-term fallout for the critical missions of these organizations and, in the case of Chernobyl, impacts that shook the very foundation of the Soviet state.[4]

What Perrow was getting at by calling these tragic and catastrophic events "normal accidents" has relevance to the study of all organizations, including law enforcement organizations. Perrow looked at the extremely complex equipment of high tech enterprises, and the elaborate network of gauges, back-up systems and personnel required to operate, monitor and maintain that equipment. Such systems had an extraordinary number of failure points, not all of which were knowable, and many of which resided along the turbulent interface between subsystems (think of your computer and printer and internet connection). Because of how interconnected everything was and just how quickly things worked, when even a small thing went wrong the situation could rapidly spiral out of control. The human operators would be hard put to respond correctly, and might just accelerate the disaster.

Most police work is slow-paced, routine, and can be done in serial fashion, characteristics Perrow identifies with linear interactions. Police find themselves in an "expected and familiar production or maintenance sequence."[5] But when a police action goes awry, the circumstances are often rapidly evolving and non-routine, and all sorts of things are going on at once, characteristics Perrow identifies with complex interactions. Police find themselves in "unfamiliar sequences, or unplanned and unexpected sequences" that may not be "immediately comprehensible,"[6] but which also may demand on-the-spot decisions from stressed personnel.

Perrow said that we should expect accidents, sooner or later, in such situations. Thus, the accidents at the Three Mile Island and Chernobyl nuclear plants, as well as the loss of NASA's Space Shuttles, were "normal." For instance, any number of the 2.5 million parts on the space shuttle was bound at some point to malfunction without anyone knowing. Even if the personnel responsible for an errant part did know, as was the case for both Challenger and Columbia, they could misinterpret and downplay any malfunction's impact.[7] Eventually that part fails at a mission critical point when no human intervention can stave off disaster. So, when a faulty rubber seal exploded the Space Shuttle Challenger in 1986 and a flying hunk of insulating foam doomed the Columbia shuttle in 2003, human operators on board and on the ground could only watch in horror.

Similarly, sooner or later a nuclear reactor gauge might give a false reading, causing operators to enact corrective procedures unnecessarily, which in turn starts the reactor down a dangerous path to meltdown. Operators, now "outside the box" with two sets of gauges going south (the "false report" gauge and the gauges now redlining because of the unneeded corrections), run through a whole inventory of corrective procedures. Some corrective responses will not work and others accelerate the reactor's collapse, as still other gauges go into the red.[8] At this point, operators may improvise, as they did at Chernobyl, while an exponential chain reaction gains momentum by the second.[9] The result: meltdown, explosion, radiation release and, in Chernobyl, death, sickness and instant ghost towns rendered unsafe to humans for generations to come.

Perrow wrote specifically about the inescapable pitfalls of managing high-risk technology. His definitions and distinctions were developed in relation to NASA or to the nationwide power grid,[10] not the FBI. The concept of normal accident, however, has wider applicability, as Perrow suggests in pointing out how accidents can damage "symbols, communications and legitimacy" in organizations such as universities.[11]

And, certainly, Perrow's ideas are applicable to law enforcement. Pursuits, raids, sudden confrontations with suspects, and the management of unruly crowds put officers, their vehicles and weapons into high intensity, fast paced and unpredictable situations that may well defy standard operating procedures, plans and capabilities. When this happens, an officer or supervisor is thrown upon his or her own devices in order to make split second decisions in a rapidly developing situation where equipment and/or procedures may have already failed, and where confusion often reigns.

In Perrow's terms, things have gone complex and non-linear.[12] Possibilities multiply; predictability plummets. At this point, the police officer might as well be in front of a nuclear reactor's control panel where several of the readings are rapidly going south for reasons nobody quite understands. If the officer makes a wrong choice, "normal accident" may sufficiently explain any failure that results. A variety of forces, however, tend to focus post-failure analyses in more critical and punitive directions, with hapless officers and supervisors paying a price.

# Congenital Error in Organization

The fact of the matter is that organizations, even small organizations working on simple tasks, are intrinsically failure prone. Complex organizations managing technical projects, and police agencies handling critical incidents, are subject to "normal accident," but all organizations in general are subject to what might be termed congenital risk.

Think of the congenital risks of organization this way. A single tailor might miss a critical stitch on every hundredth garment. If that tailor has his or her own shop, the garments are created with a 99% success rate. If you convince that tailor that he or she would be better off teaming up with nine other equally talented tailors to produce suits faster using an assembly line, their level of perfection is likely to decline. Why? Because each of the ten tailors on the assembly line will not make that "one in a hundred" mistake on the same garment. Tailor A will screw up the zipper on suit number five, tailor B will mess up the vest on suit number six, and so on.

This is not to deny the advantages of creating larger organizations. As each tailor becomes a zipper or a vest expert, the error rate on each of those tasks will likely decline, and overall production should increase. Similarly, if one tailor becomes the administrative expert, and another becomes the marketing specialist, each job overall should be done a bit better and less expensively than when each tailor had to carve time out from their stitching and fitting to do these tasks. These advantages of organization are known as "economies of scale," and are one reason organizations, including police departments, choose to merge.

Even though creating a new or larger organization usually increases production and diminishes per unit cost, the risk of error increases. More and more pieces have to come together successfully to create a finished product; more employees are involved. This, in turn, leads to further elaboration of the organization. Supervision, audit, quality control and automation are all responses to the increased errors that occur when more and more tasks must be combined to create a finished product. However these new layers of organization created to control error require more hand-offs and communications, which carry their own inescapable error quotient.

Not only can new structures for controlling error fail but the new technologies that facilitate work are often a double-edged sword as well. New gadgets tend to take over ever greater shares of the organization's reliability load, so the consequences of their failures are also greater—think about how a hard disk crash can destroy months of work or how the shutdown of the intra/internet connection can bring an organization skidding to a halt. And new gadgets expand limits, and failure zones, as cars go faster, databases get vaster and surveillance techniques allow for greater intrusion. If employees don't test the envelope on their own, they are likely to be pressured towards the edge of the envelope by managers seeking productivity gains from the new technology. In this new territory lie failure risks that may well exceed the gains coming from productivity programs or improvisations by employees.

# The "At Risk" Law Enforcement Organization

Taken together, the ideas of normal accident and congenital error tell us that organizations will inevitably fail as a matter of course. Not because Officer Jones is a psychopath, or because Supervisor Smith is derelict, or because the use of force policy was doomed to fail, or the city's purchasing department wrongly signed on for that crash-prone police cruiser. Not because the cops as a group had thrown up a blue wall of silence, or were enforcing the law with a heavy and uneven hand, or because the mayor, city council, the ACLU, or community activists tied the police department's hands.

Though all these elements can and do contribute to police failures, they are not necessary conditions for any given failure by a law enforcement organization. Even official blame pinned on one or more "usual suspects" may be more about developing an explanation that gets everyone past the situation than about getting at the real causes. In addition, though the idea of accountability all but demands that chiefs identify and discipline "responsible parties" in order to drive the organization towards greater reliability, some who are punished are little more than symbolic sacrifices to the wrong-headed notion that organizations are perfectable.

The bottom line is that failure will inevitably occur in law enforcement as a consequence of the very nature of organizations. As was written about a firearms training accident in Illinois that wounded an officer, "a series of events, despite extensive planning, precautions, training, redundancy, protective devices, policies and procedures came together in just the right way in an unforgiving environment."[13]

In other words, things sometimes will go wrong just because.

* * *

**Normal Accident Defined:** Normal accidents occur when complex machine elements malfunction, either individually or interactively, and human operators misjudge what is happening and respond with actions that accelerate the deterioration of the situation.

## Runaway Police Van at the Holiday Parade

On December 4, 1998, in Minneapolis, twelve citizens were run down on the sidewalk by a police van as they awaited the start of a winter festival parade known as Holidazzle. Two died, including an infant. Two of the injured were an off-duty police sergeant and her daughter.[14]

The van had arrived on the scene to pick up several drunks who, after staggering loudly through the family crowd, had fallen. Two of the drunks, who were well known to the police, were either disinclined or unable to get up.[15]

Both officers had left the van to survey the scene. The officer who had been riding in the passenger seat went back to move the van closer to where one of the drunks lay. That officer hopped up in the van, door open, to roll it closer to the fallen alcoholic. At that point all hell broke loose. The van accelerated forward at a high rate of speed, striking another police car. The van's airbag then deployed, pinning the officer to the driver's seat. The collision redirected the van onto the sidewalk where it ran down a dozen people, including babies in carriages, as it slid along a building wall. A concrete pillar stopped the vehicle's forward motion but not the screech of the tires, which were continuing to try to accelerate the van forward.

An off-duty lieutenant, who was the husband of the police sergeant the van had struck, rushed over and, shouting over the engine roar, told the dazed officer behind the wheel to turn off the ignition. He did, and the killer van went silent.[16]

## The Obscure Origins of Normal Accidents

The officer who had hopped into the van was the initial target for blame. An investigator from the National Highway Traffic Safety Administration was skeptical of claims, advanced by Minneapolis' police chief and other department officials, that something went wrong with the van.[17]

The investigator had checked out the van and found its mechanical systems in order. He concluded that the officer had initiated a "driveway maneuver" which occurs in vehicles with automatic transmissions when someone unfamiliar with the foot pedal placement only partially seats himself before trying to drive a short distance.[18] The fact that the van had a failsafe transmission — no foot on brake = no shifting into drive — caused the investigator to conclude also that the officer had simultaneously depressed the brake and the accelerator in order to set the tragic event in motion.[19]

Six weeks after he made his report, the investigator learned the full story. The investigator happened to be giving a talk on vehicle safety at a suburban Minneapolis hotel and alluded to failsafe automatic transmissions on police vehicles. A Minnesota State Trooper in the audience took issue with this, saying that he could often shift his cruiser into drive without having his foot on the brake. Sure enough, the investigator went out into the parking lot and watched the trooper shift into drive without touching the brake.

This startling revelation led the NTSB to investigate further. It turned out that mechanics working for police agencies in various parts of the country were piggybacking an after-market "wig wag" device on the circuit that controlled the failsafe on the transmission. The "wig wag" flashed the brake lights on and off each second when the vehicle's emergency lights were lit, as they had been on the killer van. What no one knew was that, for each half-second the brake lights flashed on, the transmission failsafe was disabled. So when the emergency lights were flashing, or every other half-second, a police vehicle with modified brake lights could be thrown into drive with the accelerator depressed. This finding led to the National Highway Traffic Safety Administration (NHTSA) issuing a nationwide warning urging police departments to test their vehicles and to check for modifications that could turn their cruisers into deadly missiles.[20]

This is a classic "normal accident." A small circuit innocently modified in order to enhance the visibility of patrol vehicles created a dangerous risk. But nobody knew about it. The mechanics didn't think they'd compromised the failsafe, even if obscure manufacturer's notices warned against piggybacking on the circuit. For troopers in the field, the added lights were a benefit, the easy shifting transmission merely a curiosity.

Nothing went wrong, until exactly the right circumstances came together. A cop in a hurry and slightly out of synch with the driver's side configuration was unlucky enough to catch the failsafe in its disabled half second. The result was a tragic accident, but a normal one because the obscure glitch in the modified technology needed only a slight misstep by the human operator to set disaster in motion.

* * *

We will next look at a case where the "normal accident" explanation emerges as one of several possible explanations of a racially charged, high visibility instance of a police operation gone terribly awry. Equipment failures play a minor yet critical role. The case involves erroneous information, complex interactions between organizations, split second response times, and a situation spiraling out of control. The case also illustrates the limitations on human operators trying to mount a measured response in a complex, rapidly developing situation where little is going as expected.

## The Tragedy of Eleanor Bumpurs

Eleanor Bumpurs was an African-American woman living in a New York City Housing Authority development. In her mid-60s, Bumpurs was emotionally disturbed, overweight, not in the best of health, and she had fallen behind on her rent by less than $100, which was enough to set the wheels of New York City's housing bureaucracy in motion.[21]

A letter was promptly generated, asking Mrs. Bumpurs for the back rent under the threat of eviction. She ignored this. New York City Housing Authority officials knocked on her door. She wouldn't let them in, shouting through the locked door that appliances and fixtures in the apartment weren't working and she wouldn't pay the rent until they were. The repair crews came but Mrs. Bumpurs wouldn't let them in either. The amount of rent she owed grew.[22]

The phone worked better, at least for communicating with Mrs. Bumpurs, who remained adamant about not admitting anyone into her apartment. Her reasons simply confirmed Mrs. Bumpur's tenuous hold on reality. She was afraid to open the door because she believed that enough people were already infiltrating her apartment through the walls and floors.

Housing Authority officials persisted, actually getting Mrs. Bumpurs to open the door. Since Mrs. Bumpurs held a knife as she recited a litany of what was wrong inside the apartment, housing officials chose not to enter.[23] The legal steps proceeded apace, however, inching closer to where the Housing Authority would have the right to summarily evict Mrs. Bumpurs from her apartment. Less relentlessly, housing officials solicited help from the Human Resources Administration and tried to get in touch with Mrs. Bumpurs' relatives.[24]

Housing officials and maintenance workers finally gained entry into the apartment, as Mrs. Bumpurs watched with knife in hand. Fighting their way through noxious odors, workers found human waste festering in cans in the bathtub with flies flitting all about. The things Mrs. Bumpurs had claimed weren't working, were. She blamed all of this on, among others, Ronald Reagan, who was president at the time. The Human Resources Administration engaged a psychiatrist/consultant to go see Mrs. Bumpurs.[25]

But things were moving on yet other administrative tracks, none of them involving the police. The eviction process reached the Sheriff's Office, which enforces the civil judgments of the New York courts. The sheriffs were gearing up for an eviction even as the psychiatrist managed a face-to-face interview with Mrs. Bumpurs, who greeted him knife in hand, though she did put it down at one point. The psychiatrist ended up more concerned about Mrs. Bumpurs' seriously deteriorated mental state than the knife, which she seemed to carry more as a reserve weapon against her imaginary demons than against people. The alarmed doctor recommended that Mrs. Bumpurs be hospitalized, a request that the city's Human Resources Administration began to dutifully process.[26]

All the bureaucratic processes were coming to a head simultaneously, so it was decided to evict and then hospitalize Mrs. Bumpurs all at once. A convention of sheriffs, Housing Authority officials, New York City Housing police (a separate department, since incorporated into the NYPD), movers, social workers and psychiatric personnel convened outside Mrs. Bumpur's apartment door, lending credence to her delusion of being assaulted from all sides by demonic legions seeking entry to her home.[27]

Mrs. Bumpurs acted predictably. She wouldn't let the officials in, and raged at them from behind the door, threatening to "fix" them if they entered. The gaggle of officials, laborers, housing police and medical personnel were thwarted so they began to speculate about what Mrs. Bumpurs had inside. Perhaps the smells now emanating from Mrs. Bumpurs' apartment related to her "history of lye throwing." (No such history existed; the smells came from roach spray.)[28] Perhaps this defiant woman was going to furiously fling her considerable bulk, and perhaps her knife and blinding lye, at anyone in her vicinity.

Then, and only then, were the police called. Two members of the NYPD Emergency Services Unit responded, as was routine in such cases. The officers had the means to deal with emotionally disturbed persons. Their equipment was designed to restrain and pin a disturbed person in close quarters. The emergency service officers had body armor to protect themselves, "moon suits" for entering toxic spaces, and, if all else failed, a shotgun.

A chorus of warnings and concerns greeted those first two emergency service officers. Earlier speculation had grown to near factual status. Mrs. Bumpurs, in keeping with her non-existent "lye throwing history," could very well have been cooking up some lye in her apartment by that time. Though Mrs. Bumpurs had yet to strike out with that ever-present knife, she was now presented as the slasher behind the door. All of this seemed to be confirmed when officers punched out the lock, and peeped through to see Mrs. Bumpurs standing with her knife in what looked to them like a cloud of mist or steam.

The two ESU officers called for backup.[29]

An ESU sergeant arrived, along with three additional officers. The warnings about Mrs. Bumpurs were repeated, so the sergeant told the officers to gear up. That meant, for the first officer through the door, a protective vest, goggles, gas mask and a large U-shaped bar with a long handle designed to pin and help subdue an unruly individual. The next two officers bursting into the apartment also had on vests, masks and goggles and carried plastic shields. Their job was to help subdue Mrs. Bumpurs once she was pinned by the bar. The fourth cop through the door carried a shotgun, a reserve but ready weapon should any of the cops come into harm's way. The sergeant was the last of the five officers to enter the apartment. The sixth cop remained on guard in the hall.[30]

The cops bursting into her apartment "must have been quite a sight for ... Eleanor Bumpurs, who had imagined that people were after her.... Here were six men, all but two dressed like spacemen, carrying bizarre equipment and pleading with her to drop her knife."[31] Mrs. Bumpurs, knife in hand, resisted and tried to fend off the oncoming cops.

Nothing worked; Mrs. Bumpers maneuvered around the pinning bar, so the officer tried to use it as a ram. Another officer tried to use his shield to disarm Mrs. Bumpurs and then to pin her arm against the wall. She was neither pinned nor disarmed. This roiling mass of cops and the emotionally disturbed Mrs. Bumpurs struggled across the living room. As Mrs. Bumpurs pushed back against the shield being pressed against her, the officer with the iron bar fell and, according to the cops in the room, Mrs. Bumpurs advanced on the fallen officer with her knife. From a distance of two feet, the shotgun-wielding officer fired, pumped, and then fired again. With only seconds having elapsed since the officers had burst through the door, the incident was over and Eleanor Bumpurs lay dying.

## Criminal and Organizational Post-Mortems

The Eleanor Bumpurs case played out as a high profile failure and embarrassment of the NYPD. Eleanor Bumpurs was African American; the cops were white. The case became a cause célèbre for activists, was featured in a book-length rendering of "racial atrocities,"[32] and remains a mainstay in activist litanies of racially motivated police brutality. A Bronx grand jury returned a second-degree manslaughter indictment against the cop who shot Mrs. Bumpurs.[33] The grand jury concluded that the second, lethal shotgun blast was an excessive and needless use of force because medical evidence indicated that Mrs. Bumpurs' knife hand had been hit by the first shot. The ESU officer was acquitted more than two years later.[34]

As a result of the Bumpurs case, the NYPD endured a storm of criticism and instituted a number of new policies for dealing with emotionally disturbed persons. These included mandatory simulation training for ESU officers in which actors played mentally disturbed individuals, the acquisition of better equipment, and the development of more deliberate approaches during interactions between police and emotionally disturbed individuals.[35]

Trials, new policies and required training can minimize but can never eliminate outcomes such as occurred in the Bumpurs incident. That is because officers will always confront dynamic situations that unfold in seconds. Their ability to accurately read such situations is limited, and may well be complicated by false reports. Equipment will fail, and so will procedures, forcing officers into time-pressured improvisations as likely to fail as to succeed. Situations threatening to spin out of control will also elicit from officers responses that have worked in the past, even if those responses may violate procedures. In all of this, disaster lurks, with its occasional emergence all but certain.

But these disasters often flow from a larger organizational context, as did the tragedy of Eleanor Bumpurs. The mess that the Emergency Services cops walked into that day had been created by a variety of organizations. The Housing Authority's rent collection mechanisms had relentlessly painted Mrs. Bumpurs into a legal corner that took no account of her mental incapacity. The local housing officials, who did realize Mrs. Bumpurs' precarious mental state, engaged the sluggish social service bureaucracy on her behalf but did not disengage the eviction process bearing down on her.

Involved social service workers could have put the eviction on hold with an emergency rent payment but wrongly thought that Mrs. Bumpurs had to be interviewed first.[36] The psychiatrist, who days before helped settle Mrs. Bumpurs at least a bit while interviewing her, neither recommended nor attended the simultaneous eviction-hospitalization that was sure to set her off.

Outside Mrs. Bumpurs' apartment on the day of the eviction, frustrated, agitated officials created a highly charged atmosphere, which they compounded by providing false information that was critical in determining how the police officers entered the apartment. The mayor's bottom line analysis was that Mrs. Bumpurs death came not "because of brutality, but because of something much more complex—a chain of mistakes and circumstances that came together in the worst possible way."[37]

## Identifying Normal Accident Characteristics

Let's keep the Bumpurs tragedy in mind as we look briefly at America's worst nuclear accident, the partial meltdown of the reactor at Three Mile Island. Three Mile Island is a nuclear power plant that sits in the Susquehanna River just south of Harrisburg, the capital of Pennsylvania. When the accident occurred in 1979, the plant had been operating for five years but its second reactor, the one that failed, had been on line for only six months. The power plant personnel were highly trained and working with reliable equipment, since brand new Reactor # 2, along with its turbine room and cooling tower, was a twin of Reactor # 1.

At four o'clock on the morning of March 28, 1979, a pump feeding water to the steam generator shut down—a very serious situation, since the most critical job in any nuclear plant is to make sure that nothing overheats. An overheated nuclear reactor is on the way to meltdown, which is catastrophic. Superheated steam, which builds to tremendous pressures without coolant, can blow concrete containment structures apart, so water is needed in abundance.

Within two seconds of the pump shutting down the water flow, the water pressure and temperature in the reactor started to rise. One second later, a relief valve opened to blow off steam but then it failed to close, as it should have, when the pressure had been reduced to acceptable levels. The valve began bleeding coolant instead of steam. As a result, the reactor started to overheat. Then, control rods, which dampen nuclear reactions, were automatically inserted into the reactor core. The nuclear reaction slowed.

All this had taken nine seconds, without human intervention.[38]

At the same time it was trying to right itself, the reactor was alerting the human operators. The control room was ablaze with warning lights and alarms were going off left and right. However, two problems confronted the operators, problems that also confronted the cops outside Mrs. Bumpurs' apartment.

The first problem was information overload. Of the control panel's two thousand gauges, indicator lights and switches, many of the indicators were flashing red and a number of gauges were outside of normal range.

The second problem the power plant operators faced was that the control panel was generating false and contradictory information. The control panel falsely reported that the still open valve bleeding off vital coolant had closed. The temperature of the water in the vicinity of the valve was also being misreported in a way that reassured operators that the valve was working as usual. But because the reactor had decided to take itself down a few notches, which required less coolant, the operators reduced the water flow. This, plus the leaking valve, brought the coolant to a level below the reactor core, which now began superheating itself, generating excess steam and setting off chemical reactions that produced radioactive gases that began blowing through the relief valve and out into the world. At this point, the operators were thoroughly perplexed, and ran through a variety of actions, none of which seemed to work.

The operators' predicament was similar to what the police officers faced outside of Eleanor Bumpurs' apartment. When the cops arrived on the scene they had to make sense of the various members of the thwarted eviction committee, who were excitedly sounding multiple alarms with an air of authority, even though some of those alarms were patently false. When the cops entered the apartment in a manner partially responsive to the false data, their tactics not only didn't work, they helped fuel Mrs. Bumpurs' agitated, weapon-wielding response that was ended by the fatal shotgun blast.

Three Mile Island killed no one, but came close. With the incredible heat the reactor core was generating, the water in other pipes running in and out of the reactor building began to overheat. Filled with steam and superheated water, the pipes began banging and shaking, ready to blow. Just as in Eleanor Bumpurs' apartment, nothing was going right.

What the Three Mile Island operators still had—and the ESU officers didn't have, after they had entered the apartment—was time. Though the power plant operators acted urgently not knowing what their time cushion was, the scene was not the one of split second chaos and improvisation that accompanied the attempted seizure of Mrs. Bumpurs. Still, the control room operators made a number of wrong decisions, some of which "over-steered" the reactor.

Over-steering is a common decisional blunder in time-pressured crises.[39] Think of the tendency to jerk the steering wheel back to the left when your car starts to skid to the right. At Three Mile Island, over-steering involved, among other things, reducing the injection of coolant into the system nearly to zero. Fortunately, this occurred with enough time to correct the skid. In 1986, however, operator over-steering helped the Chernobyl nuclear reactor in the Ukraine blow sky high, with numerous fatalities and radiation spewed over much of Europe.[40]

The second shot that killed Eleanor Bumpurs may or may not have been a case of over-steering by the officer handling the shotgun. Testimony by the police officers described Mrs. Bumpurs as still aggressive after the first shot, while autopsy evidence indicated that the first shot disabled her knife hand.[41] However, the two shots were seconds apart, and over-steering not only involves misjudgment but misperception as well. In general, over-steering by police officers in close-quartered, chaotic confrontations that transpire in a matter of seconds can be expected. Even continuous, careful training can do little more than reduce the frequency with which such situations produce erroneous judgments and misapplied force that may well be deadly.

The Three Mile Island reactor was finally brought under control by an operator who had been called in from home.[42] With a fresh eye, he looked at elements of the system that his fellow operators had categorized as non-problematic, including the true culprit; the stuck open relief valve whose indicators reported a closed condition with near normal temperatures. When the operator isolated that valve from the system, temperatures started going down, as did the pressure inside the reactor building and the piping that serviced it. Thus was complete disaster averted.

Three Mile Island was still a major failure. The reactor had partially melted into itself, creating a radioactive slagheap that took more than ten years to clean up and then seal forever. Similarly, the Bumpurs incident, despite its predominant "normal accident" characteristics, was a major failure that helped create racially charged imagery that hobbles the NYPD, and policing in general, to this day.

* * *

Perrow's conclusion about nuclear power plants was that the risk of "normal accidents," however small, presented too great a potential for catastrophe. He argued against any further investments in nuclear power and proposed that serious consideration be given to shutting down nuclear power plants already in operation.[43] Perrow's argument was buttressed by the meltdown at Japan's Fukushima Daiichi plant after the tsunami of March 2011, when conditions engineers hadn't accounted for overwhelmed all protections to create a wide-ranging catastrophe that will take decades to fix.

## The Death of Amadou Diallo

The NYPD shooting of Eleanor Bumpers in 1984 was set up by ill-advised moves and misleading information generated by multiple agencies that had dealt with her case for months. When, on the day of her eviction, stymied authorities called for reinforcements, the police got the last minute call to deal with the desperate and delusional Mrs. Bumpers.

The large cast of government agencies and the months of robotic, tunnel-vision actions that set the stage for Eleanor Bumpers' death is not the usual formula for controversial police shootings and assaults. Most often the questionable use of force involves just two characters—the police (one or more officers) and civilians (again one or more) that those officers feel are suspicious or threatening—and these cases play out, start to finish, in minutes.

Over a decade after Eleanor Bumpers death, two high-profile NYPD cases occurring within eighteen months of one another followed the one act/two-character model while repeating the racial subtext from the Bumpers case. In both cases, adrenalized white cops misinterpreting a situation delivered grievous injury or death to black males who had committed no crime.

The first case, in August 1997, involved Abner Louima, who had been a spectator to a fight between two women that had spilled out of a club where Louima had been partying. When the police waded in, Louima was caught up in the action and one of the officers, Justin Volpe, mistakenly believed Louima had hit him. With Louima in his custody, an enraged Officer Volpe, along with other officers, beat Louima on the way to the station house. There Volpe sodomized Louima with a broomstick.[44]

The Louima case was not a normal accident—it was a case of brutality with malice aforethought delivered in a rogue moment by an officer who had lost all professional bearings. The patent excessive force and lack of restraint by Volpe, along with the victim's race, were front and center as the case played out in the courts, the media and public discourse.[45] Four other officers were charged with covering up for or abetting Volpe, with all but one acquitted at trial or on appeal. His criminal trial earned Volpe a thirty-year prison sentence; civil trials ultimately cost the City of New York $9 million.[46]

The fallout from the Abner Louima case was ongoing when, in February 1999, Amadou Diallo, a twenty-two-year-old immigrant from West Africa was killed in a fusillade of 41 shots fired by four plainclothes officers on anti-crime patrol in the Bronx.[47]

Diallo had been standing alone just after midnight atop the entryway stoop of the row house where he lived. The cops, driving by in an unmarked car, decided something was amiss with this man outside a building entrance in the middle of the cold night. The unmarked car reversed and stopped in front of Diallo's building, with the officers quick-stepping out of the vehicle and shouting commands meant to freeze Diallo. As the cops swarmed towards him up the stairs, Diallo backed into the vestibule while reaching for his wallet, which the cops mistook for a gun. The firing commenced, and ended only when the first two officers up the steps had each emptied their 16 round magazines, and the other two officers had followed-up with nine more shots. Amadou Diallo was dead.

The Amadou Diallo shooting echoed the Bumpers case in some respects: white officers, black casualty; misapprehension by the officers about the individual before them; a chaotic, split-second and tragic denouement. A major difference in the Diallo case was that no other agency contributed to the misunderstandings that determined the tactics employed by the officers. The Diallo case strips police encounters with citizen/suspects down to the bare essentials. Namely, how do officers think, perceive, analyze and react under intense time pressure in uncertain situations? When do officers' thoughts, perceptions and interpretations combine in ways that produce deadly consequences for innocent individuals such as Amadou Diallo?

Diallo, of course, had every right to be taking in the air outside his dwelling, whether at high noon or midnight. The officers, however, did not think about Diallo's behavior in this way. The most experienced Street Crimes officer, from the front passenger seat, set the tone: "Hold up! Hold up! What's that guy doing there?" So, the first articulated thought about Diallo, who belonged on the stoop, was that he was out of place in a way that required some kind of rapid response. "Hold up! Hold up!" was enough to send the unmarked cruiser into reverse, coming to a stop in front of Diallo's building.

The tone of the encounter was thus set.

The two officers on the passenger side, including the officer who first spotted Diallo, flung open the car's doors and advanced between parked vehicles towards Diallo's stoop, announcing themselves as police, with one officer flashing a badge. Whether the multi-lingual Diallo understood right away it was police approaching him is unknown. Language barriers may have been in play, but aggressive body language by the cops may also have set off alarms in Diallo that drowned out their words. Cops are trained to convey commanding posture and tone to control situations that might turn dangerous. And the officer who set the encounter in motion led the charge believing that Diallo might be a push-in burglar or a long-sought serial rapist whose general description Diallo matched.

Whatever he saw or heard, Diallo said not a word but instead turned and ran into the vestibule.

This only put the two cops in the lead more on edge as they arrived, guns drawn, at the top of the stoop where they encountered Diallo at the inner door of the vestibule. Diallo had one hand on the doorknob as he turned towards the cops who were now in full-throated shouts—"Don't make me shoot you!" yelled one—to make Diallo to show his hands. And then one of the closest officers saw Diallo reaching in his pocket and drawing out a black object that … had … to … be … a … GUN! The officer shouted out "GUN!" and then emptied his weapon at Diallo, as did the officer alongside who, in the chaos of ricocheting bullets, tripped backwards and fell, which convinced the two officers bringing up the rear that their partner had been shot, so they started shooting into the vestibule as well.

Forty-one shots and seconds later Amadou Diallo lay dead, and one of the officers could only repeat, as he gazed at the wallet in Diallo's hand, "Where's the f***ing gun?"

## When What We See Isn't

What the cops thought they saw was totally wrong, but nonetheless mobilized them to a series of actions that left them cursing over an innocent corpse.

Malcolm Gladwell, in his book *Blink*, uses the Diallo case, among others, to explore how people perceive, interpret and respond to rapid-fire situations, and what kind of training might help us, or officers on patrol, get fooled less often.[48]

As the Diallo case shows, misreads that intensify situations increase the potential that things will end tragically. Witness the Trayvon Martin case in Florida, whose legal resolution remains up in the air as this book goes to press. In that "policing" encounter, George Zimmerman, a community resident on neighborhood watch saw, in Trayvon Martin, a crime waiting to be committed, and initiated an encounter. Though emerging facts indicate each individual misread the other to some extent, only George Zimmerman, who ended the encounter with a fatal shot, remains alive to justify what he saw and believed.

Law enforcement is, of course, held to a much higher standard in such situations. So, it is not surprising that the police dispatcher asked Zimmerman to back off pending the arrival of officers. Officers are better trained and more experienced in recognizing and correctly interpreting signals that suspect and/or agitated individuals convey. These abilities are critical since, as the Diallo case demonstrates, even with police an initial "false read" can set things on a tragic path where the first misinterpretation produces erroneous responses and further wrong assumptions as the situation gains velocity and grows more intense.

The cascading misinterpretations went like this for the officers in the Bronx that night. Diallo's relaxed posture on his own porch became the arrogant ease of a felon lying in wait. *Let's go check him out!* Retreat to the vestibule became escape. *Don't let him get away!* A cowering, diminutive Diallo twists around to see what's coming. *A shooter's crouch!* Out the wallet comes to placate his pursuers. *He has a gun!*

Every interpretation is wrong, but understandable, especially as an incident races on chaotically, each action a second or two after the last, and the officers were in fact acquitted after trial. But "normal accident—law enforcement style" doesn't cut it as a general explanation for such cases. What went on in the Diallo and similar cases needs to be addressed by modifying tactics, re-thinking deployment policies and training in techniques that help officers better read and manage individuals and themselves so as to prevent encounters from needlessly escalating. Officers should be as versed in techniques for decelerating and moderating situations as they are in techniques for forcefully controlling them.

This author helped develop a program mandated by the New York City Council in 2001 as a result of the Louima assault, the Diallo shooting and the death of Patrick Dorismond, another minority club-goer who ended up in a fatal struggle with an undercover officer in 2000.[49] John Jay College of Criminal Justice, where I teach, was selected to mount a credit-bearing program where NYPD officers, studying together outside any "official training," could consider how issues of organization, management, psychology, and community dynamics shaped their jobs.

Some classes explored how subtle, reflexive and unconscious stereotyping based on difference, which often translates to race, influences decisions. Those classes incorporated research approaches that Gladwell referenced in his incisive analysis of the Diallo shooting. As Gladwell convincingly argues in the context of the Diallo case, stereotyping is in motion from the moment we set eyes on a situation or individual. Understanding the power of stereotypes, and reflecting on how they get established and operate *in us*, can raise the threshold against instant misreads that lock incidents on to tragic paths. Such "training aforethought," by making snap judgments based on stereotypes less likely, buys time for the application of tactics designed to keep officers safe while preventing situations from spinning out of control.

The NYPD also made organizational changes after the Diallo shooting that were designed to make encounters between special unit officers and citizen/suspects less combustible. First, street crime unit officers were put in uniform. Diallo, who as a street vendor dealt with officers on regular patrol, would less likely have fled the approach of uniformed officers that night. It's not clear if Diallo realized at first, or at all, that the men rushing at him in street gear were cops. The all-units-in-uniform mandate was later modified, however, with some units reverting to plainclothes. [50]

Next the NYPD moved to decentralize the Street Crimes Unit, setting up eight commands across the city. Before Diallo the street crime teams operated under a central command that sent units to crime "hot spots" across the city. Identifying a "hot spot" could mean rapid deployment of a hastily put together unit within a precinct or across the boundaries of several precincts without local commanders being notified. Diallo was shot by four officers — three were street crime unit "rookies" — who had never worked together before and were patrolling an unfamiliar neighborhood.[51] Other African immigrants who worked long hours lived on Diallo's street, but the officers didn't have such "local knowledge" to help them see Diallo for what he was rather than what they wrongly made him out to be.

## When What We Want Can't Be

The Diallo killing also occurred as productivity pressure was intensifying on the street crimes operation. Officers were being added in an attempt to maintain the high rates of crime reduction that such units had helped the NYPD achieve throughout the mid-1990s. But the pressure to keep reducing street crime at the mid-90s rate was pushing operations up against mathematical and practical limits by 1999.

Mathematically, if your operations reduce crime by 10% a year for five years (Year One: 1000−100=900; Year Two: 900−90=810; Year Three: 810−81=729; Year Four: 729−73=656; Year 5: 654−65=589) you're doing just fine except with that senior commander who wants to know why the 100 solved cases from the "Year One" glory days shrank to a paltry 65 last year. Crime reduction rates also slow as the "pool" of crimes diminishes, but that doesn't stop bosses from obsessing about keeping up those 10% declines. Such a command mentality in the NYPD was fueling pressure on the Street Crimes operation to keep its numbers up.

Practically, any new crime-fighting program will have difficulty maintaining its initial crime reduction rates. When the program starts, crime is everywhere and a good percentage of criminals are so blatant, drug-addled or inept that they are easy pickings. As the program goes on, the "low hanging fruit" perpetrators go to jail or find more legitimate pursuits. The remaining criminals occupy higher ground. Smarter to begin with, they are also smart enough to adjust to a given anti-crime program's techniques.

When you add the mathematics to the practicalities, any anti-crime approach is likely to have a point of diminishing returns, where more troops will not mean higher crime reduction and previously successful tactics can be stalemated as the criminal element changes how it operates. In the stalemated condition especially, it often makes more sense, despite a program's historical successes, to radically overhaul or even end a program—which eventually occurred with the street crimes approach.[52]

William Bratton, who as NYPD Commissioner was an early architect of the NYPD's "street crimes" approach, had some interesting thoughts on how to deal with a program with a history of success that reaches a point of diminishing returns. Bratton, three years after he left the NYPD, had just finished a presentation to graduate students at John Jay College when he was pointedly asked about the very recent Diallo shooting. In response, Bratton was dubious about adding street crime officers in pursuit of ever more elusive productivity goals. He suggested instead redeploying some street crime unit officers to community policing and other assignments that would help solidify and build upon the remarkable crime drops the program had achieved. Bratton termed the redeployment a "peace dividend," a way of looking at things that, had it won out over "keep those numbers up," might have spared the life of Amadou Diallo.[53]

* * *

Our next "normal accident" focus will be police chases. The pursuit by police of vehicles whose occupants are suspected of some offense is the single most dangerous activity of law enforcement—for the suspects, for the police and for innocent bystanders. Police chases that go wrong carry a small, but real, risk of ending in catastrophic accidents with multiple fatalities, years of lawsuits and substantial liability judgments against agencies and even officers. Just like the nuclear power plants that Perrow felt should be put in mothballs, many law enforcement agencies have taken steps to severely limit the pursuit of suspects fleeing in their vehicles.

## *Pursuit to the Death in Minnesota*

Everett Contois was drunk and on a joyride one August night in 1995. He and three other teenagers were careening down a rural road in Blaine, a suburb of Minneapolis, when they passed a police cruiser occupied by Officer William Bott, who clocked the speeding car at 111 miles an hour. Bott gave chase.[54]

The car full of teenagers kept ahead of Officer Bott by running lights and stop signs at speeds between 60 and 80 miles an hour. Then Contois sped past a second officer, John Burch, who joined the chase, becoming the closest pursuer.

With Burch hot on his tail, Contois went through four more stop signs and ended up on a dead end street in a residential neighborhood. To get away, Contois drove over two lawns and a retaining wall in order to get to the next street over and then sped off again. Officer Burch was right behind as the pursuit wound its way back to main roads.

What Officer Burch did next was right out of the police chase videos we see on TV. He drove alongside the rear fender of the fleeing vehicle then cut his wheels in order to ram Contois' car. The purpose of the maneuver is to throw the suspect's vehicle into a spin, bringing it to a stop. On the third try, Officer Burch did indeed throw the fleeing car into a spin. The car spun across the median of the highway to the other side where it ended up facing oncoming traffic. Contois sped off again anyhow, now going the wrong way on the divided highway, putting innocent motorists in deadly jeopardy.

Officer Burch then rammed Contois' car a fourth time, and spun it onto the median again. This put Contois onto the side of the highway he had originally been on. The car full of teenagers kept on going, this time with the traffic flow, at speeds of 80 to 100 miles an hour. Contois then sped off an exit onto another highway, and soon exited that roadway and entered the town of Spring Lake Park, where another police cruiser joined the chase.

In Spring Lake Park, Contois ran his last red light. Entering the same intersection was a pick-up driven by Timothy Helseth, who was riding with a friend. The two vehicles collided at high speed. The passenger in Helseth's car was killed. Helseth was paralyzed for life. The three teenage passengers in Contois' car were seriously injured.

The aftermath of this chase went on for years. Contois was convicted of third degree murder, criminal vehicular operation and fleeing a police officer. Timothy Helseth sued Bott, Burch and the City of Blaine. The legal cases dragged on for seven years until 2002, when the Supreme Court of the United States declined to review the split Appeals Court decision dismissing Helseth's claim that his injuries were a result of improper police action. Though the claims against Officer Bott were dismissed early on, Officer Burch was enmeshed in legal action and the prospects of financial ruin to the very end.

## High Speed Pursuit of the Normal Accident

The tragic outcome of the police chase outside of Minneapolis was not exactly an aberration. Once a police pursuit starts, the likelihood of an accident occurring is about 30%, and casualties occur in fifteen of every hundred chases. A 1996 National Institute of Justice Report,[55] one of the first to summarize research into high-speed police pursuits from selected jurisdictions across the nation, found:

- A collision of some type occurred in 32% of pursuits.
- 20% of pursuits resulted in property damage; 13% in personal injury.
- A fatality occurred in approximately one of every hundred police pursuits.
- Occupants of the pursued vehicle represented 70% percent of pursuit-related casualties (injuries plus fatalities); law enforcement officers and innocent civilians driving, or standing, in the wrong place at the wrong time each represented half of the remaining 30% of those injured or killed.

The first edition of this book looked at Pennsylvania's pursuit statistics from 2000–2004.[56] Pennsylvania law requires local departments to report their pursuits, and the State Police then aggregate the figures into a statewide annual report. Pennsylvania was not one of the several states studied by the 1996 NIJ Report, but Pennsylvania's 2005 figures echoed the earlier study's findings. For this edition, we looked at Pennsylvania's most recent police pursuit data, from 2010.[57] While the overall number of pursuits is down, the percentage of bad outcomes is not.

- 1413 pursuits produced 583 crashes, a 31% rate;
- Total injuries were 205. Nine people were killed;
- The casualty rate—injured plus killed—was 15%;
- Property damage approached $1,600,000, with 32% of the damage inflicted on innocent motorists.

These are sobering numbers that actually understate how dangerous police pursuits are. That is because Pennsylvania police gave up the chase about a quarter of the time, sometimes early on under supervisors' orders. These chases ended before damage could be done. The longer a chase goes on, the more likely it is to end in a collision.

The downside of police pursuits is influencing the policies of departments across the country. Some jurisdictions are swearing off high speed pursuits for most observed infractions and other departments are limiting when, where and how pursuits can be conducted no matter what the crime. The daylight police chase of fleeing vehicles through crowded city streets is increasingly becoming an artifact. Pennsylvania's police chases have dropped nearly 40% since 2000–2004, which almost certainly reflects the accumulation of policies limiting vehicular pursuits.

The chases that still occur, however, can be just as deadly as ever. In March 2012, a stopped motorist in Philadelphia allegedly produced a gun instead of a license and then took off leading police on a 20 minute chase across densely populated neighborhoods, through parking lots, up on sidewalks, racing wrong way against traffic before T-boning a car containing a family, killing the father and badly injuring his wife and baby, who ultimately recovered. Philadelphia's pursuit policies, which had been tightened up earlier after two officers died in chase-connected accidents, were slated for further review.[58]

The tragic Philadelphia pursuit shows in microcosm how difficult it is to bring normal accident dynamics under control and keep them there. And the larger picture is no more encouraging. An International Association of Police Chiefs' study in 2008 surveyed 56 agencies in 30 states; the results pretty much matched Pennsylvania's pursuit outcomes.[59] In a report prompted in part by the deaths of four civilians in three chases within two months in Milwaukee, USA Today looked into ten years of innocent bystander death and injury statistics from the U.S. Department of Transportation, which showed virtually no change from 1999 to 2008.[60]

The accidents arising out of police pursuits underscore the factors that create "normal accidents." These factors, illustrated below in terms of the high-speed vehicle chase, are the same systemic factors that can cause any number of police operations to crash and burn.

- Multiple systems—vehicles, operators, roadways, traffic controls—are interacting.
- The pursuit system, specifically officers, cannot control other systems—the flow of unaware, innocent motorists; the unconcerned strolling of pedestrians.
- Various elements in each system have differential reliability—ranging from police officers trained in pursuit driving, to officers with little or no such training, and on to fleeing drivers who may be drunk, panicked or in unfamiliar stolen vehicles.
- As the number of elements involved goes up the accident potential increases—the more police cars in a chase, the heavier the traffic, the more likely an accident.
- Technical error is made more likely, as are accidents, by radios on different channels, multiple dispatchers and jurisdictional issues that arise when chases, as they often do, cross departmental boundaries.
- Complexity in the surrounding system increases accident risk; in the case of pursuits more accidents occur on city streets than on limited access highways.

It is no wonder that police pursuits so often end in accidents. Pursuits involve split-second decisions by officers engaged in high intensity situations involving racing vehicles that can suddenly confront obstacles that must be avoided or else. And split-second decisions in these dynamic circumstances must be made by everyone else: suspects, innocent drivers and pedestrians. There may be no better normal accident model in law enforcement than the police pursuit.

A police organization deals with failure when a police pursuit results in injury or death to civilians or officers. Failure looms even if only the suspect is injured, or nothing worse than property damage occurs, especially if officers violated procedures when starting, continuing and concluding the chase. Everett Contois—who emerged relatively unharmed from the fatal wreckage at the end of his drunken joyride—maintained that, after playing "cat and mouse" with Officer Bott, he feared for his life in the face of the "deadly force" Officer Burch was applying.[61] A more sympathetic or more championed defendant than Contois can easily become a rallying point for protests against "excessive" police behavior. Whether or not the fleeing motorist is reprehensible, claims of emotional distress, rights violations or injury may well translate to million dollar lawsuits against local governments that can ill-afford to pay.

# What *Went* Wrong versus What *Is* Wrong

From this point forward in the book, we will be looking at larger organizational contexts as a source of law enforcement failures. The areas we will consider are:

- Basic organizational structures
- Quality control and oversight
- The power and influence of organizational culture(s)
- The institutional leverage organizations exercise over the surrounding environment
- How public positions and policies shape incumbents' attitudes and integrity

These are big issues and, as we will see, when something is wrong in any of these areas the law enforcement agency is on track for a big fall.

This 'normal accident' chapter has been more about what can go wrong in the everyday world of policing.

"What happened?" is *the* question for a police supervisor arriving at an incident in which his or her officers have been involved.

If the incident looks like any of the cases in this chapter, the "What happened" question becomes "What went wrong?"

As we have seen, there is a lot to tease out in order to answer this question, from the mechanics of equipment, to the quality of information, to the imagery our brains seize upon under stress.

Sometimes answering "What went wrong?" takes a while, as the Holidazzle Parade case shows.

Even with the simple issues in that case, a rush to judgment about bad positioning by a careless cop/driver threatened to end the inquiry with the wrong answers—a result that would have kept lots of officers in harm's way behind the wheel of their defective cruisers.

The Minneapolis chief stood up by holding out for the possibility of equipment malfunction. He was both right, and fair to the officer involved. He displayed leadership in resisting the quick, easy answer that promised to get the agency off the hook but would have left the accused officer twisting in the wind. Not all chiefs would have made that choice.

And the pressure on chiefs to move from the "What happened/went wrong?" question to the "What *is* wrong?" question is constant.

High profile incidents involving police are magnets for those who think they have the answer to "What is wrong?" with policing. Even as commanders begin to figure out "what happened" in the deaths of an Eleanor Bumpurs or an Amadou Diallo, they are fielding critiques of their department's structure, culture and attitudes towards the community. These critiques are legitimate speech, and quite often are on to something, but should not cause departments to short-change the "What happened/what went wrong?" question. The answers to that question are critical for reducing mistakes, whether from normal accidents or other factors.

The "what is wrong" inquiry, our focus from here on, should never exclude "normal accident" as a possible explanation. To take just one iconic case, that of Rodney King, there were several "What is wrong" issues. From the top down, the LAPD had consciously adopted an aggressive stance towards criminal suspects. In addition, several police agencies showed up at the King stop, and figuring out who was in charge affected how King was approached. These are issues of structure and culture that we will closely look at in coming chapters.

The King case also featured "normal accident" factors we've looked at in this chapter. Extended pursuit at high speed over long distances preceded the King stop. Officers arrived with adrenaline pumping. The aggressive posture of the LAPD officers was accentuated by their supervisor's speculation about the drugs King had taken. The Taser hits that should have immobilized King didn't. Hardly any of the multiple baton strikes, also designed to subdue an unruly individual, were correctly delivered or had the desired effect.

The Rodney King incident initiated a wholesale review of the policies, procedures and training relating to the use of Tasers and batons and the conduct of high speed chases and apprehensions, and rightly so. Similarly, with regard to cases in this chapter, the "fail safe" circuit in police cruisers no longer serves double duty as a means for flashing emergency lights. Police tactics with emotionally disturbed individuals have been refined, and officers in forward-looking departments are being trained to recognize how stereotypes can unconsciously dictate their approaches to individuals and communities.

So, as we go on to view failure through a structural and cultural lens, readers should remember that much of what "goes wrong" in organizations is rooted in mundane, ordinary elements whose degradation is little noticed. The best preventive medicine against such failures lies in continually enhancing the reliability of personnel and equipment, smoothing the interactions between organizational components, and insuring that accurate and timely information gets to personnel responsible for choosing the correct course of action in critical situations.

# Endnotes

1. Allen Feuer and Jim Dwyer, "City Settles Suit in Louima Torture," *New York Times*, July 13, 2001, A1.

2. Charles Perrow, *Normal Accidents: Living with High Risk Technologies* (New York: Basic Books, 1984).

3. Charles Perrow, *Normal Accidents: Living with High Risk Technologies*, (Princeton, NJ: Princeton University Press, 1999).

4. Nicholas Daniloff, "Media Developments In The Soviet Union," Harold W. Anderson Lecture, (Washington, D.C.: World Press Freedom Committee/ Center for Strategic and International Studies, November 30, 1987). See also, Nicholas Daniloff, "Chernobyl and Its Political Fallout: A Reassessment," *Demokratizatsiya*,(Winter 2004) http://www.find-articles.com/p/articles/mi_qa3996/is_200401/ai_n9358348 (Accessed April 16, 2005).

5. Perrow, *Normal Accidents,* (1984): 78.

6. Ibid.

7. Diane Vaughan, *The Challenger Launch Decision: Risky Technology, Culture and Deviance at NASA,* (Chicago: University of Chicago Press, 1997): 153–95. Vaughan's chapter on the "normalization of deviance" nicely explains how organizations settle comfortably into high-risk routines.

8. Perrow, *Normal Accidents,* (1984): 15–31.

9. Gregori Medvedev, *The Truth about Chernobyl,* (New York: Basic Books, 1991): 67–73.

10. Perrow, *Normal Accidents,* (1984): 66.

11. Perrow, *Normal Accidents,* (1984): 64.

12. Perrow, *Normal Accidents,* (1984): 75–78.

13. Michael T. Charles, "Accidental Shooting: An Analysis," *Journal of Contingencies and Crisis Management* 8, no. 3, (September 2000): 157.

14. James Chiles, *Inviting Disaster: Lessons from the Edge of Technology* (New York: Harper Business, 2002): 235.

15. Chiles, *Inviting Disaster,* 233.

16. Ibid.

17. Anna Wilde Mathews, "A Simple Case of Sudden Acceleration—Or So It Seemed at First to Bob Young," *The Wall Street Journal*, November 1, 1999.

18. Chiles, *Inviting Disaster,* 238.

19. Mathews, "A Simple Case."

20. National Highway Traffic Safety Administration, VEHICLE ADVISORY for Law Enforcement Agencies, Washington, DC: April 1, 1999.

21. Mario Merola, *Big City D.A.* (New York: Random House, 1988): 9

22. Ibid.

23. Merola, *Big City D.A.,* 10.

24. Selwyn Raab, "Eviction Death Leads the City to Demote Two," *New York Times*, November 21, 1984.

25. Merola, *Big City D.A.*, 11.

26. Ibid.

27. Merola, *Big City D.A.*, 12.

28. Ibid.

29. Ibid.

30. Merola, *Big City D.A.*, 13.

31. Ibid.

32. Alphonso Pinkley, *Lest We Forget—White Hate Crimes: Howard Beach and Other Racial Atrocities*, (Chicago: Third World Press, 1994).

33. Selwyn Raab, "Officer Indicted in Bumpurs Case," *New York Times*, February 1, 1985.

34. Frank J. Prial, "Judge Acquits Sullivan in Shotgun Slaying of Bumpurs," New York Times, February 27, 1987.

35. Jesus Rangel, "Panel is Shown Devices for Use with the Disabled," *New York Times*, November 29, 1984.

36. Selwyn Raab, "Head of HRA Faults Actions in Eviction Case," *New York Times*, November 10, 1984.

37. Selwyn Raab, "Eviction Death Leads the City to Demote Two," *New York Times*, November 21, 1984.

38. Dawn Fallik and Tom Avril, "TMI: Legacy of an Accident," *Philadelphia Inquirer,* March 25–28, 2004. This three part series is the source for the time line and other descriptive elements in this section. The series and interactive graphics are also available at http://www.philly.com/mld/inquirer/news/special_packages/phillycom_teases/8257351.ht m (Accessed on April 1, 2005). See also U.S. Nuclear Regulatory Commission, "Fact Sheet on the Accident at Three Mile Island," (Washington, D. C.: March 2004) http://www. nrc.gov/ reading-rm/doc-collections/fact-sheets/3mile-isle.pdf (Accessed April 30, 2005).

39. Dietrich Dorner, *The Logic of Failure: Recognizing and Avoiding Errors in Complex Situations*, (New York: Perseus Books, 1996): 30.

40. Ibid.

41. Selwyn Raab, "Autopsy Finds Bumpurs Was Hit by Two Blasts," *New York Times*, November 27, 1984.

42. Chiles, *Inviting Disaster*, 58–61.

43. Perrow, *Normal Accidents* (1984): 350.

44. _____, "Chronology of Events in the Abner Louima Case," New York Daily News, July 13, 2001.

45. Sewell Chan, "The Abner Louima Case, 10 Years Later," The New York Times, August 9, 2007.

46. Ibid.

47. The description of the Diallo case below is drawn from several sources, including: Jane Fritsch, "The Diallo Verdict: The Overview, 4 Officers in Diallo Shooting Are Acquitted of All Charges," *The New York Times,* February 26, 2000, B6; _____, "At Diallo Trial Justice Is Weighed in Different Measures," CNN.com, February 17, 2000. The principal source, however, is Malcolm Gladwell, *Blink: the Power of Thinking without Thinking*, New York: Back Bay Books, 2005, 189–244.

48. Gladwell, *Blink*.

49. Kevin Flynn, "Shooting Raises Scrutiny of Police Antidrug Tactics," The New York Times, March 25, 2000.

50. Julia Vitullo-Martin, "The Legacy of Amadou Diallo." GothamGazette.com—Citizens Union Foundation, February 4, 2002. http://www.gothamgazette.com/iotw/diallo/ (Accessed January 25, 2012).

51. Ibid.

52. Robert Kolker, "Street Fight," *New York Magazine,* April 22, 2002.

53. William Bratton, Spring 1999 Graduate Lecture, John Jay College of Criminal Justice.

54. The materials for this case are drawn from the fact pattern presented by the concurring and dissenting judges in *Helseth v. Burch,* 258 F.3d 867 (8th Cir. 2001). See also Don Kidd, ed. "High Speed Pursuits—Intent to Harm Standard," *CJI Legal Briefs* 6, no. 3 (Fall 2001): 7–10.

55. National Law Enforcement and Corrections Technology Center, "High-Speed Pursuit: New Technologies around the Corner," (Washington, DC: National Institute of Justice, October 1996) http://www.nlectc.org/txtfiles/speed.html (Accessed July 22, 2004).

56. Pennsylvania State Police, *Police Pursuit Reporting System* (Harrisburg, PA: 2005) http://ucr.psp.state.pa.us/UCR/Reporting/Pursuit/Annual/AnnualPursuitUI.asp (Accessed April 30, 2005).

57. Pennsylvania State Police, Bureau of Research and Development, *Pennsylvania Police Pursuits: 2010 Annual Report.* Harrisburg, PA: 2011.

58. Inquirer Editorial Board, "Review of city's police-chase policy justified," *The Philadelphia Inquirer,* April 4, 2012.

59. Cynthia Lum and George Fachner, *Police Pursuits in an Age of Innovation and Reform,* Alexandria, VA: International Association of Chiefs of Police, 2008.

60. Larry Copeland, "Deaths Lead Police to Question High-Speed Chase Policies," *USA Today,* April 23, 2010.

61. *Helseth v. Burch,* 18, as cited by a dissenting judge, who felt Officer Burch had gone beyond his authority in the conduct of the chase.

# Chapter Three

# Structural Failure in Law Enforcement: Design Defects in Organization

## Basic Structures of Organization

Organizations consist of a deliberate arrangement of people doing specific jobs following particular procedures in order to accomplish a set of goals determined by some authority. Law enforcement agencies divide their sworn officers into ranks, from officer to chief, or from trooper to superintendent. Regardless of the terminology, superior officers direct the subordinate officers. Civilian employees are similarly arranged. Some clerk, others supervise.

Law enforcement agencies also, with the exception of very small departments, divide up the core task of maintaining order while preventing and solving crime. Officers patrol, detectives investigate. Some headquarters personnel plan deployments and tactics, directing officers where to go and what to do. Training officers school members of the force in those tactics before they are deployed and throughout their careers. Some civilian employees staff the 911 call center, others process the paperwork generated by arrests.

Rank (hierarchy) and task division (specialization) comprise the superstructure of the law enforcement organization. Rank provides for direction and resolution of issues while specialization creates component tasks that should combine logically to achieve the mission of the agency.

The central mission of any organization, which is order maintenance and crime prevention for local law enforcement agencies, is carried out by the operating core, which for municipal police agencies consists of units such as patrol and investigations and emergency services.[1] Just about anything else layered onto an organization is in service to the operating core, or to the outside authorities that chartered and continue to sanction the organization.

For instance, a crime scene investigations (CSI) unit may set forth the steps for securing a crime scene before CSI personnel arrive. These steps govern the behavior of officers first on the scene, and the protocols followed by detectives who come along later. The legal division may chime in with advice about the treatment of witnesses and maintaining the chain of custody with respect to evidence. Still, the function being served is investigation and, when the culprit is apprehended, an "operator" such as a detective will likely make the arrest.

The CSI and legal units are but two that help the operating core do its work better. What the public relations unit is doing is helping get out a clear message about what the operating core is doing. What the personnel office does is make sure the operators are getting paid and are treated in accordance with employment law and union contract. What the chief or, in a large agency, the legislative relations unit does is to work with legislators to insure that the authority and money granted to the police department are being used as intended. While he or she is at it, the chief may also reassure the legislature that the police department is coordinating nicely with prosecutors, corrections, and the courts.

# The Haphazard Design of Organization

Organization charts come across as tidy arrangements, as logically structured designs for organizational effectiveness. This is often not the case. The organization chart may have features that represent the legislature's most recent dictate, or the outcome of last month's struggle between deputy commissioners. The chart may show lines of reporting authority that no one pays attention to and offices that exist in name only. An organization's operating structure starts deviating from the blueprints from day one. While "we make it up as we go along" may not be any top executive's motto of choice, it is frequently the way organizations get constructed.

Organizational charts often belie the actual power being exercised by the offices illustrated. In the mid-1990s, Michael Ovitz looked more powerful on paper as president of the Disney Corporation than he really was. The chief finance officer welcomed Ovitz by announcing that he wouldn't report to him, but would continue reporting to Michael Eisner, Disney's chairman.[2] Then Ovitz and Eisner had a falling out, which caused Eisner to run even more of the show right around Ovitz who nonetheless hung on for almost another year.[3] On the other hand, when Bill Gates stepped aside as president of Microsoft in favor of Steve Ballmer, an industry news report said that, in the view of some observers, "Ballmer has effectively been running Microsoft for some time."[4]

Compared to private firms, public agencies, and particularly law enforcement agencies, tend to have more enduring structural elements. Many interests help create a government agency, and these interests stay active trying to keep structural elements they value from being modified. Where civilian complaint review boards or other offices for independently reviewing the propriety of police actions have been established, they are likely to endure because of the substantial and continuing support these offices receive from minority communities and their elected representatives. A variety of laws also help determine the organization of law enforcement agencies, as well as the other parts of the criminal justice system.

The LAPD, from the 1950s through 1992, presents a good example of laws affecting organizational structure that, in turn, impacted law enforcement policy. For decades, until the 1991 Rodney King beating and the associated 1992 riots, civil service laws granted tenure to Los Angeles police chiefs. Thus insulated, chiefs such as Darryl Gates could and did operate with little regard for input from, and even public criticism for, mayors, the City Council and community groups. Thus, LAPD structures and policies changed slowly and mostly to the extent that chiefs recognized and chose to respond to changing political, social and legal climates. So, by the time of the 1992 riots, long-standing LAPD tactics and attitudes had alienated many of the city's minority communities.[5] The acquittal of the officers who had arrested and beaten King thus ignited a days-long incendiary riot for which the LAPD had no adequate response.[6]

After the devastating riots, criticism of the LAPD was widespread; city officials forced Gates out and the chief's job protections were sharply reduced.[7] A new chief was brought in from Philadelphia and given five years to impose change on a demoralized force whose members were understandably suspicious of the new regime. This, in turn, had its own ramifications, one of which was the Rampart scandal, which we will address further along in the book.

The hasty LAPD reforms in the wake of the riots illustrate a general truth about the structuring of organizations. Flawed organizational structures are predictable results of a creation process that is more art than science, and more often a function of happenstance and forced choice than of carefully thought-through design. The legacies of the haphazard structuring of organizations include divided authority, inappropriate tasking, communications failures, questionable personnel selection, perverse incentive systems and poorly designed processes. Alone or, just as likely, together, these structural flaws can cause critical performance failures in any organization.

Apart from executives and external authorities and constituencies, organizations are also shaped by the very units that compose them. Who does what in an organization has much to do with the differential leverage of units favored by performance and/or circumstance. The resulting organizational structure, as well as the employee incentive structure, may reflect power rather than functionality. The 9/11 Commission took the FBI to task for how the dominance of the criminal investigation division meant that anti-terrorism work, though touted by FBI brass, became a backwater. Most agents saw counter-terrorism as a career dead end, which starved this important function of talent. That changed when fuel-laden airliners piloted by Al Qaeda operatives brought down the twin towers of the World Trade Center. In this chapter, a new case, "The First 9/11," addresses the struggle among functions that went on in the FBI before that attack.

We will also look at the Philadelphia Police Department's assault on the radical group MOVE. That operation failed, killing eleven and burning down two city blocks. The planning for that assault largely bypassed top-level headquarters' staff but instead was delegated to units with narrowly drawn mandates located in remote facilities. As a result, sergeants and police officers ended up doing much of the planning in spite of, not because of, what was called for by the organization chart.

## Viewing Organizations Realistically

Organizations are perpetually under construction. Units are disbanded and created, downsized or expanded, split apart or merged. They are given new duties, relieved of old duties, have their reporting responsibilities modified, and get new bosses with new ideas about how things should be arranged. Communication links get severed and no one thinks to reestablish them. New computer systems and old computer systems are meshed but blind spots and glitches lurk. Organizational memory, which resides mostly inside people's heads, gets transferred out, retires, or is wiped out by new bosses unable to elicit what their subordinates know. All these factors create structural weaknesses in an organization. Aspiring law enforcement managers need to understand and look out for the range of factors that can compromise the readiness of their organization to meet challenges both large and small.

Vigilance is necessary because, in an organization with serious structural flaws inborn or developed slowly over time, members are often blind to just how problematic things have become. We will look at an immigration case where enforcement structures had been compromised over time as the agency adjusted to external pressure. By the standards applied after 9/11, the Immigration and Naturalization Service (INS), since incorporated into Homeland

Security, had been ineffectual. But for those managing the agency and doing the job prior to 9/11, the mediocre level of enforcement and results was simply normal, and had been for a long time. Important stakeholders were endorsing the INS's enforcement choices. All seemed well. In such delusion failure lurks, and is almost certain to catch the agency unawares and unprepared.

Chiefs, commissioners and high-ranking commanders are no less prone to these delusions, or to the deliberate blindness of those who see a problem but choose not to deal with it. Though one might think that an aware police official would quickly recognize and overcome active or passive resistance to putting more effective operating structures in place, this is frequently not the case. Executives refrain from jumping into the fray to make peace between warring units, to reconcile practice with policy and bring prodigal operations back into the fold. Instead, conflicts fester or resolve themselves, which may not be a pretty sight and quite often ends up restructuring the organization in unintended ways. Though executives may end up "approving" the new arrangements, they often have had little or nothing to do with creating them.

When executives keep their distance from internecine squabbles, or keep their eyes deliberately closed to poorly designed structures, they may consider the price of getting involved as too high. New laws or organization-wide policy changes demand tremendous effort; issues within the organization can be all but intractable. For instance, the dominance of patrol units in a state or local police department is not easy to change. Nor are the high-profile SWAT and Emergency Service jobs that tend to generate positive press and happy bosses but may also generate resentment from officers grinding away on patrol under supervisory glares.

Since law enforcement executives have a relatively short tenure in which to wrestle with a host of critical issues, few choose to seek major policy changes affecting powerful organizational elements almost certain to resist. Most executives live with the status quo, however problematic. But those chiefs who do the opposite, who confront reality and take on the powerful, established organizational groups, are the leaders who better prepare their organizations to move towards long-term effectiveness.

# Defining Structural Failure

We are going to use four cases in this chapter in order to look more closely at how the structures of law enforcement organizations break down. These cases are the JonBenet Ramsey murder investigation, the Immigration and Naturalization Service's (INS) failure to keep tabs on two 9/11 terrorist hijackers, the FBI's struggle to right-size its counter-terrorism efforts pre-9/11, and the Philadelphia Police Department's 1984 confrontation with the fringe group MOVE.

The JonBenet Ramsey case shows us the volatile psychodynamics of human hierarchical and inter-group relations erupting to wreak havoc on a high profile murder investigation. This case should help the reader better understand how the potential for damaging organizational conflict lurks along the lines that divide superior from subordinate, as well as along the lines that divide Unit A from Unit B. These conflicts are always ready to explode with the right combination of individuals and circumstances. This combination clicked in the JonBenet Ramsey case, which featured resource scarcity, withering media scrutiny and standoffs between aggressive detectives and more cautious prosecutors.

The INS case demonstrates failures of execution, coordination and follow-through. Several 9/11 hijackers entered and remained in the US despite issues concerning their eligibility for entry, their sudden decision to seek student status (for flight training) after arriving as visitors, and multiple entries and exits that should have initiated new INS reviews. But the hijackers represented only a few of the millions of anomalous blips on the INS radar. Since the INS was taking upwards of a year to check out irregularities and process status change paperwork, the terrorists moved about with impunity.

The case of "The First 9/11" underlines the difficulties law enforcement organizations face when historically dominant units remain powerfully positioned in the face of new challenges such as terrorism. Dominant units can have enough sway to deny resources and authority to units created to meet those challenges, or to take the play away from those units altogether on "big cases."

The 1985 Philadelphia Police assault on the MOVE cult shows starkly how not to conduct an operation requiring carefully planned tactics, coordinated police action and multi-agency cooperation. Years of inaction by two mayoral administrations had emboldened MOVE in its disregard for neighbors, the building codes and sanitary laws. When the neighbors' long-standing complaints against MOVE became a media event, the mayor ordered police to undertake an eviction/warrant execution forthwith. During the hastily planned operation, police tactics set off a conflagration that burned down nearly two city blocks. Six MOVE adults died, as did five children who were still in the house because of miscommunications between the police, courts and social services. Firefighters stood by as the blaze spread because their commanders were waiting for a go-ahead from the police. The police officials believed that the fire officials were free to order that the fire be fought. And the mayor watched on TV as a situation he had long ignored and then urgently ordered to be fixed turned into a deadly disaster.

* * *

**Structural Failure Defined:** Structural failure occurs when operations, procedures and processes that are functioning according to design lead to failure.

## Battling Bureaucracies in Boulder

In Boulder, Colorado, on Christmas night 1996, John Ramsey carried his sleeping daughter, JonBenet, up to her bedroom. The Ramseys were affluent, lived in a large house in a nice part of town, and doted on their six-year-old daughter, who was pretty enough to have been entered in local child beauty contests.

Early the next morning, a frantic 911 call from the Ramsey residence summoned the Boulder police. Patsy Ramsey, JonBenet's mother, had discovered a lengthy ransom note near the bottom of a rear stairway leading from the first floor to the upstairs bedrooms. In the note, a "small foreign faction" claimed to be holding JonBenet, and was prepared to exchange her for $118,000.[8]

A Boulder patrol officer was the first to respond. Soon several other officers arrived, along with a victim's advocate who was soon joined by a colleague. Two couples that the Ramseys had called upon for support had also shown up, as had the minister from the church the Ramseys attended. When Detectives Linda Arndt and Fred Patterson arrived just after 8 AM they joined eleven law enforcement officers and civilians already in the house.[9]

Since a kidnapping was indicated, the FBI was notified, and agents were on their way to Boulder police headquarters. The Colorado Bureau of Investigation had also been alerted. At the house, however, Arndt's partner and the uniformed officers had cleared out just after 10 AM because the phone call promised by the ransom note never came. With detectives on the case, the officers went back on patrol. The department had 130 sworn personnel and those on duty the morning after Christmas were stretched skeleton thin.

Supervision was also minimal. The Commander of Detectives, John Eller, was on vacation but in town, so he was notified and started in to headquarters. Detective Sergeant Larry Mason, who was on call as acting commander, had arrived at the office, where he soon received an urgent call from Linda Arndt, who requested assistance in managing all the individuals at the Ramsey house. Patsy Ramsey was distraught and physically ill; her husband had been wandering off into other parts of the house.[10]

When Commander Eller arrived at headquarters he was confronted with presumptive FBI jurisdiction in this kidnapping case, as well as the Colorado Bureau of Investigation's potential involvement. He found Boulder detectives searching the files unsuccessfully for the FBI's standard operating procedures on kidnapping cases. Eller chided Mason about his FBI training and then rejected Mason's suggestion that specially trained K-9 units from an adjoining jurisdiction be called in to begin searching the hills that rose up behind the Ramseys' neighborhood. The Boulder dogs would do, said Eller.

About one o'clock in the afternoon, Detective Arndt asked the two men in the group of friends consoling the Ramseys to accompany John Ramsey around the house, checking for things that might be out of place. In the basement, while checking a small room that had already been looked in, but apparently not very carefully, John Ramsey came upon his daughter's body wrapped in a blanket, with mouth taped and hands tied above her head. Removing the tape from JonBenet's mouth, and partially untying her hands, John Ramsey picked up his daughter and went upstairs. John Ramsey placed his daughter's body down on the hallway floor where an anguished Patsy Ramsey embraced her.

The kidnapping locale was now a crime scene, and a disturbed one at that. The body had been partially unbound and moved from where it had originally lain, and then was moved a second time by Detective Arndt to get it out of traffic. Three people had handled the body and still others had been near enough to touch it in all the commotion, and preserving evidence couldn't have been more important for eventually apprehending the killer or killers. JonBenet had been strangled and had received a blow to the head. Vaginal penetration had occurred. The way the body was clothed and wrapped in a blanket suggested that care had been taken after the child had died. The family members and friends in the house became suspects, which is normal practice in such cases. Detective Linda Arndt was still alone.

The modestly sized Boulder Police Department was facing a bear of a case, so Detective Sergeant Mason readily allowed the FBI agents to accompany him to the scene. Their expertise in handling kidnapping cases and profiling perpetrators might come in handy. When Mason arrived, the Ramsey house was swarming with cops and being roped off as a crime scene. Warrants were being drawn up for a search of the house. Family and friends were out of the residence. Things were more or less under control when Mason returned to headquarters, where Eller awaited.

Eller was bothered that the FBI was still involved.[11] Boulder had a murder case on its hands, and Eller at that point showed as little interest in FBI involvement as he had in enlisting a K-9 dog from the neighboring police department. He was no more enthused about the involvement of the Colorado Bureau of Investigation, the Boulder County Sheriff's Office or of the Denver Police Department, each of which had greater resources than the Boulder department and stood ready to help.[12] By late evening on December 26th, the investigative ball was solidly in the court of the Boulder police, who had conducted their warrant searches in a tidy six hours and were ready to turn the house back to the Ramseys.

The short search horrified the Boulder County district attorney's representative on the scene, who put in a call to the head of the DA's felony division, Pete Hofstrom. Hofstrom, who had held his post for fifteen years, in no way viewed six hours as sufficient to search a huge three-story house, large portions of which had been transited by JonBenet in the grasp of her killer(s). He protested to Commander Eller, who had recently rotated into the detective command without ever having been a detective. In a heated and acrimonious exchange, Eller again stood his ground, threatening to close the DA's office out of the investigation altogether.[13]

Hofstrom then went over Eller's head and appealed to Police Chief Tom Koby. Koby overruled Eller, and the six-hour search extended to ten days. But this was the opening salvo in an extended struggle between Eller, backed up by most of his detectives, and the district attorney's office. This struggle featured Eller's lockdown of information generated by his investigators, his scrutiny of media revelations to determine the source of leaks, and a rocky working relationship with other criminal justice agencies.[14]

While Eller strongly fortified the Boulder Police Department's jurisdiction, the investigation started weakly. In the immediate aftermath of the crime, opportunities to interview key figures, most notably JonBenet's parents, were lost in part because the police initially viewed the Ramseys as both victims and respectable citizens to whom deference should be shown. By the time the police started viewing them principally as suspects, the Ramseys had lawyers who did most their talking.[15]

To get the Ramseys talking, Eller, after the autopsy, tried to hold on to JonBenet's body as a bargaining chip. This horrified the Ramseys legal team, already gearing up for a protracted struggle and it also didn't sit well with other law enforcement officials. The coroner refused to hold the body hostage, the district attorney told Eller the move was illegal and even Detective Sergeant Mason, who was heading up the investigation, objected to Eller. The body was released, but Eller was not happy, a view expressed most forcefully to Mason, the only subordinate who directly questioned Eller's ploy.[16]

Eller's campaign against leaks soon had a victim and it was Mason. Word got out that the Ramseys had consented to be interviewed by the Boulder police. Eller accused Mason of being the source of the leak and pursued formal charges despite Mason's denial and a Ramsey attorney's claim to be the source. Mason was suspended for several weeks, ended up back on patrol, and hired a lawyer to pursue complete exoneration (which he eventually got). Amidst all this commotion, Mason let lay any raw notes, untranscribed audio tapes, draft reports, leads and theories he had generated in the ten days he led the JonBenet murder investigation. It was six months before the Boulder Police Department harvested Mason's work and asked him to write a report.[17]

The battles in which the Boulder police asserted its ownership of the investigation and fought to exclude other law enforcement agencies, most notably the Boulder County District Attorney, only grew more intense over time.[18] A joint "war room" where Boulder police investigators and the DA's investigators worked side by side was less notable for its contributions to apprehending the killers than for the hostilities between investigators, who often wouldn't make case-related phone calls from the room for fear of being overheard. The demise of the "war room" as a joint effort came after Eller called in the Colorado Bureau of Investigation (CBI) because a police computer in the room had apparently been broken into. Eller suspected personnel from the district attorney's office, with whom he exchanged harsh words, but the CBI determined that the computer itself was malfunctioning and generating the peculiar outputs to which Eller had reacted.[19]

Largely shut out from the Boulder Police Department's investigation, the DA hired retired detectives and borrowed investigators from other agencies to examine JonBenet's case independently.[20] For its part, the Boulder police hired its own lawyers to act as an in-house DA because it had lost faith in the advice coming from the Boulder DA. Unable to influence each other directly, the warring sides resorted to the media, leaking one or another "nefarious" move by the other side. These leaks were compounded by the Ramseys' ongoing public relations campaign to counter an investigation they believed had focused primarily on them from day one.

While JonBenet's killers were no closer to being caught, the criminal justice system in Boulder was awash in embarrassment. Late night talk show hosts made jokes; newspaper columnists and editorial writers ripped the investigation. The FBI, which had finally been asked for its advice, declared that there was more work to do. The "Police DA's" weighed in that no prosecutable case yet existed. Sergeant Mason was vigorously pursuing complete vindication, including administrative retribution against Eller. Finally, two Boulder detectives secretly taped a tabloid reporter, who revealed the Boulder district attorney as his source for published information critical of the Boulder Police Department. Eller played the tape for Police Chief Koby. The chief, however, did not see the reporter's admission as a nuclear bomb with which the DA could be destroyed. Instead the chief saw the tape as the last straw from Eller, and removed him from the case.[21]

Eller retreated to his office, putting in his hours and marking off the days to his impending retirement.[22] Chief Koby appointed a new leader for the investigative team and announced his own resignation shortly thereafter.[23] With new leadership, the police investigation moved forward, identifying suspects who had opportunity to commit the murder, though any motives apparently remained murky. Then the Boulder police handed off the investigative files to the Boulder DA's office, which predictably kept the police in the dark about what was going to happen next. For the detectives who had put the case together, their history with the DA made them worry that what might be next was nothing.

This was all too much for Detective Steve Thomas, a member of the investigative team who had worked on the case night and day from the beginning, getting sick in the process. Thomas submitted his resignation on JonBenet's birthday in a long and passionate public letter excoriating the district attorney's office.[24] The letter was filled with media ready headlines like "politics seemed to trump justice," and "failure of the system in Boulder," which got the attention of no less a personage than the governor of Colorado. After a panel of fellow DA's intervened at the governor's behest, Alex Hunter, the Boulder DA referred the JonBenet Ramsey murder case to a grand jury. The grand jury, in the end, didn't indict anybody. The DA, another casualty of the case, chose not to run for re-election in 2000.[25]

## Challenging Case, Challenged Agencies

The JonBenet Ramsey case remains open to this day. After years of work, the criminal justice system in Boulder was left with more questions than answers. Was there a kidnapping attempt at all? Was it a murder? Or an accident covered up to look like a crime? Perpetrated by somebody in the house? Or committed by an intruder? Was this a crime intricately plotted by a shrewd perpetrator who wove misdirection within misdirection to throw investigators off the scent? Or was the killing and its aftermath a slapdash improvisation?

What factors contributed to the inability of Boulder's criminal justice system to wrap up the JonBenet Ramsey case? Certainly, the investigation was challenging. Evidence that some investigators thought might implicate family members consisted of ordinary household objects the Ramseys would have handled frequently. Various subjects of the investigation were wealthy and sophisticated, hiring high-powered attorneys and mounting effective public relations campaigns to defend themselves and blast the quality of the investigation. Perhaps even the best investigators and prosecutors working under ideal organizational conditions would have been incapable of solving the JonBenet Ramsey case.

Conditions in Boulder, however, were far from ideal. The investigative resources of the Boulder Police Department were sorely taxed by the case. The department did not take advantage of opportunities to augment those resources. Conflict, not cooperation, characterized the relations between law enforcement agencies, and between the Boulder Police Department and the Boulder County District Attorney. Inter-organizational combat diverted energies from the case, and all but consumed key individuals in the investigation. The intense media scrutiny on the case skewed organizational actions every which way and had a debilitating long-term effect. These organizational dysfunctions were more than enough to jeopardize the successful prosecution of this case, regardless of how challenging the investigation might have been.

When we consider what went wrong organizationally to torpedo the Jon-Benet investigation, structural factors predominate. We'll consider three separate issues: resource inadequacy, hierarchical dysfunction, and inter-organizational conflict. None of these issues are unique to Boulder, or to Colorado, or to a particular region of the country. What sunk the JonBenet Ramsey investigation is, at this very moment, retarding law enforcement efforts in towns, cities and counties across the U.S.

## Resource Limitations of Smaller Departments

Boulder's population is just under 100,000. In 1996, the Boulder Police Department had 130 sworn officers.[26] With JonBenet's death on December 26th, Boulder detectives had their first homicide of the year. From the moment a kidnapping was reported, and then turned into a homicide with the discovery of the girl's body early in the afternoon, Boulder police had to scramble to keep up. The kidnapping had been called in early on the morning on the day after Christmas. When the call came, few officers were on duty and a sergeant was the tour's ranking officer.

The patrol personnel who were the first to arrive searched the house briefly, not looking for a body, but for evidence kidnappers might have left behind. So an officer searching the basement passed by the darkened room where JonBenet's body was found six hours later, but did not go in. With shifts changing and other regular posts in need of coverage by a skeletal staff, uniformed officers soon gave way to detectives. The detectives found themselves managing the distraught parents and several neighbors and friends awaiting an expected call from the kidnappers. When no call came, the whole situation went on hold. With things in abeyance, one of the two detectives left, leaving the other in charge of nine civilians. At 1PM that detective alone had to handle the explosion of confusion and grief that accompanied the discovery of JonBenet's body by her father.

The JonBenet Ramsey case would have been a major challenge for any police department, let alone a small police department operating in a community like Boulder. Boulder saw precious few homicides, and fewer still that were as challenging as the Ramsey case. Solving this crime required forensic capabilities that a department like Boulder's simply cannot maintain in-house. Keeping the investigation on track and uncompromised required sophisticated media management, and neither the Boulder Police Department nor the district attorney had the wherewithal to parry the non-stop, sensationalized national media onslaught brought on by JonBenet's death. Investigators went to Georgia, where children from John Ramsey's first marriage lived, and Michigan, where the Ramseys had a vacation home, taxing the BPD budget, as well as the energy and patience of those assigned to the case. At times, thirty officers—about 25% of the Boulder police—were involved. The Boulder Police Department needed all the help it could get because it lacked the capability to handle the case alone.

The resource shortcomings that hobbled the Boulder Police Department are rooted in the way law enforcement is structured throughout the United States. With 14,000 police agencies averaging 47 sworn officers apiece,[27] most police departments in the United States are considerably less well equipped to handle a JonBenet Ramsey case than the Boulder department. And most of these police departments do not enjoy Boulder's ability to seek assistance from a robust state police agency, a county sheriff's office twice its size and a well-resourced police department in a nearby metropolis like Denver.

The United States is a country with nearly 39,000 county and local governments, not to mention special purpose districts,[28] many of which choose to have their own law enforcement units. Because local prerogative is part and parcel of governmental structure and philosophy in the U.S., such choices are likely to continue. As long as the local police department handles cases within its design capabilities, such as a small resort town police force sticking to traffic control and order maintenance, small is not necessarily a handicap. But small is a handicap when a particular case, such as JonBenet's, or an emergent law enforcement issue, such as gang-sponsored drug dealers invading smaller Midwest cities, exceeds the capacity of the local police agency to mount a full and effective response.

When this happens, the challenged police agency is likely to fail unless it pursues a more cooperative strategy with other police agencies. Cooperation may occur on a case-by-case basis with minimal formality, as happens all the time when police personnel from different jurisdictions share intelligence and lend each other resources. Cooperation may sometimes be formalized. Adjoining small towns, for instance, may consolidate their departments into a regional police force, or two agencies with overlapping jurisdictions may come to a formal, written understanding about what each will do.

A resource-pinched police department may also make plans to draw upon the services of another, which the Boulder Police Department did beginning in 2003. Under budget pressure, the Boulder police had just eliminated its in-house K-9 unit, and was going to call upon the Boulder County Sheriff's Office for its future K-9 needs.[29] The irony is that in December 1996 Commander Eller rejected out of hand the suggestion that another department's specially trained K-9 unit be used in the search for JonBenet. In addition to calling upon neighboring public safety agencies, a police department may also formally request help from above: the county police, the state police, or even the FBI. Whether assistance is rendered depends on a number of factors, including jurisdiction and capacity (not to mention political considerations), but a stymied local agency loses little by asking for help.

The Boulder Police Department rejected working with other law enforcement agencies in the first days of the investigation and took a wary approach to subsequent offers of assistance as the investigation progressed. The department's obsession with leaks, combined with Mason's punishment, was more than enough to limit potentially productive chats between Boulder officers and law enforcement personnel elsewhere. The initial "go it alone" approach, combined with continuing high levels of wariness and suspicion, transformed resource limitations the Boulder Police Department could do little about into major handicaps of its own making. Not only did the murder investigation suffer as a result, but those very visible handicaps also became fodder for those who blamed the dead end investigation on a colossal failure of law enforcement.

## Dealing with Hierarchical Dysfunction

In the JonBenet Ramsey case, Detective Commander John Eller was a key figure. Eller was driven, an ambitious "cop's cop." He was on the rise as the newly appointed Detective Commander, sitting one level below chief, a position to which he aspired. The JonBenet Ramsey murder was the first homicide case that Eller, who had never served as a detective, supervised. Eller was not the lead investigator in the first weeks of the case; Detective Sergeant Mason was in charge initially. But Mason's tenure as lead investigator was cut short when Eller filed charges that Mason was leaking information about the investigation to the media.

Eller butted heads with Mason from the first moments of the investigation. Mason's FBI training became an issue, as did Mason bringing FBI agents to the Ramsey house on the afternoon of December 26th after the kidnapping had morphed into a murder. Eller had also, that morning, shot down Mason on the K-9 issue.

The charges against Mason filed by Eller, who then stuck to his guns in the face of exculpatory evidence that quickly emerged, disrupted the leadership of the investigation at a critical point. In addition, an indignant and mobilized Mason trained his sights on Eller for the next year. When all was said and done, Mason's ultimate vindication ended up being a nail in Eller's coffin.

Mason wasn't the only individual alienated by Eller, who rarely hesitated in asserting his view about police prerogatives. Right or wrong, diplomacy was not Eller's strong suit. Even Eller's natural allies in law enforcement were taken aback by his determination to hold JonBenet's body hostage to elicit the testimony of the parents. They were little more enamored of his cyber-theft charges against the district attorney's staff. When all was said and done, relations had broken down between Eller's investigators and the DA's office, between Eller and Mason (and Arndt as well), and between the Ramsey defense team and the Boulder Police Department. All of this ultimately led Chief Koby to see Eller as an obstruction to the investigation who needed to be taken off the case.

After being relieved, Eller was still Detective Commander but that seemed to mean little. With his hopes of moving up to chief dashed, Eller announced his retirement. The chief mourners were Eller's detectives, who had battled with him for nearly a year in extremely high-conflict terrain that Eller had done much to create.

The dynamics of hierarchical relations in police organizations help us illuminate Eller's behavior, and the behavior of those with whom he dealt. Hierarchy in organization is so necessary and ubiquitous that it tends to be taken for granted. Hierarchy is not just a technical problem of organization, on the order of creating a steel skeleton capable of supporting a towering skyscraper. The behaviors arising from hierarchical structure have a powerful impact on organizations. Poorly managed hierarchical dynamics is one of the most corrosive threats to the effectiveness of any organization. To explore just how the effectiveness of police organizations can founder on hierarchical dysfunction, we need some basic grounding about hierarchy.

Hierarchy is an inescapable feature of organizational life. Ultimate responsibility for all that goes on in an organization ultimately rests with the individual who occupies its top position, whether the CEO of a firm or the Chief of Police. "The buck stops here," President Harry Truman once famously said, but it also makes a lot of stops along the way. The training officer is accountable when a rookie fails to perform as required. The training sergeant or lieutenant is responsible for making sure that the training officers are up to date on practice and procedure, and are doing the job of keeping everyone else current. A command executive for employee development is required to monitor performance, practice and complaints, and will be held accountable for deviations from what the department expects from well trained, motivated officers. When "the buck" finally stops on the chief's desk, how it has been handled on the way up becomes a factor in determining how well the chief is doing the job.

Hierarchy distributes directive authority as well as accountability. While a police officer trained for every contingency would be ideal, no such animal exists. In policing, as in any enterprise, the officers on the beat, the detectives on a case, the undercover officers in a squad will encounter unique situations all the time. In the first hours of the JonBenet case, confronted with a kidnapping that quickly turned into a murder, officers and detectives on the scene continually touched base with superiors. Questions with no clear answers had to be resolved. How should one treat the grieving Ramseys, who were distraught parents but also material witnesses in a kidnapping? How should one manage the crowd of family and friends in the house? How many officers need to stay at the kidnapping scene? What are the marching orders once the child's body has been found? Someone in charge has to give direction when the way to go is not clear.

So in order to achieve accountability and direction, hierarchy is a major element whereby organizations are structured, and in few places is this more apparent than in police departments, where hierarchy is very visible. Police chiefs arrive with stars on their shoulders and gold braid on their hats. Captains and lieutenants have bars on their shoulders and sergeants have stripes on their arms. The symbols and rewards of hierarchy are highly prominent in police organizations.[30]

Hierarchy also is amplified when police organizations view themselves as paramilitary. No small debate revolves around the need for police organizations, which are designed for maintenance of order and crime prevention and which mostly deploy personnel one and two at a time, to adopt paramilitary forms. That debate includes the extent to which departments must adopt rigid hierarchical structures with punitively enforced norms of unquestioned obedience, a practice designed principally for combat. Nonetheless, almost all police organizations feature military-type rank structures which, in turn, provide tacit or explicit endorsement for the expectation that subordinates must unquestioningly comply with directives from superiors, or else.

More rigidly structured hierarchies are more likely to enable, and thus encourage, "my way or the highway," and "because I am the boss, that's why" managers. This is even more likely in police organizations, where basic training for every recruit focuses on how to take control of situations. By the time most officers embark on a promotional path, taking control has usually served them well on the job and can seem just as promising as a supervisory strategy in a rank-focused hierarchy.[31]

This is exacerbated by another inherent characteristic of organizational hierarchy. Hierarchy is not just a structure for managing; it is the playing field on which employees advance to greater authority and rewards. Hierarchy as career path is a progressively tougher game with a guarantee of more losers than winners at each stage. And the stakes keep escalating. Money and rank are just a few of the rewards. For many advancing through the ranks, ego gratification is the major payoff. Directing a complex, high profile investigation is its own reward, an adrenaline-rushed "big one" that may, in the bargain, vault investigators further up the ranks. So being taken out of the game can be devastating, even for those who keep their title and salary. The pain is not only from the blow to one's ego but also from being summarily ejected from a prime spot for hierarchical advancement. Eller's successor, in fact, ended up as chief. Eller's retirement thus was no surprise. It would have been more surprising had he stayed.

Chief Koby could have tempered Eller's drive to dominate the investigation early on. Eller's combat with the DA, which spoke volumes about Eller's drive for dominance and control, landed in Koby's lap on the very first day of the investigation. Eller's conflict with Mason, the initial lead investigator, was an issue with which Koby had to deal two weeks after the investigation started. Had Koby reined in Eller early on (instead of banishing Mason), the Boulder Police Department could have avoided much of the inter- and intra-agency friction that hobbled the investigation. Instead, Eller was affirmed by these early struggles, and could rally his investigators who, by dint of their own skirmishes with their counterparts in other agencies, needed little convincing to go forward in warlike fashion.

So Eller ended up on top and in control, with his troops seeing what he saw and pledging their solidarity. Eller had triumphed in a hierarchical game that had no necessary connection with, and further complicated, the investigation. Chief Koby might have benefited early on from the advice of Jack Welch, who led General Electric for two decades. Welch observed that the results obtained by hard driving supervisors weren't worth it if they were obtained by riding roughshod over values, norms and relationships crucial to the organization's overall functioning and long-term success. Welch said that these individuals ought to be moved aside for the good of the organization.[32] When Koby finally divined this message, it was too late. He was on the brink of announcing his resignation and the damage to the Boulder Police Department had long since been done.

## Understanding Inter-organizational Fracture

The Hatfields and the McCoys had nothing on the Boulder Police Department and the Boulder District Attorney's Office. The conflict began with a bang on the first night of the investigation, when the Boulder DA's felony chief appealed to Koby in order to extend the search of the Ramsey residence after Eller was ready to declare it complete. Eller was not a half-hearted combatant and neither was the head of the felony unit at the district attorney's office. Sparks flew from day one and quickly ignited a conflagration of mutual accusations, near-paranoid suspicion, and bureaucratic thrust and counter-thrust in the battle over the direction of the investigation. As this went on, relations between the police department and the district attorney's office gyrated between icy and non-existent. The combatants also sucked in others, including media representatives who were happy to oblige, and other law enforcement officials who were less than happy to be dragged into a very messy situation.

The conflict between the police and prosecutors greatly handicapped the JonBenet Ramsey investigation. Like the hierarchical dysfunctions that were also in evidence, the inter-organizational conflict helped divert, almost completely at times, the energy and attention of investigators and prosecutors. The problem was not that tension existed. Some tension is normal. But when that tension is allowed to spiral so out of control that mission failure looms, fundamental organizational breakdowns have occurred. Let's look at how organizational conflict can come about, first generically and then with respect to the criminal justice system.

Create a group—and divisions or units within an organization are no exception—and you are creating an entity strongly disposed to think highly of itself. This is natural and helps bind together any group in any setting. Organizations, in fact, try to exploit this tendency. "The few, the proud, the Marines" is a slogan that, in the service of organizational goals, seeks to instill a positive group self-image. When this feat is pulled off the result is esprit de corps, a concept as relevant to Microsoft or the FBI as it is to the Marines.

A culture of pride, excellence, or customer service works best when spread more or less uniformly throughout an organization. But this is rare and more likely to be found in newer, smaller, narrowly focused organizations. As organizations grow they specialize, creating units that generate their own cultures and worldviews rooted in the work they do. Organizations over time increasingly become amalgams of distinct groups of people doing different things, and thinking in different ways.

A work unit's perception of its worth is likely to be considerably higher than anyone else's, including that of management and other organizational units.

This lofty self-image is natural, and not just because of egotism. Employees know their own work best, the jobs of others less well or not at all. Unit managers usually reinforce their workers' thinking, praising their unique skills and emphasizing how crucial the unit's contributions are to the organization.

The flip side of a unit's elevated sense of contribution is a negative perception of the contributions of others. Such attitudes can easily degrade into direct critiques and obstructive behavior when units work together. When conflict escalates into win-lose mode, one or both units can become alienated from the overall organization, as well as fiercely resistant to management control.

Anthropologists have terms for these dispositions that tend to splinter the ties that bind groups to a larger social structure. The terms are ethnocentrism, basically group self-absorption, and xenophobia, distrust of the other. At the extreme, these tendencies can cause groups to separate themselves in righteous fury from their evil neighbors, only to renew contact by warfare designed to subjugate or eliminate the foe.

Ethnocentrism and xenophobia are at work in all organizations. Mostly these dynamics simmer, well hidden beneath surface niceties, a mere squiggle on the organizational Richter scale. When ethnocentrism and xenophobia rumble, however, organizations quake, and may well be torn apart.

If we think of organizations as spread across a landscape where some locations are stable and others are highly unstable, then law enforcement organizations are located atop an earthquake zone. Relations between many law enforcement agencies feature enduring distrust. Wary coordination is interspersed with occasional periods of intense cooperation and highly charged instances of standoff and severed relations. For instance, the history between the FBI and CIA spans more than half a century and was kicked off by fierce battles over which agency would do what to rein in foreign agents on U.S. soil. The agencies have continuously struggled over the murky dividing line between counter-intelligence and criminal investigation, and which agency may operate where. Poor information sharing between the agencies played a role in the failure to identify and take action against terrorists in the U.S. who were preparing to take part in the 9/11 attacks.

The conflict between the Boulder Police Department and the district attorney took place along a major organizational fault line in law enforcement. Police and prosecutors have different standards for dealing with suspected felons. Cops make arrests based on probable cause, which requires an arresting officer's reasonable belief, based on sufficient facts and circumstances, that the person charged has committed the crime. Prosecutors, however, need to prove that same case beyond a reasonable doubt. That means a level of proof that will convince jurors and/or a judge that, after a close and impartial look at the evidence, no meaningful doubt exists about the defendant's guilt. Even if prosecutors can meet the "beyond a reasonable doubt" standard, police improprieties, such as an illegal search, can torpedo the case.

Just as prosecutors have good cause to cast a critical eye on cases brought to them by the police, police experience with prosecutors also provides a basis for skepticism. DA's can and do toss cases carefully developed for months by cops who have put themselves in harm's way in making the arrest. Though cases like this are relatively few, that's enough to set cops against prosecutors, and generally sour their working relationship.

But differing standards, incentives and perspectives for police and prosecutors are a design element of the criminal justice system, not a structural flaw. The Constitution of the United States, and the constitutions of individual states, very deliberately set a high hurdle for prosecutors seeking to deprive an accused person of life, liberty or property. On the other hand, the police are under enormous, and quite legal, pressure to combat crime with all available tools including the aggressive application of probable cause.

The structure does fail, however, when the police and/or the prosecutors act as if the other does not exist. Structural failure also occurs when the management of either institution, or both, allows naturally diverse perspectives and inevitable frictions to degenerate into a bitter, adversarial and counterproductive relationship. This came to pass in Boulder as the relationship between the police and district attorney's office hit rock bottom, along with progress on the case. Also at rock bottom was public opinion, swayed by the tales of infighting and ineptitude headlined in the supermarket tabloids and critiqued on the editorial pages of Denver area newspapers.

The distinct mandate of police and prosecutors is unlikely to change. What can change is the degree to which these offices work with each other to insure that "good" arrests become "successful" prosecutions. This requires understanding and communication, and the support of police chiefs and DA's. Cops need to be kept up to date on courtroom developments by prosecutors and prosecutors need to keep abreast of the realities of policing. Jurisdictions across the United States do this on a regular basis, even assigning prosecutors to police units in order to make sure that day-to-day investigative tactics and pending arrests pass court muster. The result is better arrests and more cases closed by guilty pleas or convictions.

A cooperative approach strengthens the structure of the police/prosecutor interface and makes the criminal justice system more effective. But, as Boulder clearly demonstrated in the JonBenet Ramsey case, the structure of the police/prosecutor interface can also be so seriously undermined that cases collapse, and the careers of dedicated public servants get crushed in the wreckage.

\* \* \*

## Terrorist Welcome Wagon at the INS

Terrorists Mohammed Atta and Marwan al-Shehhi each flew a plane into the World Trade Center. They had come into the United States in late spring 2000 on visitors' visas and were routinely admitted, as were almost all the 230 million visitors arriving that year. In July 2000, Atta and Alshehhi enrolled in flight school in Florida. That September the two terrorists requested a change of visa status from "visitor" to "student" to reflect their flight school enrollment.[33]

The INS took a nearly a year to adjudicate the two requests. Though the movement of the applications was slow, it was also sure. Despite incomplete, sloppy applications, and suspect educational choices, an INS adjudicator ultimately approved the change of status.[34] The approval turned out to be moot. The two terrorists had finished their flight training long before approval was given and the men had been in and out of the country twice, voiding the original status change requests. But the INS adjudicator knew none of this when he approved the status change in July 2001.

The official INS approval for Atta's and Alshehhi's enrollment arrived at the flight school six months after they flew hijacked planes into the Twin Towers, ten months after the adjudicator had first ruled, more than a year after they finished their flight training, and a year and a half after they first applied. The INS contractor that handled these notifications was backlogged, much like the INS adjudication process. The INS was duly embarrassed but was in fact just one of several agencies, including the FBI and CIA, whose poor performance gave terrorists the breathing room to carry out their heinous crimes.

### Managing Chronic Task Overload

Much like the JonBenet case overwhelmed the Boulder Police Department, the work of immigration law enforcement taxed the INS beyond its limits. Over a half-million student visa holders were in the U.S. during the 2000–2001 academic year. Student visas issued during the 2001 fiscal year totaled 320,000. The INS was responsible for keeping track of the educational status of this multitude, the bona fides of the thousands of schools they were attending and the continuing validity of each alien's status as foreign students went in and out of the country. In addition, of the 232 million foreigners entering the United States in 2000–2001 as visitors or tourists, some 29,000 applied for student status *after* arriving, as did Atta and Alshehhi. The system of determining and monitoring status required coordination with educational institutions, other government agencies, and foreign embassies. It required reviewing applicant credentials, checks on entering and exiting visa holders, communications with school officials and, from all concerned, a multitude of forms, some of which had to progress from applicants to sponsors to educational institutions and on to the INS with signatures added at every step of the way.

The crush of student status business swamped the INS, which proceeded to waive interview requirements, adjudicate incomplete and sloppy applications and generally give applicants the benefit of the doubt. Many of the waivers and perfunctory reviews, which the terrorists exploited, were permitted by INS rules. Even waivers that skirted regulations seemed justified by the generally tolerant INS approach and the need to process the flood of work. In addition, supervisors might well overrule and chastise inspectors who flagged suspect visitors. And none of this was simply a matter of administrative convenience. Pressure was being felt from the very top levels of the INS, where the airlines and their supporters in Congress were pushing hard for expedited international travel.

Resources inadequate to ballooning tasks created structural weaknesses that hampered INS enforcement of immigration law. The press of business was more than the INS could handle, creating cracks though which foreign nationals slipped despite their disqualifying histories and, more ominously, their destructive intentions. The INS was stretched to the breaking point.

## The Burden of Conflicting Mandates

The INS was not just overwhelmed by too much work. Law enforcement at the INS competed with other priorities concerning how to treat foreigners entering and residing in the United States. The INS was often not clear about how vigorously immigration law should be enforced in a whole range of situations, not the least of which concerned foreign nationals seeking education in the United States. Colleges and trade schools lobbied vigorously for liberal application of immigration policies with respect to students from foreign lands. Colleges kept the pressure on even though it was clear that many foreign nationals were exploiting their educational status, as well as lax monitoring by their schools, in order to remain in the US for other, usually economic, reasons.

So, sheer numbers aside, facilitating foreign enrollment at US colleges while watching out for fraudulent and/or dangerous individuals proved to be a balancing act beyond INS capabilities. Consequently the INS leaned towards facilitation to a far greater degree than gate keeping, and all sorts of individuals were illegally in the country under the cover of "student."

The INS was not the architect of its contradictory mandates, Congress was; the president and the courts helped with the construction. The result was an agency with a conflicted mandate. Legal immigrants were to be welcomed and facilitated. That was the "nice guy" INS. On the other hand, many immigrants were illegal, and employers often exploited them. INS inspectors were required to round up and repatriate illegal aliens, or turn them back at the border in the first place, while cracking down on exploitative employers. That was the "tough cop" INS.

This dual and contradictory policy blueprint would have been difficult enough to follow. Congress and the president, however, compounded the basic policy design flaws with wings and additions that further confused the central mission of the agency. Congress, the president and even the courts encouraged gentler treatment of illegal aliens for diplomatic (better relations with Mexico), economic (illegal immigrants sustained certain agricultural and domestic labor markets) and constitutional reasons (due process). Even for visitors and visa holders, the INS might be encouraged to go by the book for citizens from certain countries while being accommodating towards citizens from other countries considered important allies, such as Saudi Arabia — where most of the 9/11 hijackers were from — or Egypt and the United Arab Emirates, the respective home countries of Atta and Alshehhi. The INS didn't know on any given day whether to concentrate on its welcome wagon or its paddy wagon, and consequently did neither very well. Add budget pressures, increased contracting out and ever more entries and exits and it is no surprise that terrorist pilots received a clean bill of health from the INS.

## The Subordination of Law Enforcement

By the year 2000, the job of immigration law enforcement, as designed, had built-in structural weaknesses ready to give way under enough pressure. And airlines, airport operators, travelers and even other government agencies had been ratcheting up the pressure on the INS for years. Thus, the INS contended not only with resource limitations and conflicting mandates, but also with other organizations that had gained a substantial measure of influence over how the INS operated. These organizations included the U.S. Department of Transportation and the Federal Aviation Administration, as well as organizations representing the air travel industry and its passengers. Because these organizations interacted constantly with the INS, and had for years, they were a major influence on how the immigration agency approached its tasks.

Prior to 9/11, lax security practices had taken hold in the air transport system. Travel had skyrocketed through the 1980s and 1990s, no U.S. hijackings were occurring and communist regimes, so long the enemy, were melting away. The FAA, airport operators and airlines smoothed the flow of passengers with minimally disruptive security at the gates. And, at international airports, where the customs desk and immigration clearance sometimes became chokepoints, the FAA and air industry allies successfully encouraged Customs and the INS to speed travelers along as well. So, in a subtle and seemingly benign process over a period of years, the INS relaxed its enforcement practices at international airports to, literally and figuratively, go with the flow.

Practices modified in a negotiated process tend to calcify. Calcification occurs because the parties with whom an agency negotiates tend to hold on to their place at the table. Not only do they stay around, they develop a sense of entitlement to policies shaped for their benefit, and not just for existing policies but for future policies as well. The law enforcement agency thus contends with the powerful presence of organized non-law enforcement interests in its policy-making process. This presence limits enforcement options, slows their implementation and dilutes their impact.

The INS and Customs contended with these pressures throughout the 1990s as the Department of Transportation, the Federal Aviation Administration (FAA) and their Congressional allies pushed for checkpoint policies that moved travelers along. More lenient enforcement policies were the result. Immigration and Customs agents at border crossings, and particularly at gateway airports, increasingly saw themselves as an obligatory, highly unpopular rubber stamp stop in the increasingly traveler-friendly U.S. entry system. Morale plummeted, along with the effectiveness of immigration enforcement.

Some agents complained about the gaping enforcement holes at the nation's international gateways. Their complaints died on the desks of immediate superiors committed to speedy processing or, more rarely, on the desks of higher-ups for whom an enforcement policy change meant reopening settled understandings with other agencies. Agents, predictably, complained less and less. Though a few concerned agents expanded their definition of "suspicious" traveler and rigorously inspected documentation and baggage, this slowed things up, usually drew supervisory attention and invited a reprimand. So "traveler-first" policies prevailed until the 9/11 hijackers hurled not one but four airliner-bombs through the porous security perimeter patrolled by the INS and the FAA.

No agency exists in a vacuum. Agencies need to work—and work well—with others. This is particularly true, as the JonBenet case demonstrates, when the agencies involved are all within the criminal justice system. Some crimes are better dealt with by close cooperation with non-criminal justice agencies, as when police work with family services agencies on child abuse cases. None of these situations seriously impede the police agency's pursuit of its core enforcement mandate. But in the case of the INS, its enforcement mandate was subordinated in part to goals being pursued by agencies and private organizations outside of law enforcement. This resulted in the dilution of enforcement programs designed to protect air travel from criminal assault and secure our borders against illegal entrants.

The law enforcement agency's effectiveness will almost certainly be diluted when core policies are substantially determined over an extended period by those for whom law enforcement is a low priority. In the case of the INS (and Customs) at international airports in the U.S., the FAA and airline industry wielded enough influence to elevate processing speed over investigative diligence. Similarly, in New York City in the 1980s, the Metropolitan Transportation Authority was very concerned about calling even more attention to rampaging subway crime, and thus encouraged reactive transit police tactics that kept the arrest rate just about as low as the morale of officers.[35] Likewise in Washington, DC in the 1990s, enforcement diligence and police morale plummeted as Mayor Marion Barry, a long time police antagonist reelected after a drug conviction, imposed lower recruiting standards, installed ethically challenged commanders and kept up his general criticism of law enforcement.[36] Whether the case involves Marion Barry with the Washington Police Department, the FAA/Department of Transportation/airline industry with the INS, or the MTA with its transit police, when police practice is overly subordinated to external concerns the enforcement structure is weakened, potentially in profound and dangerous ways.

The 9/11 Commission recognized immigration screening and airport security as fragmented pieces of an enforcement and travel system puzzle solved by the terrorists.[37] It is thus no surprise that immigration enforcement, as well as airport gate security, is now part of Homeland Security. This new, huge and complex agency was created to pull together law enforcement functions spread throughout the government. This consolidation was a powerful structural response to law enforcement weaknesses caused by conflicting mandates in the multi-tasking agencies that previously housed these functions.

## The First 9/11: February 26, 1993

The incorporation of immigration and customs enforcement into the new Department of Homeland Security reflected the wrenching changes in the federal law enforcement landscape after 9/11. Consolidating agencies into Homeland Security was designed to break down the narrow silos in which agencies operated and jealously guarded prior to 9/11.

A more subtle, but no less important issue, was the low priority law enforcement agencies generally had given terrorism prior to 9/11. The fixes, though not so public as a Homeland Security takeover, were often as dramatic. Federal law enforcement agencies, such as the FBI, reassigned thousands of agents to counter-terrorism and got funding to add even more agents. In most large U.S. cities, cops who once walked beats started doing counter-intelligence and anti-terrorism work. Within a year of 9/11, the NYPD had over 1,000 officers in such roles, and had assigned officers to posts in England, Germany, Israel, Canada, and at Interpol's headquarters in France.[38] So, after the deaths of several thousand innocent civilians in three states, countering terrorism became a first order law enforcement priority—a decade too late.

It is easy to forget, given the enormity of 9/11, that Islamic terrorists made an earlier attempt to bring down the World Trade Center. In February 1993, a truck bomb was detonated in the parking garage underneath the World Trade Center's North Tower. The explosion did tremendous damage, taking out three garage levels and caving in part of a public concourse above, creating a crater the size of a hockey rink. Over one hundred cars, and the truck that carried in the bomb, were totally destroyed. Steel beams went flying, obliterating walls as they went. Electricity, water, and hardwired communications were cut, and the fire caused by the explosion sent thick smoke throughout the North Tower and filtered through shared underground spaces into the South Tower as well. Tens of thousands had to be evacuated, some by helicopter from the top of the World Trade Center. The human cost: Eight were killed, over a thousand injured.

That so few were killed was due to luck as much as anything. The conspirators, short on cash and time, had to downsize their truck bomb, which then failed to blow away the massive support columns holding up the North Tower. Taking out those columns at their base had been the terrorists' hope, not only to bring down the North Tower but to have it crash sideways into the South Tower, toppling that as well.[39]

The FBI and the Joint Terrorism Task Force, made up of police detectives as well as agents from the ATF, FBI and other federal agencies, made fast work of most of the 1993 bombing suspects, thanks to the quick, needle in a haystack recovery of a small, scarred ID plate from the rented truck blown to bits by the bomb it carried. So, at the New Jersey truck rental location, agents arrested one of the plotters as he was trying to get back his rental deposit. Others involved were soon arrested, except for Ramzi Yousef, the bomb-maker, who managed to board a flight out of the U.S. within hours of the explosion.

The 1993 bombing had been solved—by good police work.

Just three years before, good police work had also wrapped up the assassination of militant Zionist Rabbi, Meir Kahane, after an alert U.S Postal Service police officer shot and wounded the assassin, El Sayyid A. Nosair, who was fleeing the Manhattan hotel crime scene with smoking gun in hand.[40] "Everything indicates he was acting alone," the NYPD Chief of Detectives said that night.[41]

The "case closed, lone gunman" theory was not the only possibility. The assassin's apartment featured a bullet-riddled target, and lots of literature on firearms and explosives. Receipts from a suburban gun range indicated the assassin practiced regularly. The apartment also contained substantial handwritten materials in Arabic but a small sample translated by an officer was judged innocuous. For the Chief of Detectives these loose ends only fortified the conclusion that the angry and politically minded Nosair, fixated on guns and ordnance, lost it when the Rabbi Kahane came to town. "There was nothing that would stir your imagination," he said, "We've got witnesses and we've got evidence. At this point it looks like he was a lone gunman who committed a murder. Why he did it we may never know."[42]

So, in the early 1990s the good news was that the cops were locking up assassins and bombers. They were getting the bad guys. Cases were being closed; the criminal investigation mission satisfied.

The bad news was that the closed cases obscured critical connections that, if looked at from a counter-terrorism perspective, as opposed to a criminal one, pointed towards much more going on.

The 1993 plotters were connected to the nascent Al Qaeda organization. The builder of the truck bomb, Ramzi Yousef, had honed his skills in Pakistan and Afghanistan and then, with Al Qaeda support, took his show on the road. Yousef's accomplices included "Afghan Arabs," men from the Middle East who had gone to Afghanistan to wage jihad against the Soviet Russian occupiers. Other accomplices worshipped at New York area mosques where Sheik Omar Abdel Rahman, a religious inspiration for jihadists, gave his blessing to the violent overthrow of Egypt's government, the destruction of Israel and attacks against any country supporting these regimes, starting with the U.S. The conspirators also had ties to the Al-Kifah Refugee Center, the Brooklyn, New York branch of a "charity" Osama Bin Laden had started for securing funds and volunteers for the anti-Soviet struggle in Afghanistan. As suggested by the "Refugee Center" label, Al-Kifah had also become involved in the return of Afghan fighters, not a few of whom came back ready to carry on jihad against the "un-Islamic" regimes of their home countries or against infidel regimes in "refuge" countries such as the United States.

It also turned out that two of the 1993 conspirators had been at the house of El Sayyid Nosair when police investigators showed up after Kahane's 1990 assassination. Those documents seized from Nosair's house, which sat around in boxes since they weren't needed to convict Nosair for murder, turned out to be anything but innocuous when more completely translated and examined after the 1993 bombing. They included World Trade Center schematics, tracts in Arabic containing calls from Sheik Rahman to destroy the "high world buildings" of the "enemies of Allah," and instructions and formulas for creating the kinds of explosives used by the 1993 bombers.

Even as the investigation of the 1993 World Trade Center bombing was exhuming the Nosair documents, another plot was discovered. More zealots, guided by Sheik Rahman, were planning to blow up the two main Hudson River tunnels from New Jersey into Manhattan. They hoped to breach the tunnels, letting the river rush in to drown trapped motorists and sending a flood tide out into surrounding streets to wreak more death and destruction. Prosecutors dubbed this conspiracy, which also targeted the United Nations and the FBI's New York office, the "Landmark Plot." In a wide-ranging conspiracy charge that incorporated the Kahane assassination and the bombing plot, ten individuals were tried and convicted, including Nosair and Rahman, who each received life sentences.[43]

As all this was going on, Ramzi Yousef turned up in the Philippines planning to blow up airliners. A small test bomb he planted on a Philippines Airlines jet to see if his design would work killed one, wounded five and severed flight control cables running under the floorboards.[44] He was also planning to kill the visiting Pope when one of his chemical brews ignited a fire in his apartment, which brought in Philippine authorities just a few steps behind Yousef, who fled the country.[45]

Law enforcement was not blind to the intricacy and global scope of this terrorist web. But that knowledge did not significantly refocus law enforcement agencies, even as some resources were shifted to counter-terrorism. Resources alone didn't elevate the prestige or clout of agents working in counter-terrorism. Compiling dossiers on terrorist suspects still didn't have the cachet of arresting bad guys.

And the issue wasn't just a matter of intramural jealously among the ranks; it was also a matter of organizational image. The FBI, for instance, long presented itself as a criminal investigation agency. The FBI's annual crime reports and statistics embellished this image. Career advancement came easier to crime-fighters than analysts. Rare was the FBI executive who had not spent the bulk of his or her career pursuing traditional criminals. So, as the FBI devoted more resources to counter-terrorism in the mid-1990s, it remained to be seen how much real impact that would have on the FBI's overall approach to its business.

In early 1995, John O'Neill was one up-and-coming FBI official who had been moved into counter-terrorism work when he was assigned to take over headquarters operations for monitoring and investigating foreign and domestic terrorist threats. O'Neill had been working in the FBI's Chicago office, where he spearheaded investigations into abortion clinic bombings. Driving overnight from Chicago, O'Neill arrived at the FBI's Washington headquarters on a February Sunday and took an urgent call from Richard Clarke, who worked on counter-terrorism in the White House. U.S. operatives had just tracked down Ramzi Yousef in Pakistan. Clearances, forensic confirmation and coordination spearheaded from Washington would be necessary to affect the arrest and get Yousef back to the United States. O'Neill jumped into action, beginning his work in FBI counter-terrorism by doing much to affect the arrest of the "most wanted" terrorist, not only by the U.S. but by several other countries as well.

So from day one O'Neill was immersed in all things terror-related. A month after Yousef's February 1995 arrest, a deadly poison gas attack was unleashed on Tokyo's subways by devotees of a doomsday cult. The next month, on April 19, Timothy McVeigh blew up the Murrah Federal Building in Oklahoma City, killing 167 and wounding over 1000, which focused presidential and Congressional attention. The FBI was given the lead role in responding to terrorist attacks, and more funding to do that job, which kept growing. By the end of 1995, Saudi Arabian offices where U.S. personnel worked had been bombed, as had the Egyptian embassy in Pakistan. Al Qaeda sympathizers had also kidnapped U.S. and European tourists in India.

The steady increase in the number of terrorist acts, homegrown and foreign, convinced O'Neill—who in turn convinced the FBI command—that a single counter-terrorism unit no longer made sense.[46] O'Neill's unit was split into two. The unit focused on domestic groups was handed over to one of O'Neill's deputies and O'Neill stayed in charge of pursuing Al Qaeda and other foreign groups, bringing in a CIA official as his deputy.[47]

Soon, both in U.S. government councils and within the FBI itself, O'Neill was shouting the loudest about how Bin Laden and Al Qaeda were intent on escalating and spreading the violence and casualties and bringing it home to the United States. O'Neill was "The Man Who Knew," which was a chapter title in his biography,[48] as well as the title of a Frontline documentary about O'Neill.[49] His warnings were borne out when, in June 1996, terrorists blew up a high rise barracks in Saudi Arabia full of U.S. military personnel—killing 19 and wounding 400 others, mostly American soldiers.

From FBI headquarters in Washington, O'Neill helped strengthen FBI efforts in foreign counter-terrorism by working across agencies to coordinate intelligence and driving his investigators, more by example than command, to work as hard and fast as possible to develop solid cases.

O'Neill was less successful in moving counter-terrorism higher on the FBI agenda, and it was not for lack of trying. He was opinionated, forward, tireless and obsessive about having command of the facts. Some who needed convincing saw O'Neill as arrogant, others were wary because John O'Neill clearly did not fit the FBI mold. A flashy dresser who played hard, stayed out late and lived a busy bachelor life-style, O'Neill was dubbed "The Prince of Darkness" by rivals in the FBI's staid Washington headquarters, who were not above using the grapevine and gossip as weapons in hierarchical competition.

By the end of 1996, O'Neill had been promoted to Special Agent in Charge of National Security Programs and was on his way to the New York Field Office, the Bureau's largest, from which the National Security Program had long been managed. He was replacing Thomas Pickard, who left to head the FBI's Washington Field Office, a fast-track assignment that, within four years, vaulted Pickard to head of the FBI's Criminal Division and then to Assistant Director of the FBI.

New York was the center of the universe in a lot of ways for O'Neill. New York, unlike Washington, was a world city, and not just because of the United Nations and the various member country missions, a major reason the FBI had headquartered the National Security Program Office there. New York was an international business crossroads and the kind of 24/7 town that fit O'Neill's style.

O'Neill thrived, forging relationships with local law enforcement, other federal agencies and foreign officials stationed in New York and visiting from abroad. He did this as much by force of personality as anything else—often after hours, which only reinforced the views of FBI headquarters officials inclined to believe that O'Neill might just be too slick and non-conforming for prime time roles.

In 1998, Al Qaeda simultaneously bombed U.S. embassies in Kenya and Tanzania, constituting the highest casualty terrorist crimes against the U.S. to that point. John O'Neill was not allowed to lead the investigation, which instead was handled from Washington, much to O'Neill's chagrin. Interestingly, Thomas Pickard, O'Neill's predecessor, ended up making the call that the Washington field office would take the lead.[50] The investigation ultimately led to Al Qaeda operatives, and from them straight back to Osama bin Laden—linkages that O'Neill, "the man who knew," was on top of from the moment he received news of the bombing.

O'Neill was not only held back from Africa but also was under a three-year promotion hold due to a recent minor rule violation, which basically consisted of allowing his significant other to ride in an official car after his personal vehicle had broken down near an FBI garage in New Jersey.[51] The FBI had a "bright line" policy regarding such violations so O'Neill spent a month off without pay in addition to the promotion hold.[52]

O'Neill was getting discouraged. His aspirations for moving up in the FBI were stymied. And it was a blow to be denied the lead in a major investigation that he, along with others such as the US Attorney for the Southern District of New York, strongly felt should be his as a matter of jurisdiction, expertise and leadership.[53] It also no doubt grated on O'Neill that the call had been made by his plain vanilla predecessor—now risen to the FBI's top ranks—who three years earlier, and New York-based, had been designated the FBI lead for extricating Ramzi Yousef from Pakistan.[54] Though the embassy bombing investigation was eventually transferred back to the New York office, O'Neill was not allowed to go to Kenya to directly oversee the investigation.[55]

What happened next on O'Neill's watch was pretty much what had been happening since his arrival on the FBI's counter-terrorism desk in 1995 and, in fact, what had been happening since 1990. In 1999, a "Millennium Plot" to blow up Los Angeles Airport was foiled, and the bomber, a free-lancing Al Qaeda sympathizer, led to other suspects in the U.S., Canada and Algeria.[56] Early in 2000, in Aden harbor in Yemen, two Al Qaeda members detonated a huge bomb alongside the USS Cole killing 17 sailors, wounding 39 and nearly sinking the ship.[57] Again, the New York FBI Office laid claim to the investigation. And again, Pickard, by now FBI Deputy Director, thought not. This time, however, an appeal to FBI Director Louis Freeh landed the investigation with the New York Office with the investigation led on the ground in Yemen by John O'Neill.[58]

Meanwhile, Bin Laden, who had taken up residence in Afghanistan as a welcome guest of the Taliban, was operating large-scale training camps for Al Qaeda fighters and plotting future strategy with senior Al Qaeda operatives. One of these operatives was Khalid Sheikh Mohammed, Ramzi Yousef's uncle, who late in 1998 proposed crashing planes into U.S. buildings, including the Twin Towers his nephew had failed to topple five years earlier. Bin Laden approved, paving the way for two years of meticulous planning that culminated in 9/11.[59]

By summer 2001, O'Neill had "put in his papers." He retired from the National Security Programs post he had held since 1996 just three weeks before the 9/11 attacks. Had O'Neill advanced further, his goal of reshaping FBI priorities to meet the game-changing challenges of global terrorism may have also advanced. We will never know. What we do know is that right up until 9/11 the criminal investigation role continued to dominate the FBI's priorities and mindset despite a decade of incessant and escalating terrorist assaults. We also know that, in the months before 9/11, credible information relating to the attack, including a suspect under arrest, never got translated into action thanks to FBI headquarters' button-down, make-no-mistakes, risk-averse, strict silo approach.

While these opportunities were missed, "the man who knew," the man who made a mistake or two, the man who took risks and rushed at cases, the man whose interagency and international networking broke down silos, that man, John O'Neill, was on his way to a new job outside the FBI—Director of Security at the World Trade Center. There O'Neill died, on September 11th, 2001, when the Trade Center's South Tower, which he had just entered, collapsed.

## Making a Policy Difference in the Organization

"Maverick' was a label pinned on John O'Neill, and it comes up in the Frontline documentary, "The Man Who Knew," which was viewable online when this book was written and is definitely worth a look. One suspects that "maverick" was used most often by O'Neill's organizational adversaries. O'Neill didn't go with the flow, and that threatened the status quo. Some of this had to do with personal style; O'Neill looked different and lived differently. But a lot had to do with O'Neill championing a mission, correctly as it turns out, that the FBI was not well structured to embrace.

O'Neill's story took place in the FBI, but the analytical meaning goes beyond the FBI and even government agencies. Any organization invests a lot into getting to wherever it is at a given point. Executives who have built or thrived in that environment tend to be skeptical about proposals for course corrections and can be incensed at units and/or employees that appear to have set off on a new course without permission. When this happens it is not unusual for terms like "freelancer," "loose cannon" or, more formally, insubordinate to be tossed about. These epithets can be thought, if not flung, before anyone has gotten around to seeing if a new course makes sense.

In many ways this is where O'Neill found himself. He didn't ask to land in the middle of the battle just as jihadist terrorism was growing fast and morphing into something monstrous. Neither did O'Neill craft his "man about town" persona for FBI purposes but, as compared to the stiff and formal FBI social style, the O'Neill persona came in handy for cementing relations with foreign police officials, visiting dignitaries and local cops. O'Neill's intensive networking across agencies and up and down hierarchies, including above his bosses, also ran counter to the FBI's historically closed and guarded approach to outsiders in general. O'Neill was "off base" yet, in the fight against terrorism where intelligence is king, this kind of networking is critical, and was formally implemented after 9/11 with near universal endorsement. In other words, and sadly, had he stayed with the FBI, the networking John O'Neill would have been on-target, not off-base. In lavishly cultivating foreign counterparts and socializing extensively with other U.S. law enforcement personnel, O'Neill more likely would have been seen as a skilled relationship manager, as opposed to a "maverick."

So what are the lessons here for the aspiring law enforcement manager?

Lesson one is to appreciate the factors and pressures that make police agencies change-resistant.

Some of these factors and pressures are inherent to the organizational form. Establishing a comprehensive anti-narcotics operation, for instance, means assigning and shaping staff over an extended period of time into complex arrangements with specified funding streams. Narcotics operatives—the undercover cops, officers and detectives—grow comfortable in and identify with their roles. Their commanders likely have a say in the agency's policy councils and, if they are worth their salt, push hard for maintaining and growing their anti-drug operations.

As you multiply the narcotics operation by the patrol division, the detective division, and emergency services division and so on, the law enforcement agency is challenged to adjust quickly to change, especially change that has little meaning for the great bulk of employees and their leaders.

What's the John O'Neill lesson here? Know these pressures. Even better, get to know the principal players in these units, listen to what they face, show that you get it, and help if you can, even in little things that may not directly relate to the job. Show how serious you are about your unit, and the hard work that's done, and what others might do to make your objectives easier to achieve. These kinds of conversations are best when they are informal and relaxed. Though an O'Neill level after-hours social calendar is beyond the endurance of most, try never to eat lunch alone.

O'Neill had this level of understanding that helped him advance his unit's agenda. As noted earlier in this chapter, an organization haphazardly structures itself to produce, at any point, a mosaic of units that are both puzzle-like and puzzling. Few look beyond their own piece, even fewer understand how all the edges fit together and fewer still, like O'Neill, get down to the ways unit members think about what they do—the mostly hidden force that can bind or break the mosaic. This level of knowledge may not guarantee success in rearranging the organization for the better, but without this knowledge the odds of crashing and burning against inertial forces are very high.

After you've got a handle on the operating units and structures, figure out the agency's executive leadership, and where its priorities lie. O'Neill thought the powers at headquarters had it in for him, and he had his reasons for believing this, true or not. Thomas Pickard certainly made major decisions on the African and Yemen bombings that O'Neill took personally but that Pickard said were a matter of precise bureaucratic interpretation. O'Neill saw these calls and the disciplinary actions as of a piece, the play-it-safe headquarters versus maverick John O'Neill.

However, "Maverick" O'Neill may well have been thwarted had he been "St. John" O'Neill. An ever-present issue in the organizational scheme of things during this period was that counter-terrorism was an "upstart" function competing against the criminal investigation function that had been the FBI's core business from day one. The criminal investigation function dominated in the

FBI's everyday operations and in the executive suite. Historically, and through the 1990s, the top career executives in the FBI rose through the criminal division. Indeed, during O'Neill's time in counter-terrorism, even the FBI Director, Louis Freeh, had been an FBI special agent, as well as an Assistant U.S. Attorney and Federal Magistrate—cop, prosecutor, judge.

In the FBI, and in any agency or private organization for that matter, arriving at the executive suite should mean leaving any parochial favoritism behind. In reality, and for reasons not at all sinister, this is pretty much impossible. You can put a street cop in the executive suite but you can't expunge years of gut level connection with that role. You can elevate a life-long detective to an administrative post but you can't prevent a sympathetic ear, a longer visit or warmer feelings when the commander of detectives comes to propose that a new investigative initiative be funded. It matters where the bosses come from. When Tom Pickard closely parsed FBI rules to determine that those overseas terrorism investigations belonged to the Washington, D.C. field office, he determined that the assignment belonged with an office that he had just recently led.

No doubt O'Neill could scope out the lay of the land above as well as anybody. Still, he dutifully and forcefully pushed for his division, as well as for his own seat on high councils, but his terrorism portfolio only carried so much weight with a leadership more attuned to the FBI's traditional mandates. And, to top things off for the often flamboyant O'Neill, a straight-laced and low-key image was projected at FBI headquarters, from Freeh on down.

This kind of leadership analysis, which helps gauge the receptivity of superiors to one or another policy proposal, is not rocket science. For the most part, where your superiors come from, right up to the top, is an open book. It is a "must-read" for those who want to get ahead in organizations.

Finally, O'Neill, always a man in a hurry, chose not to wait for an unsympathetic leadership to depart, which, in fact, it did shortly after 9/11. But no one reading this should forget that "waiting them out" is as much an option as appealing to the preferences and skirting the prejudices of leaders on whom you've done your homework.

## The Philadelphia Police Assault on MOVE

Early on the morning of May 13th, 1985 on a residential street in Philadelphia, Police Commissioner Gregore Sambor got on a bullhorn and said: "Attention MOVE. This is America. You have to obey the laws of the United States."[60] Sambor's declaration was the opening salvo in what became a day-long police siege of the MOVE cult, a "back-to-nature," anti-establishment group of African Americans living communally in a small row house down the street from where Commissioner Sambor stood.

Sambor was backed up by several hundred heavily armed cops, water cannons and a State Police helicopter on standby. Firefighters and their equipment also stood at the ready. The police came in force because armed confrontations between MOVE and the police had occurred before. In 1978, a MOVE confrontation with the police had left Police Officer James Ramp dead and the MOVE house leveled.[61] As was the case in 1985, the earlier MOVE-police confrontation had occurred after MOVE members had fortified their house, stopped paying utility bills, violated numerous health and housing ordinances, harassed their neighbors, brandished arms and set up street-side sound systems that broadcast tirades against "the system" at all hours of the night and day.[62]

In the run-up to the 1985 confrontation, a focal point of MOVE protests was the freeing of the nine MOVE members who had each been sentenced to prison terms of 30–100 years for the death of Officer Ramp. MOVE demonstrated anywhere and everywhere, whether it was in the middle of a main Center City artery during rush hour, in court during a hearing for a member, or at midnight over booming loudspeakers in their middle-class, predominantly African-American residential neighborhood.

MOVE's neighbors were annoyed by more than the midnight harangues. MOVE held animals in high regard, including rats and roaches which, feasting on food scraps left for them by MOVE members, multiplied and migrated.[63] MOVE children went around barely clothed and did not attend school, images other parents on the block didn't want their children to see. The MOVE house was often illuminated by candlelight, an unsettling circumstance in a long block of houses each attached to the other in ways that could rapidly draft fire up and down the street. MOVE also constructed a fenced-off animal pen whose high walls blocked the common alleyway through which residents drove to the garages at the rear of their houses.[64] Finally, MOVE members started bringing in tree trunks from nearby parks, metal plates from street construction sites and other materials with which they fortified their house inside and out.[65]

Neighbors who complained to MOVE about its behavior were verbally abused and confrontations between MOVE members and others on the block erupted.[66] Though the neighbors' complaints to MOVE members were unproductive and unsatisfying, their entreaties to the Philadelphia city government fared no better. The residents grew angrier at the city than at MOVE. While MOVE was philosophically committed to an in-your-face, code-violating lifestyle, residents saw the city's job as protecting them against this.

On May 1, 1985, MOVE's fed-up neighbors held a press conference in which they directly appealed to the Republican governor of Pennsylvania, to whom they had written the day before threatening to take the matter into their own hands if the City of Philadelphia didn't act soon.[67] This made the papers and the TV news, and Philadelphia Mayor Wilson Goode, a Democrat, decided that something had to be done.

After nearly two years without effective action by the Philadelphia city government, the mayor was ready to mobilize. As a practical matter, this meant police action. At least one MOVE member residing in the house was a parole violator, but his parole officer had been driven away from the premises by threatening MOVE members.[68] MOVE had unpaid bills for water and gas, both city-owned utilities, but utility workers were in jeopardy if they approached the house to collect bills or shut off service. The City's Department of Licenses and Inspections considered the MOVE house a no-go zone for its workers.[69] Enforcement of existing warrants, code violations and payment obligations would require the intervention of the police, who secured additional warrants against MOVE members in the week prior to the assault.

The Philadelphia Police Department had the year before created a detailed plan for dealing with MOVE at the Osage Avenue location.[70] The plan had even been put in motion the previous summer in an attempt to execute a warrant against a MOVE member who had assaulted a neighbor. At that time, the Philadelphia Police had fully deployed, taking up positions in nearby houses and on roofs. A negotiated settlement was reached. But not, however, before police had tipped their tactical hand to MOVE, which further fortified the house with, among other things, rooftop bunkers.

Nonetheless, the existing plans would have been a good starting point in preparing to execute the May 1985 warrants. The plans would have been a good starting point except for two things. First, they were nowhere to be found. Second, the officer who had drawn up the plans had retired, and couldn't be reached. So, under pressure from the mayor, with D-Day less than two weeks away, the Philadelphia Police Department started planning anew for an operation against individuals in a fortified structure who had given every indication they were prepared to violently resist.

The police commissioner, Gregore Sambor, had ascended to the top more through staff positions than operational posts, and had headed the Police Academy for years before becoming commissioner in January 1984. Sambor came across as a somewhat eccentric figure, frequently going about in full commissioner's regalia instead of the suits favored by his predecessors and successors.

Many at Police Headquarters viewed Sambor with bemused detachment, which was not a good thing in Philadelphia, where civil service law, union contract and even political sponsorship protected all but a handful of ranking commanders. For Philadelphia police commissioners, long-standing fraternal relationships with their commanders went a long way in helping get things done.

Sambor had few such relationships, and ended up delegating the critical job of planning the MOVE assault to personnel with whom he was familiar from his police academy days.[71] The planning group included officers he knew who worked in squads, such as bomb disposal, which just happened to be housed on the remote Academy grounds. There the planning got parceled out even further, to the point where patrol officers were designing key elements of a complex assault involving hundreds of officers, massive firepower, explosives, armor, helicopters, evacuations and fire equipment.[72]

Time pressure was acute, which meant that key plan elements were developed in days and hours, and received cursory review from ranking commanders. One police officer, having ended up a key planner, briefed the brass at headquarters on the weekend prior to the operation. He received little feedback other than nods of thanks from commanders, who perfunctorily accepted the plans as they had been drawn up.

The plans featured explosives to breach the interior walls of the MOVE house so that assault teams could insert tear gas to drive MOVE members from the house. Water cannons would be used to drive MOVE members out of the front porch sniper's nest, and to try to dislodge rooftop bunkers the group had built. High-powered automatic weapons would lay down covering fire.

The plans the police drew up also relied on other agencies. Young children were in the MOVE house and the mayor wanted them out. So Sambor needed to make contact with the commissioner of the city's Department of Human Resources to set things in motion so that only adults would be in the house when the operation began. On a similar track, representatives from the district attorney's office would draw up warrants and arrange for a judge to be at the ready for any court orders necessary to authorize removing the children.

Evacuations were also part of the plan. The MOVE house was part of a long block of attached row homes, with similar lines of homes on the other side of narrow Osage Avenue and across a small alleyway to the rear. Hundreds of residents had to be removed for their safety but also because police planned to occupy several homes as part of the assault. The Philadelphia Fire Department would also be at the ready, since plans included the use of a high pressure water cannon and flooding MOVE out of the basement. Finally, with all the firepower and high explosives involved in the operation, firefighting might be necessary.

Plans began to unravel even before the assault. Four days before, when Sambor called the human resources commissioner about removing the children, she replied that she needed evidence of neglect or abuse in order for her agency to act. The imminent danger posed by Operation MOVE could also warrant the seizure of the children. But Sambor, wanting to keep the plans secret, did not tell the human resources commissioner about it. Sambor also didn't reveal that "a deputy city attorney had obtained permission from a Family Court judge to take the children into custody in advance of obtaining a court order."[73] Nor was the mayor's sense of urgency conveyed to the cops manning the barriers on Osage Avenue, who were also in the dark about the upcoming operation. Those officers had an opportunity to take MOVE children from a vehicle days before the assault, but were never clear on their authority to act. So, when the operation got under way, the children were still in the house with the adults.

In contrast, the evacuation of the neighbors proceeded smoothly. The displaced residents, who were eager to see something done after years of inaction, moved in with relatives and friends for what everyone expected would be a day or two.

The police spent Sunday putting equipment in place, establishing firing positions, and deploying the hundreds of personnel who would participate in the operation. Fire trucks and emergency rescue vehicles were also deployed. The police commissioner and the fire commissioner ran the show. Philadelphia's managing director was away for the weekend. The mayor continued to stay out of operational planning and execution.

The stage was set. The curtain rose early Monday morning when Commissioner Sambor announced through his bullhorn, "This is America." The reply came not long after, as bullets were fired from the MOVE house, and the police, in turn, fired thousands of rounds at the house to little effect. Gunfire continued sporadically from the front porch fortifications MOVE had built, raking the street with a field of fire that precluded any frontal assault.

The explosive/gas insertion teams had moved into the adjoining attached houses under cover of smoke charges and cascades of water. From left and right of the MOVE home, their explosive charges knocked down parts of the walls. What remained, however, were the tree trunks and other huge pieces of wood and metal with which MOVE had fortified their side of the dividing walls. Gunfire then began coming through slits in MOVE's interior fortifications. One insertion team, driven back, began to hurl the remaining explosive charges, grenade-style, towards the MOVE residence. The other team retreated to where the wall separating the houses had not been breached, and then shaped a powerful charge which they affixed to the wall and then detonated. The net effect of all the explosives was the near-complete demolition of MOVE's porch-side fortifications. Gunfire, however, still continued from inside the house. The tear gas tactic for driving out the MOVE members also didn't work.

The equipment that the planners of the operation had lined up also had less than their desired effect. The water cannon and fire hoses, which were supposed to drive the defenders back from and possibly dismantle their commanding firing positions, could neither get close enough nor draw on enough water pressure to do the job.

Osage Avenue was a war zone; the battle, a standoff. Displaced neighbors close enough to hear or see what was going on began to have doubts. Houses on the block were now pockmarked with bullet holes. Homes near the MOVE house were waterlogged. No end was in sight.

As evening drew near, the strongest card left in the police's tactical deck was using a helicopter to drop explosives on the bunker on the roof of the house, an option that had been briefly considered but not adopted during the planning. With the situation stalemated, bombing the bunker was looking more attractive to the police command. Not only would a rooftop sniper's nest be put out of commission but, if the bombed bunker fell through the roof and the floors below, that might fully disrupt the occupants' defense and drive them outside.

"Bomb on roof" was pretty much the understanding of the decision-makers who gave the go-ahead. They did not know that the bomb would be crafted using C-4, a powerful military explosive, in addition to other explosives. The Philadelphia Police Department generally used small amounts of C-4 for training purposes, but the bomb squad had obtained a large quantity several months earlier in an unrecorded exchange with an FBI agent. The officer crafting the bomb had created a charge the power of which few, if any, fully appreciated.

The decision-makers were also oblivious to the containers of gasoline stored on the roof of the MOVE house. Photos existed of the containers being hoisted up and then sitting on the roof. Neighbors had alerted the city. The information had made it to mid-command levels in the police department. The bombing plan, however, did not take the gasoline into account. And everyone in authority later claimed to have been unaware of the gasoline's presence when planning and then authorizing the bombing of the bunker.

The bomb was dropped at 5:27 PM. The ensuing explosion was huge and fiery. The bunker did not fall through the roof, though the blast had created a hole. Soon flames were seen coming from the MOVE house. Fire personnel, however, stood down. The fire commissioner said he was awaiting the all-clear from Sambor, the overall commander on the scene. Sambor later expressed the view that the fire commissioner was free to act. After half an hour, the city manager, speaking by phone to the police commissioner, ordered the fire put out. But the police commissioner, in consultation with the fire commissioner, decided to let the bunker burn down to eliminate the threat it posed to police and firefighters.

The extra minutes of inaction proved critical. Soon the flames engulfed the entire MOVE residence. The adjoining houses, linked structurally in ways that allowed the rapid spread of fire, were soon ablaze as well. Sparks from the blaze ignited more houses across Osage Avenue and on Pine Street across the back alleyway. When the Fire Department finally mobilized close to 6:30 PM, it could do little but contain the holocaust.

A firefight was also blazing. As the MOVE house became fully engulfed, several occupants tried to exit through the rear alleyway. Two staggered towards police lines and survived. The rest ended up back in the house, where they perished. Just how they died stirred a controversy that endures today. Police claim the residents emerged firing weapons and retreated, either of their own accord or in response to return fire from the police. Surviving MOVE members claim that police deliberately drove the surrendering MOVE members back to their deaths, and that some may have been shot in the alleyway by police and then buried by the collapsing, burning structure

Sixty-one families on Osage Avenue and Pine Street saw their houses and all their possessions burn to the ground. Six MOVE adults and five children, several burned beyond recognition, perished.

## Miscommunication and Crisis

One semester an NYPD deputy chief happened to be in my "Bureau-pathology" course. He ended up analyzing the MOVE debacle and was aghast. In the NYPD, he said, for something like Operation MOVE, we would have talked and planned, and then talked and planned some more. The plan would be thoroughly vetted by the commanders of any operational units that would be involved and any staff units—legal, planning, community affairs, public information—with advice to give. Everyone involved would thoroughly understand who did what and who reported to whom. In short, there would have been extensive and effective communication.

The MOVE operation, from start to finish, was a primer in how ineffective communications can precipitate law enforcement failures. To read the MOVE hearings and the half-dozen books written about the tragedy is to come time and again across officials who were not on the same page, subordinates confused about what their supervisors wanted, and superiors who were content to nod their heads at high-risk plans hastily developed by subordinates.

The decision-makers were clueless about the composition, power and impact of the explosives, especially the improvised aerial bomb. Were enough questions asked to determine these things? No. Was much information volunteered by subordinates? No. Should those in authority have been surprised when the bang was bigger than expected? No. Did these same decision-makers serially plead ignorance, or delegation or innocence when questioned by the investigating commission? You bet. The bombing authorized by the mayor, mediated by the managing director, ordered by the police commissioner and flown in by state police pilots was carried out by the head of the bomb squad who was clueless about ingredients his subordinate had added to ramp up the power of the bomb. In the end, no one in authority had the same perspective about how exactly this came to pass, due in no small part to failures of communication before the event.

The commission impaneled to study the MOVE debacle found that the failure to get the children out was a result of unclear and poorly communicated directives, and that going forward with the children still in the house constituted gross negligence on the part of the mayor.[74] Did the police commissioner tell the human resources commissioner enough to justify her agency's intervention to take custody of the children? No. Did she inquire sufficiently to determine whether an imminent danger to the children loomed? No. Was a brief phone call sufficient to thrash through the nuanced issue of how and why children might be legitimately removed from the house? No. Charles W. Bowser, a member of the Philadelphia Special Investigative Commission, excoriated "the narrow parameters of the concern for the children at every level."[75] Bowser was referring to the technical rationales that allowed managers to withdraw from difficult problem-solving dialogues and wash their hands of responsibility for any dire results.

The communications dysfunctions in the MOVE case are practically legion. Did some police personnel know about the gasoline on the roof? Yes. Did this critical piece of information get to the decision-makers who ordered what they thought was a surgical strike at the rooftop bunkers? No, at least if you asked them. Did Commissioner Sambor think that the officers manning the end of the block checkpoints, or their supervisors, had been advised that the children should be taken into custody at the first opportunity? Apparently yes. Did the officers at the checkpoints clearly understand this? No.

It goes on. The managing director gave his first directive of the day at 6 PM when he ordered the fire put out. Several minutes later, the mayor, watching long distance as he had all day, incorrectly believed that the snow on his TV was water being poured on the blazing Osage Avenue residence.

What also is utterly striking about the communications is just how little of anything was written down. Some failures to record were deliberate. Sambor didn't want certain aspects of the plan written down in the interest of preserving secrecy,[76] but in general the paper generated was minimal. This, in turn, minimized careful prior review and meaningful feedback by commanders not intimately involved in the planning. The main opportunity for input was during verbal briefings to audiences hearing for the first time about an operation presented as an imminent done deal. At these meetings, perfunctory nods of approval were pretty much the norm. In writing about a similar verbal fog of communications at mayoral meetings about the MOVE operation, Robin Wagner-Pacifici saw "a process of communication more appropriate to a small-scale, informal organization."[77]

Information is the lifeblood of organization. Information travels through the organization via the communication system. The organization is healthiest when the communication system is:

- Robust—more rather than less information is transmitted;
- Widespread—any unit that needs information gets it;
- Well-exercised—all parties freely contribute, extract and clarify information.

In this case, communications within the Philadelphia city government, including the police department, were virtually the antithesis of robust, widespread and well-exercised. There is no substitute in a law enforcement organization for systems that circulate information of a quality and quantity that best informs the decisions of personnel from the lowest to the highest ranks. Without such communications systems, the most elegant and logical organizational structure is susceptible to unmitigated disaster.

## The Impact of "Shadow Structure" on Organizations

Big city police departments, state police and federal law enforcement agencies will inevitably confront highly delicate situations whose resolution requires sophisticated strategizing and careful, detailed tactical planning. The MOVE crisis in May 1985 was just such a situation but the Philadelphia Police Department found itself under the gun because the mayor wanted MOVE out forthwith.

On the other hand, the haphazardness with which the Philadelphia Police Department planned for the MOVE assault was due to more than the mayor's sudden urgency. While smaller police departments, like Boulder's, may lack the resources to effectively deal with complex situations, Philadelphia's 7,000-strong police department had the personnel and budget to come up with a carefully calibrated plan to deal with MOVE. And given the department's long and troublesome history with MOVE, there was every reason to be prepared, regardless of the stance taken by one or another mayor at any particular point in time. The ways in which the department was structured and operated helped insure the planning failures that turned the extraction of MOVE members into a deadly disaster.

In the 1980s, the Philadelphia Police Department had—and to some extent still has—an administrative structure that weakens the Office of the Police Commissioner. Civil service protections and union protections extend into the very highest ranks. Compare this to New York City, where civil service protection extends only to the rank of captain. Anyone in a higher rank serves at the pleasure of the commissioner. Though an inspector or deputy chief with whom a commissioner is terminally dissatisfied usually chooses to retire gracefully, their exit is facilitated by the possibility of demotion back to captain at a lower salary and pension base. In Philadelphia, however, asserting control over resistant executive staff can embroil a commissioner in battles that go on for years, as John Timoney learned, starting in 1998.

Timoney, as NYPD First Deputy Commissioner under William Bratton, helped give birth to COMPSTAT, which combined computerized incident mapping with a real-time analysis of crime patterns, followed by the rapid deployment of officers in response to what the research showed. COMPSTAT produced dramatic crime drops in New York and has been subsequently adopted, with considerable success, by numerous big city police departments.

When Timoney took over in Philadelphia, he naturally wanted COMPSTAT up and running but quickly learned that he wasn't in New York anymore. Listen to him tell it:

> One of the biggest challenges I have had in Philadelphia that we didn't have in New York has been the unions and the strong civil service system. It's hard to reward good work when all you have to do is pass a test to get promoted, and I've had lots of run-ins with the union. This is a very powerful union that represents every level and rank. I can't even transfer people who are not performing, without union approval. We have created one of the best crime mapping and analysis units in the country by using graduate students from Penn State to develop the technology, but the union sued us for using non-cops in this role and won. We are appealing that ruling, but the whole mindset is disgraceful! It goes against everything we are trying to do here.[78]

Not that the union was against applying geographic information systems to fight Philadelphia crime. The union was, however, adamantly opposed to bringing in civilians and/or outsiders, no matter how qualified, to do the job. If the assigned cops weren't up to snuff—and many weren't—the department would just have to educate the officers in the requisite electronic mapping and data analysis skills, however long it took. Timoney eventually prevailed on appeal after nearly three years, and another small chunk of the Philadelphia Police Department came under the control of the commissioner.

Timoney took an equally aggressive approach towards the department's crime reporting. He was greeted on his arrival by a series of exposes in the *Philadelphia Inquirer* highlighting dramatic drops in auto theft that seemed not to conform to any possible reality,[79] and the routine downgrading of sexual assaults for the previous decade. Timoney ended up disavowing, recalculating and resubmitting Philadelphia's Uniform Crime Reports and reining in his commanders, both for submitting bogus figures and independently dealing with the media about crime statistics.[80]

Timoney had advantages. As one of only two Philadelphia police commissioners in the previous fifty years not up from the ranks (the other, Kevin Tucker, took over from Sambor), Timoney could look at the department with a fresh eye. Timoney had also been on the cutting edge of urban police practice. And, coming from a department where the high command exercised great control over staff units and mid-rank operational commanders, Timoney was willing to battle for authority that many of his predecessors, including Gregore Sambor, had effectively conceded.

In 1985 Gregore Sambor was laboring under multiple handicaps. As a product of the system, he was ill prepared to look either critically or creatively at the department he now led. He took over a "weak" commissioner's office and had bypassed most operational commands on the way to the top. Leading a department where leverage over policy and personnel was widely dispersed and having few "buddies" in high command, Sambor could not augment his limited authority by drawing upon the long-term loyalties of top commanders.

The result, according to Charles Bowser, a member of the MOVE Commission, was that "Sambor assigned the critical planning work to his cronies in the department and eliminated any chance of utilizing the experience and expertise of his top commanders."[81] The MOVE Commission concluded that having officers with limited planning experience design an operation against an armed, battle-seeking, motivated group like MOVE was clearly, and predictably, a mistake.[82] But it was a mistake rooted in an agency structure so potentially unresponsive that the Commissioner may well have felt it necessary to reach far down the ranks to find personnel he could trust and effectively direct in a time-pressured situation. Better perhaps to rely on low-ranking but loyal soldiers than on possibly detached and bemused commanders who could pick and choose the extent to which they would lend him their expertise and support.

In any event this process pretty much closed out key commanders, such as the civil affairs chief, who may have been able to constructively criticize the assault-centered plan. Instead, bomb squad and stakeout personnel effectively put their imprint on the plan that remained essentially unchanged during truncated reviews by higher-ups as D-Day loomed. And when Plan A went awry absent any contingency plan, this narrowly drawn group remained front and center in drawing up, in less than two hours, the ill-fated helicopter bombing.

What Sambor wrestled with was a parallel structure of authority and influence that diluted his command of the formal structure of the organization. The union held great sway over staffing; commanders protected by civil service had a measure of independence in operational matters. This power of these "shadow structures" could translate into control over one or another issue regardless of what the commissioner wanted. Such phenomena underpin the rich literature on "informal organization," which considers both emergent structures and sub-cultures that do not buy fully into the official goals, practices and norms of the larger organization.

A critical management lesson of the MOVE tragedy in Philadelphia is that police executives often have to deal with, and try to manage, "shadow structures" that are all but invisible to outsiders yet do much to determine a law enforcement agency's direction and decisions. And because these "shadow structures" have power independent of the official organizational structure, the all but inevitable conflict of purposes, commitments and motivations can skew policies and influence decisions in ways that set up the law enforcement organization for major failures.

# Leading the Structurally Challenged Agency

We have looked at several ways in which the organizational structure can fail in its job of supporting an adequate and effective response to the challenges that confront a law enforcement agency. They are:

- Resource inadequacy
- Task overload
- Conflicting mandates
- Subordination of law enforcement
- Hierarchical dysfunction
- Inter-organizational dysfunction
- Flawed communications systems
- Shadow structures

Resource inadequacy and task overload are related concepts with important differences. When we looked at resource inadequacy in the JonBenet Ramsey case, the issue for the Boulder Police Department was the quality and variety of resources it could devote to the case. Bottom line: The Boulder police lacked the sophisticated mix of investigative skills the case required and refused for months to call upon better equipped law enforcement agencies that stood ready to help.

In contrast, the INS suffered from task overload. Verifying eligibility to enter the country is a rather straightforward clerical/investigative task best performed by well-trained officers with time to interrogate incoming individuals. Unlike the Boulder Police Department, which ended up bringing in ransom note analysts, criminal profilers and DNA specialists, the INS needed more personnel with basic training in order to accommodate the flood of entrants into the U.S. But additional personnel were not forthcoming and, because there was pressure from other government agencies to ease the entry of foreign nationals, immigration law enforcement was ramped back by the existing cadre of inspectors.

The subordination of law enforcement also played a role in the INS case, and should be a concern to any law enforcement executive whose unit is nested in a larger system whose main concerns are far from law enforcement. In transportation systems, in hospitals, in housing complexes and in universities, the police force may face pressure to under-enforce laws and under-report crimes because doing so is seen as protecting the larger enterprise. However, accepting this subordination is often an invitation to disaster that paves the way for medicine more bitter than what the larger institution sought to avoid in the first place. Colleges now have to report crime annually, and are subject to severe penalties for misreporting, because for years campus police departments routinely "disappeared" most crimes that occurred on campus. When student deaths capped off unacknowledged crime waves at certain colleges, parents won massive liability judgments and set off on a crusade to make all colleges come clean about crime on campus. Law enforcement executives who give in to pressure to soft-pedal enforcement or downplay crime are planting the seeds of disaster. And while resisting such pressures may jeopardize one's career prospects, it's a principled stand that sometimes has to be made to preserve the integrity of the law enforcement function.

Conflicting mandates, which also plagued the INS, are akin to a congenital handicap because they are built into the system in an authorized way. Congress and the president handed down idiosyncratic, shifting and even conflicting advice about whether the INS should come on as Dr. Jekyll or Mr. Hyde towards particular groups coming into the country. Law enforcement administrators should know when their mandates conflict and should stand ready to publicize the dilemma this poses for the agency. This puts the ball back in the court of legislators and chief executives, where it belongs. Whether legislators and executives were clueless or cynical in saddling the agency with a Hobson's choice, the solution to the structural handicap of conflicting mandates lies with them.

Hierarchical dysfunction is likely to rear up at some point in just about everyone's organizational career, in or out of law enforcement. The same can be said of inter-unit and inter-organizational friction that reaches dysfunctional levels. Morbid hierarchical and inter-unit combat can paralyze any law enforcement agency, and can arise suddenly out of seemingly benign conditions. Hierarchical and inter-unit struggle can be seen as cancerous in the sense that previously useful elements—hierarchical authority and division of labor—get some gene turned on that causes them to go out of control. Like a cancer, these struggles often call for, but can also be resistant to, aggressive treatment by management. Ultimately, in Boulder, the principal actors struggling over the JonBenet case were surgically removed, and the governor convened a statewide team of law enforcement specialists to stitch back together the torn relationships of Boulder's criminal justice system.

The John O'Neill case also featured hierarchical and inter-functional struggles, at the very highest executive and policy levels, over the long-term direction of the FBI. Operational and personnel decisions became weapons in this struggle; and whether or how a particular weapon was used often depended on what positions, past or present, were held by those involved in the decisions.

Inadequate communications bedeviled the MOVE decision-makers. A robust, widespread and well-exercised communications system is a must for every law enforcement agency, particularly for the planning and execution of critical operations. Without this level of communication, critical information will be lost. Law enforcement managers should also be alert for the spread of a dysfunctional communications ethos among cynical and self-absolving employees. When information "falls through the cracks" because speakers are secretive and untruthful and listeners are distracted or hear only what they want to hear, vigorous treatment is called for. Communicating well is an obligation that must be shouldered by every member of a law enforcement organization.

The last structural problem we addressed was the "shadow structure" of the Philadelphia Police Department with which Commissioner Sambor contended in 1985 and which John Timoney fought somewhat more successfully thirteen years later. "Shadow structure" is a chronic condition in law enforcement agencies, especially larger ones, throughout the country. Whether one talks about the Boston Police Department being run from City Hall in the 1970s[83] or a Philadelphia Police Department where union officials and protected senior commanders could effectively stymie policy, the formal executive structure of the agency is not nearly as in charge as outsiders might believe. Rather the "boss," usually out of public view—which saves embarrassment all around—has to bull and/or negotiate his or her way through entrenched organizational elements seeking to hold onto prerogatives they have long enjoyed. As a chronic, embedded condition that is widespread yet unique in its agency-by-agency symptoms, a full understanding of shadow structure is something aspiring law enforcement executives need to acquire as they climb the career ladder in their agency. Executives brought in from the outside are also well advised to get quickly up to speed on the agency's shadow structures. A law enforcement executive not fully versed in an agency's formal and informal structures and power centers risks being neutralized or marginalized, with little power to control the drift of the agency, even if that drift is towards disaster.

# Endnotes

1. Henry Mintzberg, "The Five Basic Parts of the Organization," in *Classics of Organization Theory*, ed. Jay Shafritz and J. Steven Ott (New York: Harcourt, 2001): 222–33. Mintzberg's abstract organization chart, which places the "operating core" front and center, is very much on the mark in conveying the essential elements of organization. See also James Q. Wilson, *Bureaucracy: What Government Agencies Do and Why They Do It* (New York: Basic Books, 1989): 31–110. Wilson talks about "operators" in great detail. Reading all of Wilson, as well as Mintzberg's *The Structure of Organizations* (Upper Saddle River, NJ: Prentice-Hall, 1979), will educate anyone about the basics of organizations and, thanks to Wilson, the essential dynamics of public agencies.

2. Rita K. Farrell, "Ovitz Was Odd but Diligent, Former Disney Officer Says," *New York Times*, November 23, 2004.

3. James B. Stewart, *Disney War* (New York: Simon and Schuster, 2005): 257–79.

4. Joe Wilcox, Michael Kanellos and Aimee Male, "Gates Turns Over Reins Of His Empire," *C-Net News.com* http://news.com.com/Gates+turns+over+reins+of+his+empire/2100-1001_3-235639.html?tag=nl (Accessed April 2, 2005).

5. Wellford W. Wilms, "From the Age of Dragnet to the Age of the Internet: Tracking Changes Within the Los Angeles Police Department," in *California Policy Options*, ed. Daniel J. B. Mitchell, (UCLA School of Public Policy and Education, 2004): 157–72.

6. Walter Shapiro, "Lessons of Los Angeles," *Time* 139 (May 18, 1992): 38.

7. Wilms, "The Age of Dragnet," 159.

8. Lawrence Schiller, *Perfect Murder, Perfect Town: JonBenet and the City of Boulder*, (New York: Harper Collins, 1999): 8

9. Lawrence Schiller, *Perfect Murder, Perfect Town*, 9.

10. Ibid., 12.

11. Ibid., 18.

12. Kevin McCullen and Lynn Bartels, "Denver Chief Offered Help To Boulder After Slaying," *Rocky Mountain News*, Feb 14, 1997.

13. Schiller, *Perfect Murder, Perfect Town*, 23–24.

14. Charlie Brennan, "Ramsey Case a Tragedy of Errors," *Rocky Mountain News*, June 8, 1997.

15. Ibid.

16. Schiller, *Perfect Murder, Perfect Town*, 50.

17. Ibid., 87.

18. Hector Gutierrez, "Assistant DA Apologizes to Boulder Cops," *Rocky Mountain News*, February 15, 1997.

19. Schiller, *Perfect Murder, Perfect Town*, 404.

20. Charlie Brennan, "A Fresh Look At Ramsey Case Boulder Seeks Outsider To Investigate Killing," *Rocky Mountain News*, Feb 23, 1997.

21. Schiller, *Perfect Murder, Perfect Town*, 339–41.

22. Kevin McCullen, "Detective Taken Off Ramsey Case To Quit," *Rocky Mountain News*, Nov 22, 1997.

23. Kevin McCullen, "Boulder Police Chief To Retire In December 1998, *Rocky Mountain News*, Nov 19, 1997.

24. "The Thomas Resignation Letter," *Rocky Mountain News*, August 8, 1998.

25. Kevin McCullen, "Hunter Decides To Call It Quits," *Rocky Mountain News*, March 10, 2000.

26. Boulder Police Department, *2003 Fact Sheet*, http://www.ci.boulder.co.us/ police/crime/fact_sheet_02.htm (Accessed November 20, 2004).

27. Federal Bureau of Investigation, *Crime in the United States, 2003*. Washington, D.C.: 2003, 364.

28. U.S. Department of Labor, Bureau of Labor Statistics, *Career Guide to Industries, State and Local Government*, Washington, D.C., 2004, 254. http://www.bls.gov/oco/cg/ cgs042.htm (Accessed April 4, 2005).

29. Boulder Police Department, *2003 Annual Report*, http://www.ci.boulder.co.us/police/directory/AR2003-newest1.pdf (Accessed November 20, 2004).

30. Dorothy Guyot, "Bending Granite: Attempting to Change the Rank Structure of American Police Departments," *Journal of Police Science and Administration* 7, no. 3 (1979): 253–84.

31. John P. Crank, *Understanding Police Culture* (Cincinnati, OH: Anderson, 1998): 261–64. Crank illustrates just how problematic hierarchy can be in policing.

32. Noel Tichy with Eli Cohen, *The Leadership Engine: How Winning Companies Build Leaders at Every Level* (New York: Harper Business, 1997): 262–64.

33. U.S. Department of Justice Office of Inspector General, *The Immigration and Naturalization Service's Contact with Two September 11 Terrorists*, Washington, D.C., 2002 http://news.findlaw.com/hdocs/docs/doj/dojoig052002insrpt.pdf (Accessed April 12, 2005). The description of this case is drawn from material in this volume.

34. Ibid., 9.

35. William Bratton, *Turnaround: How America's Top Cop Reversed the Crime Epidemic* (New York: Random House, 1998): 143–47.

36. Carl T. Rowan, Jr., "Badge of Dishonor: DC Confidential," *The New Republic* 218, (January 19, 1998): 20–23; See also Carl T. Rowan, Jr., "The Death of a Police Department," *LEEA Advocate*(Spring 1996): 30–34.

37. National Commission on Terrorist Attacks Upon the United States, *The 9/11 Commission Report: Final Report of the National Commission on Terrorist Attacks Upon the United States* (New York: W.W. Norton, 2003): 383–93.

38. Craig Horowitz, "The NYPD's War on Terror," *New York Magazine*, February 3, 2003 http://nymag.com/nymetro/news/features/n_8286/index2.html (Accessed March 22, 2012).

39. Federal Emergency Management Administration, United States Fire Administration, *The World Trade Center Bombing: Report and Analysis,* Washington, D.C., 1993, 18–19. This FEMA report was reprinted of the December 1993 special issue of Fire Engineering.

40. John T. McQuiston, "Kahane Is Killed after Giving Talk in New York Hotel," *New York Times*, November 6, 1990, A1.

41. Ibid.

42. John Kifner, "Police Think Kahane Slaying Suspect Acted Alone," *New York Times*, November 8, 1990, B17.

43. Joseph Fried, "Sheik Sentenced to Life in Prison in Bombing Plot," *New York Times*, January 18, 1996, A1.

44. Murray Weiss, *The Man Who Warned America,* (New York: Harper Collins, 2003): 84.

45. Ibid., 8.

46. Weiss, *The Man Who Warned America,* 119.

47. Weiss, *The Man Who Warned America,* 121.

48. Weiss, *The Man Who Warned America.*

49. Michael Kirk, director, *The Man Who Knew,* (Boston: Frontline—WGBH, 2002) http://www.pbs.org/wgbh/pages/frontline/shows/knew/ (Accessed March 20, 2012).

50. Weiss, *The Man Who Warned America,* 208.

51. Weiss, *The Man Who Warned America,* 199.

52. Weiss, *The Man Who Warned America,* 200.

53. Weiss, *The Man Who Warned America,* 209.

54. Weiss, *The Man Who Warned America,* 87.

55. Lawrence Wright, *The Looming Tower: Al Qaeda and the Road to 9/11,* (New York: Vintage Books, 2006), 310.

56. Ibid., 337–338.

57. Weiss, *The Man Who Warned America,* 290.

58. Lawrence Wright, *The Looming Tower,* 361–362.

59. Ibid., 348.

60. Jim Quinn. "MOVE v. the City of Philadelphia." *The Nation* 242, (March 29, 1986): 440.

61. John Anderson and Hilary Hevenor, *Burning Down the House: Move and the Tragedy of Philadelphia* (New York: W.W. Norton: 1987): 37.

62. Anderson and Hevenor, *Burning Down the House,* 9–16.

63. Charles W. Bowser, *Let the Bunker Burn: The Final Battle with MOVE* (Philadelphia: Camino Books, 1989): 72–73.

64. Robin Wagner-Pacifici, *Discourse and Destruction: The City of Philadelphia versus MOVE* (Chicago: University of Chicago Press, 1994): 64.

65. Anderson and Hevenor, *Burning Down the House,* 78.

66. Wagner-Pacifici, *Discourse and Destruction,* 57.

67. Bowser, *Let the Bunker Burn,* 84.

68. Ibid., 83.

69. Ibid., 82.

70. Ibid., 61.

71. Ibid., 62.

72. "Excerpts From Commission's Report on Bombing," *New York Times*, March 7, 1986.

73. Bowser, *Let the Bunker Burn*, 54.

74. *New York Times*, "Excerpts From Commission's Report."

75. Bowser, *Let the Bunker Burn*, 53.

76. Anderson and Hevenor, *Burning Down the House*, 93–94.

77. Wagner-Pacifici, *Discourse and Destruction*, 84.

78. Tod Newcombe, "An Interview with Philly's Top Cop, John F. Timoney," *Government Technology*, April 2000. http://www.govtech.net/magazine/crimetech/Apr00/CTEInterview.php (Accessed on May 1, 2005).

79. Mark Fazlollah and Craig R. McCoy, "Crime Stats Target of 2d Probe," *Philadelphia Inquirer*, May 24, 1998.

80. Mark Fazlollah and Craig R. McCoy, "Timoney Throws Out Crime Stats as Faulty," *Philadelphia Inquirer*, July 26, 1998.

81. Bowser, *Let the Bunker Burn*, 63.

82. *New York Times*, "Excerpts From Commission's Report."

83. Bratton, *Turnaround*, 113.

# CHAPTER FOUR

# OVERSIGHT FAILURE IN LAW ENFORCEMENT: MARGINALIZING THE GUARDIANS

## The Challenge to Internal Control

Oversight is important in all organizations, and critical in policing where the price of error and wrongdoing can be lost lives, tainted justice and shattered organizational legitimacy.

The oversight function is usually set apart from, yet is responsible for assuring lawful compliance by, the overall organization. Accountants, internal affairs, external auditors and quality control units all provide organizational oversight. The critical role and unique positioning of oversight warrants a separate structural failure analysis, which this chapter undertakes.

We typically think of oversight in law enforcement in terms of Internal Affairs guarding against criminal or rule-violating cops. Oversight is broader than that, however. Oversight investigations can focus on issues such as excessive overtime because of budget strain, not illegality. Other issues, such as dating between superiors and subordinates, may not violate any rule but are under review, for instance, because lawsuits and large judgments arising from the issue elsewhere may signal rising liability risks for the agency.

Oversight, in the most general sense, is about monitoring the integrity of a range of organizational systems in order to spot and address aberrant behavior that diminishes performance, damages morale or may bring the agency into disrepute. In law enforcement, the job of identifying and rooting out aberrant behavior most often rests with internal affairs, though other units, such as personnel and employee assistance programs, also monitor employee behavior with respect to certain problems.

The first problem with entities that oversee error-prone organizations is that they are themselves organizations, which means they are as subject to accident and error as the entities they oversee, perhaps even more so. Normal accident factors easily combine with structural deficiencies to hobble oversight units.

Police internal affairs investigations are a case in point. Allegations are numerous. Suspect personnel and fellow officers may be aggressively uncooperative. Witnesses to alleged violations may include only the involved officers and complainants. The motives and veracity of complainants may be suspect, and their willingness to cooperate can be variable. Investigators often must pursue a case over extended periods while other cases compete for attention. Meanwhile, grapevine scuttlebutt alerts targets. The investigators themselves may be reassigned, and those taking over a case may not be up to speed. As a result, investigations are often "blown" because a single critical thing goes wrong, collapsing a corruption investigation that, in order to be successful, requires that so many things be done just right.

The second problem with oversight units is that they tend to be small and poorly funded relative to the organizational activities they monitor. Organizations naturally give priority to their core operations. Oversight is necessary but, absent a scandal, far from the head of the line for personnel and funding. Oversight units thus find themselves overstretched or overmatched. In the first case in this chapter, a constant refrain, both from internal affairs investigators and their superiors, was lack of resources. Corrupt officers were doing their dirty business 24/7. However, due to limitations on overtime for internal affairs investigators, suspect officers were only watched, as it were, from 9 to 5. Officers under investigation also traveled in and out of the city, and even abroad, to further their schemes. The internal affairs investigators hadn't the travel funds to follow them. Whether it's a lack of high-tech recording equipment, miniature cameras, forensic accountants or simply officers, the internal affairs function is often under-resourced.

The third problem is that overseers can be co-opted, becoming overly responsive to top management and/or overly sympathetic to the people they oversee. An internal affairs operation under the thumb of an image-conscious commissioner or police chief is less likely to aggressively attack impropriety, even if widespread. The empathy investigators can have for line personnel— "there but for fortune go I"—also mutes aggressive oversight. Internal affairs officers who continue to identify with their previous rank-and-file roles are sorely tempted to shelve or downplay investigations into practices they may once have engaged in or tolerated, or to give a heads-up to old buddies whose unit has become an investigation target.

The cases in this chapter involve all of these issues. Structural and resource issues emerge center-stage in the case of "The Watcher," as do internal affairs policies that reflect top management's rosy views. In "The Secret World of David Brame" a very high price was paid because police officials closely identified with a very troubled member of the department, failing to see his slide towards disaster as something actionable. We will also take a look at the brief tenures of internal affairs chiefs in Philadelphia and Baltimore, cases underscoring that the internal affairs function is the first place in which the image of integrity must be absolutely assured. Finally, in "Friends of the Police," we'll look at how oversight is challenged by deeply embedded and generally accepted improprieties like ticket-fixing.

* * *

**Oversight failure** occurs when supervisory levels and staff units responsible for oversight fail to detect and/or address organizational conditions that depart significantly from the norm.

## The Watcher: Internal Affairs and the Case of Michael Dowd

Joe Trimboli had a lonely job. He sat in a car watching other cops work. He went to file rooms to examine their employment history. He monitored officers coming to and from the job. He talked to community residents who knew the cops. He talked with informants who interacted with cops and criminals. Joe Trimboli worked Internal Affairs as a NYPD detective in a field unit in Brooklyn in the 1980s.

Field internal affairs units were spread throughout the NYPD from the 1970s until 1993. They had come about in the wake of the landmark Knapp Commission hearings, which had exposed systematic, "grass-eating" corruption in the department.[1] This corruption was not so much a matter of big time felonies by notorious "meat-eating" cops as it was an accumulation of petty bribes routinely extracted from legitimate and illegitimate businesses by lots and lots of ordinary cops, so many in fact that station houses had systems in place to collect and redistribute the proceeds.[2]

After the Knapp Commission, Field Internal Affairs Units (FIAU) were given the job of nipping corruption in the bud before it could again take root and spread. Much of the work of FIAU detectives consisted of investigating allegations that "grass-eating" cops were abusing time and leave, pocketing valuables at crime scenes or not paying the local grocer for their coffee and donuts. Occasionally, an FIAU detective stumbled across a big case, where "meat-eating" cops were in league with mobsters or were committing their own crimes for big bucks. These cases usually ended up being run from Internal Affairs Division headquarters, which oversaw the Field Internal Affairs Units but also had considerable resources to devote to "big" cases. Additional resources for major police misconduct cases also were available from the New York State Special Prosecutor for Criminal Justice, established after the Knapp Commission primarily to prosecute major cases of police corruption.

Joe Trimboli came across a "meat-eater" in 1987. Michael Dowd had a malingerer's profile, which accounted for some of the raw material in the case file Trimboli was building. Dowd's sick leave was excessive. For a patrol officer in a high crime precinct, his arrests were minimal. He had a reputation for alcohol abuse, and would often close a local bar in the precinct almost at dawn after his 4 PM to midnight tour was over. Most 75th Precinct officers saw Dowd as a frequently out-of-control substance abuser, unreliable at best.[3] Darker suspicions were held by cops who knew that Dowd sometimes didn't pick up his paycheck for weeks at a time. And then there were the corruption complaints, most of them identifying a nameless cop who matched Dowd's description, but also one called into the department's Crime Stopper Hotline fingering Dowd by name, and filled with details about Dowd's behavior on and off the job.[4]

It wasn't hard to find evidence that pointed to much more than malingering. Dowd drove a $35,000 red Corvette[5] (2012 cost: $70,000). He drove that Corvette to and from his several houses on Long Island, at least one of which was in the same league as the Corvette.[6] When Dowd drank until closing at that bar at the edge of the precinct, it was with a motley crew that included bartender ex-cops, cops close to Dowd who were also attracting internal affairs attention, and drug dealers. Soon two of those ex-cops and one still on the force, though not Dowd, were arrested—they had held up and then strong-armed a grocery store owner "at the behest of a drug dealer," as Trimboli later discovered.[7]

Trimboli became obsessed with the Dowd case. Dowd seemed to be in the middle of so many things. His commanders were zeroing in on Dowd for drug abuse.[8] Cops he hung out with got arrested. Known drug dealers were his buddies. Indicted cops[9] and, later, drug suspects[10] showed up as tenants and guests of Michael Dowd, the real estate baron. Internal Affairs cases kept being generated that had Dowd on the list of players. According to Trimboli, "You can't go into the office and meet an investigator who isn't working on a Michael Dowd case. And they are not even working together on them."[11] This perspective impressed itself upon Trimboli's FIAU captain who, in the summer of 1988, consolidated the various Brooklyn internal affairs investigations involving Dowd and assigned them to Trimboli.[12]

The pursuit of Dowd, however, was slow, and not at all sure. About to be drug tested in 1988 on the orders of the precinct commander, with a positive test warranting immediate dismissal, Dowd claimed alcoholism. This claim stopped the test and won Dowd a 30-day stint in rehab, followed by departmental psychological counseling.[13] It also earned him "gun-free" assignments to the motor pool and the police pound for more than a year.

Trimboli would occasionally monitor Dowd from a roof near the police pound in Whitestone, Queens. There he met yet another Internal Affairs cop on Dowd's trail who clued Trimboli in on federal investigations into a drug-dealing network in which Dowd seemed to be involved.[14] Remarkably, there were still other Queens Internal Affairs investigators curious about Dowd. But Trimboli didn't know this because he worked for a Field Internal Affairs Unit in Brooklyn, not Queens. Trimboli had no idea that Dowd's PBA card, which he had sold, had turned up, along with other police property, in the possession of a civilian arrested in Queens for impersonating an officer.[15]

But the greatest impediments that Trimboli faced came not from Dowd, or from the scattered investigations, but from his bosses at Internal Affairs. Trimboli stayed a one-man show, despite the fact that Dowd was clearly at the center of an unsavory ring that included other cops. Trimboli's weekend surveillance of Dowd, and other suspect cops, was called off. Trimboli's entreaties to the Internal Affairs Division and to the Special Prosecutor's office produced little information and no real help. He was assigned, full time, to other cases for extended periods.

Then, things got worse. In March 1989, the brass at Internal Affairs Headquarters in Downtown Brooklyn summoned Trimboli. Facing nine superiors, Trimboli listened as they took turns intimating he was corrupt himself, denigrating his investigation as unproductive, bemoaning its length and generally sending Trimboli the message that he would be better off doing other things. He responded on the spot by giving them two more names of cops that seemed to be in the web connected to Michael Dowd.[16]

Shortly after this inquisition, Trimboli got the opportunity to grill Dowd's former partner, Kenneth Eurell, who ultimately was arrested along with Dowd on drug dealing charges. Eurell was taking disability retirement. To be cleared for retirement, officers had to answer any questions they might be asked about ongoing investigations. So Trimboli set up an interview. Literally at the last minute, however, Trimboli's boss told him not to ask any questions about Dowd or crimes connected to Dowd, which produced a meaningless interview. Off the Police Department hook, Dowd's partner walked away with a lifetime tax-free pension.[17]

In 1990, his Internal Affairs Division superiors ordered Trimboli's cases on Dowd closed. Carefully crafted reports, based on Trimboli's less diplomatic drafts, went out under the signature of superiors. The cases against Dowd were deemed "unsubstantiated."

The Dowd case was far from over, even in the NYPD, where allegations about Dowd kept rolling in, generating yet other case files being lackadaisically worked. In contrast, Dowd and the retired Eurell were very active out on Long Island, where they both lived. By 1991, they were supplying a local drug dealer with product from the streets of Brooklyn, which came to the attention of the Suffolk County Police and District Attorney. After a short, intense, and not particularly difficult investigation, Suffolk cops arrested Eurell in May 1992, along with his brother, an active-duty New York City cop. Then the Long Island officers came in and arrested Michael Dowd, as well as his new partner, who were on patrol in Brooklyn.[18]

Trimboli in the end stood tall. He was lionized in the press and was promoted.[19] The corruption he had tracked so doggedly gave rise to the 1993 Mollen Commission probe into NYPD Internal Affairs failures. Trimboli was a star witness before the commission, and so too was Dowd, who expressed contempt at the Department's inability to uncover his wrongdoing.[20] Lee Brown, the police commissioner on whose watch the scandal broke, resigned and took a post in the Clinton Administration. New York's mayor, David Dinkins, had the unenviable task of running for reelection against crime-fighting former prosecutor Rudy Giuliani just a month after the hearings. Dinkins lost and Michael Dowd was sentenced to fourteen years in federal prison on charges stemming from his years as a criminal cop.

## When the Structure of Oversight Fails

The NYPD oversight system failed in the Dowd case, Trimboli's heroic efforts notwithstanding. As Police Commissioner Raymond W. Kelly noted at the time, "The system is not functioning as it should. This is the type of thing that happens in a bureaucracy when there's no monitoring of a system that's been in existence for twenty years."[21]

The Dowd case was replete with evidence that all was not well with the structure of the Internal Affairs Division (IAD) of the NYPD during the late 1980s and early 1990s. Dowd was on IAD radar as early as 1985, and the allegations were serious from the start. Dowd, moreover, was registering numerous blips year after year, with seventeen complaints landing here and there in the department. Some complaints, including those worked by Detective Sergeant Trimboli, generated big, fat radar tracks that stood out even more because of Trimboli's perseverance and refusal to be intimidated by superiors.

A key structural problem encountered by IAD was its decentralization. The Field Internal Affairs Units (FIAU) may have been the perfect response to the chronic, widespread "grass-eating" corruption uncovered by the Knapp Commission. Spread the Internal Affairs detectives out; pervade them through the department. Let every officer know that someone nearby is watching, ready to nail anyone who takes $10 a week from the grocery store owner, or dares try organize a penny ante racket that all the cops are in on. That type of corruption did, in fact, fade.

But the decentralized structure clearly failed in the Dowd case. Trimboli started off with one Dowd complaint, but inherited others previously handled at some length but limited depth by other investigators in his FIAU. Another internal investigation involving Michael Dowd began (and ended) in Queens without Trimboli knowing. Trimboli also was not privy to complaints against Dowd at Internal Affairs headquarters. As the official NYPD report noted, there was a "failure of coordination and the shortcomings of an internal investigative system built on overlapping responsibility and bifurcated authority."[22]

IAD headquarters had its own problems. An Internal Affairs headquarters lieutenant remembered the Dowd case getting the attention of superiors as early as 1989.[23] The IAD Chief at the time had no such recall.[24] Headquarters was also challenged in keeping track of the numerous Dowd investigations going on across the agency.[25] To one of Trimboli's closed-out, "unsubstantiated" case files relating to Dowd, one boss added a contradictory note citing the investigators' belief that the complaint had substance.[26] It is very likely that cases were closed to reduce the Dowd inventory, or even to shut out Trimboli, because cases with similar allegations against Dowd remained active.

Getting the right resources to investigators was another problem with the decentralized internal affairs structure. The new breed of corrupt cops, as exemplified by Dowd, did not operate within precinct, borough, city or even national lines. Dowd brought drugs in Brooklyn that were wholesaled fifty miles to the east on Long Island. His spread out network of crooked cops (they called themselves "The Losers") did not dissolve when Dowd was sent from Brooklyn's 75th precinct to the Queens auto pound, or when he came back to patrol in the far northeast corner of Brooklyn. But the IAD bosses could and did consider Trimboli off base and over budget when he tracked, or wanted to track, Dowd to far flung places. This was especially true when Dowd traveled to the Dominican Republic, to the hometown of the Dominican drug dealers he was in business with. Trimboli wanted to follow, but his bosses' "No" was emphatic.

Trimboli and the FIAU offices generally were under-resourced for the type of investigation that is often necessary in cases like Dowd's. In 2012 dollar terms, Dowd was driving around in $70,000 cars to $700,000 houses whose taxes alone amounted to more than a third of an officer's take-home pay. He treated his paycheck as an afterthought, not even picking it up at times.

To Trimboli, and others, the smell of corruption around Dowd was ripe. But sensitive noses are not enough. Official administrative inquiries into possible criminal profiteering by employees often require financial statements, bank statements, tax returns, and forensic accounting. So, often, do trials; not every corrupt cop is caught on videotape passing drugs through the squad car window. The Field Internal Affairs detectives could not perform sophisticated financial analyses. And, as Trimboli found out when he went to central Internal Affairs and to the Office of the Special Prosecutor, detectives seeking assistance from offices that could provide forensic accounting and sophisticated surveillance were often dismissed out of hand.

Police Commissioner Raymond Kelly came to some of the same conclusions in his 1992 report on what went wrong in the Dowd affair. "I think a lot of the problems in field units had to do with lack of resources, and lack of people."[27] In microcosm, that statement is about Trimboli, who for years pursued a complex, major case virtually on his own, with few tools, to the point of exhaustion. As Commissioner Kelly remarked at Trimboli's promotion ceremony, the sergeant's most important tools were his "respect for the law, pride in the department and steadfast faith in what is right above all else."[28]

## The "Independence" of Internal Affairs

Organizations are, on the whole, tough machines. You can restructure them and, if that doesn't work out, you can restructure them again—as one management consultant once told me, "If centralized, decentralize. If decentralized, centralize." While it is not quite as simple as that, most of the basic structuring of organization—number of ranks, number and type of specialized units, how resources are distributed to organizational components—involves limited and reversible choices, and mostly comfortable margins of error, mainly because the costs of those errors are usually not excessive.

The structuring of Internal Affairs has much less tolerance for error, and the costs of those errors can be enormous. Nothing should be constructed and maintained with such care as the role, positioning and standing of the Internal Affairs function in the law enforcement agency.

The Dowd case highlighted an internal affairs function in the NYPD that had degraded. Later on in this book we will review the case of "The Buddy Boys," cops that, in the early and mid-1980s, ran a criminal enterprise in Brooklyn's 77th Precinct, next door to Michael Dowd's station house. Internal Affairs and the Office of the State Special Prosecutor took "The Buddy Boys" down in 1987. Thirteen cops were indicted. One committed suicide. Half the others were convicted, but administrative actions continued to go forward against the remaining officers. The police commissioner transferred everybody—every officer and commander—out of the precinct.

Thieving cops, fraternization with killers and drug dealers, suicide, mass transfers, the steady drip of pleas, trials, convictions, acquittals, disciplinary hearings—the commissioner had had enough! Charles Hynes, the state special prosecutor, wanted to look into other precincts that matched the 77th's profile of brutality complaints, which Hynes correctly surmised was a precursor and/or co-symptom of corruption. These precincts were the 73rd and the 75th, the home of Michael Dowd. The police commissioner, Benjamin Ward, would have none of it. "My department is clean. I don't want to hear about any more corruption."[29]

Leaders' words have dramatic and rippling impacts. What Ward said was not just conveyed to the Special Prosecutor, but to the department, and most especially Internal Affairs. The message was conveyed not by a memo, perhaps not even by a direct verbal order, but word got around. No more systematic corruption, no more cabals of rogue officers—the commissioner doesn't want it, and says it doesn't exist.

Approaches to policy and operations are shaped all the time in organizations by employee interpretations of what they see as signal statements by the boss. NASA's approach to risk analysis before the 1985 Space Shuttle Challenger disaster supposedly had its origins in how Apollo-era NASA Administrator James Webb had reacted when a rigidly quantitative risk analysis indicated that one out of five attempts to reach the moon would kill everybody on board. "I never want to see one of these again," said Webb, as he dramatically threw the document down. The message got out. Mushy math was applied to produce rosier numbers. So when Challenger did kill everybody, it was, NASA said, a 1 in 100,000 fluke. The real number, developed after the accident by rigorous risk analysis? It was below 1 in 100, as the more recent Columbia space shuttle accident seems to confirm.

Commissioner Ward's message put the NYPD at risk and Internal Affairs in a dilemma. Corruption was out there, this they saw. But the Commissioner didn't want to hear about it. This, it turned out, Internal Affairs could see even better. The Internal Affairs chief through most of the Dowd years testified, "When I went up with bad news that two cops would be arrested in the morning, or that three cops would be indicted, I felt like they wanted to shoot me."[30] There was, he said, a strong and pervasive desire to avoid the negative publicity for the department—and for individual commanders—that would be associated with uncovering pockets of corrupt officers.[31]

Internal Affairs' role was severely compromised. The integrity of internal affairs depended on not worrying about embarrassing the Department, or the top bosses. Once Internal Affairs elevated avoiding embarrassment on its list of priorities, it was vulnerable to pressures that impeded, rather than advanced, investigations.

Trimboli certainly felt it was no accident that his pursuit of Dowd was curtailed, or that superiors blocked his vigorous questioning of the retiring Eurell, or that he was dressed down and essentially threatened at a sudden command appearance before gathered senior officials at Internal Affairs headquarters. Trimboli's "paranoia" made sense. Once staving off embarrassment becomes an Internal Affairs priority, investigators who are getting too close to uncovering systematic corruption become a "problem."

Internal Affairs, indeed any quality assurance function, must guard against being drawn too far into the orbit of the operational leadership. Clark Kent Ervin, the Department of Homeland Security's first Inspector General, claimed that he had had to educate his boss, Homeland Security Secretary Tom Ridge, about the role of the Inspector General's (IG) Office. According to Ervin, Ridge wanted Ervin's reports, some of which concerned the agency's law enforcement units, spun in ways favorable to the Department.[32] While Ridge denied the allegations, Ervin made them as the former Inspector General. Agency executives, in law enforcement and other functions, are sorely tempted to think that Internal Affairs should be an arm of management, with leaders who should be loyal members of the management team.

After the Knapp Commission, John Guido ran Internal Affairs in the NYPD for more than a decade. Guido, whose persona matched his tactics, staked out a fiercely independent role for the Division, maintained its offices apart from police headquarters, worked closely with the state special prosecutors, and let the chips fall where they may. One observer noted, only partially in jest, that any commissioner who suggested to Guido that internal affairs do it management's way might well be arrested on the spot.[33] And, indeed, the retired Guido faulted leadership, not structure, for how poorly Internal Affairs performed in the Dowd case.[34]

Most Inspector General Offices are structured to institutionalize the independence that Guido's personality and leadership achieved for NYPD internal affairs. While an Inspector General has a presence in a department, and usually keeps departmental management apprised of ongoing studies and inquiries, the primary reporting responsibility goes beyond the department. In the federal government, Inspectors General submit their reports to Congress. Inspectors General housed in New York City agencies report ultimately to the New York City Department of Investigation. The Office of New York State

Special Prosecutor for Criminal Justice, which went out of business in 1990, also served as an outside partner that helped NYPD Internal Affairs leverage its independence within the department.

Law enforcement executives are well advised to respect and protect the independence of Internal Affairs, and grant that independence where necessary. If this does not happen, the likelihood increases exponentially that someday, sooner rather than later, the Internal Affairs function will break down, as happened in New York City in the late 1980s.

After such breakdowns, chiefs end up explaining why corruption and police misconduct charges filed against officers went from 112 in 1987 to zero in 1990. Or why a special set of files, never shared with prosecutors, were kept for complaints against commanders, and for complaints against cops related to key commanders. The damage such revelations do to the credibility of the agency, the legitimacy of its leadership, and the level of employee trust can take years to fix.

In New York City, reforms instituted by Commissioner Ray Kelly in 1992 included personnel changes, the elevation of Internal Affairs to Bureau status under the leadership of a Deputy Commissioner, creation of a computerized case data base, additional resources, and the consolidation of field units into the overall integrity control effort. Commissioner Kelly left the NYPD in January 1994, only to return again in 2002. Kelly's return probably served no function as well as Internal Affairs, which, as we have seen, is always vulnerable to the vicissitudes of successive management regimes.

\* \* \*

Our next case concerns the shifting intersection of the law enforcement work world and the private lives of officers. At this intersection we find domestic violence and sexual harassment, and an oversight conundrum that many police agencies across the United States have yet to solve.

## *The Secret World of David Brame*

David Brame, a member of the Tacoma, Washington Police Department, had secrets. One secret sat in Brame's personnel file. The file showed that the psychologist who screened him for employment in 1981 had serious reservations, and that the interviewer-investigator who handled the overall application had given Brame a qualified pass, expressing doubt that Brame would survive probation and recommending continued attention to the issues the psychologist had raised. Those issues included Brame's "tendency to exaggerate to the point of deception," as well as "his difficulty in evaluating situations and acting appropriately."[35]

Another secret resided with veteran police personnel, some retired. Fifteen years earlier, they had looked into a rape allegation against Brame. Their investigation had foundered on the shoals of "he said (consensual)/she said (rape)," even though investigators felt the charge was credible. Though the 1988 investigation files had been purged, the rape charge had resurfaced in a 1999 lawsuit against the Department by an officer. After that trial had come to an end, the court file had been sealed at the urging of a city attorney.[36]

His wife, Crystal, shared many secrets with David Brame. Few made her comfortable. David Brame had abused her, pointed guns at her and threatened her with death. One domestic incident in 1996 led Mrs. Brame to call 911, but she "did not want her husband to get in trouble at work," so nothing had come of the complaint.[37] Crystal Brame also fielded and rejected her husband's diverse sexual propositions, which included her having sex with another man while he watched, as well as a ménage a trois with him and another woman.

The "other woman," despite refusing repeatedly, was also being harassed by David Brame about having three-way sex with him and his wife.[38] "No" didn't slow Brame down; neither did the fact that "the other woman" had a boyfriend. Having to refuse placed the woman in a difficult position, because she was a police officer and David Brame was her boss. And not just any boss—David Brame was her police chief in Tacoma, Washington's third largest city.

Brame's wife and the female officer were not unknown to each other, thanks to his relentless attempts to pull off his fantasy. Brame introduced them in November 2002 when he and his wife chanced upon the female officer on duty outside a mall.[39] Brame so badgered his wife to call the officer that eventually she did, but their talk was not about the sex that neither was interested in. Crystal Brame was candid about her disgust over her husband's manipulations in the matter.[40]

This late January 2003 conversation was just about the last straw for Crystal Brame and she began talking divorce. This elicited thinly veiled and ominous threats from her husband, which included aiming a gun at her head and saying, "Accidents happen."[41] These threats only stiffened her resolve and, by the end of February 2003, Crystal Brame filed for divorce. She demanded custody of their two young children, as well as child support and property settlements that would claim about half of Chief Brame's income and wealth.

The divorce proceedings sent David Brame downhill fast. He became inattentive to his duties for long stretches, and obsessed about his plight for hours on end in conversations with police employees with whom he was close. "He told anyone who would listen that Crystal was going to destroy him," one said.[42]

This had an impact on the police employees in Brame's inner circle. Just as they were on Brame's team at work, several high level employees seemed to be on David Brame's team in his domestic battle. One assistant chief, trying to encourage reconciliation, called Crystal Brame proposing that they have lunch.[43] Though Brame's wife declined in a testy exchange, she also revealed some important things that the Assistant Chief recorded in notes that investigators later obtained.[44]

Crystal reportedly told the assistant chief of Brame's ménage a trois obsession and his pursuit of the female officer for that purpose, as well as death threats Brame had been making.[45] Technically, Mrs. Brame was talking to exactly the right person. The assistant chief, Catherine Woodard, was the department's Equal Employment Opportunity (EEO) officer and also handled sexual harassment complaints. Assistant Chief Woodard, who also knew of Crystal Brame's 1996 call to 911 about a domestic dispute, took no official action as a result of what she learned, and she continued to be involved with Chief Brame relative to the ongoing divorce proceedings.[46]

The assistant chief did discuss Chief Brame's personal difficulties with the city manager. So did the chief. The participants in these conversations aren't talking, but a City of Tacoma investigation concluded that these and other conversations were sufficient to let the city manager know about allegations of abuse in the Brame household, as well as about the chief's deteriorating performance.[47] In any event, those who met regularly with the chief could hardly help but notice his eccentric behavior, changed appearance and deepening depression.

Yet Chief Brame stayed in place, even as he told yet other senior commanders about his attempts to add a female Tacoma police officer to his marital bed.[48] On April 10, Chief Brame showed up at a divorce hearing with three subordinates—Assistant Commissioner Woodard, a detective and the department's spokesperson.[49] Crystal Brame's family perceived this police department phalanx as inappropriate, particularly with respect to Woodard, from whom they sensed hostility. When Chief Brame brought clothes to his wife the next day—he was still in the marital residence, she was at her parents—Woodard also went along, which led to words being exchanged and a 911 call by Crystal Brame alleging intimidation. When David Brame finally did move to his own apartment, the moving crew consisted of three other assistant police commissioners.[50]

By the last days of April, rumors of Brame's alleged sexual harassment, domestic violence and kinky proclivities were racing through Tacoma's grapevine, in and out of city government. Brame, with increasing depression and anger, contemplated the financial and career costs of his impending divorce. He was ready to snap. Still, his loyal allies in the department didn't see Brame as the problem. Not true, said one ally, a lieutenant, to another officer inquiring about the domestic violence rumors, "Crystal's crazy."[51]

The next day, in a drug store parking lot, in the presence of their two young children, Chief David Brame shot his wife in the head, and then turned the gun on himself.[52] The chief lived three hours. Crystal Brame lingered on for a week. Then she, too, passed away.

## Identification with Offenders

David Brame was a time bomb. He went off, tragically, killing his wife, devastating his children and his wife's family. The damage Brame did to them, and himself, is irreversible. The substantial hurt Brame inflicted on the agency he led, however, is reversible, and we will discuss below the steps the Tacoma Police Department took to prevent a repeat of this tragedy. But for now we will consider the oversight failures that allow problematic employees to continue their aberrant behavior, and even flourish, in police agencies.

Police departments should expect to have personnel who are abusive to spouses, dependent on alcohol, or wrestling with other demons they cannot shake. These are not conditions peculiar to police personnel, but occur more than in most professions due to job-related stressors. So any police agency needs to be on the lookout for employees, and especially officers with firearms, who are becoming a threat to themselves or those around them. Internal affairs, or units such as human resources, generally field such complaints, or stumble across issues since troubled employees are also more likely to break the rules. Once official note is taken of troubled employees, there is a duty to get them help. Failing in this duty can, as Brame case shows, have tragic consequences.

To the very end, police officers and executives who worked with David Brame had a hard time seeing him as an abusive husband or as a sexual harasser. Attitudes and behaviors that shelter problem employees are not unique to law enforcement. In law enforcement, however, the consequences can be greater, as the high rate of police suicide and alcoholism attests.[53] Dissecting the David Brame case helps peel back the layers of insulation that shield problematic law enforcement officers in agencies throughout the country.[54]

David Brame slid very far very fast at the end. The murder-suicide may have occurred even if his department had taken formal action to address his increasingly morbid fixation on his domestic struggles, the workplace sexual harassment and his enlistment of departmental personnel in his divorce battle. But we will never know, because no oversight action was initiated.

The instinct to not report a fellow officer's transgressions was certainly operating. Brame's subordinates were bound to him by loyalty that was cemented, in some cases, by fear arising from Brame's well-deserved reputation for taking down "enemies."[55] But whether they feared Brame or feared what might happen to him, personnel in a position to see Brame's unraveling kept it to themselves. In the next chapter, we'll look at a case where a sexually disturbed, criminally abusive Pennsylvania state trooper was enabled by willfully blind and/or protective superiors and peers, and detached internal investigators.

Brame's colleagues quietly took up the slack for his nose-diving performance. And as Brame slid deeper into depression, most of his close colleagues were reassuring—to him and to others who expressed concern. This "help" actually hurt. David Brame, who needed psychological help, was instead validated, given more time to obsess about and plot against Crystal's career-threatening divorce filing. At the very end, at least one Tacoma officer, not a part of Brame's inner circle, complained to the city manager that Brame was being carried by his staff.[56] The complaint was too little too late, yet better than nothing, which is what still occurs in many departments where co-workers help hide the severely diminished capacity of troubled officers.

Brame's staff, by standing in solidarity with him, muted Crystal Brame's expressed fears for the very agency that could have given them credence. Tacoma Police Department veterans working with the chief knew of the 1996 domestic dispute and the 1988 rape allegations. The chief's pursuit of the female officer in 2002 and early 2003 was something that he had mentioned to work colleagues. And, having been pursued by Brame at all hours of the day and night, at home and in her car, alone and with her boyfriend, on duty and off, the officer's version of the story was likely in the Department grapevine as well. Crystal Brame broadcasted Brame's escalating threats, his pointed firearm demonstrations in her presence, and his sexual adventurism. But, in Brame vs. Brame, key police officials stood foursquare with the chief.

From an oversight perspective, what thwarted the exposure of Brame's serious issues on and off the job might be called identification with the offender. Identification with the offender is similar to identification with the aggressor, a concept from prison research that helps explain the intimidating sway Brame held over his staff (and, until early 2003, his wife).[57] But Brame also had a hold on staff members who supported him out of long-term solidarity, not fear, and out of empathy, not subordinate position or marital obligation.

Identification with the offender operates in police departments everywhere. It is in stark relief in the Brame case because of the tragic circumstances. It is all but certain that somewhere, on this very day, police officers have decided not to report a fellow officer's drinking problem or its impact on his or her work, or have decided not to pass along a spouse's pleas or other indications of domestic abuse by a fellow officer. And possibly in that same department, and certainly in others, internal affairs officers are not eager to receive or aggressively pursue such complaints. Penalties may be viewed as too Draconian, especially for common human foibles that implicated officers may well work out on their own.

Such thinking insulated David Brame, just as it will in the future insulate other abusive officers, or officers at risk for running down a pedestrian while coming home from four hours of end-of-shift cocktails. Addressing this thinking, and the co-optation of oversight sustained by it, is a crucial task for law enforcement.

## Addressing Domestic Abuse by Law Enforcement Officers

Before the Brame tragedy, the Tacoma Police Department did not have in place a comprehensive set of rules for dealing with officer-involved domestic violence, let alone sexual harassment by a chief trying to blend his marriage with an unrequited workplace infatuation.

The lack of guidelines doubly handicapped Tacoma police executives already hobbled by their identification with the offender. Without a clear roadmap, it was difficult to break free of that identification in order to rein in the Chief. Some brave soul would have to improvise in a very grey area to take actions that might or might not have succeeded against a very vindictive and unstable superior.

To its credit, the Tacoma Police Department worked hard to create such guidelines to avoid a repeat of the Brame tragedy. The new policy "calls for immediate notification of supervisors when a domestic violence call or incident involving a Tacoma officer is reported. In the event that the alleged abuser is an assistant chief, then the chief is notified. If the information is about the chief, the policy calls for the command duty officer or shift lieutenant to immediately notify the city manager, the mayor and the Pierce County prosecutor."[58]

The policy also requires sending at least three officers, including a supervisor, to the scene of an officer-involved domestic violence complaint. At the scene, all firearms are to be seized. Complainants are put in touch with agencies serving domestic violence victims, and the confidentiality of any safe house placement is strictly observed, even to the point of not being provided to the police at all. Employees are forbidden from going to court with fellow workers who are domestic violence defendants because "their mere presence ... may appear intimidating to the victims."[59]

The new policy calls for dual track investigations of domestic violence allegations. This seeks to insure that cases bound for court also get administrative review and that administrative review is not allowed to stand in place of a criminal referral, which is what happened with the 1988 rape allegation against Brame. The policy empowers the chief to designate an outside agency to conduct the administrative review, a handy option if high-ranking officials are under scrutiny.

The policy also empowers the department to respond proactively with referrals when employees or members of their families express safety concerns. Psychological and background screening for recruits has been intensified, with zero tolerance for anyone with a history of domestic violence. Officers are required to tell supervisors of any domestic violence in which they are involved, or which they observe.[60]

This policy was formulated in concert with the police union, advocacy groups and even survivors of officer-involved domestic violence. Interestingly, for reasons we will discuss further below, domestic violence involving officers is not treated as a zero-tolerance offense, although dismissal is an option even where criminal charges have not been filed. Though the Brame tragedy provided the impetus, the approach adopted by the Tacoma Police Department has been praised as a model policy for victim protection by Renae Griggs, who directs the National Police Family Violence Prevention Project.[61] On a national level, Congress in 2005 passed the "Crystal Judson Domestic Violence Protocol Program," which makes grants available nationwide to help public and non-profit agencies develop better ways for dealing with domestic violence.[62]

Many law enforcement agencies are not yet close to Tacoma's accomplishment. Addressing problems such as domestic violence in police households or alcohol abuse by law enforcement officers requires careful definition, education about the dangers posed, and very specific steps to be taken in dealing with distressed individuals. Agencies that are behind the curve in these areas are ill-equipped to identify and deal with troubled employees who might just have the tragic potential of a David Brame.

## Zero Tolerance and Measured Administrative Response

A very interesting alliance surrounds the issue of officer-involved domestic violence. Activist groups are often in league with police officials—and the International Association of Chiefs of Police—in demanding zero tolerance and career capital punishment for offending officers. Hit your spouse; lose your job.

Activists view termination, along with protection orders and criminal prosecution, as just punishment. Police executives view zero tolerance/termination as a vaccine for alleviating, if not eliminating, the scourge of liability judgments stemming from abusive behavior by troubled officers. The affliction they want to be immunized against is very real: Crystal Brame's family filed a claim for $75 million—later settled for $12 million, Brame's alleged 1988 rape victim was seeking $2 million and the female officer Brame harassed filed a $1.5 million damage claim.[63]

While the stance taken by some activists, as well as by the International Association of Chiefs of Police on behalf of its members, is understandable, the zero tolerance/capital punishment approach hobbles effective oversight, and may well endanger those it seeks to protect, mostly women (who are the main, but not the only, victims of domestic violence) in abusive relationships.

The last thing Crystal Brame wanted was for her husband to lose his job. That was true after their 1996 domestic dispute, when she repeatedly told officers that she did not want her complaint to hurt her husband at work. And it was true in 2003, when her future welfare and that of her two children was dependent on her husband's salary as a law enforcement executive. Lurking in the background in 1996 and 2003, and quite likely in the intervening years, was Crystal Brame's fear about what might happen if David Brame saw her as the ruination of his career. As we saw, her murder at his hands is what could, and did, happen.

Zero tolerance policies have "ratcheted up the lethality potential a great deal," according to Renae Griggs.[64] Griggs, with a graduate degree in forensic psychology, is Founding Director of the National Police Family Violence Prevention Project. She is also a former police officer whose profound job-related depression drove her to the edge of suicide. Her concern about zero tolerance workplace policies for officer-involved domestic violence also extends to federal legislation that forbids those convicted of domestic violence from owning guns or ammunition. Stripping officers of their jobs or their ability to work robs them of their identity. "He is," she argues, "his job."[65] Take it away and there is nothing left to lose.

David Brame frighteningly fit Griggs' analysis. He obsessed constantly about what he saw being taken from him: his job, his possessions, and his reputation. The closer this came to reality, the more ominous were Brame's threats to his wife, and the more his turmoil revealed itself at work. To the extent they believed Brame's doomsday scenario, his subordinates may have rallied to his side to save his unfairly threatened career. Their already tortured boss, at 44, was a rising star and not, as far as they were concerned, singularly responsible for discord in the Brame household. This tragic case, with its stark profiles, underlines a structural flaw that can seriously undermine the effectiveness of oversight.

The flaw is excessive sanctions in general, and particularly with respect to behaviors long considered "personal problems." As these problems are legally recast as serious transgressions, police executives often respond with policies carrying heavy penalties and enforcement that makes "an example" of the first violators. The "get tough" approach fits well with police culture. Zero tolerance/harsh penalty policies also spin a positive story for outsiders who have specific concerns related to problematic police behaviors. Mothers against Drunk Driving (MADD) will cheer strict workplace penalties for alcohol-related transgressions by officers on or off the job. Women's advocates may well cheer if spousal abuse becomes a one-way ticket out the door for law enforcement officers.

But officers will not cheer, and may actively resist, for reasons that go well beyond "the blue wall of silence." If being identified as a cop with a drinking problem means automatic banishment to the "bow and arrow" squad, or if pushing one's spouse during a spat at the precinct picnic ends a career, few cops will be willing, on grounds of fairness and common sense, to implicate a fellow officer. Cops understand that alcoholic colleagues may go dangerously beyond being an underperforming annoyance, and that hitting a woman is wrong. But they also understand that mandatory harsh sentences are not a measured response to the range of behaviors and complex dynamics that constitute alcoholism, domestic violence, or sexual harassment.

Sanctions arising from oversight findings are a form of discipline. Like any form of discipline, these sanctions need to be measured and consistently applied.[66] Punishments seen as excessive or meted out to some and not to others are largely self-defeating. This is especially true in emerging areas of specialized oversight that seek to address employee abuse of legal substances, violence in off-duty relationships and sexual harassment in the workplace. Yesterday's normal has become today's deviance and, in the process, employees' previously private emotional issues become an even more stressful matter of organizational concern, peer attention and career jeopardy. That is why determining how to deal with these emergent abuses is best done, as it was in Tacoma, with the involvement of labor, management, victims and advocates in a deliberate process.

\* \* \*

Our next two cases involve seemingly minor missteps. In Philadelphia, the residency requirement for officers appeared at first blush to have been skirted by a commander. In Baltimore, pictures from a social event surfaced which showed another commander alongside a car dealer with a rap sheet, as well as an already suspect officer later convicted of drug dealing. But these were not just any commanders. When these two stories broke, each was in charge of internal affairs.

## *In Residence at Philadelphia Internal Affairs*

Frankie Heyward had a very short tenure as head of Internal Affairs for the Philadelphia Police Department. Appointed to head the office in April 2003 and promoted to acting deputy commissioner in the beginning of June 2003, by the end of that month Heyward was out of Internal Affairs, had reverted to chief inspector, and was the subject of reviews by the district attorney and the city comptroller's office.[67] It was, by any standard, a meteoric rise and fall.

As the head of Internal Affairs, Frankie Heyward was responsible for enforcing a number of rules and regulations that Philadelphia police officers are required to live by. For instance, Philadelphia has a residency requirement. Its police officers must live within the city limits. Violators are subject to dismissal. Lying about one's housing situation, or other matters relating to qualifications for employment, is also prohibited; so is taking your city car back and forth to suburban locations when not on official business.

Chief Inspector Heyward officially lived in the West Oak Lane section of Philadelphia. The residence was a modest row house, picked up for $13,830 from the U.S. Department of Housing and Urban Development.[68] The Philadelphia Inquirer decided to do some internal affairs work of its own, and sent out a reporter. Early on two successive weekday mornings the reporter found Heyward and his unmarked city car, but not at the Philadelphia house. The Internal Affairs Chief was spotted and photographed coming out of another house in Elkins Park, a Philadelphia suburb decidedly outside the city limits.[69]

The paper did some digging. The $150,000 Elkins Park house belonged to Heyward and his wife. His son went to school in the suburban district. Heyward's personal car was registered and insured to the Elkins Park address. His wife and son lived there, as Heyward freely admitted when questioned by the reporter.[70] He told the reporter that, although he resided in the city house, he made brief visits during the week to the suburban house, and stayed there on weekends. This helped explain what the reporter already had learned from Heyward's suburban neighbors: They saw him often.[71]

The newspaper kept on the story the next day, reviewing the water bills for Heyward's city residence, which showed minimal amounts most months and zero billing in two others.[72] The reporter talked with the District Attorney's office, which was going to look into the discrepancy between where Heyward said his personal car was kept—the city house—and were it was insured—the suburban house. The reporter checked with the City Comptroller's Office, which was interested in whether Heyward had a bona fide city residence. The reporter talked to two City Council members, who were interested in everything.[73]

The story did not, as they say, have long legs. The first story ran on June 20th, the second on June 21st. Before the second story ran, Heyward was out as commander of Internal Affairs. Three days later, his nomination as Deputy Commissioner was withdrawn, and the extra $15,000 he got for serving in that title in an acting capacity was gone as well. The Philadelphia Internal Affairs Bureau had a new chief within a month. Her name was Charlotte Council and she immediately had two connections to Frankie Heyward. One of the cases her new bureau was working was Heyward's; and she lived in Philadelphia's West Oak Lane, not far from Frankie Heyward's city house.[74]

## Social Affairs and Internal Affairs in Baltimore

In January 2012, the Baltimore Police Department got itself a new Internal Affairs chief. He was Grayling Williams, who had spent most his career in federal law enforcement with the DEA.[75]

Williams was an outsider coming into a department that long had promoted from within. Promoting from within had lost some of its luster, however, especially with respect to internal investigations. Internal Affairs had burned through three career-officer directors in three years amidst a string of scandals starring rogue officers and a general approach to officer discipline that critics believed downplayed transgressions.[76]

Williams came on board six months after another Internal Affairs commander, Major Nathan Warfield, had been replaced. In July 2011, a Baltimore Sun reporter had uncovered a 2009 Facebook photo album titled "Nate Warfield Party" where two photos placed Major Warfield cheek by jowl with individuals later indicted on felony drug charges. Photo number one posed Warfield, who became IA chief a few months later, alongside an officer in his district command by the name of Daniel C. Redd. Redd was already a major blip on the department's internal investigations radar, having been denied promotion due to suspicions later borne out by his July 2011 indictment for the sale of heroin from, among other locales, a precinct parking lot. Redd pled guilty to federal charges in March 2012.[77] Photo number two featured Warfield and one Sam Brown, an auto salesman with a criminal history. Brown was also on the court calendar in 2011 thanks to heroin distribution charges not connected to Redd's indictment.[78]

Warfield was placed squarely on the hot seat by the photos, but also was criticized by a Baltimore Sun editorial for how he ran Internal Affairs. "What is needed here is greater transparency. (Police Commissioner) Bealefeld has to start answering questions about what's been going on in internal affairs—not just in regard to Major Warfield's relationship with Messrs. Redd and Brown but also about the division's efficacy in general, which is difficult to gauge given the paucity of information that the department has released about its investigations since Mr. Warfield took command."[79]

The skepticism in the editorial was sharpened by concerns over the ongoing investigation into the January 2011 "friendly fire" death of an undercover officer, as well as a scandal that erupted in February 2011 involving kickbacks to more than a dozen police officers by a tow truck operator/car repair shop in return for officers filing exaggerated accident reports and steering car own-ers to the shop for repairs.[80]

Major Warfield was reassigned days after the photo album surfaced and, as had been the case in Philadelphia, a critical issue was the image the IA chief's earlier behavior projected. [81] Though not yet in internal affairs, Warfield was nonetheless a ranking commander photographed socializing with an already-suspect officer under his supervision who ended up as the 2011 bad cop poster child for the Baltimore PD. As a police source told the Baltimore Sun when Warfield was reassigned, "Just being associated with Redd in any way shape or form—there's questions that need to be answered there. In that position, there's no room for errors."[82]

After Warfield, an interim chief ran internal affairs as a steady drip of guilty pleas from the towing kickback scandal continued through the end of 2011. So it should be no surprise that when the Baltimore PD named a permanent internal affairs director to kick off 2012, it was Grayling Williams, by way of the DEA and Homeland Security, who was very unlikely to have Facebook photos of himself cavorting with BPD officers he might someday investigate.

## Role Modeling in Internal Affairs

In Philadelphia, Heyward was in and out faster than a blink in the rank-and-file's collective eye. Cops still noticed. Twelve city employees, including two cops, had lost their jobs for residency violations in the prior year.[83] Now the top police official responsible for enforcing residency rules was caught up in residency issues.

Now as far the law enforcement missteps in this book go, this was minimal and quickly corrected, involving a cop with a long and distinguished career. Indeed, Heyward retired honorably in 2005, the tempest of 2003 having re-sulted in nothing beyond the commissioner's actions immediately following the *Inquirer's* revelations. Internal Affairs later cleared Heyward on the resi-dency issue while declaring that where his personal car was insured was out-side the jurisdiction of the police department.[84] Even an *Inquirer* columnist couldn't help but be sympathetic because the Heyward's purchase of the Elkins Park home afforded their son educational opportunities not available in Philadelphia's troubled public schools.[85]

As was the case with Frankie Heyward, Nathan Warfield later retired hon-orably from the Baltimore PD, the episode that ended his Internal Affairs tenure little more than a hiccup on a distinguished record.[86]

Both departments did, however, sustain damage. In Philadelphia, Internal Affairs was left with a botched leadership transition, not to mention an active case file on the recently departed chief. In Baltimore, Warfield's party pictures made the news right after Officer Redd's mug shot, and set off general media questioning about what Internal Affairs was up to.

By default, every person who serves in internal affairs is a role model. And role models cannot afford even the appearance of non-compliance with departmental rules and regulations or behavioral expectations that they are in charge of enforcing. Any "Do as I say, not as I do" imagery is almost certain to make dealing with existing internal affairs cases harder, and may even create more cases. After the Heyward story broke, cops were whispering to reporters about the suburban residences of yet other higher ups; and grumbling about how rank-and-file employees had been dealt with harshly in similar circumstances.

These were Philadelphia and Baltimore stories, but Internal Affairs' credibility can be undermined anywhere. After Michael Dowd's arrest, the Mollen Commission investigation disclosed an NYPD Internal Affairs "tickler file" warehousing complaints against commanders and, in one case, a commander's relative.[87] These files were held so close to the vest, said Internal Affairs officials, because they contained minor allegations against subjects who might well visit Internal Affairs. Rank-and-file officers, who felt targeted by Internal Affairs for the slightest infractions, were dubious.

It is the responsibility of police managers, and especially Internal Affairs supervisors, to avoid any behavior that gives credence to the notion that disciplinary actions are arbitrary, capricious or unfair. The even-handedness of the process, and more importantly, the unquestioned probity of top investigators, is crucial to the credibility of Internal Affairs. Even perfectly legitimate behavior can generate invidious comparisons that negatively impact the job of integrity assurance. In a later chapter, we will look at overtime abuse by cops in Ohio, where investigators had a difficult time penetrating and rolling back widespread schemes to inflate pay. Perhaps the resistant officers in Cleveland knew that their recently retired Internal Affairs Chief had been the department's highest paid cop from 2000 to 2003—thanks to overtime.[88]

## 'Friends of the Police'—Ticket-Fixing at the NYPD

Maybe the New York Yankees connection made everyone pay attention.

A wiretap picked up the Yankee's Vice-President and security chief asking a police union delegate for help in getting another member of the Yankee's front office out of a speeding ticket.[89]

The wiretap on that Yankee-friendly union delegate was one of more than two dozen placed on union delegate officers during a two year investigation by NYPD Internal Affairs and prosecutors whose initial investigation into ties between a Bronx cop and a reputed drug dealer had mushroomed as evidence of ticket-fixing kept sprouting up.[90]

Ticket-fixing, it turned out, was not rare—if you hit the right connection. And the connection turned out to be those union delegate officers whose job it was to keep their fingers on the pulse of the rank and file in their precinct or in a specialized unit such as highway patrol. Union delegates occupy key nodes in the day to day working culture of the NYPD and other major unionized police agencies.

The union delegate possesses currency of considerable value to officers on the job. It's the union delegate who knows the rules, regulations and contractual provisions that can trip up or protect officers in the course of their duties. It's the union delegate who can quietly back off an aggressive supervisor with hints of a formal grievance or by networking that causes the supervisor's bosses to pull in the reins. And if formal action is taken, such as a grievance against actions by local managers or a general challenge to departmental rules, most union delegates will make clear their finger was on the trigger.

The delegate's job is also highly social. Union affairs, retirement parties, holiday picnics, after-work drinks, union-management committees, and police family funerals—few cops hit more of these events, or end up knowing more about the various players in a given law enforcement agency than the union delegates. Through their inherent potential to back off bothersome supervision and the considerable social capital they build, union delegates have inherent value for the cop on the beat. This value can be traded upon.

When the union delegate asks for an officer's help regarding a citation that officer issued to someone with "family on the job," or who is a "stand-up guy who takes care of the cops on the ballgame details," what's a small favor—such as "forgetting" to show up for the court hearing or "remembering" the radar gun was malfunctioning the day the ticket was written? And, since networks have extensive reach, officers in the bureaucratic chain leading from precinct to court can also be called upon to "lose," "misfile," or "accidently mutilate" the ticket or other records required at court. Judges routinely and summarily dismiss citations when such flaws arise, as was the case in the NYPD ticket-fixing scandal.

As the ticket-fixing investigation moved forward, and witnesses paraded before the grand jury week after week, two things became evident. First, a large number of officers were going to be implicated—sixteen ultimately faced criminal charges, most for ticket-fixing, and administrative charges were filed against others. Every officer indicted on ticket-fixing charges either was, or had been, a union delegate.[91] Second, the practice was widely accepted among the rank and file, several hundred of whom showed up at the arraignment to express support for the charged officers and disgust at the prosecution of a 'professional courtesy' that, according to the head of the police union, "had been accepted at all ranks for decades."[92]

There was a decidedly ugly side to the happy face of professional courtesy that the union head painted on what his delegates allegedly had done. The Bronx DA estimated that the "courtesies" that had just turned into indictments added up to millions of dollars in lost revenue for the city.[93] At one point, prosecutors were contemplating racketeering charges against the union because of how pervasive and blatant the ticket-fixing was.[94]

The "professional courtesy" mindset apparently existed even in Internal Affairs where a lieutenant was indicted for leaking information about the probe to those under scrutiny, an embarrassing turn that probably increased the intensity of the investigation as well as the disdain officers directed at it. Indeed, the broom swept so broadly that, when all was said and done, the internal affairs detective who blew the whistle on the lieutenant also faced administrative charges for conducting an unauthorized "sting" that exposed her.[95]

Predictably, the microscope was turned on Internal Affairs and the general ability of the department to police itself as the ticket-fixing scandal blossomed and other indictments were handed down against NYPD officers during the same period for smuggling guns, planting drugs and false arrest.[96] While police officials argued that Internal Affairs was doing its job, and in fact had uncovered the ticket-fixing scandal, other alleged crimes by NYPD officers during this period had been revealed through investigations by other law enforcement organizations.[97]

This scrutiny resurrected long-standing but historically neutralized concerns about the structure of oversight for the NYPD. A Civilian Complaint Review Board had long been in place in New York City, but both NYPD management and the unions representing the various ranks had fought successfully to limit the degree to which the Board, and other external oversight bodies such as the Commission to Combat Police Corruption, could independently review and pass judgment on allegations of police misconduct. Though often at loggerheads, NYPD management and its unions, when working together, were more than formidable and their arguments for in-house oversight had over the years carried the day.

Perhaps it was only a small step but, in response to the scandals of the previous year, New York's Mayor, Michael Bloomberg, kicked off 2012 by tripling the legal staff—from two to six—of the Commission to Combat Police Corruption. [98] Those favoring more external oversight of the NYPD applauded the move but also called for even more muscle for the Commission in the form of subpoena power that could plow through any NYPD stonewalling.[99]

## External Oversight of Law Enforcement

This case brings us full circle for the chapter. It started with the case of NYPD Officer Michael Dowd, whose criminal activities across the geography of the city and in surrounding counties were, for quite a while, more than a match for the decentralized NYPD internal affairs operation and its locally focused investigators. As we saw, centralizing internal affairs was one response for improving the identification, monitoring and apprehension of crooked cops who worked their schemes across NYPD divisional borders and outside, as well as inside, the City of New York. Speaking of circles, the NYPD Commissioner who oversaw those reforms in the early 1990s was Ray Kelly who, as the ticket-fixing scandal broke in 2011, was approaching the tenth anniversary of his second stint as NYPD's top official.

Commissioner Kelly had forcefully ushered in structural change in internal affairs in the wake of the Dowd affair. Like every NYPD Commissioner, however, he consistently fought the idea that any outside agency should be performing any part of, or overseeing, the NYPD internal affairs function. And, were you to poll police chiefs across the land Commissioner Kelly's position would win hands down. You would get the same, if not a stronger result, if you polled officers. Their rationale would be that only police professionals have the training and background necessary to judge whether the actions of officers cross the line, and what the appropriate sanctions should be. There is fear, not unfounded, that an outside overseer may be directed and staffed by individuals ignorant of, or hostile to, the police function.

If we look back on some of the cases addressed in this book so far, it is plain to see why cops would want to be investigated by cops. There are some very fine lines between what is and isn't good police practice in dealing with an emotionally disturbed individual like Eleanor Bumpurs or chasing a reckless Eliot Contois at high speed on city streets. There is also, as we have discussed in this chapter, good reason to hesitate when outsiders call for "zero tolerance" after a tragedy like the David Brame murder-suicide. A deep understanding of police organization and the operational realities of enforcement is essential to getting the involved officers a fair shake, and making sure revised policies don't backfire.

But ticket-fixing is not some core police activity, nor is it a high-intensity encounter begging for the understanding of other professionals who have had similar experiences. Nor is it, despite what union officials imply, some grey area that only enemies of the police would criminalize. Ticket-fixing is not legal and, what's more, it is fundamentally corrosive to the legitimacy of the police, which rests on the majority of citizens trusting that the law will be enforced even-handedly. When the Yankee executive's speeding ticket disappears, or the breathalyzer isn't administered after the weaving motorist announces his brother's "on the job," everybody who has ever gotten a ticket or been stopped at a DUI checkpoint "gets it" in a way that demolishes the standing police need to do their jobs effectively.

Police transgressions such as ticket-fixing are really not about policing, they are about an organizational culture that adopts and normalizes particular practices that then become just part of what goes on. When that happens it is easy to get to "everybody's does it," pretty much the position NYPD union officials took. Even those who advance to supervisory or even oversight roles can suddenly develop a combination of amnesia and selective blindness regarding the practice. In extreme cases, sworn officers investigating such practices may just give a heads up to the targets who, after all, were only acting *normally*.

So, when it comes to exposing and correcting practices that are culturally entrenched, and thus resistant to internal oversight, the answer may well be adding more muscle to external oversight bodies, as was done in New York City with respect to the Commission to Combat Police Corruption.

## Finding the Correct Vectors for Oversight

The organizational placement of oversight units is critical to their success.

As we have seen, an Internal Affairs unit insufficiently independent from top management may be seriously compromised when the commissioner pronounces corruption extinct. If the vector from which Internal Affairs attacks corruption precisely tracks the line taken by the police chief, the corruption fighters may have to trim their flaps when the chief does. Similarly, identification with the offender turns Internal Affairs into an empathetic peer of those being investigated. Here, too, investigations can veer off course, or never get off the ground, so as not to crash into sympathetic suspects.

Ideally, internal affairs should enjoy very elevated status in the agency that is nonetheless quite apart from the office of the commissioner or chief. And internal affairs must maintain a similar separation from operating personnel at all ranks, not just as a matter of investigative confidentiality but also as a matter of the guardianship, detachment, and objectivity so crucial to effective oversight. And because probity and role modeling is so vital, Internal Affairs personnel and, most of all, their leaders must be above reproach, with departments well-advised to conduct entry-level type investigations for Internal Affairs commander candidates.

External oversight is also a necessary vector from which police malfeasance should be examined. When problematic practices are deeply entrenched, and have become just part of the organizational landscape, internal investigators may be blind or willfully ineffective. Under such circumstances, external reviews will more likely reveal practices and beliefs that support arbitrary, capricious and unfair enforcement of the law.

Finally, internal affairs offices and law enforcement oversight units generally must be committed to constant renewal. The tactics of miscreant officers, the organizational structures they exploit and the legal, administrative and social norms distinguishing acceptable behavior are continuously in flux. If oversight in law enforcement does not keep up, the gap will grow between what is being monitored and what ought to be monitored. In this gap, failure lurks.

# Endnotes

1. Knapp Commission, *Knapp Commission Report on Police Corruption* (New York: George Braziller, 1972).

2. Peter Maas, *Serpico*, (New York: Viking Press, 1973). *Serpico*, and the movie based upon it, chronicles the young cop who helped expose long-standing, chronic and widespread corruption in the NYPD.

3. Mike McAlary, *Good Cop, Bad Cop*, (New York: Pocket Books, 1994): 88.

4. Ibid., 87.

5. Ibid., 88.

6. Ibid.,19.

7. Ibid., 95.

8. Ibid., 90.

9. Ibid., 117.

10. Government's Sentencing Memorandum, United States v. Michael Dowd, SI 92 Cr. 792 (KMW). From McAlary, *Good Cop, Bad Cop*, 244.

11. McAlary, *Good Cop, Bad Cop*, 94.

12. Ibid., 98.

13. Ibid., 90.

14. Ibid., 131.

15. Ibid., 126–27.

16. Ibid., 149–50.

17. Ibid., 154–58.

18. Ibid., 184.

19. George James, "Back From The Edge: Vindication For An Officer Who Stood Alone," *New York Times*, October 30, 1993.

20. Selwyn Rabb, "Ex-Rogue Officer Tells Panel of Police Graft in New York," *New York Times*, September 28, 1993.

21. Robert McFadden, "Commissioner Orders an Overhaul in Fight against Police Corruption," *New York Times*, November 17, 1992.

22. Ibid., B5.

23. Steven Lee Myers, "Panel Is Told Of A File on Police Graft within Internal Affairs," *New York Times*, October 5, 1993.

24. Ibid.

25. McAlary, *Good Cop, Bad Cop*, 214.

26. Ibid., 184.

27. McFadden, "Commissioner Orders an Overhaul," B5.

28. James, "Back from the Edge," 24.

29. McAlary, *Good Cop, Bad Cop*, 56.

30. Myers, "Panel is Told of File," B2.

31. Ibid.

32. Pete Yost, "Ridge Allegedly Fought Criticism," *Philadelphia Inquirer*, March 14, 2005.

33. McAlary, Good Cop, Bad Cop, 56.

34. Selwyn Rabb, "Police Official Will Reopen Graft Cases," *New York Times*, October 6, 1993.

35. "Two Shots Echo in Tacoma," *Law Enforcement News*, May 15/31, 2003.

36. Sean Robinson, "Inside David Brame's Police Department," The News Tribune (Tacoma, WA), September 14, 2003.

37. Attorney General of Washington, "Re: Criminal Referral Pursuant to RCW 43.10.232 (Assistant Chief Catherine Woodard)," November 14, 2003, 13 http://www.atg.wa.gov/pubs/brame/criminal_referral.pdf (Accessed April 14, 2005). This eighteen-page letter/report to the Pierce County Prosecuting Attorney found no criminal wrongdoing by Assistant Chief Woodard. However, the Attorney General's office did recommend further investigation into the possibility of administrative misconduct by Woodard, which the City Manager's Office undertook, only to be stymied by Woodard's retirement.

38. Robinson, "Inside David Brame's Police Department."

39. Ibid.

40. Sean Robinson, "David Brame's Life, Career Crumble When Wife Seeks A Way Out," *The News Tribune* (Tacoma, WA), September 15, 2003.

41. Ibid.

42. Ibid.

43. Ibid.

44. Attorney General of Washington, "Re: Criminal Referral," 5.

45. Robinson, "Brame's Life, Career Crumble."

46. Attorney General of Washington, "Re: Criminal Referral," 11–13.

47. Sean Robinson, "City's Early Findings Law Blame on Corpuz," *The News Tribune* (Tacoma, WA), December 15, 2004.

48. Robinson, "Brame's Life, Career Crumble."

49. Attorney General of Washington, "Re: Criminal Referral," 15.

50. Robinson, "Brame's Life, Career Crumble."

51. Martha Modeen, "Brame Ends Wife's Hopes for a New Life," *The News Tribune* (Tacoma, WA), September 16, 2003.

52. Ibid.

53. Robert Fox, "The Blue Plague Of American Policing," *Law Enforcement News*, May 15/30, 2003.

54. Peter B Kraska and Victor E Kappeler "To Serve And Pursue: Exploring Police Sexual Violence Against Women," *Justice Quarterly* 12, no. 1 (1995): 85–111.

55. Robinson, "Inside David Brame's Police Department."

56. Robinson, "Early Findings Blame Corpuz."

57. Jay Frankel, "Exploring Ferenczi's Concept of Identification with the Aggressor: Its Role in Trauma, Everyday Life, and The Therapeutic Relationship," *Psychoanalytic Dialogues* 12 (2002): 101–39.

58. "Tacoma Unveils New Focus on DV by Officers," *Law Enforcement News*, January 2004.

59. Ibid.

60. Ibid.

61. Ibid.

62. Rick Anderson, "Review of Tacoma Confidential," Seattle Weekly, January 4, 2006.

63. Sean Robinson, "City Faces More Legal Problems Over Brame," *The News Tribune* (Tacoma, WA), December 1, 2004.

64. "The LEN Interview: Renae Griggs," *Law Enforcement News*, January 2004.

65. Ibid.

66. See Frank Anechiarico and James B. Jacobs, *The Pursuit of Absolute Integrity: How Corruption Control Makes Government Ineffective* (Chicago: University of Chicago Press, 1996).

67. Mark Fazlollah, "Police Official Stripped of His Rank and Salary Increase," *Philadelphia Inquirer*, June 24, 2003.

68. Mark Fazlollah, "Officer Drives Home—To Where?," *Philadelphia Inquirer*, June 20, 2003.

69. Ibid.

70. Ibid.

71. Ibid.

72. Fazlollah, "Police Official Stripped of Rank."

73. Ibid.

74. Mark Fazlollah, "Johnson Taps Leader for Internal Affairs," *Philadelphia Inquirer*, July 23, 2003.

75. Justin Fenton, "Baltimore Police Hire Ex-DEA, Homeland Security Official to Oversee Internal Affairs," *The Baltimore Sun,* January 17th, 2012 http://www.baltimore sun.com/news/maryland/crime/blog/bal-baltimore-police-hire-exdea-homeland-security-official-to-oversee-internal-affairs-20120117,0,6579215.story (Accessed January 20, 2012).

76. Ibid.

77. Meghan McCorkell, "Baltimore Police Officer Pleads Guilty to Heroin Trafficking," *WJZ News-Baltimore*, March 17, 2012. http://baltimore.cbslocal.com/2012/03/17/baltimore-police-officer-pleads-guilty-to-heroin-trafficking/ (Accessed March 29, 2012).

78. Justin Fenton, "Amid Questions, Police Commander Reassigned," *The Baltimore Sun*, July 26, 2011. LexisNexis Academic Web (Accessed: January 20, 2012).

79. "Policing Internal Affairs: Our View—Police Commissioner Bealefeld Needs to Say More About His Efforts to Root Out Corruption or Risk Losing the Public's Trust," *The Baltimore Sun*, July 27, 2011. LexisNexis Academic Web (Accessed January 20, 2012).

80. Justin Fenton, Peter Hermann, Julie Scharper, "More than 30 Cops Charged, Suspended in Towing Scheme," *The Baltimore Sun,* February 23, 2011.

81. Fenton, "Amid Questions, Police Commander Reassigned."

82. Justin Fenton, "Former Baltimore Police Internal Affairs Commander Retires," *The Baltimore Sun*, February 8, 2012. http://www.baltimoresun.com/news/maryland/crime/blog/bal-former-internal-affairs-commander-retires-20120208,0,2646097.story?track=rss (Accessed March 29, 2012).

83. Erin Einhorn, "Residency Rules Widely Resented," *Philadelphia Daily News*, June 23, 2003.

84. Mark Fazlollah, *Philadelphia Inquirer* reporter, in discussion with the author, May 11, 2005.

85. John Grogan, "He Did City Wrong to Do Right by Son," *Philadelphia Inquirer*, June 30, 2003.

86. Ibid.

87. Steven Lee Myers, "Panel Is Told of a File on Police Graft within Internal Affairs," New York Times, October 5, 1993.

88. Mark Gillispie, "Police See Overtime as Perk of the Badge," *The Plain Dealer* (Cleveland, OH), March 14, 2004.

89. Kevin Deutsch, "Ticket-Fixing Scandal: Yankees Executive, Sonny Hight, Expected to Testify before Grand Jury," NYDailyNews.com, June 18, 2011. http://www.nydailynews.com/new-york/ticket-fixing-scandal-yankees-executive-sonny-hight-expected-testify-grand-jury-article-1.129591 (Accessed February 7, 2012).

90. Kevin Deutsch, "Cops under the Gun in the Massive Ticket-Fixing Scandal 'Nervous' as Grand Jury Mulls Indictments," NYDailyNews.com, September 21, 2011 http://www.nydailynews.com/news/crime/cops-gun-massive-ticket-fixing-scandal-nervous-grand-jury-mulls-indictments-article-1.956488 (Accessed February 8, 2012).

91. N.R. Kleinfield and John Eligon, "Officers Unleash Vitriol as Peers Are Charged in Ticket-Fixing," New York Times, October 29, 2011, A1.

92. Ibid.

93. Al Baker and Joseph Goldstein, "Unsealed Indictments Shed Light on Procedures for Ticket-Fixing by Officers," New York Times, October 29, 2011, A19.

94. N.R. Kleinfield and John Eligon, "Officers Unleash Vitriol as Peers Are Charged in Ticket-Fixing."

95. Joseph Goldstein, "Detective Who Led Ticket-Fixing Inquiry Faces Internal Charges," New York Times, December 11, 2011, A18.

96. William K. Rashbaum, Joseph Goldstein and Al Baker, "Experts Say NYPD Isn't Policing Itself," New York Times, November 3, 2011, A1.

97. Ibid.

98. Al Baker, "Vow to Fight Misconduct by Police Faces Skepticism," New York Times, January 13, 2012, A20.

99. Ibid.

# CHAPTER FIVE

# CULTURAL DEVIATION IN LAW ENFORCEMENT: CLOSED WORLDS THAT DAMAGE AGENCIES

## The Power of Culture in Policing

Law enforcement organizations are structured entities: arrangements of people and things and processes to get some job done. Organizations, however, are not just the sum of their designed parts. Off-target efforts and wasted expense are reduced by standardized service delivery, as well as by careful supervision and oversight units to keep things on track. Centralized administration creates economies of scale, reducing those expenses that support, but do not directly deliver, the law enforcement agency's core services. And the synergy of well-designed organizational structures and policies meshing with highly motivated employees can produce skyrocketing returns on an organization's human and material resources.

The key element in this last equation is the "highly motivated" employee. William Bratton, who has been a chief or commissioner in Boston, New York and Los Angeles, has a talent for getting the most out of his officers. Through equipment upgrades, face to face talks and videotaped messages and, perhaps most importantly, by clearing away administrative impediments so cops could concentrate on fighting crime, Bratton motivated officers towards better, more focused performance. Bratton exploited, in a positive way, the group dynamics of the personnel under his command.[1]

Bratton did not have to flip an "on" switch to get cops grouped together and motivated. These conditions always exist. Management can only influence the degree and direction of employee motivation, from less to more positive and, hopefully, never towards the negative. Little that management does is more important than aiming the motivational energy of employee groups in a positive direction. Nothing has a greater impact on how organizations behave and perform, for better or for worse, than the irrepressible need of human beings to interact with each other as social animals in all settings, including law enforcement agencies.

Because humans interact continuously from birth, recruits come to law enforcement already shaped in numerous ways that will influence how they approach the job. Rookie Police Officer Smith may be a trained member of the department but her life experiences have also trained her. Before coming to the job, she may have gone to public school or parochial school, been a Girl Scout or a cheerleader, a clerical administrator or a waitress. She may or may not have completed college. She may be an African American raised in Brooklyn, New York who has seen aggressive police tactics first hand, or she may be a newly minted citizen who grew up in London, where unarmed police patrol mostly on foot. Whatever her history, she would enter the police academy with a very distinct perspective on policing and retain much of that perspective when she graduated.

And law enforcement academy training itself is but a brief and somewhat abstract chapter in the overall socialization of an officer. The much lengthier, and absolutely real, training and socialization takes place "on the job." The veteran's archetypical greeting to a rookie, "Kid, forget everything you learned at the academy," symbolizes that day-in and day-out police work is the major determinant of how an officer thinks, performs and relates to others.[2]

This socialization is not conducted by any official trainer but is orchestrated by the officer's peers. Classes take place on the streets. The lessons feature real-time dealings with supervisors, service contacts with the general public and encounters with complainants and suspects. And, above all, the new officer learns how cops look at each other and at their jobs.

Law enforcement officers operate continuously under conditions that no other profession faces. Their workdays combine numbing routine with occasional doses of adrenaline-rushed chaos. Their fellow citizens have given law enforcement officers tasks that, by their very nature, involve bothering people, stopping them in their tracks, seeing them at their worst or depriving them of their liberty. Because the job gets done at odd hours, often in run-down areas and can feature dangerous encounters with scary individuals, most of their fellow citizens not only won't do an officer's job but would rather not know exactly how it is getting done. So the world of policing becomes tightly closed. Cops play with cops, talk with cops, and hang out with cops—on the job and off. Few work groups in any profession bond as tightly as law enforcement officers.

The strong bonding of police work groups presents a special challenge and opportunity to law enforcement executives. For chiefs like William Bratton, who so often pushed the right buttons, cadres of police officers produced bursts of focused energy that got the job done better and elevated their departments in the eyes of the public and law enforcement professionals alike. Chiefs like Willie Williams in Los Angeles, a Bratton predecessor who missed more motivational buttons than he hit, end up disconnected from rank and file officers, increasing the possibility that some will drift towards damaging behavior.

The cases in this chapter focus on how groups of law enforcement officers sabotaged the operation, reputation and morale of police agencies in Los Angeles, New York City, Pennsylvania and New Orleans. These cases reveal how work groups operate, how they adopt renegade behavior, what management does (or doesn't do) to let things fester, and what damage law enforcement agencies suffer as a result. And, as we will discuss, these cases also point the way towards preventing renegade behavior and turning the natural energy of law enforcement work groups towards positive accomplishment.

# The Concept of Cultural Deviation

Cultural deviation occurs when a group of employees operate in disregard of organizational rules and official norms as matter of daily process and moral value. When this condition is acute, culturally deviant elements of an organization operate largely unto themselves and for themselves. This chapter is anchored by four cases that clearly fit this description: the Rampart scandal that rocked the LAPD in the late 1990s; the Buddy Boys scandal in the NYPD in the mid-1980s; the "sex scandals" in the Pennsylvania State Police that broke in 1999, reverberating for five years; and the 2005 Hurricane Katrina disaster that exposed toxic cultural issues in the New Orleans Police Department that are still being addressed in 2012.

A close reading of each of these cases reveals enduring cultural dynamics that shaped employee behavior across twenty-five years and from coast to coast. While the case circumstances are different, each scandal was rooted in the work group culture of front-line policing. These cases acquaint us with common cultural elements in policing and also highlight particular elements of culture that came to the forefront in each case.

We will also describe ways in which management failed in these cases and offer suggestions for how law enforcement executives might avoid similar scandals in the future. Executives and mid-level managers bear primary responsibility for checking any excesses of the rank-and-file culture.

Front-line law enforcers confront circumstances more or less stable over time; police executives are paid to see and adjust their agencies to larger social changes that may be invisible to their officers. Because many heads create its collective consciousness, employee culture does not easily change its mind; executives are empowered to think outside the box and change things if need be. Front-line employees operate with a "twenty year and out" time horizon that mutes pressures to change; executives operate under short time horizons, "two years and out" is more like it, and have to quickly prove themselves and improve their operations if they want to stay even that long. And even the executive who is an operational wizard may well become a casualty of poorly managed organizational cultures. It is a rare thing, indeed, for a group of rogue officers to be exposed without taking down senior commanders, including chiefs and commissioners.

The work group culture of Brooklyn's 77th Precinct in 1984 is more alike than different from the LAPD Rampart culture of 1994 or the barracks culture of Pennsylvania State Troopers in 2000 or the culture that drives rank and file New Orleans officers. Those cultures, shaped by the jobs officers do, proved quite stable and change-resistant, even when change was urgently needed. It was law enforcement leadership that changed most radically before and after each case broke, going from facilitating failure to implementing reform. By being bold change agents, and by understanding how police culture works, these law enforcement executives coaxed their employee cultures in a positive direction. Hopefully, present and future law enforcement leaders reading this chapter will come away with a sense of the messages that can either repel or resonate with police work cultures, and a sense of the actions that can either precipitate or head off destructive actions by employee work groups.

## LAPD Blues: The Case of Rampart CRASH

Frank Lyga was not your typical, clean cut LAPD officer.[3] His pony-tailed hair went past his shoulders. His angular face featured the stubble of a beard, framed by a droopy moustache. His clothes were street, as was his attitude. Lyga worked undercover, and was good at staying in character, which was lower class hustler operating on the fringes of the law.

So Lyga was in character when he exchanged glances and then words with a jump-suited, goateed African American who had pulled up in an SUV alongside Lyga's unmarked car. The dispute escalated. In heavy, slow-moving traffic, the cars separated and then came side by side again. Then, guns were drawn and pointed and two shots rang out on the busy street. Both shots were fired by Lyga. Lyga's second bullet hit its mark and killed one Kevin Gaines, who just happened to be an off-duty LAPD officer.

One cop shooting another dead under any circumstances will rock any law enforcement organization. And that's without factoring in race, or the fact that the killing occurred as not one but two professional police officers let a road rage incident escalate to a deadly conclusion. The LAPD dealt with a flood of questions and an earthquake of criticism from the moment the incident occurred. And revelations kept coming that caused the ground under the LAPD to shake ever more violently. Gaines, it turned out, had moonlighted as a bodyguard for Death Row Records, was living with the estranged wife of Death Row founder Suge Knight, was driving a car registered in her name and had pulled his gun during other street disputes with civilians while he was off-duty. Gaines was also close friends with another LAPD officer involved with Death Row, Gregory Mack, who soon afterwards was arrested in connection with a Los Angeles bank robbery.

So the LAPD went from investigating the tragic death of one officer at the hands of another—for which Lyga was later exonerated—to an extended investigation into a web of officers connected to criminal activity on the job and off. As yet other officers turned out to have Death Row Records connections, something that stood out was that many had been assigned to the Rampart Division of the LAPD and, more specifically, to the Division's anti-gang unit.

The CRASH (Community Resources Against Street Hoodlums) Unit had a motto "We intimidate those who intimidate others." And the motto had considerable currency. Suspects complained of being beaten by Rampart officers while handcuffed and having had drugs and guns planted on them. Rumors of over-the-top tactics circulated on the LAPD grapevine.

Investigators were making some headway but had little cooperation from Rampart personnel. Corrupt Rampart CRASH officers may have been few but Rampart personnel in general maintained a fierce protective shield around their culture of aggressive street enforcement. Even supervisors attempting routine operational audits had been rebuffed. Then, six pounds of cocaine turned up missing from the LAPD property room, and evidence soon implicated Rafael Perez, a Rampart CRASH officer who was close to Gregory Mack. Investigators also believed that Perez had walked a seventh pound of cocaine out of the property room, but he was prosecuted for the theft of the larger weight, and the trial ended up with a hung jury that was leaning towards conviction. As prosecutors moved towards a retrial, eleven additional instances of purloined cocaine, all bearing the Perez M.O., turned up. This, along with his pending retrial on various charges associated with the six-pound theft, was enough to "turn" Perez. Seeking a lighter sentence on the cocaine theft charges, Perez agreed to tell what he knew about illegal activity by Rampart officers.

And what a story it was.

Perez said that most of the officers in Rampart CRASH, starting with himself and partner Nino Durden, were "putting crimes" on suspects. Perez testified that he and Durden had shot an unarmed drug suspect named Javier Ovando and then fabricated an assault charge to cover up what they had done. Ovando, left paralyzed by their bullets and then sentenced to 23 years as a result of their perjured testimony, was eventually released and awarded $15 million in damages. Far from being an aberration, Perez said, planting guns and drugs and fabricating charges against suspects was common practice in Rampart CRASH. And the cops who weren't setting up or beating up suspects were brought "into the loop" when the miscreant officers made sure the "straight" cops knew what was going down. Knowing just enough for long enough made even the uninvolved cops culpable and afraid to talk. Over the course of nearly a year, Perez implicated seventy other Rampart officers in a variety of misdeeds ranging from felonies to drinking on the job, filing false reports and being "in the loop."

Perez' confessions led to the prosecution of eight other officers, including his partner, Nino Durden. Four of those officers, including Durden, were either convicted or pled guilty to some of the charges against them. And over 100 convicts, their trials tainted by testimony from Rampart officers implicated by Perez, walked out of California prisons. Most headed straight to civil attorneys who filed lawsuits against the City of Los Angeles for a cumulative amount that made the $15 million awarded to Javier Ovando look like pocket change.

The fallout from Perez' testimony also had a profound impact on the management of the LAPD. Separate reports by the LAPD command and an independent commission lambasted the department's hiring practices, personnel assignments, supervision, training and leadership. The investigations confirmed much of what Perez had said: Rampart CRASH selected its own members, fended off supervision, marked the killing and injuring of suspects with plaques and enabled some officers to act as a law unto themselves. Civil rights lawyers from the United States Department of Justice were circling because Rampart practices had clearly violated citizens' constitutional rights, whether one measured those violations by Perez' sweeping claims, or by actual convictions and pleas, or by the findings of the investigating commissions. Although the department's leadership resisted for a time, a November 2000 consent decree authorized a federal judge to oversee the LAPD for five years to make sure that it cleaned up its act. In 2002, in large part because of the Rampart scandal and his handling of it, Chief Bernard Parks was replaced by William Bratton.

## Unit Transformations from Supportive to Subversive

The Rampart case illustrates how a group of law enforcement officers can develop a culture so deviant from organization-wide norms that their actions de-legitimize and damage the agency. Within deviant cultures, rule-defying behavior becomes a matter of daily process and moral value. Every day in states and cities across the U.S. small groups of officers guiltlessly, and even righteously, subvert the principles and practices of their law enforcement agencies.

Rampart cops did not start as renegades. Rampart CRASH was set up in the early 1990s to combat gang crime in South Central L.A. And that is what they did, cutting crime more than 50% from 1992 to 1999.[4] As CRASH's crime fighting success went up, however, the thinking and behavior of the members was increasingly at odds with LAPD rules and regulations and, ultimately, the law.

The Rampart Independent Review Panel reported, "Rampart CRASH officers developed an independent subculture that embodied a 'war on gangs' mentality where the ends justified. the means, and they resisted supervision and control and ignored LAPD's procedures and policies."[5] In this finding, the Review Panel echoed the Los Angeles Police Department's own findings: "Rampart CRASH had developed its own culture and operated as an entity unto itself. It routinely made up its own rules and, for all intents and purposes, was left with little or no oversight."[6]

The Rampart CRASH motto "We intimidate those who intimidate others" enabled members to adopt personas barely distinguishable from the gang members they policed. The group gave awards to members who wounded or killed suspects—the killing award being more prestigious.[7] Rampart's most notorious cops, who were outright criminals, made sure that their compatriots were "in the loop"—knowing just enough so that their silence was assured, not only by cop-to-cop loyalty but also by fear of being indicted for not quickly reporting what they knew.

The Rampart CRASH culture glued itself together just like any other culture would. CRASH adopted a unifying worldview and employed symbols of belonging as well as ways of recognizing outstanding members. While all cultures construct themselves similarly, what results is unique. When a strong employee sub-culture becomes isolated from the larger organization and increasingly operates according to its own rules, as Rampart CRASH did within the LAPD, the effect can be cancerous. The unique subculture of Rampart CRASH featured beliefs and practices that subverted the overall LAPD mission, as well as the organization-wide culture that management sought.

The law enforcement executive needs to be aware of the distinct subcultures operating within his or her agency. Every law enforcement executive is in the business of culture management. The principal culture being managed is the overall culture of the organization. Law enforcement agency mission statements are devices for building culture. The NYPD seeks to build a culture of the "finest" dedicated to preserving law and order and protecting the citizenry through police services delivered with courtesy, professionalism and respect. The LAPD "official" culture seeks to preserve and protect while emphasizing quality through continual improvement. Getting and keeping the membership engaged in a culture dedicated to accomplishing the official mission is crucial. That is why commissioners and chiefs give speeches, hold awards ceremonies, design distinctive uniforms and emblazon police cruisers with slogans that are messages to the rank-and-file as well as to the public.

Law enforcement managers also need to devote thought and energy to managing the subcultures that will invariably spring up within their agencies. The natural processes from which subcultures in policing emerge start with personnel being grouped together in order to perform certain activities. A group of emergency service police officers, for instance, will likely value risk-taking more than members of the patrol ranks. They'll also value their equipment more: Emergency service officers who as patrol officers used to be cavalier about the condition of their cruisers wouldn't think of starting their tours today without checking their emergency equipment. And emergency service officers are also more likely to have strong teamwork norms because they must often closely coordinate in rescues and other emergency situations. Such subcultural norms help the law enforcement agency to the extent that they reinforce and facilitate the job of the units involved without clashing negatively with the larger organization's values and goals.

But subcultures don't always remain benign. Since they are continuously in the process of creating themselves, any law enforcement subculture can start down a track that deviates increasingly from what the larger organization, or even the law, intends. An emergency services unit can become isolated and arrogant, seeing its members as the "real action heroes" in contrast to the "pencil pushers" and "beat walkers" in the rest of the department. Similarly, emergency medical service and fire rescue personnel are seen and treated like fifth wheels that ought to stay out of the way because the "real work" needs to be done by the emergency service cops.

This attitude is all well and good for shaping cops in the emergency services culture into tightly knit groups whose members feel good about themselves. This attitude is counter-productive, however, when the emergency services cops must work closely with their patrol officer brethren or with fire rescue and emergency medical workers. Then, the emergency cops' pride and arrogance can fuel animosity that leads to mistakes and even disputes between various emergency services personnel over who is in charge at a particular disaster scene.

When subcultures begin to significantly deviate, in a mission-damaging way, from the culture of the larger organization, management should act. Managers who keep their finger on the pulse of their organizations will often sense the emergence of problematic subcultures and take steps to reinforce mainstream organizational attitudes and behaviors in deviating units. For managers who do not watch and listen as closely, things may go very wrong before the cultural deviance is recognized and addressed. When management fails to see the deviation or, as is often the case, ignores it, then the potential skyrockets that the deviant subculture will operate in ways that turn out poisonous for the whole organization.

With respect to Rampart, the LAPD executives were either blind or looking the other way. Rampart CRASH achieved remarkable crime reductions over its first five years, and gratified superiors were not inclined to look too hard at the CRASH culture. Achievements aside, however, enough stories were floating around the department about the wild and wooly style of CRASH officers to pique the interest of any superior who wanted to look into things. And, indeed, a few mid-level managers did try. But they didn't get very far. Rampart personnel actively resisted the inquiries, and top management apparently did little to back up the thwarted investigators.

When things unfold as they did in Rampart, management bears the brunt of the blame. Unit cultures do what they do, including developing in ways inimical to overall organizational interests. The members may be oblivious to the damage they are causing or may simply discount the damage as necessary given the righteousness of their chosen path. Managers are, by default, the first, and often last, line of defense in such situations. When managers fail to act, the responsibility for a Rampart scandal lies squarely on their shoulders.

## The Dangers of Cultural Autonomy

Rafael Perez talked to investigators *ad nauseam*, naming so many names and citing so many crimes that police defenders, pointing to how few indictments came out of so many accusations, say that Perez sang a mostly false song to save his skin. This may well be, but even the convictions and pleas that were achieved bespeak an operation that was way over the line. However accurate he may have been in fingering almost all the cops in Rampart CRASH, Perez' voice rings true when he talks about the Rampart culture.

As Perez tells it, Rampart CRASH largely controlled its own membership. A prospective member came on board because he or she had already been vouched for by someone associated with CRASH. This is the way one usually joins a country club, but ought not to be the way to join an elite anti-gang unit at the center of a major metropolitan police department's crime reduction efforts. Allowing the unit to select its own members was guaranteed to widen the cultural divide between Rampart CRASH and the rest of the LAPD. A unit allowed to choose its own members has a strong tendency to bring in "people like us." Perez had arrived at Rampart on a recommendation from Sammy Martin, an LA police officer who was a close friend of David Mack, with whom Perez soon partnered.

Perez' final partner, Nino Durden, came to Rampart thanks to Perez' wife. Her close friend, who happened to be Durden's girlfriend, had lobbied Mrs. Perez. Despite having reservations, Perez brought Durden's nomination forward, not wanting to displease his wife. Squaring the Durden-Perez-Mack circle even further, Perez took Durden on as his partner.

It speaks volumes that in this particular chain of selection, Mack, Perez and Durden, all ended up as convicted felons. Whether Rampart solicited aggressive and edgy street cops, which was typical, or brought in officers easily turned to criminal conduct under cover of the badge, as was the case with Perez, Mack and Durden, the rest of the LAPD had little say. The Rampart CRASH unit, for better or worse, was free to perpetuate and strengthen a culture whose attitudes and practices were departing, in ever widening arcs, from lawful policing as envisioned by the LAPD.

Not only did Rampart CRASH have the informal authority to select members in, it also flexed its muscles to shut out the prying eyes of superiors. Rampart actively fought off overhead control. "Rampart CRASH was not audited for ... two years. The Operations-Central Bureau lieutenant who was responsible for auditing Rampart CRASH made it known that ... Rampart detectives refused to provide him with statistics and sergeant's log books necessary to complete the audit."[8]

Complaining to higher-ups in Rampart command got the harried lieutenant no further. Overall, the department was reluctant to come down hard on the highly productive Rampart cops, even though "it was generally known throughout the Department that Rampart CRASH was difficult to supervise and had developed its own culture and aggressive approach to the gang problem."[9]

Rampart CRASH operated with a huge measure of autonomy thanks to its control over personnel selection, the operating freedom that CRASH unit members enjoyed on South Central's streets, and the immunity the unit gained by parrying oversight attempts. Elements of Rampart CRASH were not only out of control, they were also largely beyond the effective control of the LAPD management. In the end, major felonies had to be committed by cops in order to enlighten ranking LAPD officials that things were very wrong at Rampart CRASH.

Forget that a cadre of Rampart CRASH officers moved in Death Row Records social circles, and moonlighted as bodyguards for the talent and the music impresarios. Forget even that Rampart enforcement activities were generating more than the usual level of brutality complaints from arrestees, and that some of the complaints were sticking. A manager might steer clear of inquiring into officers' private lives, or might not catch a spike in brutality complaints. But few executives would be oblivious to units that pick their own members and that send departmental auditors packing. These are events that reverberate strongly at managerial and administrative levels. That being the case, it is all but certain that at least some LAPD managers made informed choices to let Rampart CRASH be.

But these are choices that, as a rule, should not be made. Allowing an on-the-edge operation the freedom to clone its marginal members is a recipe for cultural deviance. So is letting a hard to oversee unit more or less throw out the auditors sent in to take a look. The message to the unit is that "you are free to do whatever you are doing" and the subtext is "because what you are doing is good" which, even if that is not what management intends to say, is certainly what the renegade unit will hear.

It is incumbent upon law enforcement executives to scan the agency for units resisting and breaking away from administrative control, for units operating on the edge of the law and police practice, and for units whose norms and codes of conduct are at odds with those of the larger agency. In some cases, this monitoring will discover units that have found better ways of operating within the law to fight crime, which is a good thing that ought to be emulated. In other cases, this monitoring will uncover deviant organizational subcultures poised to plunge the agency into a whirlwind of controversy, which is a bad thing that ought to be eliminated. In either case, the law enforcement executive is leading responsibly, as opposed to managing passively, in the face of cultural deviations with enormous downside potential for the agency and its members.

## The Buddy Boys: Brooklyn's Bandits in Blue

In the mid-1980s, Brooklyn's 77th Precinct was Siberia, a deteriorating, high crime landscape to which officers were shipped if they screwed up, were difficult to supervise, or had bad attitudes. There they joined veteran officers in place since the precincts' better days, or officers for whom the precinct meant a convenient home to work commute. Commanders and ranking officers might also end up in the 77th if something went wrong on their watch in a prior command.

Whether they were exiles, cynical veterans or commuters of convenience, most officers of the 77th shared a siege mentality. Criminals operated brazenly in the Bedford-Stuyvesant precinct, and officers contended with extremely high crime rates in categories ranging from drug sales to assaults to homicides. More mundane criminals like drug users, prostitutes, muggers and bookmakers operated in broad daylight. Crime was so ingrained in the fabric of the neighborhood that a raucous crowd could appear at the precinct gates in response to an arrest, whether the suspect was a drug dealer whose ill-gotten gains supported an extended family or a petty crime suspect believed to have been roughed up by the cops. Thanks to the occasional siege and the precinct compound's eight-foot high walls, officers took to calling the 77th "The Alamo," and even wore "Alamo" T-shirts under their uniforms.[10] Officers may have fashioned the 77th as a bastion but it was also their clubhouse, where officers hung out, lifted weights, told war stories and drank beer—before, during and after their tours.

Like the real defenders of the Alamo, most of the officers of the 77th Precinct saw themselves in a losing battle. Crime seemed intractable and the neighborhood was not only hostile but positively foreign to the cops, mostly white, who motored in from the suburbs to put in their eight hours. And beyond each cop's individual story of exile, the cops of the 77th saw themselves as abandoned by higher-ups who, they felt, had conspired with liberal courts and spineless politicians to handcuff enforcement efforts, to bend over backwards for suspects and to establish a revolving door justice system that put criminals back on the street before the arresting officer had returned to duty.

If the 77th was a gulag for some cops, it wasn't exactly a fast track for their managers. A succession of commanders simply accepted that the precinct was demoralized or, after an ignored memo or two to higher-ups, realized that there was no support from above for a rebirth of police professionalism in the 77th. Just as the rank-and-file retreated from the community behind the walls of the precinct and the interiors of their police cruisers, their executives managed mostly from behind closed doors, where they did not have to confront the depressing array of burnt-out cops, rejects and station house lawyers waving union rule books.

Amidst the gloom, one could miss the fact that some of the cops in the 77th precinct were absolutely energized. They referred to each other as "Buddy Boy" and, for them, life in the 'hood was a blast. As much as they could, the Buddy Boys worked the night shift—12 to 8—in part because of the minimal and perfunctory supervision on the midnight tour. Flying below the radar was something they valued highly. No Buddy Boy wanted blips to show up on the screen of anyone in authority who might care enough to crack down on what had just about become their principal activity at work. The Buddy Boys had become criminals.

Their slide had started with little offenses. Frustrated over a criminal justice system that failed to mete out the punishment they believed their arrestees deserved, some officers took the shoes of suspects, drove to a remote area and dropped the suspects off. Soon the nascent Buddy Boys progressed beyond shoeless suspects hiking back home, and reveled in the anguish of junkie suspects who had just had their drugs flushed down a toilet, thrown down a sewer or scattered to the winds.

Then a light bulb went off in some cop's head in 1981, if not before. "Why throw this stuff away? We already have relationships with the dealers we keep wagging our fingers at saying 'we know what you are doing and we'll get you someday.' But you know what, someday may never come, and these drugs we're flushing down toilets can fetch good money from our professional acquaintances in the drug trade. Why not cash in?"

And that the Buddy Boys did.

At its simplest, their system worked like this; nab drug suspect, seize the drugs and any money, release suspect, split up money, and resell drugs. Everybody makes out, even the hapless suspect/victim, whose arrest goes away in exchange for some drugs and cash. The "Buddy Boys," ever energized and innovative, created elaborate variations on this basic M.O. In teams of two, three and four, the Buddy Boys started to raid big-time drug operations that employed upwards of a dozen individuals. The raids would be carefully orchestrated to leave an escape route for the suspects. All of the Buddy Boys might come crashing through the front doors and windows of a drug location, "forgetting" to guard the back door through which the relieved drug dealers fled. Sometimes the Buddy Boys ended up with an unwanted prisoner who had been sleeping in a back room or who had wandered in off the street after the "raid." These accidental prisoners usually found themselves escorted outside, away from the "crime scene," where their police officer/guard invariably suffered a brain freeze and wandered back into the building.

The Buddy Boys were a tight and cohesive group who worked well together and liked what they did. Robbing felons was lucrative and fun and punished bad guys. Some Buddy Boys actually felt they were succeeding where the criminal justice system had failed. If it occurred to them that their behavior constituted a net increase in crime, the Buddy Boys didn't show it. They were too busy running their franchise in the neighborhood's drug trade, which continued apace along with its devastating impacts on local residents.

The officers of the 77th were so out of control that tales of their escapades could not help but filter up the chain of command. Those tales revealed the 77th as wacky, with practical jokes featuring officers "wounded" by starter pistol shots at roll call and powder-only shotgun blasts in the squad room.[11] And the denizens of the 77th could be laughably inept, as one veteran cop proved by crashing a cruiser into the precinct's vestibule, having destroyed two steel doors on the way in after accidentally throwing the vehicle into reverse while gunning the accelerator.[12] But what most concerned those superiors who even considered taking a close look at the 77th were tales of cops blatantly robbing drug dealers, and using and selling drugs themselves.

But getting the goods on the Buddy Boys was easier said than done. The occasional sergeant or lieutenant who arrived at the 77th vowing to "clean up Dodge" soon backed off. All it usually took was a punctured tire or two, threats scrawled on lockers or a dead rat bearing the supervisor's name nailed to the bulletin board.[13]

Captains fared little better when seeking guidance from superiors on how to deal with the intractable zoo the precinct had become. Usually no response was forthcoming from these zone commanders who had been complicit in stocking the 77th with "drunks, duty shirkers, wife beaters, drug addicts, rule benders and discipline problems who were not quite bad enough to fire."[14]

The 77th was on the radar at NYPD Headquarters in Manhattan throughout the early 1980s, but its Internal Affairs investigations were compromised at almost every turn. Officer William Gallagher, a leader among the Buddy Boys, was also a long time union representative with extensive contacts throughout the Department. A heads-up on impending investigative activity could come from anywhere in the network into which Gallagher was wired, from a fellow union delegate or a headquarters cop who "heard something" or from an Internal Affairs officer more sympathetic to the officers on patrol than to the job of assuring integrity.

As a result, the Buddy Boys were forewarned about upcoming Internal Affairs surveillances and integrity tests. In one such test, a van laden with cartons of cigarettes was parked overnight, doors open, in the 77th precinct. Several Buddy Boy officers were ordered to patrol up and down the deserted street in the hopes that they would succumb to temptation. Instead, the Buddy Boys added another box of the same brand of cigarettes to the cache on the van, which they duly inventoried and brought back to the station house. They also pounded on the sides of the nearby undercover van in which Internal Affairs officers sat hoping to film members of the Buddy Boys stealing the cigarettes. The flummoxed Internal Affairs investigators had been "busted" by their targets. Adding insult to injury, the Buddy Boys had also screwed up Internal Affairs accounting for the bait cigarettes.[15]

The Buddy Boys were finally undone in 1986 and the first Buddy Boy to fall was Henry Winter. When the New York State Special Prosecutor for Criminal Justice pounced, Henry Winter was a Buddy Boy through and through, even though he had arrived at the precinct in 1981 as a distrusted outsider. Winter had come from the nearby 75th precinct where his brother-in-law, also a cop, had cooperated with Internal Affairs. Winter, guilty by association, was shunned by colleagues and given lousy assignments, such as patrolling remote piers on foot, which prompted him to request a transfer to the 77th precinct.[16] Even though Winter knew nothing of his brother-in-law's Internal Affairs work, rumors that sped ahead of the transfer told a different tale. Winter was no more accepted at the 77th precinct than he had been at the 75th.

All that changed when Winter learned that Officer William Gallagher and a partner had stolen money from a suspect's home, where the officers were by reason of a fabricated complaint that they themselves had phoned in anonymously. Gallagher, a driving force behind the Buddy Boys, realized that Winter knew and decided to test his loyalty. In a showdown, Gallagher patted Winter down, looking for a recording device. But Winter was not wired and assured Gallagher that he had no interest in broadcasting anything about his fellow cops.[17] From that moment forward, Winter was in the Buddy Boy's loop and was generally accepted by the 77th's cops, beginning a corrupt slide that only got steeper when he became Gallagher's partner for a while.

By 1986, Winter and the other Buddy Boys came to work more to steal than to police. Whole nights were given over to a succession of criminal acts. The Buddy Boys honed their techniques for robbing drug dealers, fencing stolen goods, fending off radio calls and trading-off time consuming arrests to other officers. They also took bribes. When Winter and his partner were finally caught on tape, they were accepting money from a neighborhood drug dealer with whom the Buddy Boys had enjoyed a long, profitable relationship.

The Buddy Boys did not know that the dealer, having been arrested in possession of major felony weight cocaine, had gone to the DA through his probation officer and had offered up the 77th Precinct's dirty cops in order to get a better plea deal. The DA went to the Special Prosecutor, bypassing the NYPD and Gallagher's widespread network of informants. The bribe-taking videos were filmed soon after. Winter and his partner were then picked up and escorted to the world premiere of the tapes at the Special Prosecutor's office. The tapes were so damning that two officers agreed immediately to gather evidence and testify against other corrupt cops in the 77th.[18] When all was said and done, over a dozen cops were indicted; most were convicted or pled guilty prior to trial, and one Buddy Boy killed himself. Departmental charges were filed against more than two dozen additional officers.

Pulling itself out of the wreckage of the scandal, a wounded NYPD cleaned out the 77th precinct totally, scattering its personnel across the city. The Buddy Boys were no more.

## Concentrating Problem Employees

The Buddy Boys were a creation of management. Unlike Rampart CRASH, which largely created itself as management stood back admiring the unit's crime reduction figures, the Buddy Boys emerged from a chaotic 77th Precinct that NYPD commanders had turned into a dumping ground for problem officers. One New Jersey police lieutenant, after reading about the Buddy Boys, wrote in a paper:

> In a normal organization, managers can expect to spend 80% of their time dealing with 20% of their people, the problem workers. What do you do in a unit where 80% of the workers are problem children? Add to this the fact that the supervisors had been dumped there just as the officers, and for similar reasons, and it becomes apparent that this unit needed supervision the most, and got it the least. There was a critical mass of bad officers, and no one was watching.[19]

It couldn't be better put—critical mass. It wasn't a matter of whether something was going to blow in the 77th, but when. Most managers have all they can do to extract a productive, motivated effort from a work group with one or two problem workers. At the 77th, with dozens of uniquely problematic officers, precinct management essentially abdicated, which left—and this is barely a metaphor—the inmates to run the asylum.

Many officers of the 77th had gotten there because of deliberate, if informal, personnel policies that were operating at middle and upper command levels of the NYPD. The 77th was "Siberia" because exiling problem employees made life easier for most NYPD commanders, with the exception of the hapless CO's and executive officers of the 77th or other dumping ground units.

The exile option made life easier at command levels, where personnel actions against problem officers invariably involved a difficult, paper-laden and lengthy process that only got harder if, as was most often the case, the employee invoked union grievance procedures or alleged violations of civil service rules. Exiling officers with drug and alcohol issues or emotional problems also avoided an employee assistance program referral, which was seen as stigmatizing by officers and bosses alike. Referred officers could be stripped of their firearms which, for some, meant also being stripped of second jobs in private security that provided needed income. So bosses were understandably leery of such referrals.

So, for managers in general, transferring that malcontent or alcoholic employee to some agreed-upon "Island of the Lost" worked all around. The transfer, on its face, was benign. A vacancy was created that could be refilled. And a major employee headache was gone—from the sending unit, at least. But the headache reappeared, pulsing and ready to blow, as a critical mass of problem employees in an impoverished, minority community for whom the legitimacy of law enforcement was already in doubt.

The dynamics that produced the 77th Precinct are not unique in law enforcement. The incentive system that operated so powerfully in the NYPD in the 1980s all but demanded that commanders mask the jettisoning of difficult employees as routine transfers. The disincentives for discipline included the ability of a charged officer to tie a supervisor in knots for months or years by aggressively wielding union and civil service rules against even minor reprimands; the collective ability of officers to contract the "blue flu" or otherwise punish superiors seen as pushing too hard; and a residual empathy that made commanders think twice about disciplining or referring out problem cops.

In contrast, the incentives for "backdoor" discipline included the relatively speedy elimination of problem employees, the minimization of confrontation and recrimination, a peer network of commanders ready to facilitate the lateral transfer of unwanted employees and, finally, the availability of a "dumping ground" where few cared about performance and nobody listened to those in the community who did.

When this combination of incentives is fully or partially in play, management will group problem officers together in organizational backwaters where little attention is paid to what is going on. In these conditions deviant cultures can coalesce and thrive until, quite often, they burst forth in scandals that consume officers and executives alike.

## The Power of Obstructionist Cultural Networks

Officer William Gallagher acted like an intelligence chief for the Buddy Boys. Just as the CIA works a worldwide network of spies and informants, Gallagher cultivated an intelligence network in the NYPD. Gallagher gathered information that helped guide the Buddy Boys' tactics, such as the timing of their crimes, and achieve their strategic purpose of growing their illicit enterprises.

It is hard to overestimate the role such intelligence gathering can play. The Buddy Boys christened themselves in the early 1980s, but the egregious criminality and misconduct stretched back to the 1970s and involved many of the officers, including Gallagher, who were finally brought to justice in 1986. Over a decade or more, the scale of misconduct grew, as did the number of participating officers. But somehow, over that time, no investigation by Internal Affairs or Special Prosecutors made a real dent in the criminal enterprise being operated by rogue officers of the 77th. They were, as they liked to joke among themselves, "bullet proof." [20]

On the whole, oversight investigators did not fail for lack of trying. Information would be received, and duly noted. Surveillance operations and stings would be arranged. But, when these operations went down, the Buddy Boys would be on their best behavior, enforcing the law—which they were pretty good at when they chose to be. As the case described, the Buddy Boys sometimes learned enough about stings designed to ensnare them that they arrogantly toyed with the Internal Affairs investigators.

The intelligence flowed to the Buddy Boys through Gallagher because he was wired into a larger cultural network that spanned the Department, pervading just about every nook and cranny, including Internal Affairs. A cultural network is composed of individuals scattered throughout an organization who have loyalty to each other on the basis of shared characteristics and/or beliefs. A cultural network is not an aggregation of work group cultures, since each work group culture is unique. Rather, a cultural network is glued together by more general symbols and principles that nonetheless subsume key characteristics and beliefs shared by many of the organization's work groups and/or individual members in all parts of the agency.

There are three critical things to understand about cultural networks, especially if you are a manager. First of all, cultural networks operate autonomously. A chief will occasionally lose sight of this, demanding that rumors cease, launching investigations into leaks, and wondering aloud why everybody can't be on the same page. This is just about guaranteed to have no impact other than to create a sharper division between the targeted cultural network and agency management.

The second thing to keep in mind is that the symbols that bind a cultural network together may resonate more strongly with its members than any competing symbol put forth by management. This brings us to the third thing, which is that members of a cultural network can, without compunction, subvert and obstruct organizational initiatives seen as violating key tenets in the network's belief system, or seen as harming employees exhibiting a characteristic valued by the network.

The NYPD was, and is, awash in cultural networks. Benevolent or endowment associations, which serve as unions, exist for patrol officers, detectives, sergeants, lieutenants and captains. These associations are a powerful presence, with union delegates in every command. In addition, a large proportion of uniformed officers either formally belong to or move within the orbit of ethnically based associations—which exist for, among others, Latino, African American, Irish, Italian and Jewish members of the NYPD. Similar networks take in female officers, gays and lesbians, and the list goes on. And the NYPD is by no means unique. Cultural networks exist in every law enforcement agency and, indeed, in every public agency and private organization with more than a handful of employees.

In any event, Gallagher was wired into both the largest Benevolent Association network and the large and influential Irish network and was a likable guy who got around besides. Since the Buddy Boys, and their affiliated rogue cops at the 77th, were a diverse bunch in rank and ethnicity, Gallagher was not the only member who could mine information from cultural networks. A heads up about an impending investigation could, and did, come down through an "Italian" or an "African American" or a "Sergeant" network.

The binding belief that both glued these networks together and disposed them to subvert the formal investigations of the Buddy Boys was this: Our members are good cops doing a tough job that is little appreciated, least of all by managers playing "gotcha" with hard-working officers instead of owning up to their own responsibilities and errors.[21] While a core belief needn't be true to bind a network and move it to act, the culpability of commanders in creating the mess that was the 77th made this belief more true than not. And so for years information just fired across various cultural networks to officers in the 77th, who thwarted, time and time again, the formal initiatives of the NYPD to expose and put an end to the ongoing criminal activity by the Buddy Boys.

## Institutional Racism as Management Policy

Bedford-Stuyvesant was an overwhelmingly African-American neighborhood, although that label covered people from a diversity of cultural backgrounds including French-speaking Haitians and a large contingent of recently arrived residents from the English-speaking islands of the Caribbean. There were pockets of Latinos, mainly Puerto Rican and a few remaining white residents, mostly elderly, who had lived in the area for decades. Whatever your race or ethnicity, however, it was pretty certain that, if you lived in the 77th Precinct, you were poor.

It was in this largely African-American and overwhelmingly poor neighborhood that the Buddy Boys conducted a criminal enterprise under the noses of cowed and/or uncaring precinct supervisors. The heyday of the Buddy Boys, during the first half of the 1980s, also saw neighborhood crime skyrocket and a crack-fueled drug epidemic spread like wildfire. And though most cops in the 77th were not—as were the Buddy Boys—adding to the neighborhood's crime rate, their efforts had almost no impact on the upward spiral of crime in the area. In the dumping ground that was the 77th Precinct, however, it was hard to tell whether this was due to ineptitude or bad attitude or work phobia by the officers, abdication by their superiors, or a combination of everything by everybody.

The officers of the 77th Precinct were, on the whole, white, as were most of the Buddy Boys. And, since the community being so ill-served was overwhelmingly black, it is tempting to blame racist officers both for the creation of the Buddy Boys and for the low impact performance and uncaring attitude that marked policing in the 77th. This is a temptation that ought to be resisted, not because racist attitudes were non-existent but because those individual officers who may have been motivated by such attitudes were the least of the culprits.

The book, *The Buddy Boys*, was based on extensive interviews, on and off the record, in 1986 and 1987. Before that time (and to a lesser extent, still) a white officer coming on the force usually had minimal prior contact with minority group members, zero exposure to heavily minority communities and at best a textbook idea of what poverty and social distress meant. So a white officer's first assignment to a low-income minority community usually was accompanied by culture shock capable of hardening any existing stereotypes or racism.

But the cops of the 77th sounded mostly like frustrated crime fighters, as angry with their bosses, the politicians and the courts as they were with community mores that they saw as facilitating crime. Officers interviewed often struck empathetic notes when discussing the collective trials and tribulations of the community, especially when talking about hardships suffered by residents they know. Officers at the 77th for the long haul, as many were, built up a network of relationships in the community in the course of their work.

The Buddy Boys, in particular, honed their cross-cultural relationship skills. When they wholesaled their stolen drugs to or took bribes from their criminal associates in the community, the interactions could range from businesslike to a chatty friendliness. Money was being made all around and overt racial animus rarely got in the way. Nor was racial exclusion a recruitment practice of the 77th's corrupt cops, who counted African-American and Latino officers, including women, in their ranks.

All that being said, racism was a major factor in the Buddy Boys saga. The racism that counted most heavily was not in the minds of the rank-and-file officers of the 77th or even in the Buddy Boys' crimes perpetrated against African-American and Latino drug dealers. The fundamental racism was engineered by NYPD executives who dealt with misfit personnel by dumping them en masse in a precinct in an impoverished minority community unable to do much about being policed by damaged goods. This is institutional racism, and it creates Buddy Boys to this day.

Institutional racism does not require that bigots lurk in a public agency's executive suite. In fact, we can find highly pernicious examples of institutional racism in urban public school systems managed and staffed by individuals who would probably deny ever having had a racist thought. Yet, for nearly a half century, education boards and teachers unions have negotiated contracts that place the least experienced, lowest status teachers in the schools with the highest educational needs. In a nutshell, newly certified teachers brought up in suburbia, temporarily certified instructors scraped up from anywhere, and a succession of demoralized substitutes are assigned to schools in impoverished, largely minority neighborhoods where the children come to school with enormous learning handicaps.

This educational parallel to the Buddy Boys may not be criminal but is no less corrosive. Schools staffed by burnout cases, shell-shocked young adults, and substitute survivalists end up in the papers frequently. A single class has six teachers in a year. An instructor in over his or her head simply locks the door to keep the kids penned, but teaches virtually nothing. The student-victims then get socially promoted, hiding the failure of the system to have done anything for them.

Whether in policing or education, institutional racism is occurring when management chooses poor and relatively powerless minority communities as a dumping ground for bad employees, as a safe place to deliver poor service, and as a first source of economies during financial crises. These practices convey that the community does not count and that neither exiled workers nor trapped residents ought to expect much. The downward spiral in employee and community morale that predictably ensues then justifies decisions by management that takes more away. Since this process usually helps management solve problems within the organization, internal incentives for managers to keep making the same decisions are also strong.

Institutional racism is a systemic, organization-level process far more damaging to minority communities than any racist beliefs held by individual employees delivering inadequate services to residents their bosses have largely written off. In fact, by spotlighting and stringing together racially charged incidents of police misconduct and brutality into a dramatic narrative of individual, group and class animosity, the media and activists may actually help institutional racism operate with impunity in the shadows.

## Antidotes: Transparency and Performing with Integrity

In any agency where institutional racism is expressed, management has been the major force establishing and sustaining it. And management must be the key actor in dismantling organizational features that sustain racially (or ethnically) disparate service delivery.

This takes no small amount of work. Remember that the 77th Precinct became an island for lost souls because many managers found it much easier to "routinely transfer" problematic employees than to discipline them. For the sake of the community (and, incidentally, the employee), management needs to commit to whatever the personnel rules demand in order to address an employee's issues.

Management also needs to commit to working with employee unions towards positive change when contractual provisions create employee deployments that contribute to racially disparate service delivery. This process may be long, and may play out in both media and political arenas, but is necessary. A law enforcement agency's legitimacy is seriously undermined by deviant cultures, whether the seeds of those cultures have been sown by management policies, by union rules or by both.

Better management techniques may be the strongest answer to institutional racism. Since the early 1990s crime in the 77th Precinct is down by nearly 80%. This reduction coincides with the NYPD's introduction in 1994 of COMPSTAT, which came on the heels of problem-solving and community-focused policing initiatives that had gained traction in the wake of the Buddy Boys scandal. There is little doubt that COMPSTAT's real time crime statistics combined with rapid deployment of personnel to problem spots made a huge dent in crime.[22]

COMPSTAT is also a stealth bomb against institutional racism. By making every precinct commander accountable for results, and by comparing everyone's results and the tactics used to achieve them, hiding places for ineptitude are systematically eliminated. Stereotypical excuses that blame the community for intractable crime conditions are also weakened.

In the mid-1980s crime statistics appeared in periodic, low profile reports inconsistently addressed by top commanders. A captain in a persistent high crime precinct like the 77th might be called to account only rarely and might well get off the hook with a "Well, you know, it's a tough neighborhood." By 1994, everybody's numbers were being examined every week and precinct commanders came downtown regularly to explain before their bosses and peers what they were doing about crime hot spots. Nobody got let off the hook, and a subtly racist answer like "You know the neighborhood" did not fly at all, especially since Captain Smith, in a similar neighborhood in the Bronx or Brooklyn, had made great strides in combating crime. The competition among precincts also helped stiffen the general resolve of commanders against "dumping ground" personnel policies that had helped create the Buddy Boys. Now that their career progress depended heavily on precinct performance, commanders had little or no interest in managing bands of misfits.

Finally, COMPSTAT crime statistics are public, placed on the Internet as they are made available to the NYPD. Disseminating information about public safety conditions empowers the community and allows the media and elected representatives to monitor disparities in service delivery, and to zero in for a closer look.

Managerial policies that mute manifestations of institutional racism in the business of policing need to be pursued. Though racially disparate impacts continue from decisions made in political and economic realms, this is not where a police chief can make a difference. The chief who isn't afraid to manage performance and confront personnel issues directly is in the forefront of the fight against the subtle racism that can permeate public institutions.

## Sexual Predators in the Pennsylvania State Police

Michael Evans was sexually obsessed. One fellow trooper described Evans as a "hormonal freak."[23] Evans had apparently been leaving similar impressions in his wake for years. One individual interviewed as part of Evans' background check noted his "strange sexual habits."[24] Once on the job, Evans, in uniform and on duty, initiated sexual contact with women in their cars, at their homes, in State Police barracks, just about anywhere the opportunity arose. And, driven as he was, Evans did not hesitate to leverage his position in order to make crude comments, take sexual license or establish sexual relationships with women he met during car stops or investigative interviews, including cases where women were alleging abuse or assault by a boyfriend or spouse.[25]

Some advances Evans made in uniform turned into short-lived affairs that later generated complaints. Other sexual approaches Evans made generated immediate complaints from the victims or, in one case, the parents of an underage victim. Some of Evans' dalliances took a while to come to the attention of investigators. One involved a prostitute whom he had induced to pose nude in front of a marked State Police cruiser.[26] State Police investigators may have been startled by the photos they found in his locker, but Evans' fellow officers, many of whom had seen them before, were not. On at least one occasion, another Trooper joined him in a sexual escapade, apparently consensual, with a woman at a State Police training facility.[27]

Evans was generating a raft of complaints but few made it to the Office of Professional Responsibility, the central internal affairs operation of the Pennsylvania State Police. Some complaints were ignored when complainants failed to follow up, or were dismissed as unfounded by Evans' superiors.[28] For other allegations, Evans' fellow officers or his superiors got in touch with complainants to suggest they reconsider,[29] sometimes gravely intoning the penalties for making a false charge. Women who still pressed on with charges needed patience and a high tolerance for indignation, since they could wait upwards of a year, only to see local commanders punish Evans with a short suspension for sexually harassing them while on duty.

Evans, however, was generating complaints faster than his superiors could make them go away or could obscure them in the fog of investigative process and administrative adjudication. And complaints weren't only coming from Evans' victims. A sergeant in the Norristown Police Department in Montgomery County complained that Evans was hitting on a young woman at the scene of a rape investigation.[30] Soon the Montgomery County District Attorney, in whose jurisdiction most of the complaints against Evans originated, had gotten several victims to press charges. Evans pled guilty in 2000 to charges ranging from indecent assault, to corrupting the morals of a minor and official oppression.[31]

Evans lost his job and went to jail but that was hardly the end of it. With many of his victims pursuing civil actions, their lawyers subpoenaed the records of the State Police regarding complaints of a sexual nature involving troopers. Over one hundred cases were produced spanning a period of five years and eighty-nine complaints ended up as trial exhibits. Troopers were threatening their spouses, harassing women encountered in the line of duty, sexually harassing subordinates, and having sex in cruisers. As with Evans, some complaints against these officers received zero follow-up while other complaints were subject to lackadaisical investigations and wrist slap penalties. Three recently retired State Police majors headed the list.

This new information turned the attention of the victims' lawyers towards the senior executives of the State Police, and their lawsuit named the commissioner, deputy commissioner for administration and the director of the Office of Professional Responsibility. The executives pled ignorance to the extent of the problem, citing the large number of cases that had been handled solely by local commanders or by investigators who worked out of the same barracks as the offending troopers. The plaintiffs' lawyers pointed out that a substantial number of complaints, including several involving Evans, were handled or reviewed at State Police headquarters with responses that differed little from that of local commanders.

The judge in the case agreed with the plaintiffs' lawyers, decreeing that the deputy commissioner for administration of the State Police and the director of the Bureau of Professional Responsibility could be held liable for damages suffered by the women Evans had abused.[32] This motivated the State of Pennsylvania toward a settlement prior to the case going to trial, with no admission of wrongdoing on the part of the State Police defendants. The state ended up paying nearly $6 million to compensate the women victimized by Evans.[33] There was, of course, a thorough housecleaning at State Police headquarters, and a new management team that soon instituted a zero tolerance policy toward sexual misconduct by troopers.

## Peer Privilege and Cultural Immunity

Here, in the Pennsylvania State Police, we see a culture that virtually winked at sexually deviant behavior as defined by the law, and did much to enable prototypical sexual harassment by officers leveraging the power of their position to obtain sexual favors from female civilians.[34]

What was going on here?

One immediate, summary judgment is the "Blue Wall of Silence." Cops (or troopers) cover for other cops, and that's that. This, however, is of little help to managers seeking to prevent an officer's damaging behavior from being accepted within the agency's police culture. Instead, such broad and stereotypical diagnoses of revealed organizational problems tend to elicit blunt-force, after-the-fact remedies: heads roll and zero tolerance policies are created while the cultural foundations of the problem stay in place. Without culture being a part of the diagnosis and cure, however, the next behavioral disaster is just around the corner.

Another handy response to the "What's going on here" question is to attribute the behavior of Evans and other troopers to "male chauvinist culture" or similar global analyses based on race, class or gender. A gender-based analysis certainly includes, as part of a larger society wide critique, the behaviors at the heart of the Pennsylvania State Police scandal. But broad social critiques are clumsy diagnostic tools for administrative practice, and perhaps perplexing ones as well. Some supervisors who helped stall complaints against Evans were women.

It is clear that operating level police cultures can and do give succor and shelter to sexually harassing officers, to corrupt officers, and to brutal officers who vent their continuously bubbling rage on random suspects. In the main, however, these things do not occur because the sheltering police cultures are dominated by belief systems inimical to women, or to integrity or to the use of the minimum necessary force against suspects. These things occur because any operating level police culture is, first and foremost, FOR the protection of members in good standing, whatever they might do. There are limits to this, which Evans definitely tested by eliciting complaints and what should have been damning employment references from other law enforcement officers. But, on the whole, things usually must blow sky high in order to expose the destructive potential lurking in a Michael Evans, a William Gallagher or a Rafael Perez.

Evans was sheltered because his co-workers, most of whom were aware of the sexual obsessions that Evans did little to hide, had little interest in turning him in. Now this is, indeed, a manifestation of the "Blue Wall of Silence." But it is useful to look at how the foundations of "The Wall" get established in a police agency's operating level culture. Police officers, the great majority of whom are acting in good faith, will occasionally find themselves operating close to the margin that separates acceptable and unacceptable behavior. These marginal actions generate reports, either routinely or in response to complaints. As these reports go up the chain of command, officers and supervisors hold their breaths, ready to get "jammed up" if higher-ups see them as over the line. If nothing happens, everybody breathes a sigh of relief. If discipline is initiated, members of the operating level culture see it mostly as unfair persecution of a cop "just doing his or her job." In either case, the outcome reinforces the determination to avoid exposing their colleagues to a capricious disciplinary system they distrust.

As a result, operating level police cultures adopt attitudes and behavioral norms that protect the egregiously guilty along with the "innocent" transgressors and the wrongly accused. Evans becomes a "hormonal freak," a sort of excusable, even fascinating fellow whose behaviors hardly warrant a report to superiors. A brutality-prone cop is seen as a "tough guy" or an alcoholic cop gets characterized as a hard-drinking prodigy rather than as a danger to himself and others. A spouse abuser is seen as "having the usual marital problems." All the stories remain buried in the closet of the operating level culture—until they get out, often, as we have seen, tragically.

What is happening here is that *peer privilege* is being extended pretty much uncritically to all members of the operating level culture. Peer privilege means that rule-violating behavior by a member of a work group culture is excused, ignored or normalized by co-workers belonging to that culture. Peer privilege is not unique to police culture. Doctors often overlook the deadly faults of the most marginal members of their profession and may even punish others, such as nurses, who seem ready to blow the whistle on an incompetent physician.[35] And just about any teacher knows colleagues who should not be in a classroom but have been, for years, without a meaningful professional objection raised. The difference in policing, and in medicine for that matter, is that a very high price is paid for the mistakes of a very flawed, yet peer privileged, member of the work group culture.

Evans not only enjoyed peer privilege, he was also granted a degree of immunity by supervisors. Some supervisors did this passively, waiting out the extended complaint handling process and taking no action if complainants dropped out along the way. Other supervisors were more active, interceding with complainants to discuss alternatives to filing charges. But, in either case, the effect was protective of Evans. Evans was also shielded to an extent by field internal affairs investigations that began and ended at the barracks level, producing exoneration or light recommended penalties.

To understand these full and partial immunities enjoyed by Evans we need to understand two things. The first is the strength and staying power of the operating level culture. There were majors whose cases were exposed during litigation who were treated no less protectively by their bosses than Evans was by his. Whether officers move up in rank or move over to Internal Affairs, their operating level experience is almost certain to have provided the longest and most intense work culture socialization. This is a major reason for taking promoted individuals out of their former work group—the ties of solidarity are often stronger than the tenets of supervision. This brings us to the second thing. Pennsylvania is a very big state, with barracks separated by upwards of one hundred miles. Pennsylvania State Police officers, supervisors and internal investigators may well spend most of their career operating out of one or two barracks in a single region of the state.

Being deployed with the same individuals for years on end gives the operating level work culture substantial staying power even with those who ascend the ranks or move over to specialized units such as Internal Affairs. The view of Evans as a relatively harmless "hormonal freak" clearly had some currency even among the supervisors who were there to discipline him and probably among the investigators who were there to document his behavior independently of those supervisors. In a similar vein, the Buddy Boys and the "Gangsta" cops of Rampart CRASH tended to be looked upon as "peculiar" and "different," as opposed to "perverse" and "dangerous."

## Dealing with Deviant Employees and Enabling Cultures

Evans left a long paper trail, but it was scattered all about the Pennsylvania State Police. You could learn something negative about Evans by looking in central personnel files, in reports down in the local barracks or in the Bureau of Professional Responsibility offices in Harrisburg. But you wouldn't learn about all of Evans' documented problems unless you went to all three places and pieced everything together. The average citizen couldn't manage this, and neither could the Pennsylvania State Police.

The importance of centralized and complete information about personnel as an antidote to the protection of members by a work group culture is clear.

Since work group cultures are strongly disposed to hold on to information that might hurt a member, alternative sources of information need to be aggressively mined, recorded, stored and rendered accessible. In response to the discovery of inept and even homicidal physicians who continued to practice, there is now a national data bank of information about physicians with problematic histories. In Pennsylvania, the State Police now have centralized information from various personnel and investigative files on employees.[36]

Internal Affairs investigations in the Pennsylvania State Police are now centralized as well. This takes the fate of aberrant officers out of the hands of those who work most closely with them. It is now also a requirement that a record of all complaints be forwarded to headquarters. This is to prevent officer offenses from falling off the radar because victims don't follow-up or fail to correctly complete complaint forms, each of which was an issue in the Evans case. The mandatory referrals ended what the Evans case highlighted as an embarrassing exemption enjoyed by the state police. Whereas any teacher accused of molesting 14- and 15-year-old students was automatically subject to high level review, his supervisors could and did exercise discretion as to whether similar complaints against Evans would be reported upwards.

The Pennsylvania State Police are also working toward a uniform system of penalties for officer misconduct—one sanction requires termination for any proven sexual offense. This adoption of uniformity may actually soften the rank-and-file's principled opposition to command discipline. The arbitrary and uneven application of penalties is a key element in the reflexively oppositional stance that police work groups take towards disciplinary processes. In Pennsylvania, this attitude was based in reality. Major Jones of the Pittsburgh Barracks might suspend somebody for a month for failing to safeguard a crime scene, while Major Walker of the Philadelphia Barracks might hand down a reprimand for the same offense. Major Jones might never know what Major Walker had done and vice versa, but the troopers across the state sure knew. So did police union lawyers, who usually convinced state arbitrators to let officers off with the most lenient penalty for offenses where local commanders had been inconsistent in their discipline.

Managers of law enforcement organizations also need to carefully frame the offenses of deviant employees so that operating level cultures do not simply close ranks behind miscreants. This is best done by framing the aberrant behaviors as offenses against the badge and the law enforcement community, rather than against an individual rule or overall administrative process. Law enforcement personnel care about their profession to a much greater degree than they care about administration. After scandals involving criminal cops break, their peers are usually quite vocal in expressing how the badge and the profession have been shamed. The trick is to make this righteous indignation proactive and preventative rather than reactive. One step in this direction is integrity training that, regardless of the specific issue, has a global emphasis that stresses everyone's role in assuring that law enforcement is seen as legitimate in the larger community.

Topical sensitivity training also can play a role in shaping the beliefs of workplace cultures. No doubt Evans' peers could have used a deeper understanding of the nature and impacts of sexual harassment. Sensitivity training has the positive effect of raising consciousness but needs to be reinforced in practice. If such training is looked at as a rote exercise, officers shrug off the message and bosses move on to other things because the message has been sent. Finally, sensitivity training on race or gender is only part of the answer, since the general dynamics of workgroup culture operate independent of any "-ism."

## New Orleans: The Perfect Storm

New Orleans is renowned for the anything goes revelry of Mardi Gras and its "Let the good times roll" attitude the rest of the year. The city also became a poster child for natural disasters when Hurricane Katrina blew through in 2005. A delayed evacuation order left too many in harm's way. The storm came with furious winds and rain that inflicted major damage. Getting around, or out of, New Orleans became impossible. Power went down. Then the levees broke, flooding much of New Orleans proper.

City government, its communications in disarray, came to a standstill. State authorities, awaiting word from municipalities blown off the grid, did little at first and then had problems moving resources to the New Orleans region. Representing the federal government, the Federal Emergency Management Agency (FEMA) lost precious time waiting for a bureaucratically correct invite from stunned Louisiana authorities, and then stumbled into action with decisions that bottled up relief personnel and resources. It didn't help that FEMA's Director appeared unequal to the task, even as President George Bush was praising him. Few in government, excepting the military and U.S. Coast Guard officials ultimately put in charge of relief efforts, came out of Katrina looking good.

The New Orleans Police Department (NOPD) was on the ugly list. Upwards of 200 officers were AWOL, some couldn't get to work but others just walked off the job to fend for themselves or their families. MSNBC videotaped officers who appeared to be looting a Wal-Mart.[37] The NOPD later declared this an authorized mercy mission to replace officers' wet clothes but did discipline an officer for being disrespectful—to the MSNBC correspondent—

and suspended four of the involved officers for ignoring the rampant looting going on around them.[38]

Other officers, responding to looting, general disorder and reported crimes, waded in with excessive force. The resulting deaths and injuries to citizens were the focus of criminal and civil court cases through 2012. In 2011, in regard to a single incident, a federal jury convicted four officers on civil rights charges revolving around the killing and wounding of unarmed citizens, as well as on charges that those officers, along with another, tried to cover-up what had occurred.[39] Five other officers had earlier pled guilty to federal charges stemming from this same incident, which we will explore in detail below.[40]

During and right after Hurricane Katrina, NOPD's failures owed some of their extreme edge to the unprecedented disaster. However, the wrongs police committed under Katrina's spotlight were not far out of character for a force whose dismal reputation went back decades and didn't get much better post-2005. This reputation had a lot to do with NOPD officers being tried and convicted for crimes including sexual assault, kidnapping, drug dealing, bank robbery and contract murder;[41] but also with the high rate of civilian complaints against officers regarding brutality, capricious enforcement and corrupt acts.[42] This freewheeling culture endured regardless of who was in charge, including "reform" chiefs brought in because of their successes at other problematic agencies.

In 2010, a new mayor was sworn in who promised to reform the New Orleans Police Department. Mayor Mitch Landrieu brought in Ronal Serpas as the new Superintendent. Serpas, metropolitan Nashville's police chief, had implemented COMPSTAT as NOPD's Chief of Operations a decade earlier.[43] The mayor and the new police superintendent announced they would work with the U.S. Department of Justice to forge an effective consent decree regarding the department, whose operations were ultimately judged dysfunctional by a federal investigation then underway. And the new superintendent announced that the FBI had agreed to assign two agents to work full-time in the department's Public Integrity Bureau on issues of civil rights violations and official corruption.

## Death on the Danziger Bridge

As rare as it is for any police agency, or any organization for that matter, to invite in outsiders full-time to keep tabs on possible wrongdoing, this was not the FBI's first time in residence at the NOPD. The Department also had FBI agents on board during the 1990s in the wake of high-profile corruption cases and concerns about a deep-seated departmental culture enabling corruption, brutality and an almost studied disdain for lawful policing.[44] To address these concerns the NOPD even brought in the Marines, as well as U.S. Department of Justice and State Police officials, to conduct executive training in leadership and ethics.[45]

Though the NOPD in the 1990s set about to reform its practices and personnel, including a new chief from outside the Department, embarrassing scandals did not go away. In fact, allegations and indictments against police officers shortly before Katrina struck sounded a lot like the 1990s. Just a week before Katrina, a woman alleged that a traffic stop led to a sexual assault in the police cruiser, which the officer had driven some distance away after ordering her to get in. The officer, charged with rape and kidnapping, was ultimately acquitted,[46] with the jury buying his claim that the on-duty sexual encounter after the car stop was consensual. One month before Katrina, police brought a severely injured and dying man to the hospital, as the result of a "medical incident," according to police. Witnesses saw something different, a gratuitous and out-of-control police beating, which resulted in federal charges, and convictions in 2011 against two officers.[47]

Given the department's history, the paralyzing punch of Katrina did not bode well for the NOPD. Station houses were flooded, uniforms ruined or inaccessible, most cruisers were disabled, command and control centers were non-functional and communications were down. With most of the structure their agency provided stripped away, what officers had left was the rank and file culture that had seemed all too accepting of bad behavior by cops in the best of times. And Katrina was the worst of times

Equal opportunity chaos reigned. Officers' families were at risk and/or unreachable and this exerted a tremendous pull on officers. That some officers then abandoned their sworn duties is understandable, though not forgivable given their critical public safety role during the disaster. Most of their colleagues stayed on the job, acquitting themselves and living up to their oaths by rescuing the stranded and maintaining some semblance of order.

Order maintenance was a mostly thankless task for the police called on to control thousands of people suddenly thrown together in near primal conditions at hastily created evacuation centers such as the Superdome. Many of these instant refugees were justifiably angry at "government." Often police, though blameless for the conditions, were the only visible government presence at which to vent.

Beyond the Superdome, looters were at work in shuttered businesses throughout the city. Some looters, suddenly homeless, were in search of basics like food and clothing; others, whose homes may well have been intact, emerged through the same shattered storefronts carrying major electronics. Distinctions regarding this looting were not easy to make and strong anti-looting statements by officials made it harder.

From the perspective of officers left to their own devices in Katrina's alternative universe, things were spiraling dangerously out of control—crowds seemingly on the verge of busting loose glared at them, waves of looters committed felonies in front of their noses, and little direction was forthcoming from the department's incapacitated command structure. Only the thin line of officers deployed on the streets, it seemed, was dealing with the tragedy, desperation and crime. The traumatic stressors for police were high. Thrown together, often un-uniformed, driving commandeered vehicles, working round the clock in high-intensity circumstances and largely cut off from command and control, bad things were sure to happen—and they did.

Six days into Katrina's aftermath, an officer on the bridge carrying Interstate 10 over New Orleans' Industrial Canal radioed that shots were being fired in the vicinity of police underneath the nearby Danziger Bridge. Hearing this, at least nine officers piled into a commandeered rental truck and sped off to the Danziger Bridge, arriving with guns ablaze from driver and passenger side windows. The first warning shots by the officer driving the truck had caused people on the bridge to scatter. When the truck halted at the foot of the bridge and cops poured out unleashing a fusillade of bullets, their focus became an unarmed family of five who, along with a family friend, had been pushing a shopping cart on the bridge. The family scattered, some taking cover behind the concrete barrier separating the roadway from the pedestrian walkway, the youngest leaping off the bridge and fleeing underneath as police bullets flew. Only the leaper was unscathed. The family friend was dead. The other four family members, each with serious, multiple gunshot wounds, were hospitalized and charged with attempted murder.

The amped-up cops spotted two other individuals further along towards the crest of the bridge. At least one of the officers opened fire and his targets proceeded to run down the far side of the bridge. Once again in the truck, the officers drove to the crest of the bridge to re-establish a sightline, and there hooked up with a state trooper who had just arrived in an unmarked car. The pursuit resumed in the trooper's car, zeroing in on two fleeing and unarmed individuals, one of whom officers shot dead in the back. The survivor, uninjured, was arrested and also charged with attempted murder.

That's what happened,[48] but not how the initial police report, or its follow-up, portrayed events. According to the report, the radio transmission said cops had been shot, and that the armed perpetrators had been seen fleeing across the bridge. The police report had officers arriving at the bridge only to face concerted fire from these individuals, at least four of whom were armed. Five suspects went down in a blazing firefight near the foot of the bridge, said the report. The report said another two suspects had backed up to the crest of the bridge while firing at the officers, thus drawing the officers' pursuit and return fire that killed one suspect at the far end of the bridge. Pursuing officers saw suspects tossing several guns off the bridge to grassy areas below, as well as into the water. A single recovered revolver was entered into evidence more than a month later.

In the initial version of the report, the civilians on the bridge were cited for eight instances of attempted murder of a police officer. By the time a more detailed report emerged, the attempted murders had jumped to thirteen: More officers had weighed in corroborating their exposure to the deadly fire unleashed by the suspects. A sheriff's deputy from an outlying parish was one alleged target, having raced on foot to the Danziger Bridge from high on the I-10 Bridge, three football fields away, to get after the suspects, whom he identified as having shot in his direction. Investigators also took down, but did not have the equipment to record, witness statements from civilians who observed that the suspects appeared to be armed. Transient and displaced by the storm, these witnesses didn't hang around for later questioning since they were relocating out of state, exact destination uncertain.

What the official story had going for it was the number and consistency of the police witnesses. Not only had all the cops interviewed for the first report seen essentially the same event, so had other cops who were interviewed for the second version of the report. That second report also cleared up some communications issues, the radio transmission that started it all had suggested, not declared, that cops had been shot. But that revision was minor in relation to the hail of gunfire to which every police officer at or anywhere near the incident could attest, and which several civilian witnesses corroborated.

As criminal cases moved forward against the civilians on the bridge, gaping holes appeared in the police version of events.[49] The deputy from the outlying parish was an imposter, with a criminal record to boot.[50] The truck, presumably bullet-scarred by the incoming fire police took as they emerged from the vehicle, was nowhere to be found.[51] Neither were the civilian witnesses; several later turned out to be fictional. The single recovered weapon from a blazing firefight raised eyebrows and, as it turned out, the gun had been planted by one of the investigating officers.[52] And the two 'gunmen' fleeing over the bridge were very unlikely suspects. One, the survivor, was a college grad continuously employed by FedEx for more than two decades. His brother, who police shot dead, was a mentally disabled, simple individual sheltered by the family throughout his adult life.[53]

As the criminal cases against the surviving suspects grew weaker and their civil cases against the NOPD gathered steam, the tables turned. Seven officers were indicted at the end of 2006 by a state grand jury on first degree murder and attempted murder charges. At the same time the grand jury cleared Lance Madison, the FedEx employee, of the eight counts of attempted murder filed against him for the Danziger Bridge incident.[54] When the charged officers arrived at court to enter pleas, they were accompanied by a phalanx of NOPD officers loudly proclaiming their support.

The criminal district court judge hearing the case against the officers threw out all charges a year and half later, determining there had been prosecutorial misconduct in the leak of two lines of grand jury testimony to a police supervisor and rejecting the DA's argument that a contempt of court citation would have been more appropriate than a wholesale dismissal of charges.[55] But that dismissal generated sufficient impetus to land the case in the laps of federal prosecutors who could pursue the officers' conduct as civil rights violations and other federal crimes. The multiple prosecutions that emerged from the federal investigations revealed a widespread and systematic cover-up, and led, starting in 2010, to either guilty pleas or convictions for most of the officers involved in the Danziger Bridge shooting as well as other officers who played a role in the investigation/cover-up of the incident.

On April 4th, 2012 four of the officers convicted in the shootings were given sentences ranging from 38 to 65 years, while the sergeant who was at the center of the cover-up received a six-year sentence. Five other officers, three involved in the shootings and two others in the cover-up, got lighter sentences after cooperating with the prosecution and entering pleas.[56]

## Battling Intractable Culture

Police corruption in New Orleans grows in rich soil. Louisiana's political culture, going back nearly a century, has been pock-marked by corruption, ensnaring governors and other elected officials, whose popularity often was undiminished, suggesting a co-dependency with a citizenry either resigned to, or secretly admiring, public servants who find ways of profiting from office. Such is the history that an ABA Journal article could lead off with "a political corruption trial is old hat in Louisiana."[57] The trial in question involved gambling man Edwin Edwards, four-time Louisiana governor who, in between victories, was indicted about as often as he ran, with a proud part of his platform being how little prosecutors had to show for twenty-two grand jury investigations and four indictments, though they finally got their man in 2000.[58]

Nearly a decade later, after a 2009 trial, New Orleans Congressman William Jefferson — "Dollar Bill" to Louisiana political insiders — also went off to jail in a case highlighted by Jefferson's videotaped acceptance in 2006 of a $100,000 bribe in marked bills, $90,000 of which was soon recovered from a freezer in his home. None of this interfered with his reelection that year.

Louisiana's public service, public safety included, was hobbled by more than poor executive and legislative role models. As a 1996 New York Times Magazine article noted, a criminal record was not rarity among NOPD recruits.[59] Once on the job, officers in New Orleans were allowed to work second jobs, called details, providing security at bars, restaurants, strip clubs, music venues and other businesses serving the "Big Easy's" party-hearty visitors. Most officers moonlighted extensively, which made policing more like a side job, with private security becoming their "day job." In a city where civil servants, including police, were paid little, bribery, rule-bending and turning a blind official eye were not an uncommon way of doing business, and moon-lighting officers could sometimes work both sides of the "shakedown" equation.

The 1996 New York Times article seemed like a watershed moment. The analysis of the NOPD's flaws was scathing. The article quoted federal sources estimating that 10%–15% of New Orleans officers were corrupt, but unnamed NOPD insiders considered those percentages too low by half.[60] Nor was corruption the only issue. Relative to other urban police departments, brutality complaints against the NOPD were very high and the New Orleans' murder rate stood at the top of the 1990s class.[61]

In 1994 as in 2010, New Orleans had elected a mayor, Marc Morial, committed to reforming the NOPD. Richard Pennington, a Washington, D.C., police executive, was brought in to do just that, and his baptism by fire was a major focus of the New York Times Magazine piece. Pennington was the second "outsider" to lead the department. The first, in the 1970s, resigned in frustration after two years, convinced that a brutal police rampage against a black community had as much to do with getting rid of him as it did with delivering street justice for the death of an officer.

Pennington understood the reach of the NOPD culture. Those side jobs most cops had were not only moneymakers but sources of power and influence. An ordinary cop with a lucrative off-hours job at a club or sports arena could hook up his or her superior(s) with any new openings, which turned the on-the-job authority relationship upside down, making the subordinate harder to control or discipline. Pennington attempted to deal with this issue by limiting "detail hours" to twenty.[62] Then he went after bad cops, and tightened up recruitment. The in-house FBI agents for internal affairs were also Pennington's idea.

Pennington was trying to change a lot and persevered through 2002 when he resigned after a losing bid for mayor and was replaced by NOPD veteran Eddie Compass, who held the fort until Katrina hit. The incoming mayor, Ray Nagin, more business-minded than politically schooled or corruption-savvy, left the police pretty much alone, in which case, as the Times reporter had written in 1996, the New Orleans Police Department could be expected, "as always," to revert back to normal.[63] The headlines right before Katrina suggested this was so and, in the wake of the storm, police excesses, some captured by TV network videotape, added confirmation. Compass lasted exactly a month after Katrina hit. The storm stripped away his command and control, all the AWOL officers suggested a force melting away, and he had to deal with a barrage of charges against police ranging from homicide to assault to looting. He was replaced as superintendent by another New Orleans Police veteran, Warren Riley.[64]

Riley did some post-Katrina clean-up in the department. Administrative hearings were held for some 200 officers charged with being AWOL during Katrina, resulting in more than fifty dismissals after all the appeals and reviews were exhausted. New equipment and facilities replaced much of what Katrina had destroyed. Officer pay increased on Riley's watch, a significant development given how the department's historically low wages had driven most officers to side-jobs and some towards corruption.

When Mayor Nagin left office in 2010 Riley stepped down as Superintendent. It wasn't long before the new mayor, Mitch Landrieu, was characterizing the NOPD under Riley's leadership as "dysfunctional."[65] Landrieu was jumping on a crowded bandwagon. The Danziger Bridge police killings and cover-up were now front and center in federal court, as was other scandalous and criminal behavior by officers. A federal investigation of the department was underway. Even Riley began excoriating the Danziger defendants with a vigor matching his earlier defense of them before he became aware that the reports covering up their crimes were bogus.[66]

The Department of Justice report, released in 2011, was damning.[67] The report steered clear of Katrina-related incidents, including Danziger Bridge, on the grounds that conditions had been extraordinary and prosecutions were ongoing. The report began:

> The NOPD has long been a troubled agency. Basic elements of effective policing—clear policies, training, accountability, and confidence of the citizenry—have been absent for years. Far too often, officers show a lack of respect for the civil rights and dignity of the people of New Orleans. While the majority of the force is hardworking and committed to public safety, too many officers of every rank either do not understand or choose to ignore the boundaries of constitutional policing.[68]

The Justice Department report went on to make summary observations that might well have been lifted verbatim from the 1996 New York Times article. Little had changed, use of force being one example.

Our review of officer-involved shootings within just the last two years revealed many instances in which NOPD officers used deadly force contrary to NOPD policy or law. Despite the clear policy violations we observed, NOPD has not found that an officer-involved shooting violated policy in at least six years, and NOPD officials we spoke with could recall only one out-of-policy finding even before that time.[69]

It's worth noting that the Danziger Bridge incident fit the profile of a "no policy violation" officer-involved shooting. The report goes on.

We found a pattern of unreasonable less lethal force as well. We found that NOPD's canines were uncontrollable to the point where they repeatedly attacked their own handlers, compelling us to recommend immediate suspension of NOPD's use of canines to apprehend suspects. We found that officers use force against individuals, including persons in handcuffs, in circumstances that appeared not only unnecessary but deliberately retaliatory. We reviewed instances in which NOPD officers used significant force against mentally ill persons where it appeared that no use of force was justified.[70]

And investigations of use of force—what quality, what results? The Justice Department findings from a sampling of investigations from 2008–2010 suggest that the NOPD's nodding acceptance of the manufactured reports on the Danziger Bridge incident may not have been a matter of stupidity or blind faith in the officers. Even the error that ended the state murder trial of the Danziger Bridge officers—that brief but improper communication between a DA and NOPD supervisor—begs additional questions in light of the Justice Department's findings about how bureaucratic maneuvers within the NOPD inoculated officers facing homicide investigations for deadly use of force. The report noted,

Even the most serious uses of force, such as officer-involved shootings and in-custody deaths, are investigated inadequately or not at all. NOPD's mishandling of officer-involved shooting investigations was so blatant and egregious that it appeared intentional in some respects. For a time, NOPD had a practice of temporarily assigning officers who had been involved in officer-involved shootings to the Homicide Division, and then automatically deeming the statements officers provided to homicide investigators to be "compelled," effectively immunizing the use of these statements in any subsequent criminal investigation or prosecution. It is difficult to interpret this practice as anything other than a deliberate attempt to make it more difficult to criminally prosecute any officer in these cases.[71]

The report then focused on the "details," those moonlighting jobs that Superintendent Pennington had seen as so corrosive and corrupting fifteen years earlier, and had tried to limit.

> Virtually every officer works a Detail, wants to work a Detail, or at some point will have to rely on an officer who works a Detail. The effects of Details thus permeate the entire Department. It is widely acknowledged that NOPD's Detail system is corrupting; as stated by one close observer of the Department, the paid Detail system may be the "aorta of corruption" within NOPD. Our interviews with NOPD officers, meetings with other New Orleans-based law enforcement agencies, criminal justice system stakeholders, and the public, revealed that NOPD's Detail system was a significant contributing factor to both the perception and reality of NOPD as a dysfunctional organization.[72]

Other cases in this chapter have dealt with cultural deviance in pockets of one or another law enforcement agency: The Buddy Boys going rogue in a dumping ground precinct; Pennsylvania troopers winking at and enabling the sexual crimes of troubled colleagues; LAPD specialized anti-crime units whose intimidation policing model provided cover for officers who were working the dark side. The cultural deviance in the NOPD goes beyond any of that.

The damaging culture is systemic. It persists as a dominant force over decades. It outlasts reformers and outsmarts prosecutors. The culture benefits from its manipulation of bureaucratic mechanisms in ways that insures its status and immunizes its members. It thrives in a surrounding political environment so inured to corner cutting that it is not unusual for electoral and financial rewards to continue for jaunty officials caught elbow deep in the cookie jar.

So far in this chapter I've discussed ways to counter cultural deviance. In New Orleans these approaches have encountered difficulties. Performance management at the NOPD was in its infancy in 2002 when one unit boldly cooked its books to win a crime reduction award,[73] and the downgrading and misreporting of rape statistics was an issue as recently as 2009.[74] Avoiding concentrations of problematic officers is more difficult when many officers disdain "going by the book" in favor of what their culture dictates. Institutional racism can be fought with mindfulness when perpetrators are oblivious but is much harder to eradicate as a culturally sanctioned mindset for everyday operations.

As of March 2012, the federal consent decree regarding the NOPD had not been finalized and negotiations hit a snag when an assistant U.S. Attorney involved was revealed to have posted online comments under a pseudonym that were critical of the NOPD, which prompted a Fraternal Order of Police attorney to wonder whether the negotiations might have to start all over.[75]

Add this "back to square one" attitude to the historical intransigence of the NOPD culture and the repeated failure of reform, and one wonders if any consent decree could bring things under control. The situation almost begs for a law enforcement agency version of receivership. In the private sector, receiverships are imposed, whether or not a company's leadership or rank and file likes it, in order to secure a company's remaining assets, including its goodwill, in the face of existential threats such as bankruptcy. Receiverships have recently begun to be used to take over municipal governments and public authorities beset by major financial crises. Under a receivership such as the one imposed in 2010 on Central Falls, Rhode Island, there can be radical organizational and financial restructuring, personnel changes and reductions, and any other policy that might right the ship.[76] Though a consent decree for the New Orleans Police Department really needn't go that far, the protracted negotiations indicate that whatever is agreed upon might not move very far at all from a center of gravity long-dominated by the NOPD culture. And that would almost certainly mean, down the road, little real change in a New Orleans Police Department whose severe dysfunctions stretch back decades.

# Summary: Leading Means Managing Culture

This chapter has looked at the role culture plays in steering organizations onto the shoals of failure. This role is so critical that police executives are well advised to see themselves as much in the business of managing cultures as they are in the business of running a formal police organization. Police managers must continually scan the organization for evidence of subversive cultures operating outside the bounds of proper police practice. They should learn how to prevent the unique cultures of specialized units from drifting towards an autonomy and self-centeredness that impact negatively on the organization.

Under almost no circumstances should a police executive consider concentrating a large number of problem employees in a single location, which avoids confronting problems that should be dealt with today and sets off a ticking cultural time bomb all but certain to explode in the future. Police executives also need to get a good handle on the various cultural networks that snake through their departments. These networks can obstruct a whole range of initiatives, but also can be induced to sign on to programs that serve their interests. The police executive who diplomatically engages with an agency's cultural networks is more likely to formulate missions and plans that will work.

Finally, the police executive should cultivate an abiding sense of fairness. If he or she creates policies that dramatically shortchange one or another group of citizens, the message that those groups don't count is also being sent to the work group cultures delivering the department's services. The responsibility for institutional racism, or any other systematic discrimination in the organization's delivery or services, thus lies squarely on the shoulders of police executives. Similarly, chiefs and supervisors generally should strive always for even-handed, consistent application of discipline to employees. Doing so may not make allies of the operational level work groups upon which any police executive depends, but not doing so will certainly alienate a powerful culture capable of tying the organization into knots.

# Endnotes

1. William Bratton, with Peter Knobler, *Turnaround: How America's Top Cop Reversed the Crime Epidemic* (New York: Random House, 1998).

2. Arthur Niederhoffer, *Behind the Shield: The Police in Urban Society* (New York: Anchor Books, 1969): 50–51.

3. *LAPD Blues: The Story of the Los Angeles and the Corruption Scandal That Has Shaken the Once Great LAPD.* Prod. PBS http://www.pbs.org/wgbh/pages/frontline/shows/lapd/bare.html (Accessed May 1, 2005) This site, and the companion video, is a wide-ranging, vivid and hugely educational look into the Rampart scandal.

4. Rampart Independent Review Panel, *A Report to the Los Angeles Board of Police Commissioners Concerning the Operations, Policies and Procedures of the Los Angeles Police Department in the Wake of the Rampart Scandal* (Los Angeles, November 2000): 2.

5. Ibid.

6. Los Angeles Police Department, *Board of Inquiry Into the Rampart Corruption Incident Report* (Los Angeles: 2000): 62.

7. John P. Crank, *Understanding Police Culture* (Cincinnati, OH: Anderson, 1998): 282. Subcultures should take care, because the symbols can end up defining the action, which we see here.

8. Rampart Independent Review Panel, *Report to the Police Commissioners,* 9–10.

9. Ibid., 10.

10. Mike McAlary, *Buddy Boys: When Good Cops Turn Bad* (New York: Putnam, 1987): 89.

11. Ibid., 103.

12. Ibid., 98.

13. Ibid., 104.

14. Ibid., 86.

15. Ibid., 110–11.

16. Ibid., 81–82.

17. Ibid., 88.

18. Ibid., 34–38.

19. Herb Williams, "Rampant Corruption in the 77th PCT: A Study in Organizational Pathology," (Unpublished paper, John Jay College of Criminal Justice, May 2004).

20. McAlary, *Buddy Boys,* 111.

21. John P. Crank and Micheal Caldero, "The Production of Occupational Stress Among Police Officers: A Survey of Eight Municipal Police Organizations in Illinois," *Journal of Criminal Justice* 20: 344–47. This study showed that the rank-and-file need little urging to disdain management.

22. William J. Bratton and Vincent E. Henry, *The COMPSTAT Paradigm: Management Accountability in Policing, Business and the Public Sector* (Prospect Heights, Ill.: Waveland Press, 2002).

23. Nicole Weisensee Egan, "Pennsylvania Settles Two Evans Suits For $5 Million," *Philadelphia Daily News*, September 3, 2004.

24. Ibid.

25. Office of the Inspector General, Commonwealth of Pennsylvania, *Investigative Report on Sexual Harassment and Sexual Misconduct at the Pennsylvania State Police*, (Harrisburg: 2003): 3–5.

26. Ibid., 3.

27. Ibid., Appendix C.

28. Ibid., Appendix C, Chart of Complaints; Also, 13–14.

29. Ibid., 11.

30. Ibid., 13.

31. Nicole Weisensee Egan, "Ex-Trooper Cops a Plea," *Philadelphia Daily News*, October 4, 2000.

32. U.S. District Court, Eastern District of Pennsylvania, Maslow, et.al. v. Evans, et al., Memorandum Opinion and Order, J. Rufe, July 25, 2004.

33. Egan, "Pennsylvania Settles Two Suits."

34. Crank, *Understanding Police Culture*, 145.

35. James B. Stewart, *Blind Eye: How the Medical Establishment Let A Doctor Get Away With Murder* (New York: Simon and Schuster, 1999).

36. Samuel Walker, *The New World of Police Accountability* (Thousand Oaks, CA: Sage, 2005): 130.

37. _____, "Police Looting a Wal-Mart in New Orleans," Original MSNBC report by Martin Savidge, August 30, 2005. http://www.youtube.com/watch?v=cHcajIR-cBvA (Accessed March 18,2012).

38. _____, "New Orleans Police Officers Cleared of Looting," Associated Press, March 20, 2006. http://www.msnbc.msn.com/id/11920811/ns/us_news-katrina_the_long_road_back/t/new-orleans-police-officers-cleared-looting/ (Accessed March 18, 2012).

39. _____, "5 NOPD Officers Guilty in Post-Katrina Danziger Bridge Shootings, Cover-up," New Orleans Times-Picayune, August 5, 2011 http://www.nola.com/crime/index.ssf/2011/08/danziger_bridge_verdict_do_not.html (Accessed March 28, 2012).

40. Ibid.

41. Paul Keegan, "The Thinnest Blue Line," *New York Times Magazine*, March 31, 1996, 32.

42. Katie Moore, "Complaints High Against NOPD Officers," WWLTV.com, April 4, 2011. http://www.wwltv.com/news/complaintshighaboutnopd-119216154.html (Accessed April 1, 2012).

43. _____, "Biography of Superintendent of Police, Ronal W. Serpas, Ph.D.," City of New Orleans Website http://www.nola.gov/GOVERNMENT/NOPD/NOPD%20Home/Biography%20of%20Superintendent%20of%20Police%20Ronal%20W%20Serpas%20Ph%20D (Accessed March 30, 2012).

44. Paul Keegan, "The Thinnest Blue Line."

45. Federal Bureau of Investigation—New Orleans Division, "A Brief History," http://www.fbi.gov/neworleans/about-us/history-1 (Accessed March 31, 2012).

46. David Meeks, "Former NOPD Officer Cleared of Rape Charge," *New Orleans Times-Picayune*, April 15, 2007. http://blog.nola.com/times-picayune/2007/04/former_no_police_officer_clear.html (Accessed March 3, 2012).

47. _____, "Two New Orleans Cops Convicted in Death of Treme Man," *New Orleans Times-Picayune*, April 13, 2011 http://www.nola.com/crime/index.ssf/2011/04/2_new_orleans_cops_convicted_i.html (Accessed March 18, 2012).

48. Pro Publica, "Law and Disorder: After Katrina New Orleans Shot Frequently and Asked Few Questions," http://www.propublica.org/nola/case/topic/case-six (Accessed March 15, 2012). Pro Publica, in association with Frontline and the New Orleans Time-Picayune, assembled police reports, conducted interviews and followed for five years the unfolding of this case. My juxtaposed "actual" and "police" versions of the Danziger Bridge incident are drawn from these sources.

49. Laura Maggi, "New Orleans Police Department's Danziger Bridge Probe Full of Blanks," *New Orleans Times-Picayune*, February 18, 2007 http://www.nola.com/crime/index.ssf/2007/02/new_orleans_police_departments.html (Accessed March 16, 2012).

50. Ibid.

51. Ibid.

52. Gordon Russell, "Police Chief Warren Riley Shocked at News of Danziger Cover-up," New Orleans Times-Picayune, February 25, 2010 http://www.nola.com/crime/index.ssf/ 2010/02/police_chief_riley_shocked_at.html (Accessed March 16, 2012).

53. Maggi, "New Orleans Police Department's Danziger Bridge Probe Full of Blanks,"

54. Laura Maggi, "Seven New Orleans Cops Indicted in Killings on Danziger Bridge," *New Orleans Times-Picayune*, December 29, 2006 http://www.nola.com/crime/index.ssf/ 2006/12/7_no_cops_indicted_in_killings.html (Accessed, March 16, 2012).

55. Laura Maggi, "Charges rejected against Danziger 7," *New Orleans Times-Picayune*, August 13, 2008. http://www.nola.com/news/index.ssf/2008/08/charges_rejected_against_danzi.html (Accessed March 16, 2012).

56. Campbell Robertson, "5 Ex-Officers Sentenced in Post-Katrina Shootings," *New York Times*, April 5, 2012, A10.

57. Pamela Coyle, "Cajun Stew Brewing," ABA Journal, September 2000, 22.

58. Kevin Sack, "Former Louisiana Governor Guilty of Extortion on Casinos," *New York Times*, May 10, 2000, A26.

59. Paul Keegan, "The Thinnest Blue Line."

60. Ibid.

61. Ibid.

62. Ibid.

63. Ibid.

64. _____, "New Orleans Police Chief Resigns," Associated Press, September 29, 2005. http://www.msnbc.msn.com/id/9503273/ns/us_news-katrina_the_long_road_back/t/new-orleans-police-chief-resigns/#.T2ToKRGvhVI (Accessed March 17, 2012).

65. Bigad Shaban, "Mayor Landrieu Announces New Plan to Curb Gun Violence," WWLTV-New Orleans, July 16, 2010. http://www.msnbc.msn.com/id/9503273/ns/us_news-katrina_the_long_road_back/t/new-orleans-police-chief-resigns/#.T2ToKRGvhVI (Accessed March 17, 2012).

66. Gordon Russell, "Police Chief Warren Riley Shocked at News of Danziger Cover-up."

67. United States Department of Justice, Civil Rights Division, *Investigation of the New Orleans Police Department*, Washington, D.C., 2011.

68. Ibid., v.

69. Ibid., vi.

70. Ibid., vi.

71. Ibid., vii.

72. Ibid., xvi.

73. Brendan McCarthy, "New Study Calls into Question the Reliability of NYPD Crime Stats," *New Orleans Times-Picayune*, February 10, 2010 http://www.nola.com/crime/index.ssf/2010/02/new_study_calls_into_question.html (Accessed March 18, 2012).

74. Brendan McCarthy, "NOPD Admits Misreporting Rapes after TP Report," *New Orleans Times-Picayune*, May 1, 2009. http://www.nola.com/news/index.ssf/ 2009/05/ rape.html (Accessed March 18, 2012); Laura Maggi, "NOPD Downgrading of Rape Reports Raises Questions," New Orleans Times-Picayune, July 11, 2009 http://www.nola.com/ news/index.ssf/2009/07/nopd_downgrading_of_rape_repor.html (Accessed March 18, 2012).

75. Monica Hernandez, "Experts: U.S. Attorney Blogging Scandal Could Slow Negotiations to Reform NOPD," WWLTV-New Orleans, March 16, 2012 http://www.wwltv.com/ home/Experts-say-blogging-scandal-could-slow-negotiations-to-reform-NOPD-143021245.html (Accessed March 18, 2012).

76. _____, Receiver Eyes Eliminating Central Falls Mayor Post," Boston.com, March 13, 2012 http://www.boston.com/news/local/rhode_island/articles/2012/03/13/receiver_eyes_eliminating_central_falls_mayor_post/ (Accessed March 30, 2012).

# CHAPTER SIX

# INSTITUTIONALIZATION IN LAW ENFORCEMENT: RUNNING AGENCIES FOR THOSE WITHIN

We have looked at law enforcement organizations whose failures involve "normal accidents," where things go terribly wrong in carefully designed systems staffed by dedicated employees. We have also seen agencies that stumbled badly when their structures were ill-designed for the tasks at hand, or when necessary structural elements like hierarchy fueled dysfunctional behaviors that management failed to address in time to avert a debacle. Finally, we have learned that employee subcultures in police agencies can sustain attitudes and practices that undermine the very legitimacy of the law enforcement agency.

Because normal accidents and structural failures will invariably occur, organizations create oversight and quality control mechanisms to guard against them. But we have also learned that any oversight unit can be effectively neutralized in a variety of ways so that improper employee behavior goes unchecked, only to erupt as a scandal that severely damages the agency. As serious as these conditions are, a condition exists that combines many of the symptoms associated with structural failure, oversight failure and cultural deviance. The condition is institutionalization, which incorporates a range of problematic practices to create an organization that is at once pathology-prone and change-resistant.[1]

Phillip Selznick writes that, when institutionalization sets in, formal organizational goals have to compete with a highly developed system of "precedents, alliances, effective symbols and personal loyalties ... which transform the organization into something having sacred status to those within."[2] Selznick applied "institutionalization" in an organizational context while writing about the Tennessee Valley Authority (TVA). The TVA was given multistate authority by federal law to transform vast, rural areas of the South by building dams in order to provide electricity and control floods. The TVA did these things and soon assumed such a large and critical role in the region that state and local officials, as well as business and agricultural groups, were co-opted into going along with whatever the TVA chose to do, which increasingly became, first and foremost, what the TVA thought good for itself.

The institutionalized agency becomes arrogant and narcissistic. The institutionalized agency gets away with these behaviors—expressed by its employees, executives and core practices—because it is powerful enough to largely ignore the preferences of others. To get a more current perspective on institutionalization, let's look for a moment at urban public schools.

For decades, poorly performing urban public school systems managed to defy attempts at reform, and suburban public schools, which performed better than their urban counterparts, were hardly more attentive to legislators, students, parents and political executives who tried to give advice. And that thwarted advice was more than warranted. In New York City, for instance, the schools attended by children with the most severe economic and social problems were staffed by the least experienced teachers.[3] This was partly because the teacher's union and school system administrators agreed that teachers, based on seniority, could decide where they would teach. In Philadelphia, where a similar arrangement existed, unionized teachers and system administrators also, over the years, negotiated work contracts that reduced teacher time in class again and again, even as student performance stagnated and declined.[4]

Since the children, and more specifically poor and minority children, were on the losing end of these equations, their parents complained bitterly, newspaper editorials chided politely and even elected officials sometimes braved the ire of politically powerful teachers' unions by highlighting counterproductive education policies. School administrators and teachers, however, took the position, which from their standpoint was unassailable, that they were the professionals uniquely qualified to decide on all things educational.[5]

In this chapter we are going to look at powerful and/or sheltered law enforcement agencies where the executives, and their troops, adopted a similar posture in order to shut down outside scrutiny, reject reform proposals and continue doing as they pleased.

# Introspective, Insulated and Institutionalized

When we considered structural failure, oversight failure and cultural deviance, it was evident that these pathologies tended to thrive when they were overlooked, ignored, taken for granted or fatalistically accepted. Organizational pathologies are nourished by the shadows. Sunlight, as Supreme Court Justice Louis Brandeis once observed, is the best disinfectant. Yet, the institutionalized agency routinely tells outsiders, even those legally empowered to examine its workings or those affected daily by its actions, to stay out of its business. The FBI, which we shall examine in this chapter, has a history of fending off interference and inquiries that goes all the way back to J. Edgar Hoover, who ignored most Attorneys General and fought cold wars with others like Robert Kennedy, who thought that, as Hoover's superior, he could tell Hoover and the FBI what to do.[6]

Institutionalization draws a curtain around the inner workings of an agency. The more outside critics are headed off before getting within shouting distance, the less likely organization members are to question how they go about doing things. This is not to say that the employees of an institutionalized agency never agonize over a decision, or never acknowledge, to themselves at least, a mistake. But the members of an institutionalized agency believe firmly in the inherent goodness of their processes, their goals, their colleagues and their right to be largely free from outside intrusion.

And this is a pernicious mindset. With "institutionalized" thinking, a deeply flawed structure that is seen as "the way we arrange things" is likely to persist. From an institutionalized perspective, a "hear no evil, see no evil, speak no evil" oversight office is doing the right kind of job. Worst of all, deviant culture threatens to spread, with almost every member adopting attitudes and beliefs that are increasingly a handicap to effective performance in the changing world in which the agency operates.

Institutionalization sets the stage for endemic failures of performance in which the very ability of the organization to do its overall job—witness urban public schools—or a part of its job—witness the FBI Lab which we will discuss below—is seriously in doubt. Whereas normal accidents, structural failures, oversight lapses and cultural deviation are almost always treatable with targeted, localized interventions, institutionalization almost always requires a thoroughgoing, organization-wide makeover. Localized reforms aimed at a single institutionalization symptom almost always fail because the overall organization's commitment to the status quo—affirmed daily by word and deed—is strong enough to isolate, neutralize and even reverse topical cures.

We have been talking so far about professional privilege and political power setting the stage for institutionalization. Organizations also lapse into institutionalization when they operate in relatively stable worlds. IBM, through the early 1990s, was almost fatally institutionalized. Its business strategies, short-term tactics, internal relations and employee behaviors and attitudes were rooted in several decades (1950 to the early 1980s) of phenomenal growth during which IBM controlled upwards of 95% of the computer industry. IBM became deeply committed to the organizational practices and beliefs that helped establish its dominance.

IBM hardly noticed that its approach was ill-suited to the emergent micro-computing world of the late 1970s and early 1980s because the company's near monopoly kept profits up. With everything coming up roses, no one saw the rot at the roots. So IBM became a dinosaur, its practices geared to a bygone day. The management and employee culture was so focused on maintaining "the IBM way" that it not only underestimated threats from Microsoft but routinely marginalized those who suggested that IBM needed radical surgery to deal with swifter, younger, more imaginative competitors in a rapidly changing information technology market.[7]

Law enforcement agencies are prone to institutionalization for much the same reasons that IBM was. Law enforcement agencies operate in a world where many of the elements have considerable stability over time. Police in the United States have dealt with prosecutors from time immemorial—prosecutors predate the police in most jurisdictions. Throughout their long relationship, police have arrested suspects based on probable cause while prosecutors have assessed those arrests on whether the suspect's alleged crimes can be proven beyond a reasonable doubt. This disparity can cause contentious relations (recall the JonBenet Ramsey case) but demands little from either police or prosecutors in terms of major organizational changes or attitude adjustments.

Similarly, the constitutional strictures on police behavior are two centuries old and, though courts may modify police practice by requiring Miranda warnings or stricter rules for confessions, those changes do not upset basic organizational arrangements in law enforcement. But all other stability factors pale before the twin facts that (1) police agencies have monopoly status in the business of law enforcement and (2) crime fighting and public safety are held in high regard by the general public and most elected representatives.

This all means that, absent the type of disasters we have been considering so far, police agencies are under little external pressure to restructure their operations or rethink their approaches in any major way. Funding keeps coming, and so does affirmation from the parties that really count—the mayor, the media, the financiers in the legislature and most voters. So little changes in the basic way a given law enforcement agency does business. And if the chief is a student of J. Edgar Hoover, he or she will further insulate the agency with positive spin to the media, aggressive lobbying with the mayor, favors for legislators and continual assertions that policing is a job best left entirely in the hands of law enforcement professionals.

And what does an agency so insulated do? It takes care of itself, and its own, behind protective walls which few dare to assail and through which even fewer can see. And so we arrive at the definition of institutionalization.

**Institutionalization defined:** An organizational condition characterized by a widespread approach to tasks that hinges on maintaining employee status and preferences, and on insulating the organization from change and outside scrutiny.

Any organization is courting trouble when a preponderance of its units increasingly base their approach to customers or clients on what best serves the comfort or preferences of employees. This is as true of IBM as it is of the FBI. But the stakes are higher in law enforcement since the failures institutionalization produces may well shatter a police agency's legitimacy, along with the faith citizens have in their governments and public servants generally. And legitimacy, once lost, is regained only slowly, step by painful step.

Law enforcement managers guarding against the onset of institutionalization need a discerning eye. Their organizations, or units within their organizations, will naturally strive for dominance and certainty in the jobs they do. Achieving this is a positive thing but also begins to skirt a dangerous precipice. With success comes hubris, as well as self-satisfied employee comfort in the "tried and true" processes and roles that made them dominant. Increasingly, members of the organization see priority number one as maintaining their processes, their ways and each other. When this occurs, the organization invests little in searching for better practice and, more importantly, ignores the evolving views of communities, opinion-makers and elected representatives about how the agency should and should not conduct its business.

\* \* \*

Our first case study is about the FBI Lab, the original CSI whose highly technical operations and crime solving successes earned the admiration and defied the understanding of FBI superiors and the public alike. The freedom the lab thus enjoyed helped set the stage for a mighty fall that also dragged down the FBI.

The second case study concerns the New Jersey State Police, which became a poster child for racial profiling. The State Police, fortified by institutionalization, stuck to race-based profiling for years despite strictures from the State Attorney General's Office, court rulings condemning the practice, media exposes and growing outrage in minority communities.

The third case study in this chapter implicates the Central Intelligence Agency (CIA) and the FBI in harboring agent-traitors who, despite bizarre behavior and stark evidence pointing to their misdeeds, defied capture for more than a decade. The CIA-FBI spies endured, to the great detriment of the United States and their agencies because institutionalization can mask the faults of even the most subversive employees.

Finally, this chapter concludes by taking a look at institutionalization in the courts, including a Pennsylvania case where two judges engaged in toxic, criminal acts from which the reputation of their court will not soon recover.

## The FBI Lab Implodes

Fred Whitehurst, agent-chemist from the FBI Lab, faced an unhappy dilemma in May of 1989. He was in San Francisco to give court testimony at a trial for a man accused of trafficking in explosives. Whitehurst, at the request of prosecutors, had repeated tests done years earlier by another agent in the Lab who had tested for and found explosives residue on objects belonging to the defendant. That agent, Terry Rudolph, was also available to testify but prosecutors had reservations about his work. The judge, however, had disallowed the last minute substitution of Whitehurst. This presented Whitehurst, who had carefully reviewed all the earlier reports, with a crisis of conscience. He knew there were flaws in the original Lab analysis that would be used in court the next day against the defendant. Whitehurst was torn between loyalty to the FBI, as his employer, and the tenets and protocols he adhered to as a trained chemist.

Whitehurst resolved his dilemma by conveying his concerns about the original testing to the defense's explosives expert. The defendant was acquitted. Whitehurst became the subject of an FBI inquiry that was the first of many over the next seven years that ultimately revealed the full extent of deficient practice, and the need for thoroughgoing reform, at the FBI Lab.

But, in 1989, the target was Whitehurst, not the Lab. After an investigation lasting a year and a half, Whitehurst was suspended for seven days and put on six months probation for going to the defense, rather than up the chain of command, with his concerns.

The FBI punished the messenger but could not erase the message. The defeated prosecutors, one a former FBI agent, repeated it first. In a memo to the FBI after the San Francisco trial, prosecutors complained about being blind-sided by sloppy procedures, poor record-keeping and shaky testimony by the original agent-analyst.[8] The Lab's director, John Hicks, replied that he shared the prosecutors' concerns.[9] This led to a cursory audit of the analyst's work by Lab superiors. The probe found administrative shortcomings but otherwise exonerated Rudolph. Nonetheless, scrutiny of the lab was underway.[10]

One study of the Lab, begun in 1990, sought to determine the Lab's compliance with the accreditation standards of the American Society of Crime Laboratory Directors (ASCLD). This review by an ASCLD Committee revealed deficiencies that Lab management kept largely in-house. By asserting its intention to implement changes suggested by the study, Lab management mollified higher-ups in the Bureau, who had pressed for the study, and reassured the ASCLD, in which the Lab was a major player.

On a less global level, the Lab found itself returning time and again to the work of Terry Rudolph. That work kept resurfacing in problematic ways as different cases finally came to trial. So even though he had departed in 1988 for the FBI Academy in Quantico, Virginia, where he became a trainer for other forensic examiners from around the country, Rudolph was a recurring issue for the Lab. This prompted the FBI's Office of Professional Responsibility to order another audit of Rudolph's forensic work.

The audit was an eye-opener. Rudolph relied on short-cut methods, assumptions, naked-eye analysis and the substitution of memory for documentation which, when it wasn't "lost," simply hadn't been done in the first place. Cross-contamination procedures, intended to insure that an evidentiary sample of explosive powder was collected and tested in a way to keep it pure, ranged from sloppy to non-existent. Also lacking were regular verifications that equipment was properly calibrated and reporting accurate results. In fact, these verifications, routine for scales in a supermarket or pumps at a gas station, were something the Lab in general didn't do very well. Rudolph himself contended that the way he handled and analyzed evidence was more the rule than the exception at the FBI Lab.

From these inquiries there also emerged the outlines of an informal philosophy that had much to do with how the Lab was run. The FBI Crime Lab, though publicly and professionally committed to getting at the scientific truth about evidence, was staffed by individuals strongly disposed to facilitating fellow agents in efforts to help prosecutors get convictions against defendants. What criminal investigators believed to be the cause of a given crime would be transformed almost immediately by some Lab analysts into *the* governing theory that determined what evidence got analyzed and how, and what evidence got ignored or overlooked. The notes of Lab analysts, which could be weapons in the hands of the defense, often went missing or were minimal, cryptic and inscrutable so that trial outcomes were more likely to turn on court testimony. Some agent-analysts came to the Lab with little scientific training and even supervisors with such training came to "formal conclusions without acknowledging legitimate questions about their validity" and without appreciating "the importance of following authorized protocols."[11]

Though storm clouds were brewing, Lab management could use its professional expertise to deflect inquiries from on-high. Within the Bureau, only Lab managers could authoritatively answer questions about analyst qualifications or about whether particular forensic techniques were correctly carried out or appropriately applied. The FBI Lab dealt with matters beyond the ken of most Bureau superiors, who had little incentive and less ability to delve into mysteries like spectrographic analysis that the Lab appeared to handle so well. Before Whitehurst, complaints about the work of the Lab rarely elevated to executive levels of the FBI.

The FBI, as of 1992, seemed to have contained any damage from Whitehurst's charges, which had caused hardly a ripple outside the agency. But then the dam broke. The FBI Lab was publicly embarrassed in a succession of cases involving O.J. Simpson, Ruby Ridge, and the Oklahoma City bombing.

Defense experts came to trial knowing more than the Lab's experts about DNA analysis, how to determine the caliber of a fatal bullet, and just what ingredients were or were not in a particular explosive device. What these cases together showed was that the Lab was on the trailing edge, not the leading edge, in various areas of forensic science. Administratively, the FBI seemed even further behind the curve

The Inspector General of the Department of Justice, echoed by the FBI General Counsel's office, testified to Congress in 1997 that the FBI had allowed problems in the Lab to fester for nearly six years while failing to resolve multiple allegations of incompetence.[12]

Senator Charles Grassley observed that "systemic problems remain at the Lab ... because of a cultural disease within the FBI."[13] The Senator noted how Lab "science" had been distorted to help agents and prosecutors obtain convictions, concluding, "The FBI will not admit the problem exists."[14]

John Kelly and Phillip Wearne, in their book *Tainting Evidence*, summed it up.

"Convinced that it was the best, without any objective proof, certain that it made no mistakes, while refusing to publish the results of its own proficiency tests, the FBI Lab was incapable of investigating itself.... The Lab was undoubtedly one of the last redoubts of undiluted Hooverism in the FBI. No accountability, no monitoring, managed by agents, not scientists—it was the sort of environment were abuses could thrive and no one told tales."[15]

As for Fred Whitehurst, his 1990 suspension was the first of many disciplinary brushes with the FBI, the last of which kicked off in 1997 when he was placed on administrative leave, put under a gag order, and targeted with a criminal investigation for what had become his public revelations of the Lab's shortcomings. As happened after the San Francisco case in 1989, the FBI's most vigorous response was not to the Inspector General's extensive 1997 criticisms of the Lab and the Bureau; it was to the Inspector General's finding that some of Whitehurst's charges were exaggerated and/or unsubstantiated. This time the FBI did get rid of the messenger who, in his own words, " ... won in mediation. I won my salary and my retirement at a GS14 level, but I agreed to retire early. The government also agreed to pay the rest of my bills. I spent $124,000 on legal bills. They dropped the third criminal investigation they had thrown against me. And I retired."[16]

Terry Rudolph retired honorably at just about the same time, before the indictment of his work in the Inspector General's report could translate into any administrative action. Not that the FBI brass had ever been in hot pursuit of Rudolph, having followed-up one of the critical audits of his work with a mild verbal reprimand, accompanied by a five-hundred dollar bonus.[17]

## Mismanaging the Interface of Image and Reality

The FBI Lab had a great image. It also had big problems. Big problems and a great image rarely go together as long as the agency—or in this case, a major division thereof—receives meaningful external scrutiny and input. Scrutiny is necessary to expose the contradictions between image and reality. Giving leverage to input from external parties helps insure that problems that are identified are addressed and that progress is made towards a legitimate image of excellence.

In the absence of outsiders with leverage looking in, however, any imbalance between carefully hidden problems and an aggressively conveyed image of preeminence is likely to persist and worsen. The organizational value of a preeminent image is clear and very evident in the case of the FBI Lab. Through the 1980s, the Lab could hardly have been better regarded by its FBI superiors, the public, by its scientific peers and by the politicians who supported its work with budget funds and praise. The public acclaim was gratifying, and buttressed support for the FBI in Congress. Peer recognition from forensic scientists gave the FBI Lab unchallenged leadership in the field. Political support paid the bills and helped insulate the Lab and the Bureau. Superiors in the FBI gave carte blanche to a function they little understood but greatly appreciated because the Lab helped win cases.

Such an uncritical environment makes employees disinclined to stretch towards greater performance. In fact, the opposite is more likely. Marginal workers feel validated and capable performers grow careless. A Terry Rudolph can exude confidence about his work and expertise because even if his work degrades it makes little difference in successfully prosecuting cases, pleasing superiors, and being prominent in the forensic science field. Even major slipups have little consequence when the organization conspires to bury errors or sanitize them with carefully crafted justifications that satisfy the naïve and give cover to the complicit.

This drift toward mediocre performance and beyond puts the organization in a bind. Widespread or localized mediocrity that employees have normalized is not easily, nor in most cases quietly, reversed. Airing performance problems, however, undermines the agency's public façade of competence. So when problems emerge, a short term damage control strategy, which the FBI Lab adopted, is the internal review. This reaffirms the organization's special expertise, communicates an image of action and, most importantly, buys time for the institutionalized agency.

Time is the ally of entrenched forces in an institutionalized organization. Crises do pass. Public spotlights sweep towards other quarters. In time and out of the spotlight, a mistake-prone employee, like Rudolph, can be moved to a safer post. Problematic practices can be artfully modified to least disrupt the existing order, yet convey an image of reform. Stringing out internal review also stands a good chance of waiting out or wearing down critics. Reforms contemplated by top managers may drop off the radar when they depart. Big-time initiatives like gaining accreditation can be studied to death. If the agency retains powerful constituency support, buying time with minimal reform is usually enough to retain the privileges and prerogatives rooted in that support. But this is most often, as it was for the FBI Lab, an empty victory. Relying more and more on a façade that hides less and less substance paves the way for major collapse that can't be explained away and brings the organization to a painful day of reckoning.

## Self-Protection at the Institutionalized Agency

The Ruby Ridge case featured the FBI Lab as a minor player in a drama starring its parent agency. Ruby Ridge stands out as a signal example of institutionalization. The competence and image of the FBI as a whole was on trial. With the entire agency under threat, and specific individuals within the agency potential targets of criminal action, the energies of the FBI, and Lab staff, were often marshaled for self-protection. In the process, the FBI earned a contempt citation from the trial judge for obstruction of justice, assumed an adversarial role towards federal prosecutors and, in the case of the Lab, displayed a level of ineptitude and incompetence that, deliberately or not, sabotaged the case.[18]

For the FBI, the Ruby Ridge case was bad news from the start. A U.S. Marshal was shot dead on day one when surveillance of federal warrant violator Randy Weaver somehow turned into a firefight. Dead also on that first day, when the FBI was not present, was Weaver's fourteen year old son, and the family dog. A siege ensued with the Weavers and Kevin Harris, a family friend, holed up in their rural cabin. An FBI hostage rescue team was flown in and authorized to shoot any armed male outside the cabin on sight, which was a last minute change in the standard rules of engagement. Shoot on sight they did the very next day, the first shot wounding Randy Weaver who, along with Harris, fled back to the cabin. The next FBI sniper shot wounded Harris and killed Weaver's wife, Vicki, while she was holding their infant daughter.

Many things were wrong, some obvious, others less so. The collection of evidence at the scene was botched by FBI agents in multiple ways. Adding a mother clutching an infant to a list of fatalities that already included a US Marshall, a fourteen year old boy and his dog was a public relations nightmare. The "shoot to kill on sight" rules of engagement were, as the FBI itself later admitted, unconstitutional.[19] And these flawed rules of engagement had, according to Eugene Glenn, the Special Agent in charge at the scene, been cleared by higher ups at the Bureau's Criminal Investigative division.[20]

When the U.S. Attorney filed a broad array of charges against Randy Weaver and Kevin Harris in the death of the U.S. Marshall, everything about the FBI's role at Ruby Ridge—actions, orders, sketches, notes, conversations—had the potential of becoming a very public part of the trial record. This looming exposure turned the FBI from the prosecution's helpmate to nemesis and hostile witness.[21] Every copy of the Ruby Ridge "After Action Report," an internal FBI critique, was rounded up and destroyed, an obstruction of justice to which an FBI supervisor later pled guilty.[22] The Bureau told prosecutors that its mistakes, such as erroneous shooting diagrams, were not subject to discovery.[23] Testimony from agents and supervisors further muddied the murky circumstances under which the controversial rules of engagement were approved. The murder case went down in flames and so did relations between the FBI and the Justice Department.

Reverberations went on for years. The head of the Criminal Investigative Division became FBI Deputy Director in January 1995, just as he was being officially censured for managerial oversight failures in the Ruby Ridge incident.[24] To Eugene Glenn, the Special Agent in Charge at Ruby Ridge who had received a fifteen day suspension, the censure letter was unequal justice. Glenn wrote the Office of Professional Responsibility of the Department of Justice, alleging a high-level cover-up that included his superiors and the new deputy director, who Glenn believed had played a key role in revising the rules of engagement for Ruby Ridge.[25] This, in turn, fueled more investigations which, while they did not result in prosecutions, effectively ended several careers at the Bureau, including the Deputy Director's.

The Bureau's external relations also suffered. Ruby Ridge kicked off a Senate inquiry. Some agents, citing the Fifth Amendment, refused to testify.[26] Angry committee members characterized the testimony of the Lab's ballistic expert as embarrassing. A Justice Department Task Force Report was critical of the FBI, and its revised rules of engagement.[27]

In the Ruby Ridge case, the FBI was institutionally threatened. The way it did business was being probed; the behavior of loyal FBI agents and supervisors was under attack and potentially subject to criminal indictment. This intensified all the defense mechanisms associated with institutionalization. The agency fortified its perimeter, leaving even prosecutors on the outside. A broad claim of privilege was made, as exemplified by the agency's refusal to produce any "mistakes" that preceded final reports such as crime scene reconstructions. A document that could not be construed as a "draft," the After Action Report, simply disappeared. The strongly voiced doubts that Lab personnel expressed about identifying the bullet that killed Weaver's son temporarily stymied that avenue of inquiry. Then, however, prosecutors called on outside ballistic experts who quite handily did what FBI Lab experts claimed could not be done.[28]

Ranks closed on critical issues, such as the "shoot on sight" rules of engagement.[29] The FBI officials who approved the rules and personnel on down the line thought things had been done properly. Despite this, Justice Department investigators parsed out that the FBI legal counsel hadn't been consulted, the FBI's chief hostage negotiator had been left out of the loop early on and the language encouraging firing without warning or provocation was a major leap beyond existing use-of-force policies.

An institutionalized organization expects closed ranks. Agent Glenn's only transgression was violating this principle, and he was duly punished for his cover-up allegations. Like Whitehurst, Glenn broke ranks, went "outside," and exposed the Bureau to "embarrassment."

Embarrassment, to the institutionalized organization, comes from telling tales to outsiders that reveal things the organization cares not to broadcast. The mistake a Glenn or a Whitehurst makes is, fundamentally, neither operational nor a violation of a formal rule or process, though such transgressions may serve as a rationale for any punishment. The real transgression is in breaking ranks to reveal information that chips away at the organization's carefully maintained facade of professional competence. This transgression is only compounded when the revelation implicates loyal, long-term members of the organization, since tenured and comfortable organizational citizenship is a key foundation upon which institutionalization rests.

A final note in the Ruby Ridge Affair was struck in 2003. Several FBI officials flew cross-country in 1999 on the pretext of attending training but really to attend a retirement dinner for Larry Potts, who headed the Criminal Investigative Division during Ruby Ridge and was at the center of the controversy surrounding the "rules of engagement." Because the trips were charged to the Bureau, an investigation by the FBI's Office of Professional Responsibility (OPR) ensued. The Director of the OPR ended up on *60 Minutes* in 2002 to discuss resistance he encountered trying to get to the bottom of the "Pottsgate" affair. Retaliation against the OPR Director, the Justice Department Inspector General later found, followed swiftly when the FBI Deputy Director told assembled Bureau officials that the *60 Minutes* appearance had brought "discredit to the badge."[30]

## The Historical Roots of Institutionalization

An appreciation of its history helps us better understand why the FBI could play such an adversarial game against other elements in the government, close itself off so tightly and otherwise exhibit raging symptoms of institutionalization.

In 1924, J. Edgar Hoover had taken over a scandal-tinged, lightly regarded investigative agency. Hoover came in to "clean up Dodge" right after the high profile Teapot Dome scandal in which the Secretary of the Interior conspired with other administration officials to sell the oil from under public lands for personal profit. President Calvin Coolidge, a straight shooter and firm administrator, had inherited the Teapot Dome mess after President Warren G. Harding, a lackadaisical administrator with a skewed moral compass, had died in office.

The Teapot Dome scandal had been ignored by Harding's crony, Attorney General Harry Daugherty. Daugherty had also exposed the Justice Department, including the Bureau of Investigation, to external political influence regarding its administration and the appointment of personnel. Attorney General Harlan Fiske Stone was appointed by Coolidge to clean up the Justice Department and Stone, in turn, appointed Hoover to clean up the Bureau.

Hoover won a very high level of autonomy for the Bureau. Not the least of these grants of autonomy involved the personnel process, which the FBI controlled totally. The Bureau hired according to its standards. There were no appeals to the Civil Service Commission for agents who were disciplined, transferred or passed up for promotion. In Hoover's FBI, and still today, swift and sure punishment awaited those who crossed the line—especially, the bright, shining line called "embarrassing the Bureau."

This authority over personnel allowed Hoover and his successors to create and maintain an FBI workforce of very high uniformity and conformity. Such a workforce has tight cohesion built in and naturally closes ranks against outside threat. Even stragglers, with the exception of a Whitehurst—whom most in the agency considered foolhardy if not crazy—are highly motivated to fall in line by basic loyalty, not to mention discipline that is potentially limitless and difficult to appeal. Even true iconoclasts, like John O'Neill, who we discussed in the chapter three, could be torn between their strong beliefs and their loyalty to, and fear of, the Bureau.[31]

Hoover's legacy goes far beyond the personnel system. A peerless image maker, Hoover created an FBI of incorruptible crime fighters and, if that ideal fell short in practice, it certainly did not in the eyes of the public. As a lawyer skilled in the legislative process, Hoover dealt directly with Congress to secure greater FBI independence and increased appropriations. This helped the strong-willed Hoover fend off attempts to control the Bureau by its nominal parent agency, the Department of Justice.

And Hoover was quite capable of infuriating Attorneys General, especially those like Robert Kennedy, who were more interested in asserting control over the FBI. Hoover's response to Kennedy included private rages, thinly disguised blackmail attempts tied to the sex lives of Robert Kennedy and his brother the president, and subtle and not so subtle resistance to Robert Kennedy's initiatives.

Hoover, having styled the FBI as the "G-Men" or government's law enforcers, rabidly opposed most incursions on FBI turf by other agencies. His epic battles with the CIA over who would catch spies in the United States, as well as his feuds with Bureau of Narcotics head Harry Anslinger, legitimized a self-regarding, no holds barred approach when the interests of the FBI came into conflict with the interests of other agencies.

Hoover is long gone. His influence on the FBI is not. The FBI still runs its own personnel system, though aggrieved employees, now have additional, though somewhat risky, avenues of appeal. Attorneys General still encounter frustrations in controlling the FBI and its director, who is appointed by the president with the advice and consent of the Senate to a ten year term that outlasts that of political superiors. Hard-fought turf wars with other federal agencies continue, and the FBI-CIA struggle, which dates to 1947, played a real role in the U.S. government's pre-9/11 failure to draw a bead on terrorists who were in the country ready to do great harm.

So, the FBI continues to operate with legacy systems, attitudes and behaviors that help sustain institutionalization. So what happened at the FBI Lab—or, as we shall see further along, in Counterintelligence—is not surprising in light of the surrounding organizational dynamics.

Since 1996, the FBI has exposed up the Lab to greater scrutiny. This has been achieved by seeking and, in 1998, obtaining ASCLD accreditation. The Lab is now subject to periodic intense review by qualified outsiders loyal to the forensic science profession, rather than to the FBI. In addition to accreditation, professional scientists in the Lab have been given greater managerial control. Both of these measures serve as effective antidotes to the institutionalization that gripped the Lab through 1996.

Institutionalization can also be treated with one-shot leadership change, a common regimen that does not necessarily change the overall agency commitment to existing operating methods. The culture that sustains institutionalization remains in place, inviting relapses which, as we have seen, are likely.

The recidivist institutionalized agency often ends up with the strongest of medicines. That medicine is "court supervision," which, like accreditation reviews, trains a critical and authoritative external eye on suspect operations. Unlike accreditation by peers, however, supervision by judges and their special masters is continual, intrusive, often coercive and occasionally punitive. That was the ultimate medicine swallowed by our next institutionalization patient, the New Jersey State Police.

## Profiling on the New Jersey Turnpike

On April 23, 1998 a van carrying four young men was stopped by State Troopers on the New Jersey Turnpike. The van had been going 19 miles an hour over the speed limit, according to the two troopers who made the stop. With one trooper alongside the van and the other behind, the van accelerated backwards, which prompted the troopers to fire several shots into the van, wounding three of the occupants. A subsequent search of the van, and its occupants, uncovered no contraband and no weapons.

The men in the van were African American, except for one Hispanic. The troopers were white. If the stop was representative of the enforcement choices New Jersey State Troopers had been making on the Turnpike for over a decade, the actions of the troopers were based, at least in part, on race. No one waited very long to find out.

Al Sharpton soon led a group out on to the Atlantic City Expressway in a protest against the "racist" State Police policy of stopping motorists for "driving while black."[32] Ministers in predominantly African-American churches inveighed against racial profiling from the pulpit. The ACLU pointed to a 1996 New Jersey Court decision that found systematic bias in the stopping of minority motorists at the southern end of the turnpike.[33] Some pointed even further back to 1989 when the head of the Turnpike Authority wrote "sometimes a trooper stops somebody because he's black or Hispanic or 'looks suspicious' and he's a perfectly good citizen. I'm trying to stop this."[34]

Coincidentally, when the Turnpike CEO penned those words the troopers patrolling the road were learning from the Drug Enforcement Administration (DEA) how to profile drug couriers. This occurred as part of Operation Pipeline, which was an effort to intercept drug shipments on major highways such as I-95 from Florida to New York, the last leg of which runs through New Jersey along the turnpike. The profile was pretty complex and included, along with the ethnicity of the car's occupants, the number of occupants, their age, origin of the plates, type of car, whether it was a rental, time of day, five o'-clock shadows (beard stubble), occupants weary from a long haul, and other characteristics.[35]

For the troopers, the profiles were a mixed blessing. The profiles did turn up drug runners, and when they did, good things happened to the arresting troopers — commendations, pick of assignments, a bump in grade. But the profiles were also pretty complicated to apply. A trooper might sit around all day waiting for someone to drive by fitting all the criteria, or a driver might only fit a few criteria but observing Troopers knew "in their bones" that they had spotted a "drug trafficker."

In practice, the profile began to degrade. Troopers simplified things down to just a few of the profile factors, plus a good dose of trooper intuition. Down to, often, black, young and driving too nice a car, or some other very short list of variables, usually ending in African American or Hispanic. Increasingly, and increasingly out of proportion to their representation among turnpike drivers, African Americans and Hispanics were the subject of pretext stops — being pulled over for observed speeding violations or unsafe driving so that troopers can have a reason to more generally question the occupants or search the vehicle.[36] Pretext stops were particularly fruitful in New Jersey, which permitted consent searches. This meant that, if a trooper's "Mind if I look in the car?" got an affirmative shrug from a nervous driver, any contraband found was evidence that could be used against the car's occupants.

Because a less sophisticated profile was being applied, there were more stops without arrests but the arrests that did occur were good ones in terms of drug interdictions and in terms of the career boost those making the arrest enjoyed. As a result, profiling — as far as the troopers were concerned — was good, and it continued.

Profiling, however, was not viewed at all positively by African Americans and Hispanic Americans pulled out of a caravan of cars going over the speed limit, escorted to the side of the road, subjected to an interrogation with little relation to the vehicle laws, being asked to consent to a search, and then often getting a ticket for their troubles. These drivers felt, and not without good reason, that their major offense had been "driving while black."

By the mid-1990s, some of these drivers were in court seeking dismissal of their charges and complaining that their civil rights had been violated. In 1996, a judge, relying in part on statistical analyses concerning the race of drivers being pulled over in the state, found for a defendant who claimed that he had been stopped by State Police on the basis of racial profiling. This ruling in State vs. Soto was a shot across the bow of the profiling being practiced by the New Jersey State Police.

While the state appealed the ruling, various officials in the State Police and the Jersey Attorney General's office denied ever condoning racial profiling and vowed to eliminate any informal patrol practices that might constitute racial profiling. Yet racial profiling continued.

A State Police internal study found troopers still profiling minority motorists in contravention of the department's own policies despite the 1996 ruling. The report generated little administrative notice or action though considerable controversy surrounds whether high-level officials in the Attorney General's Office were aware of the report. Notice and action, however, came fast and furious in the wake of the van stop and the shooting of the minority passengers. The two troopers faced various charges, both departmental and criminal. They were ultimately acquitted of all but minor charges in court but admitted to doctoring their traffic stop documents to underreport the number of minority motorists they had pulled over, and were terminated.

As this was going on, the Superintendent of the New Jersey State Police went on radio and talked about what he saw as the obvious connections between certain ethnic groups and particular types of crime. This really blew the lid off. The New York Times speculated that, if this was what the Superintendent, a career trooper, was thinking, there might well be a pervasive mindset in the department supportive of racially skewed enforcement.[37] Civil rights activists, community leaders and the American Civil Liberties Union were not nearly so reserved in their criticisms. New Jersey Governor Christine Todd Whitman sacked the Superintendent within days. Shortly thereafter, the Governor and the Attorney General announced their discovery that racial profiling by the State Police was still going on.[38]

The ACLU, among others, had already filed suit in federal court when these admissions came. Given the admission by the Governor and Attorney General, that suit was quickly settled. So, as the millennium dawned, the New Jersey State Police found itself closely monitored by the United States Department of Justice under a consent decree designed to end practices that systematically targeted minority drivers or subjected them to a disproportionate percentage of stops.

## Institutionalizing Problematic Practice

The *New York Times* was on to something. There was a pervasive mindset in the New Jersey State Police supportive of racially skewed enforcement. A search for organizational factors influencing that mindset brings us pretty quickly to this: For those within the New Jersey State Police, profiling worked.

Profiling, even in its degraded form, worked because it produced good arrests often enough to (1) confirm the broad stereotypes troopers held about connections between ethnicity and certain crimes and (2) produce real rewards for troopers that served as positive feedback with respect to their profiling practices.

When we framed the concept of institutionalization at the beginning of the chapter, we emphasized that the condition was firmly rooted in "a widespread approach to tasks that hinges on maintaining employee status and preferences." Institutionalization is strongly indicated by the persistence of practices that primarily serve organization members. Institutionalization is all but certain when those employee-centric practices hurt clients and handicap the agency.

Let's rotate back to an educational example to illustrate this. College teachers embrace passionately their general freedom to express their educated views. This professional prerogative certainly applies to research and writing but faculty in many colleges interpret academic freedom as granting them wide discretion in putting together their individual versions of a widely taught course. This is wonderful for the teachers. It gives them the choice of innovating, which takes some curriculum development work, or teaching the same stuff year after year, which doesn't. They can use an old book, with which they are familiar, or move up to a new book, with which they are not. Depending on his or her worldview, a given teacher might take a critical or supportive view of the course's subject matter.

While this situation is wonderful for teachers, it is not nearly so wonderful for students who, when they sign up for a particular section of a widely taught course—let's say Introduction to Criminal Justice—may be unwittingly rolling the dice relative to exactly what course they are going to get. Section by section autonomy also less wonderfully serves organization-wide goals, such as writing proficiency for all students, since the same logic of autonomy that grounds textbook choices and subject matter selection also governs whether students will be assessed by multiple choice exams or writing intensive essays and term papers with detailed feedback from the teacher. Be that as it may, when faculty members interpret the principle of academic freedom as incorporating their right to freely customize courses, most sensible administrators steer a wide path around the issue and students have little say about classroom product anyway. The practice continues because it is linked to prerogatives and preferences of powerful organizational actors, in this case the faculty.

I know from painful experience that when the issue of course customization is highlighted in this way, faculty will advance a thoroughgoing and often indignant defense. Similarly, when the New Jersey State Police were accused of racial profiling, the defenses came fast and furious, ranging from denial—which tended not to hold up given emerging facts—to justifications for race-based stops, and on to the good and non-discriminatory intentions of the troopers themselves.

We can come to a better understanding of institutionalization by accepting these defenses, at least for a moment, at face value. Denial that profiling existed might seem a strange approach to outsiders, but it is a very logical step for the institutionalized agency. Like the FBI on the federal level, the New Jersey State Police is the dominant state-wide police agency. When it speaks to issues of law enforcement policy, other actors within state government tend to defer. Denial, as an opening gambit, exploits this deference and can mute the issue, at least for a time, while the police agency tries to work things out internally, and this is apparently what happened.

The justification of race-based stops also sprang from the troopers' belief that they were practicing good policing. Their approach was based on the empirical models of the DEA's Operation Pipeline and profiling, per se, is not without its place in policing. Somewhere between the FBI criminal profilers and the indiscriminate and discriminating stops on the Turnpike lies the dividing line between proper and improper police practice. Drawing that line involves deciding just what assumptions to make, what categories to compare and exactly what to count in order to prove racially disproportionate enforcement. This is a complex statistical challenge that researchers argue over to this day.[39] But the institutionalized agency needn't put such a fine point on things in order to justify particular tactics. And, as the Superintendent amply demonstrated, members may be anything but self-conscious when publicly expressing the same rickety rationales with which they reassure themselves

Finally, we have to consider the assertion that any profiling was not deliberate because it was so at odds with the general good and non-discriminatory intentions of most troopers. This assertion is also tied to the intense self-regard nurtured in institutionalized organizations. Attitudes, like practices, are presumed to be good. Whether myth or reality, this view serves a stabilizing and cohesive purpose in the organization. But it also may be pretty much true that troopers are not operating from discriminatory motives, just as urban public school teachers are not operating from discriminatory motives in adopting practices that visit disproportionately painful outcomes on particular ethnic groups. At the heart of the matter, independent of any racist attitudes that may or may not be held by employees, are the organizational incentives—which employees and managers alike buy into—and which fuel the continuation of these practices. And this was a critical factor in the persistence of profiling in highway stops on the New Jersey Turnpike: it paid off for troopers until the end.

## Agency-Environment Disconnects and Institutionalization

The New Jersey State Police got hammered over the profiling issue. Troopers went on trial, lost their jobs, and were subject to discipline. The Superintendent was dumped unceremoniously, and potential successors had their feet held to the fire for pro-profiling stands they had taken earlier in their careers. Lawsuits were filed against the agency by aggrieved citizens, the ACLU and eventually by the Department of Justice, which won the right to closely oversee the State Police practices. Rank-and-file troopers were demoralized and enforcement output declined, with troopers bending over backwards to avoid any accusation of profiling. This was not a happy outcome for the agency.

The degree of negative outcome for the New Jersey State Police had much to do with institutionalization. Institutionalized agencies, because they look primarily inward for their compass headings, can get very far off track before insiders begin to accept that major problems exist. By that time, the organization has ridden so far into the storm that raging outside elements dictate what is going to happen next.

No good captain wants to steer the organizational ship onto such shoals, yet, as we have just discussed, many do just that by failing to come to grips with entrenched practices that are increasingly problematic.

The very dangerous side effect of untreated institutionalization is an ignorance or dismissal of important environmental changes. Profiling anchored partially by race may well have been less controversial in the 1980s when the DEA was pushing Operation Pipeline by partnering with State Police agencies to capture drug couriers. But it was already being singled out for condemnation by the head of the Turnpike Authority in 1989. Lawsuits addressing racial disparities arising from public service delivery or practices were also on the rise into and through the 1990s. High profile criminal cases were turning on allegations of racial bias by police investigators, and a whole range of criminal justice issues, from treatment of prisoners to capital punishment, were being examined for disparate racial impacts. If this weren't warning enough, the state was ending up on the losing end of cases involving minority motorists who claimed discrimination. All of this happened against the backdrop of growing protests from minority communities and escalating critiques from the ACLU.

These trends found the New Jersey State Police increasingly out of touch, and increasingly vulnerable to imposed and wholesale reform. It's worth stressing again that the blindness or studied ignorance caused by institutionalization is a generic organizational issue, not unique to law enforcement or the New Jersey State Police. Institutionalized urban school systems were no less sanguine about the growing drumbeat against their dismal results, and thus seemed no less dumbstruck by major reforms that introduced standardized testing and privatized the management for public schools in some cities. IBM blithely trotted out tried and true strategies from the 1960s and 1970s to re-establish its leadership during the 1980s microcomputer revolution. IBM had to lose $5 billion in a single year to realize that the old strategies were too slow and too out of touch with the new high velocity information technology world.

The job of a police executive, or any executive for that matter, is to keep the organization connected to its environment. That means monitoring court decisions, legislative trends, community attitudes and police practices elsewhere. It means redirecting agency practice to take into account trends that, if not responded to, will put the agency dangerously out of step. In an institutionalized agency, or one approaching that state, it also means engaging in an internal dialogue about why things need to change, and how all members can best facilitate that change

In the process of keeping an institutionalized organization abreast of and responsive to environmental changes, there are challenges. One is the false "either/or" position members take with respect to imposed change. It goes like this. If we can't profile based on X, we'll just have to let everybody go by or not stop anyone exhibiting X. This often is a matter of payback from an institutionalized culture for a new policy it doesn't care for, or a self-protective reflex to perceived threat. But a whole range of issues surrounds who can be stopped for what and why, so little logic adheres to constructing the choices so that only extreme solutions are in the running. Even less logic is forthcoming from managers who allow such a dichotomous dialogue to go forward without response.

The law enforcement manager might consider William Bratton's response as New York Police Commissioner when court limitations on certain stop-and-frisk tactics caused officers to grumble that they could no longer do their jobs, and might as well not stop anybody. He reminded the officers that their sworn duty was to enforce the law within the rules, and that they irretrievably yielded the moral high ground by ignoring the rules or by going into their shells. The courts had moved the yardsticks in a notch, not taken away the playing field, and it was now the responsibility of everyone in the department to figure out how to aggressively fight crime under the new conditions. That kind of message sets the stage for a dialogue that helps adjust the agency to changed environmental conditions.

The institutionalized agency caught behind the times also has a tendency to demonize outsiders calling for change. An agency in full-fledged "us versus them" mode is almost incapable of objectively scanning the environment. Instead, incoming information is distorted, often damned, and then dismissed. Again, a leader who wants to prevent his or her agency from being isolated, cut-off and then really battered needs to legitimize an agency dialogue with external critics, and needs to be active in communicating with a range of community groups.

Ongoing communication with external forces is a vital antidote to the bunker mentality institutionalized agencies can adopt. In the absence of dialogue, community stereotypes about police go unchallenged and so do police stereotypes about what a community does and doesn't want in terms of law enforcement. It is not at all clear that minority communities, which are disproportionately affected by crime, are foursquare against aggressive enforcement of the law by police. In the Rampart case, which we reviewed in the last chapter, residents expressed concern about resurgent crime when the CRASH unit was disbanded. Even in communities critical of the police, residents usually have little interest in police abdicating their law enforcement role but a lot of interest in that role being carried out fairly. This presents a wide-open opportunity for dialogue, learning about the community's concerns, and adjusting police thinking and practice to incorporate those concerns while continuing to enforce the law.

Even bringing vociferous critics into a department's inner workings can have a salutary effect. In Philadelphia in 1999 Police Commissioner John Timoney came face to face with institutionalized practices that, for fifteen years, had systematically downgraded rape complaints to lesser offenses while generally treating sexual assault complainants shabbily. Timoney applied the expected managerial treatments—classification integrity, aggressive investigation and sensitive treatment of complainants. But Timoney also took these steps in consultation with local women's groups. Timoney then invited representatives of the groups in to monitor, case by case, how the department was doing. Timoney's actions converted former adversaries to allies who soon declared that Philadelphia's approach to sex crimes was a model for the nation. Enforcement, it ought to be noted, got better, not worse as the department adjusted to more contemporary notions of how crimes of sexual assault should be addressed.

Institutionalized agencies are often blind to another threat that is not external and does not involve broad environmental trends. This threat is right under everyone's nose, comes to work every day, and is a ticking time bomb. And no one sees it because the problem is an employee cloaked in the aura of "member in good standing," not so much on the objective record in the personnel file—that may not be so good—but on his or her conformity with the profile of an acceptable institutional citizen, like the two upstanding fellows below.

## *Separated at Birth? The CIA and FBI Spies*

Aldrich Ames worked for the CIA. He began as an intern, progressed to clerk and, after graduating from college, became a CIA Officer in the late 1960s. By the 1980s, he was rotating through responsible posts in Counterintelligence as a Russian-speaking specialist on the Soviet Union, which had been the major adversary of the United States for nearly forty years. Ames held that position in April 1985 when he strolled boldly through the doors of the Soviet Embassy in Washington, D.C. to take on a second job: spying on the United States.[40]

Ames' access to information about U.S. spies in Russia was nearly total. Soon the KGB, the Soviet Union's spy agency and secret police, knew most of what Ames knew. Within a year, over a dozen U.S. secret agents were killed. Some the KGB shot immediately. Other agents were thrown in jail and tortured, or tempted with freedom and exoneration, so that they would tell all they knew. Then, they were shot dead. Yet other spies Ames had fingered were left alone as the KGB monitored them to learn the identity and techniques of their U.S. handlers. Once this had been done, the spies were recalled to Moscow from the various embassies and cultural missions that served as their cover in the United States and other countries. Once back in Moscow, their fate was the same as the others.

By the end of 1985, the CIA had a major disaster on its hands. Its human intelligence operatives in the Soviet Union had been virtually wiped out. Aldrich Ames, the CIA Soviet counterintelligence expert, was responsible and the CIA was clueless. And since CIA-FBI relations were practically nonexistent, there wasn't going to be any help from information gathered by the FBI, namely videos of Ames entering the Soviet embassy and meeting regularly with the embassy official who doubled as Ames' KGB handler.

Thus the CIA set out in search of what went wrong. It searched in 1986, 1987, 1988, 1989, 1990, and 1991. CIA officials brainstormed about high-tech reasons for the spy network's exposure: Maybe sophisticated Soviet listening devices were intercepting CIA communications. The CIA brass considered low-tech reasons, such as U.S. Embassy support staff overseas inadvertently giving up secrets to locals with whom they were sleeping. This line of inquiry ensnared a hapless U.S. Marine Embassy guard in Moscow. But, even though the Marine was having an affair with a KGB operative, he was in no way positioned to have given up all those spies.

When the CIA wasn't zeroing in on the Marines, or the State Department, it bemoaned the FBI. Another CIA turncoat, Edward Lee Howard, had fled the United States to the Soviet Union in September 1985 after slipping away from an FBI agent who was tailing him. Howard had worked for the CIA from 1981 to 1983 while being trained to handle U.S. spies in Moscow. But Howard's CIA career was short-circuited by alcohol and drug problems, bizarre behavior and petty theft. By 1985, Howard's simmering outrage over his termination had sent him into the arms of the KGB. While his revelations did expose operatives abroad, he could not have known about most of the U.S. spies that the Soviets had arrested and killed.

Aldrich Ames had known about all of the U.S. spies that went down in 1985 and 1986. But Ames was nowhere on the CIA radar in 1985 or for several years thereafter, and was still working for the CIA and funneling information to his KGB handlers when he was arrested in February 1994. He persisted in part because he was a privileged member of the CIA family. Ames was a legacy hire. His father had been a CIA agent. Ames first set foot in the Agency as a high school intern in the middle of the 1950s. Ames was well into his third CIA decade when the agency's spies in the Soviet Union began to disappear. He would enter his fourth decade of low-profile service before he was caught.

Ames managed to keep a low profile even with behavior that might well have warranted administrative notice. When he ended up unconscious in a Rome gutter after making a drunken fool of himself at a U.S. embassy July 4th party in 1987, no institutional notice was taken. When, having previously lived in a small rental unit, he bought a $550,000 house with cash, and pulled out another $100,000 to fix it up, no institutional notice was taken. No official eyebrow was raised when Ames rolled up to the CIA in his $50,000 white Jaguar. When he failed to file required reports in his Rome assignment, including his expense vouchers, no institutional notice was taken. And none was taken when Ames decided to not be bothered with vouchers at all but instead chose to pay his own work expenses.

Some CIA employees did know of Ames' highly suspect behavior. A colleague in Rome was aware of $5000 monthly phone bills Ames' wife was racking up. Superiors and colleagues knew that his daily drinking commenced most days at lunch, which clearly affected his work. Various bosses, having given him lousy ratings, were more than happy to be rid of Ames. But they remained silent when he moved on to other CIA positions with even more responsibility and authority. Twice during his decade of spying he was evaluated relative to his peers, finishing in the bottom third on the first go-around and then the bottom 2% a couple of years later. CIA senior management was peppered with individuals who had written him off for his generally lousy per-

formance and dismal attitude, or because they knew of some of his more famous exploits—losing a CIA briefcase containing a defector's photos on a
New York City subway or getting in a DWI accident in Mexico City. Still, Ames
the traitor trudged on, his employment secure.

It took six years of stop-and-go CIA investigations before the agency included Ames on a suspect list of several dozen individuals. Then, thanks to a
CIA official who ignored the deep chill in CIA-FBI relations, FBI investigators
were alerted to Ames as a suspect. Though the CIA firmly resisted FBI attempts to gather evidence from records controlled by the spy agency, Ames
was as careless about what he threw in his garbage as he was about everything
else. With evidence gathered from his trash, the FBI fingered Ames as a spy,
which then led to the months of surveillance, wiretapping and house searches
that culminated in his arrest in February 1994.

* * *

Just after Ames' spy career had gotten off the ground in 1985, another government employee had made a decision to resume the espionage activities in
which he had first engaged back in 1980. Across the Potomac from the CIA's
Virginia headquarters, working out of a Washington building named for J.
Edgar Hoover, his agency's most famous director, Robert Phillip Hanssen was
planning to provide the Soviets with the identity of U.S. spies that Ames had
already doomed.

Robert Phillip Hanssen was an FBI Special Agent. He sold out his country
on and off for an additional sixteen years after 1985, and was finally brought
to justice in 2001, twenty years after he first took $20,000 in Soviet funds for
information compromising the interests of the United States.

The Russian-speaking Hanssen spent most of his FBI career as an intelligence
analyst and, since the FBI was responsible for countering Soviet threats on U.S.
soil, Hanssen gave the KGB more than just the identity of spies. He told the Soviet spy agency about tunnels the U.S. had dug beneath the Soviet Union's
Washington Embassy in order to intercept its communications. He provided the
KGB with the United States' continuity of government plans that detailed where
our top government officials would go in the event of an attack. He revealed
critical information about the workings of the U.S. intelligence system. Hanssen
"established himself as the most prolific source of intelligence ever on TOP SE-
CRET U.S. processes, methods and codes."[41] For this, Hanssen was not only getting cash, he was getting thank-you notes from the Director of the KGB.[42]

The thank-you notes were addressed to "Dear Friend." Unlike Ames, whose
amateurish and often drunken spy craft produced easily recordable contacts
with his Soviet handlers, Hanssen took great care in communicating with the
Soviets and successfully hid his identity to the end. Although Hanssen's cau-

tion helped him remain invisible to the FBI for twenty years, the Bureau's blind spots were also a major contributor.

Hanssen's brother-in-law, Mark Wauck, was also an FBI agent. In 1990, Wauck saw that Hanssen, though supporting six children and a wife on his FBI salary, was spending money freely. Wauck also learned that Hanssen had thousands of dollars in cash stashed in the basement. Knowing of his brother-in-law's intelligence work, Wauck put two and two together. He reported what he had seen to his FBI superiors, and offered his opinion that his sister's husband, FBI Agent Robert Hanssen, might be spying for the Russians.[43] Nothing happened.

Nothing happened when Hanssen started showering a stripper, Priscilla Galey, with gifts and attention. Galey worked at a gentleman's club in downtown Washington where Hanssen sometimes repaired for lunch. Unlike Ames, who drank his lunch, Hanssen was a sober and, indeed, highly religious individual (but with a kinky edge that drew him to strip joints as well as to church). When Hanssen latched on to Galey, he claimed to be motivated by a desire to save her from her life of sin. While saving his exotic dancer, Hanssen took her to dinner, gave her a tour of the FBI Academy, bought her a second-hand Mercedes, gave her an American Express card for the car's gas and maintenance, and paid for her to come with him to Hong Kong for two and a half weeks. In Hong Kong, Hanssen audited FBI operations by day while he and Galey did the town by night.

Even as his brother-in-law's complaint went nowhere, Hanssen, an FBI Counterintelligence Agent with top secret clearances, was lavishing significant dollars on a sex-industry worker with whom he was spending considerable time. Unlike his brother-in-law, Hanssen's co-workers in Washington and Hong Kong chose to keep what they saw to themselves. This included the sight of the middle-aged Hanssen, so dour he had been dubbed "the mortician" by colleagues, giving Galey a tour of the FBI Academy. Hanssen took Galey to eat at law enforcement hangouts, and they would take lunch hour strolls in parks often teeming with government workers, including FBI agents, but no alarms sounded within the FBI.

When investigating national security breaches, the FBI was not inclined to look inward. Agents in the Intelligence Division were not given lie detector tests. Security within the agency was extremely lax. Like Ames, Hanssen simply walked out the door with top secret documents, or with diskettes containing schematics for vital systems and facilities.

Hanssen mined information from computerized FBI intelligence files virtually at will. What he wasn't authorized to see, he hacked into. One time he brazenly intercepted a superior's data query, just to show the boss how easily he could compromise the weak system. This revelation produced nothing other than tacit approval for Hanssen to keep "testing" the system to identify vulnerabilities that outside hackers could exploit. This only made it easier for Hanssen to appear legitimate while mining the computer system for secrets to sell to the Russians.

When the FBI did look vigorously for a mole, they focused the search on other agencies. Capturing Aldrich Ames in 1994 reinforced the FBI's belief that the CIA was the sieve through which so many U.S. secrets were flowing. The CIA stayed under the FBI's investigative microscope for Hanssen's crimes until the year 2000. A hapless CIA officer, who jogged regularly through an area where Hanssen and his Russian handlers hid and picked up messages, was vigorously investigated by the FBI and suspended from his job.[44] The FBI zeroed in on Hanssen only after a Russian defector claimed that the spy they were looking for was inside the Bureau. The defector's chronology of the positions held by the spy pointed directly to Hanssen.

When FBI agents finally arrested Hanssen, he said. "What took you so long?"[45]

## Sheltering Marginal Employees in Institutionalized Organizations

The protections afforded marginal employees by institutionalized agencies augments the shelter that organizational subcultures, whether compliant or deviant, afford their members. When a work group subculture in a school, or a precinct or a division of the FBI or CIA no longer shields an odd and inept employee, organizational protections often kick in as a back-up. Supervisors choose not to file critical reports. The examination of suspect behavior is officially circumscribed, often by formal contract between management and the rank-and-file but also by informal understandings that limit the probing into the lifestyles of an Ames or a Hanssen. Finally, a communal sense of self-regard and shared empathy operates strongly in institutionalized organizations. This mitigates disciplinary penalties, especially for employees who are seen as falling within acceptable ranges of conformity and loyalty.

So Ames and Hanssen were protected. Both were the beneficiaries of reports that died at supervisory levels. Time and again, Ames' public drunkenness and lack of self-control, on the job and off, had little or no personnel consequences. Similarly, the reported suspicions of Hanssen's brother-in-law, who was both a reliable investigator and a uniquely informed source, withered on the FBI vine.

Ames and Hanssen both were insulated by the presumptive trust their agencies exhibited towards career employees. An occasional audit of Ames' document horde or Hanssen's collection of computer files would almost certainly have raised suspicions. In either agency, a general audit of document security would have revealed a broken system. The institutionalized organization, however, rarely undertakes critical self-reviews.

An institutional mindset was also evident in the approach the agencies took towards lie detector tests. The CIA's lie detector tests were part of a pro forma re-examination of the attitudes and beliefs that had qualified agents for the agency in the first place. As a legacy hire inured to the ways of the agency, Ames pretty much passed his lie detector test just by showing up. For its part, the FBI largely eschewed lie detector tests in its criminal investigations, so it wasn't going to insult agents by subjecting them to these tests, even for personnel assessments. Hanssen passed his honesty assessment because there was nothing to pass.

Finally, Hanssen and Ames show how institutionalized organizations can protect even employees shunned by their work group colleagues. Neither Ames nor Hanssen was "one of the boys." To Hanssen's crime-busting colleagues, he was an introverted, pompous techno-nerd with an arrogant streak. Many of Ames' co-workers were repulsed by his bitterness, his slovenly habits and his minimal work output. But few in either agency channeled their concerns upwards. What did go up, for the most part, evaporated.

As weird as they were, Ames and Hanssen stayed within institutional bounds in terms of performance, behavioral norms and apparent loyalty to the organization itself. Because institutionalized agencies are monopolies, the limits of acceptable performance can go very low, as Ames proved. Similarly, tenure, which is legislated for many school systems but also occurs as a practical matter in law enforcement agencies, allows disaffected individuals like Ames and Hanssen to stay at work even while undermining morale. Finally Ames and Hanssen stayed within management's definition of acceptable organizational citizenship; they did not, as did Whitehurst, rock the boat. The illusion of good citizenship can be sufficient for retention even when an employee's performance is abysmal and his or her behavior is bizarre. As Ames and Hanssen showed, the carte blanche granted to "loyal, long-term" employees can boomerang destructively for the institutionalized organization.

## The Felonious Judges of Luzerne County

This case changes our venue slightly to the courts and to, one might argue, a level of dysfunction and corruption that eclipses any law enforcement agency cases we've discussed so far. Also, this case is a nice bridge to the next chapter, which explores how individuals divert organizational resources to their own use.

The organizational setting in this case is the Luzerne County Court of Common Pleas, Commonwealth of Pennsylvania, which hears major civil and criminal cases, including those relating to adoption, divorce, child custody, abuse and juvenile delinquency.

Luzerne County sits in the heart of northeastern Pennsylvania's coal country. Coal production is not the local economic engine it once was, though the Marcellus Shale, a deep reservoir of natural gas underneath Luzerne County, holds promise of an economic resurgence.

Coal's decline dragged down a range of associated businesses. In addition, the manufacturing declines across the "Rust Belt" states, including Pennsylvania, also hit Luzerne County hard. The citizens of towns like Pittston, Hazleton and Wilkes-Barre, the county seat, were struggling.

In a limping economy, Luzerne's county and municipal governments increasingly became a major source of secure employment, business contracts and job referrals.

The growing centrality and clout of county government heightened the possibility of organizational dysfunctions such as institutionalization. And Pennsylvania's political structures and culture only increased that possibility. Citizens often express resignation, if not winking tolerance, about official abuse; a plethora of elected officials, including judges, throw their weight around; and, in many jobs in county and local governments, connections get you hired and keep you employed.

So it is not surprising that the conditions described below were there for all to see in the seven years before the central players in this case were brought to justice in 2009.

> "Things were different in the Luzerne County juvenile courtroom, and everyone knew it. Proceedings on average took less than two minutes. Detention center workers were told in advance how many juveniles to expect at the end of each day—even before hearings to determine their innocence or guilt. Lawyers told families not to bother hiring them. They would not be allowed to speak anyway.

> "The judge's whim is all that mattered in that courtroom," said Marsha Levick, the legal director of the Juvenile Law Center, a child advocacy organization in Philadelphia, which began raising concerns about the court to state authorities in 1999. "The law was basically irrelevant."[46]

The law was basically irrelevant, in large part, because two key judges involved received more than two million dollars over several years for helping the juvenile detention center get built and then making sure a steady stream of kids kept it filled.

At the heart of this case was Judge Mark A. Ciavarella, first elected in 1995, and Michael T. Conahan, on the Common Pleas bench since 1994. Ciavarella was chief juvenile court judge. Conahan, whose father had been mayor of Hazleton, was a second generation political force in Luzerne County and, not long after the kickbacks began, was also named President Judge, the administrative head of the court.

The degree to which the two judges controlled the environment in and around the court was substantial. Ciavarella, who later succeeded Conahan as President Judge, ran juvenile court with an iron fist. Conahan, as his father had before him, could powerfully assert himself on all things political in Luzerne County—who got jobs and business contracts; who got elected and defeated; what got built and where. So it was natural that Robert Powell, a Hazleton attorney whose interests in the year 2000 included the possibility of developing a for-profit detention facility, would pay a visit to his friend Judge Conahan, who turned to Ciavarella, who hooked Powell up with a developer, Robert Mericle, yet another friend of Conahan's.[47] And almost from day one, though all sorts of convoluted paths, money flowed to the judges.

The detention facility was incorporated as PA Child Care (PACC) and opened for business by February 2003. Lo and behold, detainees began arriving from Judge Ciavarella's juvenile courtroom, pursuant to an agreement with Luzerne County. Luzerne County pretty much meant President Judge Conahan since the court had considerable autonomy in contracting and purchasing, and ignored other requirements, such as bidding out proposals, that were supposed to apply to the county government generally.

PACC's business was good. In its first full fiscal year, the occupancy rate was 92%, 100% in the pricier secure beds. PACC was charging a daily rate 40% higher than similar facilities in surrounding counties. Contract provisions that state auditors found dubious allowed for aggressive billing beyond the generous daily rate. Not surprisingly, PACC turned a nice first year profit—28% in 2003 according to state auditors—and, operating at full capacity, was on track to net almost two million dollars in 2004.[48]

When Conahan had become President Judge early in 2002 he had also made sure that PACC had no competition. The competition had been Luzerne County's own detention facility, which operated under the jurisdiction of the court. Conahan's first budget eliminated funding for that facility. So when it opened, PACC was the only game in town, and was soon adding more capacity.[49]

Powell, not surprisingly, drew even closer to his judicial partners. The three became neighbors of sorts at a pricey Florida condominium complex where the judges shared a unit and from time to time, rode the waves in Powell' million and a half dollar yacht, the "Reel Justice," which was docked right below.[50]

For PACC, and the judges, the game kept getting sweeter. Steered by Conahan, Luzerne County agreed to lease the detention facility for twenty years, paying, in addition to the per detainee charges, rents that accounted for the expanded facility. The total cost of the lease, if all fell PACC's way—which had a way of happening—could approach $60 million.[51]

With both placement fees and rents flying around, Conahan and Ciavarella ratcheted up their payoff demands. Powell testified at trial that he eventually became hard-pressed to feed what he felt was the judges' insatiable appetite.[52] Not that the judges didn't do all they could to insure PACC's business. Ciavarella kept the facility filled, so the court—read Judge Conahan—began looking for additional beds. They found them—at another facility run by PACC/Powell 236 miles across the state, so Luzerne County's juveniles were sent there too, by-passing along the way similar facilities with empty beds at lower prices.

County officials, including other Common Pleas judges, hesitated to delve very far into court affairs, despite the seeming conveyer belt that led from Judge Ciavarella's juvenile court to high priced beds at the privately run detention centers. Those who did ask questions ran head on into the judges' juggernaut. Judge Chester Muroski, after raising concerns with County Commissioners about the money being spent on juvenile detentions while his Orphan's Court went begging, found that Conahan had, within days, arranged his transfer to a different court.[53]

Auditors from Pennsylvania's Department of Public Welfare, which was footing much of the bill since most of those incarcerated qualified for financial support, were stymied by the litigious PACC filing complaints in Judge Conahan's very receptive court. PACC withheld its "business secret" cost data, forcing auditors to extrapolate.[54] Judge Conahan, in his administrative role, insisted along with PACC that the country was getting a good deal. This maneuvering kept the audit in limbo for years.

When Luzerne County Comptroller Steve Flood, who had more to go on than most, saw fit to reveal some of the audit's findings, PACC sued him. Not surprisingly, the venue was the Luzerne County Court of Common Pleas, where Conahan ordered the records of the proceedings sealed.[55] Flood became persona non grata at the courthouse and, when he did have cause to enter, court officers escorted him around. Flood was defeated for reelection in 2005, a signal, intentional or not, that crossing Conahan was a bad career move. The PACC lawsuit dragged on for years, beyond the major stroke Flood suffered in 2007, and winding down not long before another stroke killed him in 2011.[56]

If Luzerne County officials were, for the most part, blind to the courthouse rot, parent after parent was coming into Judge Ciavarella's courtroom with a son or daughter and leaving minutes after alone. The 10th grader who created a Facebook page in the name of a school official she broadly satirized? Take her away! A parent watching two of her children being carted away for misdemeanors was warned to stop crying, lest she be locked up too. While Luzerne officialdom may have been blind, deliberately or otherwise, state and federal authorities were not. And by 2008, federal investigators had turned Powell, who agreed to admit his role and wear a wire for key discussions with Conahan and Ciavarella.

Since Powell had been wired, the case against Ciavarella and Conahan, as well as Powell and the developer who had constructed the facility, was very strong. Within a week of their January 2009 indictments Ciavarella and Conahan had agreed to a plea deal carrying a seven year sentence that could be shortened by good behavior, especially likely in the minimum security lock-ups for which the judges qualified as white collar criminals serving less than ten years. Formal sentencing was set for summer.

If there is such a thing as poetic justice, what occurred next was it.

When they entered their plea deals, the judges were but weeks removed from being kings of the Court of Common Pleas and political powerhouses in Luzerne County. The few weeks from charges to plea deal was not a lot of time for the judges to change how they saw themselves, or how they acted. So they didn't.

When the sentencing date arrived, the judge found that Conahan, in engaging with the pre-sentencing process, avoided "the motivation behind his conduct, attempted to obstruct and impede justice, and failed to clearly demonstrate affirmative acceptance of responsibility."[57] As for Ciavarella, he outdid Conahan, and in public no less. Ciavarella's combative response to a reporter's question was, understandably, seen by Federal Judge Edwin Kosik as evidence of zero remorse.

"You people said I took bribes, that I committed extortion, that I traded kids for cash, that I had a quid pro quo," Ciaverella told the newspaper. "Where in my guilty plea does it say that?"[58]

So, when sentencing day came, Judge Kosik rejected Ciavarella's and Conahan's plea deals — in no uncertain terms. So the judges faced a choice — throw themselves on the mercy of the seething Kosik, renegotiate their deals with re-infuriated prosecutors, or go to trial. Both chose the latter course.

In August 2011, Ciavarella was sentenced to 28 years after being found guilty at trial, ending up in a medium security federal prison in Illinois. His lawyers prepared to appeal the "cruel and unusual punishment" that had been meted out. Conahan pled guilty again, and left his sentence up to the judge. Conahan got 17 years and angled to serve his sentence in the minimum security Pensacola Detention Center in Florida, reputedly one of the "cushiest" federal prisons,[59] but ended up in a more downscale low security prison in the Sunshine State.

Fall-out from the case continued in 2012 when, at the end of February, Federal Judge A. Richard Caputo approved a preliminary settlement of $17.75

million between PACC's developer and, potentially, every juvenile incarcerated by Judge Ciavarella between 2003 and 2008. Those detained in PACC facilities could apply for a minimum of $5000, or higher depending on the circumstances. Those sent elsewhere could apply for lesser amounts, and the claims of habitual or serious juvenile offenders were limited.[60] Nonetheless, the taint attached to any sentence Judge Ciavarella handed down after 2002 ended up carrying a price tag in the tens of millions of dollars.

As for Judge Ciavarella, the U.S. 3rd Circuit Court of Appeals ruled in January 2012 that he was entitled to taxpayer-funded counsel in appealing his conviction.[61]

## Nepotism: Inbred Institutionalization

Institutionalized organizations are inclined to adopt ever stronger "us versus them" attitudes over time. "Success," whether achieved via monopoly or competitive excellence, conveys a sense of superiority and dominance to members of the organization. Collective self-esteem soars, usually helped along by increasingly negative attitudes towards competitors, critics and outsiders generally.

Another thing occurs as an organization grows to dominate its environment. More time is available for working on internal social coherence. This often ends up being expressed as rigid conformity, either at the behest of powerful leaders who demand it or through more distributed enforcement of solidarity among unionized and professional cadres.

In Luzerne County, and especially in its judicial system, many workers came on board with attitudes ready-made for an institutionalized organization. Nepotism was common. Political litmus tests were more common still. When membership in a political party or a particular party faction is a key to getting hired, the new employee arrives with a basic knowledge of what's important to do and say and from whom to take cues. And the new employee who is following onto the job a parent, sister or brother, or even Cousin Edgar or Aunt Minnie, also has almost certainly absorbed numerous lessons over the years about fitting in, and staying in, the "institution."

This inbred thinking produced by nepotistic and political hiring in Luzerne created virtually impregnable organizational fortresses, with walls that shielded not only the judges' criminally egregious scheme, but also everyday waste and cynical abuse of resources supposedly allocated to the pursuit of justice. It was, and is, enough to cause despair in those seeking to do the right thing. Witness the testimony of two Luzerne County Commissioners.

> Urban said he didn't have faith in the Judicial Conduct Board because he believed it was a "good-old-boy network" that protected judges. He

said he didn't "trust" the District Attorney's Office because of all the "nepotism and family affairs that take place in the county courthouse." Urban and Petrilla testified that they received no complaints or concerns about the juvenile justice system from court or county employees. They both described nepotism as high in the court system. Petrilla said employees hired by the "wrongdoers" kept quiet.

"The courts hired family and friends, and as a result of the hiring of family and friends, those people who may have seen wrongdoing remained silent," Petrilla said.[62]

This testimony, to the Inter-branch Commission on Juvenile Justice which was looking into the "kids for cash" case, also revealed the hubris and environmental reach that the fortress of institutionalization can enable. Commissioner Petrilla said that Judge Conahan had interceded New Year's weekend 2009 on behalf of the county's chief clerk, whom the commissioners wanted to replace. Were that to happen, Judge Conahan promised, Petrilla would be "finished." Since her predecessor as commissioner, Steve Flood, had suffered just such a fate after angering Conahan, Petrilla may be lucky the indictments came down soon after the clerk was let go. Even then, the fast-moving Conahan had arranged for the dismissed clerk to land softly in the Court of Common Pleas. The clerk's hastily created position did not, however, survive the radioactivity accompanying the breaking scandal and Conahan's suspension.[63]

## Coda: New York's Family Court

Lest readers leave this chapter equating institutionalization with criminal excess, let's close with a straightforward, non-felonious instance of a court that, through 2011, was routinely barring the public despite a major policy change fourteen years earlier that granted such access.

The court in this case was the New York City Family Courts. What generally goes on in any family court can be pretty ugly. Divorce proceedings tear families asunder. Support payments are judicially coerced from resistant and/or strapped spouses, some of whom end up in jail. Cases of child and spousal abuse fill the docket.

And, in family court, things go wrong. Violent and deadly assaults are launched, sometimes in court itself, despite restraining orders. Children die in situations of abuse and/or neglect after the court has failed to find sufficient evidence warranting removal of the children.

Most organizations understandably would prefer that their messy operations not be spotlighted. On the other hand, scrutiny is an important quality control tool, especially for organizations engaged in high-risk activities. For the public organization, including the courts, citizen and media access to proceedings and records is constitutionally guaranteed, barring some overriding privacy or safety concerns regarding parties involved in a particular case.

The forces of institutionalization, however, are not easily deterred by appeals to quality control, or the common welfare or constitutionality, especially when such appeals are at odds with how organization members believe things should be run.

Such was the case with New York's Family Courts through 1997. Business behind barred doors, except when the more egregious cases ruptured into plain sight with the corpses of serially abused children [64]and wives murdered in cold blood.[65]

In 1997, in the name of accountability, New York's then Chief Judge Judith Kaye, along with the Administrative Judge who later succeeded her as Chief, announced that "The Family Court is open to the public," and promulgated rules to that effect. Exclusions to this open door policy were few, to be determined case by case by a judge on the basis of evidence.[66]

For whatever reason, a reporter for The New York Times decided that October/November 2011 was a good time to see how the New York City Family Court was doing on its fourteen-year-old mandate to be "open to the public."[67]

Not well, it turned out. The reporter tried to enter court after court in Family Court buildings throughout the city. He was barred 90% of the time.

> Some courtrooms were locked, and many were marked with "stop" and "do not enter" signs. Court officers stationed at courtroom doors repeatedly barred a visitor, sometimes with sarcasm or ridicule, frequently demanding to know who he was and what he was doing. Armed court officers at times appeared so rattled by a visitor's efforts to enter courtrooms that, in several instances, a group of them nervously confronted the visitor, their holsters in easy reach.[68]

The actions by court personnel to keep the reporter out are symptomatic of what one is likely to encounter in a chronically institutionalized organization. The body language conveys "This is our place, with our rules; outsiders have no say and will do as we say." Not that court personnel didn't also clearly articulate this position.

> " ... an officer was asked whether a member of the public could attend—as is permitted in other New York courts. "Not allowed, not in Family Court," he said flatly. Outside Judge Susan Larabee's courtroom in Manhattan Family Court, an officer flashed his badge and said disdainfully, "You don't just walk in." In Staten Island Family Court, three officers challenged a visitor even as they stood beneath a sign that took official note of the 1997 rule: "The court is open to the public."

When the reporter challenged the court officers, he ended up referred to captains, senior court clerks, or to judges in the "off-limits" courtrooms. Institutionalization, we've seen, is a pervasive condition, so what the reporter got from the senior court officers, judges and clerks were variations of the "no access" or "limited access" themes he had already encountered.

> In her courtroom, Judge Carol Sherman immediately called the reporter to the bench and said he had to present his credentials to the court clerk on another floor. An hour later, the first deputy clerk, Nicholas Rapallo, said he had to get approval from the office of the state's chief administrative judge.
>
> When that was granted, Mr. Rapallo first instructed that access was allowed only to Judge Sherman's courtroom. After another wait, he authorized entry to other courtrooms but said, "You have to let it be known who you are."
>
> In Queens, a uniformed captain, who declined to give his full name, mocked a visitor who presented a copy of the open-court rule. "The rule here is different," the man, Captain Beneri, said. "I know the rule a little better than you do."
>
> On Staten Island, after the confrontation with the three officers, the visitor was directed to wait for the chief court clerk, William J. Quirk, to ask for permission. An hour and 20 minutes later, Mr. Quirk appeared at the clerk's window. He seemed startled when the visitor said he wanted to watch court proceedings.
>
> "You have to answer my questions," Mr. Quirk shouted after a brief conversation, saying, "The court is not public in the sense that you just walk in." [69]

Eventually the dogged reporter got high enough, namely to Family Court's Supervising Judges, where the open access policy was not only acknowledged but memos were fired off reminding court personnel that the public was allowed in, and that this policy was not new.

At least one of the supervising judges didn't seem sure the memos would have the desired effect: "I think it's a culture that has to be changed." [70]

And that is the culture of institutionalization.

# Curing Institutionalization

The "Reinventing Government" movement basically had institutionalized agencies in mind when it proposed radical restructuring of public agencies to introduce transparency, a customer focus, competition, and ongoing, rigorous assessment. Let's briefly look at how these reinvention steps help address the institutionalization ills we have seen in this chapter.

Transparency, by making most of what an agency does visible to outsiders, gets at the image-reality disconnects that perpetuate institutionalization. Protective smokescreens need to be eliminated so deviations from expected practice can be spotted more quickly. This is critical to preventing things from deteriorating quietly until they collapse, which happened disastrously in the cases we reviewed in this chapter.

Instituting a customer focus is also an antidote to the introspection so characteristic of institutionalization. As reinvention proponents point out, "customer" is a concept that needs to be broadly construed. The FBI Lab customers were in prosecutor's offices, in other law enforcement agencies, and in the scientific community that had a stake in the integrity of the Lab's work. The principal customer was not, as the institutionalized view would have it, the FBI agent who needed from the Lab a winning case on a silver platter.

A different approach towards the citizens with whom they interacted would also have served the New Jersey State Police well. As the New Jersey Attorney General's Office reported in 1999, "The Review Team observed in several cases a problem which, for lack of a better term, may be called 'occupational arrogance.' Simply put, it is the tendency for certain police troopers to approach the public with an attitude that the troopers are in no way to be challenged or questioned."[71] Variations on this theme of professional hubris are widespread among employees in any institutionalized organization. Attitudes like "occupational arrogance," however, can change, especially in organizations that choose to reinvent and reorient themselves towards clients and customers.

Competition is the most radical reinvention surgery for institutionalized organizations, one now being applied to public schools in several jurisdictions. Different educational models are now in place in Philadelphia, including charter schools, privately managed public schools and traditional, centrally administered schools. Other jurisdictions allow parents to pull their children from schools that seriously under-perform and send them to any other school in the district, a concept now enshrined in the federal "No Child Left Behind Act." If the worst schools wither and die, so be it.

Law enforcement may not yet be ready for the charter police department, but methods for introducing competition do exist. Benchmarking allows law enforcement agencies to search for and adopt best practices from other agencies. This search, and the willingness to adopt "not invented here" methods, undermines the closed and arrogant organizational culture that sustains institutionalization. Law enforcement organizations can also benchmark internally, especially through COMPSTAT-type data collection and analysis for a variety of functions.

Law enforcement agencies also need to reinvent personnel management systems. Both Ames and Hanssen were shielded by their agency's haphazard approach to reporting, recording, aggregating and analyzing negative information about employees. Some organizations have developed, for lack of a better term, "personnel-stat." All employee information is systematically collected and recorded in a central data base that can be queried to reveal patterns that might warrant further investigation or action. For instance, a search for workers with more than ten sick days, ten or more days late, two or more customer complaints but zero disciplinary actions might reveal a cluster of problematic employees in an office with ineffectual supervision. Individually, searching out worst-case employees might reveal an Aldrich Ames before he does severe damage to the agency.

Pursuing reinvention strategies serves the best interests of law enforcement agencies. It mitigates institutionalization while allowing the agency more control over, and greater ownership of, reforms that are instituted. Control and ownership of reform was taken away from the FBI Lab, the New Jersey State Police, and the CIA as a result of the cases we have just reviewed. The New Jersey State Police ended up reporting to the Department of Justice for ten years about its enforcement practices. The CIA had to grant the hated FBI considerably more investigative entrée after the Ames debacle. The FBI Lab had to undergo accreditation by external forensic scientists. At the FBI, after Hanssen's arrest, Louis Freeh was out the door and the Bureau was staring down a line-up of critical Congressional investigations. The Luzerne County Court of Common Pleas was subject to multiple state investigations and was drawn into civil litigation.

So, if you ever find yourself in charge of a law enforcement organization, or a substantial part thereof, scan quickly for evidence of institutionalization by asking the following questions.

- What are the traditions that shaped the agency? To what extent do those traditions still govern? Do these enduring traditions contribute to good practice or to practices that are out of step with present day policing? A history lesson never hurts.
- Is the professionalism of agency members used like a weapon to negate all other voices? Is there evidence of "occupational arrogance"? This will help you gauge how insular the agency is.
- Is there a dichotomy between the agency's image and the reality of how well it carries out its tasks? Do those in the agency fiercely resist scrutiny that would expose this divergence? If the answers are yes, big management challenges lie ahead.

- Are there any widespread practices that are increasingly being criticized by the media, the courts and the community? Is the attitude of agency members towards these criticisms emotional and defensive? If yes, reinvention of practice and attitude should be on the agenda.
- Finally, do records show that the organization rarely terminates anyone? Is everybody rated satisfactory? Are the first thirty employees you encounter as uniformly satisfactory as personnel evaluations indicate? If the answers are yes, yes and no, you have almost certainly entered an institutionalized agency.

If you do find yourself in an institutionalized agency, hopefully the lessons of this chapter will help you better survive and advance to leadership positions where you can take on the challenge of saving your agency from itself.

# Endnotes

1. John P. Crank and Robert Langworthy, "An Institutional Perspective on Policing," *Journal of Criminal Law and Criminology* 83, no. 2 (1992): 338–63.

2. Phillip Selznick. *The TVA and the Grassroots: A Study in the Sociology of Formal Organizations.* (Berkeley: University of California Press, 1966): 258–59.

3. Randall C. Archibold, "Worst Schools Still Seeking 400 Teachers," *New York Times*, August 22, 1999.

4. Marjorie Coeyman, "Troubled System Radical Response; A Plan in Philadelphia Would Create The Country's Largest Experiment With Private Control Of Public Schools," *Christian Science Monitor*, Nov. 13, 2001.

5. For a longitudinal, cross-country view of the problem see Maribeth Vander Weele, *Reclaiming Our Schools: The Struggle for Chicago School Reform* (Loyola University Press, 1994); Alan Bonsteel, Carlos A. Bonilla. *A Choice for Our Children: Curing the Crisis in America's Schools* (Oakland: Institute for Contemporary Studies, 1997); Lydia G. Segal, *Battling Corruption in America's Public Schools* (Boston: Northeast University Press, 2004).

6. Barry Denenberg, *J. Edgar Hoover and the FBI* (New York: Scholastic, 1993): 123–27.

7. See Paul Carroll, *Big Blues: The Unmaking of IBM* (New York: Crown, 1994) as well as Louis V. Gerstner Jr., *Who Says Elephants Can't Dance? Inside IBM's Historic Turnaround* (New York: Harper Business, 2002).

8. John E. Kelly and Phillip K. Wearne, *Tainting Evidence: Inside the Scandals at the FBI Crime Lab* (New York: The Free Press, 1998): 42.

9. Ibid., 45.

10. These investigations are meticulously chronicled in, Office of the Inspector General, Department of Justice, *The FBI Laboratory: An Investigation into Laboratory Practices and Alleged Misconduct in Explosives-Related and Other Cases* (Washington, D.C.: 1997) http://www.fas.org/irp/agency/doj/oig/fbilab1/02newrud.htm (Accessed April 20, 2005).

11. OIG/DOJ, *The FBI Laboratory: An Investigation*, (Part Five: Findings And Recommendations Concerning Individuals, B. Roger Martz) http://www.usdoj.gov/oig/special/9704a/23new5a.htm (Accessed April, 20, 2005).

12. Kelly and Wearne, *Tainting Evidence*, 160.

13. Ibid., 4.

14. Ibid., 5.

15. Ibid., 44.

16. *The City Pages*, Vol. 25, No.1244, Oct. 6, 2004. Retrieved on March 4, 2005 from http://cyberjournal.org/cj/show_archives/?id='283'&batch='16'&lists='newslog'.

17. OIG/DOJ, *The FBI Laboratory: An Investigation*, (Part Three: Analysis of Particular Matters, Allegations Concerning Terry Rudolph) http://www.usdoj.gov/oig/special/9704a/02newrud.htm (Accessed April 15, 2005).

18. Kelly and Wearne, *Tainting Evidence*, 145–55.

19. Ibid., 152

20. Richard Leiby and *George Lardner Jr.*, "Siege Guided by Hastily Revised Rules of Engagement," *Washington Post*, September 4, 1995.

21. Richard Leiby and *George Lardner Jr.*, "Government Witnesses Cause Case to Collapse" *Washington Post*, September 5, 1995.

22. George Lardner Jr., "FBI Aide Admits Obstruction," *Washington Post*, October 31, 1996.

23. Kelly and Wearne, *Tainting Evidence*, 147.

24. Sharon LaFraniere. "For FBI Chief, Big Steps and a Big Misstep: Freeh Invited Dispute by Promoting a Friend," *Washington Post*, Oct 19, 1995.

25. Kelly and Wearne, *Tainting Evidence*, 153.

26. Christopher Hanson, "4 FBI Agents Take the 5th at Ruby Ridge Hearing," *Seattle Post-Intelligencer*, September 20, 1995.

27. Department of Justice Task Force, *Department of Justice Report on Internal Review Regarding the Ruby Ridge Hostage Situation and Shootings by Law Enforcement Personnel*, June 1994 Executive Summary. Retrieved on March 7, 2005 from http://www.byingtonorg/Carl/ ruby/ruby0.htm.

28. Kelly and Wearne, *Tainting Evidence*, 142–44.

29. Samuel Walker, *The New World of Police Accountability* (Thousand Oaks, CA: Sage, 2005): 155.

30. Jerry Seper, "Justice IG's Probe of FBI Finds Retaliation against Agent," *The Washington Times* (Washington, D.C.), Feb 25, 2003.

31. Murray Weiss, *The Man Who Warned America: The Life and Death of John O'Neill, the FBI's Embattled Counter-terror Warrior* (New York: Harper Collins, 2003): 277–83.

32. Katherine E. Finkelstein, "Sharpton is Sentenced to 10 Days for Protest," *The New York Times*, March 9, 2000.

33. David M. Herszenhorn, "Reversal Has Some Questioning Attorney General's Motives," *The New York Times*, April 21, 1999.

34. SherrySylvester.com, "Bill Bradley Inspires Dream of a Different Kind of Politician," May 12, 1999. http://www.sherrysylvester.com/May%201999%20Archives.htm (Accessed on March 7, 2005).

35. Herb Williams, Jr. "Profiling," (Unpublished paper, John Jay College of Criminal Justice, 2003): 7.

36. Ibid., 8.

37. "Racial Attitudes in Jersey's State Police," *The New York Times*, March 2, 1999.

38. Herszenhorn, "Reversal Has Some Questioning."

39. Gene Callahan and William Anderson, "The Roots of Racial Profiling: Why Are Police Targeting Minorities For Traffic Stops?" *Reason Magazine* (August–September 2001) http://reason.com/0108/fe.gc.the.shtml (Accessed March 7, 2005).

40. Tim Weiner, David Johnston and Neil A. Lewis, *Betrayal: The Story of Aldrich Ames, An American Spy* (New York: Random House, 1995): 35.

41. David A. Vise, *The Bureau and the Mole: The Unmasking of Robert Phillip Hanssen, the Most Dangerous Double Agent in FBI History* (New York: Atlantic Monthly Press, 2002): 92.

42. Wise, p. 92.

43. Ibid., 96.

44. Ibid., 205.

45. Ibid., 216.

46. Ian Urbina, "Despite Red Flags about Judges, a Kickback Scheme Flourished," *New York Times*, March 27, 2009. http://www.nytimes.com/2009/03/28/us/28judges.html (Accessed March 1, 2012).

47. Ibid.

48. Bureau of Financial Operations, Pennsylvania Department of Public Welfare, Audit Report—PA Child Care, LLC (PACC), January 11, 2008.

49. _____, Report of the Inter-branch Commission on Juvenile Justice, Philadelphia, May 2010, 9.

50. Dave Janoski, "Powell Testifies Judges Demands for Kickbacks Drove Him Out of the Country" *Hazleton Standard Speaker—StandardSpeaker.com*, February 10, 2011 http://standardspeaker.com/news/powell-testifies-judge-s-demands-for-kickbacks-drove-him-out-of-country-1.1102696#axzz1qY3MC956 (Accessed March 28, 2012).

51. Dave Janoski, "Ciavarella Case Focused on Money Trail, Avoided Juveniles' Story," *RepublicanHerald.com*, February 20, 2011. http://republicanherald.com/news/ciavarella-case-focused-on-money-trail-avoided-juveniles-stories-1.1107923 (Accessed March 30, 2012).

52. Dave Janoski, "Powell Testifies Judges Demands for Kickbacks Drove Him Out of the Country."

53. Dave Janoski, "Luzerne's Other Disgraced Judge a Study in Contrasts," *The Times-Tribune.com*, September 19, 2011. http://thetimes-tribune.com/news/luzerne-s-other-disgraced-judge-a-study-in-contrasts-1.1205381#axzz1qYEx786C (Accessed March 29, 2012).

54. Bureau of Financial Operations, Pennsylvania Department of Public Welfare, Audit Report—PA Child Care, LLC (PACC), January 11, 2008.

55. Ian Urbina, "Despite Red Flags about Judges, a Kickback Scheme Flourished."

56. Hank Grezlak, "Those Who Stood Up," *The American Lawyer*, February 1, 2012 http://www.law.com/jsp/tal/PubArticleTAL.jsp?id=1202539449218 (Accessed March 30, 2012).

57. Robert Moran, "Ex-Judges Plea Deal Is Rejected," *Philadelphia Inquirer*, August 1, 2009.

58. Ibid.

59. Dave Janoski, "Conahan May Serve Time in 'Cushy' Federal Facility," *The Times-Tribune.com*, September 24, 2011. http://thetimes-tribune.com/news/conahan-may-serve-time-in-cushy-federal-facility-1.1208354#axzz1qYEx786C (Accessed March 28, 2012).

60. Michael R. Sisak, "Judge Gives Preliminary OK to Mericle Settlement," *Hazleton Standard Speaker—StandardSpeaker.com*, February 29, 2012. http://standardspeaker.com/news/judge-gives-preliminary-ok-to-mericle-settlement-1.1278789#axzz1oBWMlCLK (Accessed March 4, 2012).

61. _____, "Justice for Ciavarella," *The Times-Tribune.com*, January 11,2012 http://thetimes-tribune.com/opinion/justice-for-ciavarella-1.1255954#axzz1svWJ4Lo2 (Accessed March 31, 2012).

62. Jennifer Learn-Andes, "Petrilla: Judge Pressured Her." *The Times Leader*, December 9, 2009. http://www.timesleader.com/news/hottopics/judges/Petrilla__Judge_pressured_her_12-09-2009.html#ixzz1o02BDEka (Accessed March 2, 2012).

63. Ibid.

64. Suzanne Daley, "Agency Defended in Death of Child," *New York Times*, December 22, 1988, A1.

65. Maureen Fan, "Guilty in Slay at Court," *New York Daily News*, December 8, 1995. http://www.nydailynews.com/archives/boroughs/guilty-slay-court-article-1.701369 (Accessed March 4, 2012).

66. William Glaberson, "New York Court Says Keep Out, Despite Order," *New York Times*, November 17, 2011, A1.

67. Ibid.

68. Ibid.

69. Ibid.

70. Ibid.

71. Office of the Attorney General, *Overview, Highlights and Action Steps of the Final Report of the State Police Review Team*, Trenton: State of New Jersey, 1999. Retrieved on March 7, 2005 from http://www.aele.org/NJAG799.html.

# CHAPTER SEVEN

# RESOURCE DIVERSION IN LAW ENFORCEMENT: EXPLOITING ORGANIZATIONAL SYSTEMS

## Creative Expropriations and Compromised Agencies

Compared to the grand, systemic and frequently crippling malady of institutionalization, resource diversion seems almost benign. So police officers sometimes doctor their time sheets with bogus hours worked or back-load arrests at the end of the shift in order to generate lucrative overtime on a regular basis. So police executives may charge personal purchases to the agency's credit card, or accept rent-subsidized apartments and cross-country plane trips from civic and business leaders eager to show their appreciation. So officers gas their personal cars at the precinct pump on occasion, or the chief of administration sends off the department's laborers to paint her summer home.

So what? No big deal.

Now that was a sarcastic "no big deal." In practice, too many employees high and low take this attitude to heart. When it takes root among employees, "no big deal" does much to justify thousands of petty thieveries, determined exploitation of the system for fun and profit and, all too often, executives whose integrity becomes a victim of their increasingly grandiose sense of entitlement. As a result, the organization suffers.

The organization may suffer the slow torture of a thousand cuts when members routinely cut short their workdays or augment their salaries by systematically manipulating the payroll system. Or the organization may take a huge hit when these behaviors accumulate into a major scandal that blows like a volcano right on to the front page and the evening news. The organization may be mildly embarrassed by having the chief censured for a free plane ride she shouldn't have taken. Or it may be subject to the indignity of a commander arraigned before a judge because the several weeks' work the department's laborers performed at his house was a felony, not a perk of the office.

Resource diversion, in other words, is a very big deal, especially for law enforcement agencies. So what is resource diversion?

*Resource diversion* occurs when organizational resources end up being used for other than their intended purposes through illicit schemes or marginally legal manipulations by employee beneficiaries.

This definition is purposely broad in order to capture a whole universe of acts, both legal and illegal. The line between legality and illegality is largely irrelevant to identifying and correcting resource diversion, though the illegal kind generally presents more of a public relations headache for the law enforcement agency. If funds, equipment, personnel hours and materials have been devoted to program A but instead become ill-gotten possessions of program employees X, Y and Z, it does not matter that X stole the video camera, an indictable offense, but Y and Z routinely arranged their schedules so as to maximize each other's overtime, a breach of administrative rules only. All three employees have in their possession either dollars (Y and Z) or equipment (X) that should have been otherwise used in the program but now cannot be. The resources have been diverted.

Another reason for keeping the definition broad is that there is no end to the creativity that employees show in compromising the systems that organizations have in place to insure that resources are used according to plan. In fact, John Kenneth Galbraith, tongue slightly in cheek, once proposed "bezzle" as the generic identifier for the myriad things that employees could expropriate for themselves at work.[1] Embezzlement, stripped of its strict legal definition, can also serve as the generic identifier for the countless ways, many still to be invented, in which employees direct the "bezzle" to their own use.

The approach here uses resources, not "bezzle," and diversion, not embezzlement. But resource diversion effectively subsumes a broad class of self-serving employee behaviors. These behaviors almost always compromise the efficiency with which a law enforcement organization pursues its formal goals and the fairness with which it treats its employees. Because resource diversion erodes the twin pillars of efficiency and equity, it is first and foremost an issue of organizational management.

In contrast, terms like malfeasance, misfeasance and nonfeasance are finely nuanced legalisms designed for court action, not management reform. Irrespective of the particular crimes alleged, when resource diversions turn into indictments, organizations usually worry first, and often more, about public relations than about fixing the systems that were exploited. In the final analysis, resource diversion is extra-legal, even if it sometimes ends up in court. The following example illustrates this.

# Organizational Commonalities and Legal Nuance

Let's take a practical look at how the law might distinguish between identical actions that take place in two different organizations. Consider, for example, how West Virginia law treats public, as opposed to private, executives who divert organizational resources to their personal use.[2]

For argument's sake, let's attribute exactly the same thinking and behavior to two West Virginia executives, one in the private sector and one in the public sector. Mining executive Joyce Jones and District Attorney Sam Smith each have a taste for fine cars and a belief that their job is really 24/7. Therefore, as far as they are concerned, anything that their employer can possibly do to help them travel around ought to be done.

To make this happen, CEO Jones simply has the company lease a Cadillac for her use at those times when her corporate sedan and its assigned driver are not available. As a practical matter, the Cadillac becomes her weekend car with little connection to business activity.

DA Smith gets his Cadillac, the very same model Jones is driving, by way of an asset seizure following the conviction of its drug dealer owner. Though seized items are supposed to be used solely for law enforcement or governmental purposes, DA Smith uses the car for personal errands, especially on weekends, even though he believes that a hard-charging DA like himself is "always on the job."

What happens when one aggrieved employee in each organization blows the whistle, pointing out that the boss is enjoying additional, unreported compensation by using the company/agency car for personal purposes? The clueless CEO Jones may well keep driving. Once enlightened, she can engineer approval for her weekend rides and even see to it that the company pays the taxes on the imputed income represented by the use of the Cadillac. The equally clueless DA Smith, on the other hand, may well get indicted for embezzlement. In West Virginia, private employees must **intend** to wrongfully take an organization's resources in order to be charged with embezzlement; public employees need simply to have committed the act, knowingly or not.

From the standpoint of organizational analysis, however, we learn nothing by saying that Smith was an embezzler and Jones was not. Each came into possession of the same object, with the same sense of righteous entitlement and managed to have their organization foot the bill. In each case what they took for personal use no longer was available to serve the purposes of the organization. We better understand organizations by considering why employees come to feel entitled, how they expropriate extra rewards and what aspects of organizational command and control facilitate the process.

From an organizational standpoint, both Jones and Smith were enabled by weak organizational controls and their ability to unilaterally sanction their own benefits using self-serving logic that was transparent to almost everyone but them. For the managers in these two organizations, especially in the District Attorney's Office, putting preventative measures in place against future asset expropriations by strategically positioned employees is at least as important as pursuing criminal charges.

* * *

The cases in this chapter illustrate how, individually and collectively, law enforcement employees can divert the flow of organizational resources for their own benefit. These cases do not all involve illegality. They all do, however, show how organizational systems can be exploited.

When we look at "The Iron Men and Women of Law Enforcement," we will see that time-and-leave systems are a prime target for law enforcement officers seeking extra measures of compensation without a corresponding increment of work. And, when we look at how a corrections chief was "Getting a Good Deal on Home Improvements," we will see that high-ranking officials have ample opportunities to seize resources and the power to intimidate those who might object. A new resource diversion case for this edition dissects the fall of ex-NYPD Commissioner Bernard Kerik, iconic as New York's top cop on 9/11, but off to jail in 2010 for offenses arising from things he had already done while in public office before the horrible attack.

But first, we'll take a look at methods for "Winning the Disability Lottery," where weaknesses and loopholes in systems premised upon generosity to law enforcement officers injured in the line of duty may produce jackpot payoffs for dubious injuries that may not be job-related.

## Winning the "Disability Lottery"

Some New York State law enforcement officers called it the "disability lottery."[3] A line-of-duty injury could convert an officer's taxable pension to a tax-free pension at three-quarters pay, thanks to generous state laws. Other on-the-job injuries—twisting your knee in the precinct bathroom, jamming your trigger finger in the file cabinet—could translate to 50% tax-free pension and could also allow retired officers to draw on Worker's Compensation and other government benefit programs.[4] The disability determination system also allowed injured officers to aggressively pursue their claims, and gave hearing examiners considerable discretion in determining what constituted a career-ending injury. Thus, the winning ticket to an instant tax-free pension, the ultimate payoff of the "disability lottery," might be found in a minor, difficult-to-diagnose injury that may have even been sustained while off-duty but also, possibly, was in some way attributable to the job.

Lots of cops become disabled, certainly at a rate higher than many other professions, which is understandable given the nature of the work. But cops end up disabled more than one would expect even accounting for the heightened physical danger inherent in police work. A *New York Newsday* investigative report in 1994 estimated that, in certain jurisdictions within New York State, one-third of disability claims were false or exaggerated.[5] Officers feigned injuries, or attested to bona fide injuries lingering indefinitely. When newspapers and media outlets chose to investigate the subject, they had no problem finding disability retirees hang-gliding, playing softball or doing construction work.[6]

The disability pension system is no doubt a temptation. The complex, police-friendly pension rules in most states provide wiggle room into which a slightly sprained back may translate into a permanent disability, and a tax-free early retirement. Lawyers specializing in disability claims for law enforcement officers advertise their availability in print and online. And doctors with particular diagnostic inclinations can usually be counted on to confirm career-ending orthopedic issues.

Lots of cops take a shot at the disability lottery, most quite innocently because their dangerous jobs can buy them a chance at any time. The truly disabled retire a few years early, draw down a substantial pension and get to keep more of it. But some of the disability retirees pursue remarkably fit and active lifestyles where the maladies that cut short their career are little in evidence. The examples below are from a Pulitzer Prize winning series *New York Newsday* ran about how Long Island cops were spending their disability retirements.

One disabled ex-cop was a lifeguard at a Long Island beach. As *Newsday* reported in 1994, "the state parks system says the 45-year-old ex-cop is capable of guarding your life—able to jump from the chair, run down the beach, dive into pounding waves and pull out a drowning swimmer from the sometimes rough surf at Jones Beach."[7] Three years earlier, the officer suffered a knee injury on the job, followed by arthroscopic surgery, and then by a claim that the injury rendered him unfit for duty. This sequence of events spanned January 1991 to August 1992, when the officer was allowed to retire on disability. As *Newsday* reported, he worked as a summer lifeguard in both 1991 and 1992 while his claim was in process, came back to work at the beach as a disability retiree in 1993, and was working as a life guard yet again when the *Newsday* series was written in June and July of 1994.[8]

Another disabled cop slipped while gassing up his cruiser. That too caused a knee injury, followed by a three-year process in which his disability claim was first denied and then, after the pension board reversed itself, was granted.

The officer moved to another state, and on to another job—as a corrections officer.[9]

One officer was dryly dubbed "the golfer" by his superiors. "The golfer" had played 23 holes of golf in a day while on "sick leave" from the back injury that eventually led to his disability retirement. The injury had been suffered while the officer was responding to a car accident. According to the officer, one of the vehicles began to roll and he was thrown to the ground trying to stop it, a scenario disputed by one witness. The officer's department fought the claim, and surveillance of his golf outing was part of the offensive. Nonetheless, in 1990 the officer was awarded "an annual disability pension of $44,857, tax-free … despite the testimony of Nassau police officers who monitored him … The story … is often told within the police department, officials said, as evidence of a flawed disability pension system in which medical testimony can overrule eyewitness evidence that an applicant is capable of more physical exertion than he admits."[10] A *Newsday* report following the officer's retirement featured a recent photograph of the "golfer" at, of all places, a driving range.[11]

That tax-free $45,000 pension obtained by "the golfer" might be anywhere from $65,000 to $75,000 or more today, given the rise in police salaries over the past fifteen years on Long Island. *Newsday* in 2003 reported average police salaries and benefits of over $100,000 in Eastern Long Island.[12] Given New York's tax structure, as well as the tax-free status and high percentage of final pay that attaches to some accident-related disability retirements, the incentives in the system are often perverse. When the system was modified making disability retirement more attractive, The New York State Conference of Mayors and Municipal Officials complained of the real possibility that retired officers would "receive substantially more money in tax-free disability payments than would be received if employed."[13] This turned out to be the case. "I'd be crazy not to retire," is a common refrain among veteran officers who sustain a disability retirement-eligible but hardly immobilizing injury. So, even officers who qualify for, but have yet to take, regular retirement end up taking a chance on the "disability lottery."

## Profiling and Reinforcing Vulnerable Systems

Disability pay and disability pensions are designed to replace income that employees lose as a result of being injured on the job. The disability insurance system collects premiums from employers who, in classic economic fashion, cover that cost through the price of the goods and services we buy, the taxes we pay, or through reduced wages paid to employees. When a worker is temporarily disabled, the insurance kicks in with regular, lightly taxed payments that cover a sizable percentage of lost wages. When a worker is permanently disabled, their lifetime disability payments tap sources enriched by taxpayer dollars, like the Social Security trust fund, and public employee pension systems in the various states.

When certain disability pensions are afforded tax-free status, an additional toll is extracted from taxpayers. When one particular group, disabled police officers for example, is excused from paying taxes, the remainder of the tax-paying public makes up the difference. To the extent that disability claims are legitimate, the public at large has agreed to bear this distribution of tax burdens through their legislative representatives who passed the pension laws (although in New York the public, and probably most legislators, little understood how costly the deal they agreed to would turn out to be). Be that as it may, to the extent that disability claims are illegitimate, the undeserving recipient of a tax-free pension forces other taxpayers to shoulder extra tax burdens that no one has agreed to. Looking at the disability pension case more closely reveals features common to a wide variety of resource diversions.

First, the system being exploited is obscure and/or presumptively good. It is not seen by most as a problem. Pensions are good. Pensions for cops are even better. Who could object to enhanced pensions for cops wounded or injured in the line of duty?

Second, the system being exploited is complex. Only a few have much interest in mastering all the intricacies of the disability pension system—the system managers, police unions, the beneficiaries themselves, and the doctors and lawyers who advise the managers and beneficiaries.

Third, the system delivers substantial resources to many individuals. So a big illicit score by one person, or petty expropriations by a lot of people, has a relatively small overall impact on the system. This impact may not show up on the radar of the managers guarding the system, and may be easy to ignore or rationalize when managers do notice.

Fourth, the system's real stakeholders are hard to see. Employees see a payroll system run by "management," or by a city-wide or state-wide personnel office, and their equipment comes from "the organization" or from the jurisdiction-wide administrative services agency. But looks can deceive. Neither "management," nor "the organization," nor "the city," is the creator/owner that funds the enterprise. Public managers are direct agents of the legislature that, in turn, conveys the preferences of the public that, through its taxes, pays the freight.

Employees abusing systems usually see none of this. Picking the pockets of their taxpaying neighbors is the furthest thing from employees' minds when they take home the office's video projector. Instead, the projector is taken from an agency "that can afford it," causing "management" a problem it "deserves" anyway for having lousy control systems, and for being stingy and unappreciative towards the workers. When employees see fraud, waste and abuse as virtually victimless acts, tinged with justice, the door is open wide to resource diversion.

So what should a manager do?

First, he or she should cultivate a healthy skepticism. No system is foolproof. And systems serving noble causes like disabled officers are no more foolproof than any other. A police executive ought to act as a devil's advocate from time to time with respect to the operating principles and practices of all the operations affecting the agency. Aggressively searching for system vulnerabilities should be an ongoing task aided by feedback from rank-and-file employees. No one knows better than employees where the hidden weaknesses lie in the elegant systems crafted by self-satisfied managers.

Second, managers should give priority to knowing even the arcane and complex systems under their command. A manager need not understand the pension system as an actuary would, or the crime information system as the computer programmer would. But the manager needs to know how employees and citizens interact with these systems and how those systems interact with each other. The cases reported by *Newsday* implicated a range of systems. Some officers had time and leave problems before they suffered their disabling injuries. Other officers faced serious disciplinary charges that were automatically put on hold when their sudden injuries kicked off the disability determination process. The secondary employment of some officers belied the infirmities they used to justify their disability claims. Understanding the broader context governing employee interactions with particular processes and systems can help managers anticipate and head off problems, instead of being blindsided by issues that seem to come out of nowhere.

Third, managers need to take the position that no violation of a system's integrity can be ignored. Let's say that Officer Jones signs out his partner at the end of the shift so that she won't be docked for leaving two hours early to attend to a crisis at home. Jones is well intentioned and his partner left for good reason. Assuming that the system captures the forged signature and the hours paid without work, a manager must do something. The issue is not Jones' good intentions, nor the reasons why his partner left, but the breach of the system. Reprimands for both, and wage reimbursement by the partner who went home early, would reaffirm that the time and leave system's integrity was not to be compromised.

Fourth, managers need to educate. The field of vision of the average employee, and the average manager for that matter, tends to be narrow. This tunnel vision limits reality to what immediately surrounds the viewer. So, law enforcement officers can come to see their world circumscribed by "management" above, "perps" and "citizens" below, and their fellow police officers, "us," to the left and right. This worldview is not likely to light any motivational fires. When, as is often the case, the police officers' worldview simplifies even further to "us" versus "them," doctoring time sheets or roughing up a suspect can lose any negative connotations, becoming just another tactic with which "we" better handle "them." This degraded attitude is deadly, opening up the organization to most of the failure threats we have discussed in this book.

Education is the antidote to attitude degradation. The role of the police agency in the larger society and in the U.S. political/legal system needs to be hammered home constantly through mission statements, executive speeches, the police academy curriculum, in-service training sessions, roll call reminders, and newsletters. Everyone in the organization should come to understand that the ultimate bosses are "out there," not on the top floor of police headquarters. Management should also mount educational campaigns about the organizational systems and policies that are put into place. Time and leave systems, for instance, have equity goals, which are defeated when only some employees "beat the system." Crime reporting systems have effectiveness goals, such as crime reduction, shared by the rank-and-file. Policy changes, such as the reduction of time officers devote to arraignment, achieve "productivity," of which officers are wary; but such changes also free officers from drudgery while getting them back to their chosen profession of crime fighting. These rationales ought to be articulated and rearticulated by management. If that does not happen, policies and systems are defenseless against negative spin in the employee grapevine and become fair game for abuse.

Now that we have considered how law enforcement executives might better guard against resource diversions within their agencies, let's turn the spotlight on how executives themselves can sometimes misuse and expropriate organizational resources entrusted to their care.

## Getting a Good Deal on Home Improvements

Anthony Serra had made it nearly to the top of the New York City Department of Correction by 2002. He had progressed steadily from Captain to Warden to Three Star Bureau Chief. But as he neared the top it occurred to Serra that people on staff at the Department of Correction could do improvements on his home in Putnam County, north of New York City. After receiving tips that correction officers were serving as home improvement workers for their boss, a local TV station had secretly filmed the ongoing construction.[14] It made perfect "Eyewitness News." This mobilized city investigators who confirmed that members of the construction crew were on the clock at Rikers Island, New York City's main prison, or at other Correction Department sites and projects, while they were hammering nails some fifty miles north at Serra's home. This led to Serra's indictment in 2003 on multiple charges alleging a scheme to divert correction personnel and equipment to his personal use.[15]

As the Bronx District Attorney's office reported after Serra pled guilty to a single grand larceny charge in March 2005, the prison chief had "used Department of Correction personnel on construction projects at his home in suburban Mahopac, New York in Putnam County. The work was performed at taxpayers' expense by correction officers as well as civilian employees who were supposed to be on duty at Rikers Island. The work included the remodeling of a bathroom and kitchen, the construction of a basketball court and the installation of stereophonic loud speakers in a ceiling at Serra's home."[16]

Serra also ended up pleading guilty to a misdemeanor charge of conflict of interest. According to the Bronx District Attorney, the energetic and politically active Serra had also "used his influence to recruit subordinates ranging from wardens, assistant deputy wardens, captains, correction officers and civilian employees of the Department of Correction, to work as 'volunteers' in a poll watching operation on behalf of Governor George Pataki's primary election campaigns to win the Conservative Party and Independence Party nominations for governor."[17]

Serra was scheduled to be sentenced to a year in prison, which sentence was to run concurrently with any federal sentence for income tax evasion. The latter charge arose from the fact that Serra had not reported the substantial work on his home, as well as other income, for tax purposes. In addition to jail time, Serra was assessed some $50,000 in restitution and fines on the state charges.[18]

## The Expansive Definition of "Mine" in the Executive Suite

Stories such as Serra's are not difficult to find; we will be examining Serra's one time boss later in the chapter. Resource diversions by those in overall charge of the organization, or large parts of the organization, tend to become media events. The offending executives work in agencies with high public visibility, and often are prominent in their own right. Newspapers are sold and TV news ratings soar on an emerging scandal with the promise of tarring agencies, besmirching uniforms, and destroying the reputation of the key player or players. In a very real way, the charges alone do more damage than the subsequent proceedings and findings by courts of law or disciplinary boards. The transgressing executive charged with multiple offenses may eventually plead guilty to only a single count. The organization, however, sustains the disdain and criticism associated with all the charges through all the months and years that the proceedings drag on.

When those entrusted with leadership in a criminal justice agency violate the trust inherent in their position, it is a sorry event. And a key question is "What were they thinking?"

For a very relevant answer, let's jump several levels above Bureau Chief Anthony Serra, and move one state east to Connecticut. Within a week of Serra's guilty plea, the former Governor of Connecticut, John G. Rowland, was being sentenced on corruption charges. Rowland, who had resigned in disgrace the previous summer, told the U.S. Magistrate that he had lost his moral compass and developed "a sense of entitlement and even arrogance. I let my pride get in the way."[19]

The perks to which Rowland came to feel entitled included home improvements to his vacation cabin, as well as trips to Nevada, Vermont and Florida paid for by persons doing business with the state. Their generosity towards Rowland won favorable influence from the Governor's Office on behalf of current and potential projects with which their businesses were involved.

Rowland indicts his "sense of entitlement" as leading to his downfall. If there is one thing that persuades executives and the rank-and-file to cross the line, it is the idea that they deserve what they are breaking the rules to take. The "deserved perk" can help send FBI executives winging cross-country at agency expense to attend a party for a former colleague. A sense of entitlement was at work when a DEA Special Agent-in-Charge used subordinates and the agency's computer system in the service of the private security firm he owned.[20]

If anything, executives face greater temptations than their subordinates. Detectives or patrol officers padding their hours are manipulating a clear set of time and leave rules. They may not often think hard about those rules, having rationalized their scheme as normal and good. But when someone objectively matches the rules to their behavior, it is pretty clear that they are out of bounds.

Executives operate in territory where the lines become less clear. What's coming to top law enforcement executives by dint of their position is substantial. Things they once did for themselves get done for them. A car is always at the ready, driver too. One, two or more uniformed officers stand ready to fulfill any request the chief makes. The chief's deputies are a phone call away, ready to come on the run. The chief's staff is generally the best in the agency: appointments are expertly juggled; crafted speeches appear on the way to an event. At these events, and at a lot of other places in town, the chief is treated like a celebrity. Civilians who can are inclined to do things for celebrity police chiefs:

invite them to parties, treat them to tickets to sporting events, and send a fine bottle of wine over to their table. They, like the chief's staff, want to make the chief's day.

Here is where the chief or commissioner enters muddy and dangerous waters. When a rich array of resources is attached formally to an administrative office, the incumbents are always challenged to keep the resources that serve them in an official capacity from spilling over to benefit them as private persons. That chiefs can fail to meet the challenge is evidenced by aides who end up researching the boss' book or chauffeuring the boss' spouse around on personal errands.

Executives have another advantage over the patrol officer or detective in expropriating an organizational resource. Executives have considerable power to redefine the boundary between right and wrong in an authoritative way. No patrol officer can redefine bogus overtime as legitimate by saying "I'm always on call." Yet executives can blithely chalk up dinners with each other, time spent on airplanes, and all their waking hours at conferences as "official business." Executives can run up hundreds and even thousands of hours of comprehensive time ("comp time" = extra hours worked in a day redeemable in future paid time off) that they cash in when they leave their posts. The ability of an executive to decide for himself or herself what constitutes a "legitimate" use of organization resources only heightens what ex-governor Rowland called the "sense of entitlement and arrogance."

Similarly, when the well-heeled and well-placed civilians in whose social circles the chief now moves try to shower him or her with generosity, that chief may have a difficult time adopting the cynical and unrewarding view that these offers have nothing to do with him as a person. After all, these are dining companions, sports event buddies, and fellow members of the Chamber of Commerce. The item (pick one: subsidized rent, season tickets, low interest loan) being offered is much more ego-gratifying and conscience-cleansing when viewed as the result of warm personal friendships unrelated to the chief's job. And so subsidized rents, season tickets and sweetheart loans pop up on occasion to unseat sitting chiefs and darken the legacy of retired ones.

## The Demoralizing Impact of Executive Resource Diversion

When law enforcement executives take extra helpings from the organizational platter, a lot of people are sitting around the table. When the commissioner's car ends up at the family's summer home a hundred miles out of town, the drivers know. The secretary knows when the expense voucher includes a six-day stay in Las Vegas for that three-day professional conference. When workers are diverted to projects at the boss's home, their immediate supervisors know where they are, and so do their co-workers. Resource diversions by executives are rarely a secret, no matter how discreet or cagey the executive thinks he or she has been.

When employees witness executive resource diversions, there are inescapable negative impacts on the organization. Some employees know of the impropriety but feel constrained to keep quiet. An alleged participant in Serra's scheme told a TV news reporter: "Everyone feels totally degraded. I'm one of many and we're all drinking out of the same cup of poison."[21] Subordinates may feel a tremendous sense of inequity because they lack the leverage that their superiors use to extract side bonuses. Listen to the tone of another correction officer quoted on the same news report: "He (Serra) has several officers that ... act as personal helpers or personal assistants for him on city time ... do work on his house, run errands, personal errands and do various political jobs."[22] Such employees may not be able to do what the boss does but they can even the score in another way by doing less, with less enthusiasm, on the job.

Whether their reservations are ethical or selfish, we have seen that employee witnesses to executive excess can and do blow the whistle. Therefore, the executive engaged in resource diversion may further subvert organizational systems by seeking to prevent employees in the know from raising a hue and cry. The ways in which these executives seek to suppress whistle-blowing urges involves fear, fealty and reward.

Fear is a faint background hum in the consciousness of most employees. It is ever present in a minimal, easy-to-ignore way, yet can become immensely motivating when the employee feels in harm's way. Such exposure can result from becoming involved with or aware of executive excess, which makes an employee a potential liability to the bosses involved. Bullying bosses may directly intimidate whistle-blower candidates. But other miscreant managers simply go about their business, making few if any threats. Employees, however, know to be wary of the punitive weapons any boss possesses. Grapevine tales of whistle-blowers crushed in days gone by often reinforces this wariness. This powerful, latent danger that employees perceive makes them reluctant to report executive misbehavior through official channels. "They would have made up some sort of bogus charge to retaliate," said one correction officer in response to a reporter's question about his silence in the Serra case.[23]

Fealty is another subtle silencer. The leaders of organizations deal daily with employees who owe them a lot. Many executives, independent of any penchant for illicit enrichment, reinforce this sense of obligation by emphasizing personal loyalty at least as much as professional qualifications. This disposes underlings, in part out of fear but also out of loyalty and responsibility and duty, to give the boss what he or she wants. So, when executives offer dubious and convoluted reasons to justify their extra rewards, the subordinates who effectuate the payments may well buy in. After all, the boss says so.

But loyalty and duty, and even fear, can only go so far. This adds another wrinkle that complicates resource diversion schemes by executives. When other employees are involved in or aware of a situation that diverts substantial resources to an executive, this creates pressure to share the wealth. Either the executive or employees directly or peripherally involved can come to believe that the deal is too sweet to be hogged by the boss alone. So now the executive either splits the take or diverts even more resources to take care of associates, who end up with plum assignments, promotions and raises that yet others may notice.

The destructiveness of this in terms of organizational integrity is obvious, and the decimation of employee morale is also likely to be severe and widespread. Employees in general are highly attuned to anyone who "sucks up to the boss," or gets assigned to "special details," especially when that leaves co-workers to pick up the slack. And the employee grapevine usually has a sense of how certain bosses are exploiting their positions for personal gain. So when co-workers on special assignment to such bosses start to rise, the message is clear: Doing your job doesn't get you ahead; serving your boss, even at the expense of the organization, does. This idea is cancerous to the law enforcement organization, and spreads directly from the behavior of the resource-diverting executive.

## Justice for Resource Diverting Executives

Certainly corporate scandals in the United States have paved the way for a greater acceptance of substantial prison sentences for executive misdeeds. Harsher penalties were incorporated in various acts of Congress, including the Sarbanes-Oxley Act, designed to curb corporate wrongdoing. Since 2002, convictions of executives at Enron, WorldCom and Adelphia have resulted in long prison terms.[24] Corporate boards of directors have, in turn, put their CEOs on a shorter ethical leash. Boeing, the aircraft maker, went through two CEOs in less than a year. A major conflict of interest scandal involving defense contracts scuttled the first CEO. His successor was out the door after commencing an adulterous affair with a subordinate.[25]

Zero tolerance and sure penalties for executive misdeeds make a difference. Increasing the negative consequences associated with resource diversion makes the practice less attractive, and less practiced. This seems, at least, to be the short term impact in the corporate sector. However, the Sarbanes-Oxley Act and other federal laws passed to curb private sector abuse do not cover public agency misdeeds. Thus, while corporate embezzler Andrew Fastow, who served as Enron's Chief Financial Officer, was sentenced to ten years, spending six years in jail and pre-release facilities,[26] neither Governor Rowland nor Chief Serra served a year in jail before their supervised releases.

It can be argued that the penalties for the misappropriation of funds by governors and police chiefs ought to be at least as harsh as they are for corporate executives. Dollar for dollar, the resources expropriated by executives in public agencies may not compare to the illicit take of their private sector counterparts. However, resource-diverting public sector executives violate a solemn trust conferred upon them by the citizenry at large. And the perverse role model these executives convey can puncture agency esprit de corps and de-legitimize the law enforcement agency in the eyes of the public. At the very least, barring the toughening of laws relating to public sector malfeasance, prosecutors ought to seek the maximum penalties for such crimes under existing laws.

The effectiveness of organizational penalties in preventing an executive's diversion of organizational resources to personal use is also open to question. As a practical matter, many public agency executives caught up in such scandals are retirement-eligible, and can forestall organizational sanction by "putting in their papers." (In the disability pension case, for example, some officers short-circuited disciplinary charges with a disability filing.) When the organization's weapons against employee misdeeds are easily neutralized, they provide little disincentive to abuse. Furthermore, ripped-off agencies often have an interest in keeping violations quiet. Because media exposés and high visibility trials compound damage already done, quiet resignations by veteran executives may actually be preferred to criminal charges.

This approach sends the wrong message to rising managers with a growing sense of entitlement, who may be calculating the risks and rewards of aggressively drawing upon organizational resources they control. If resignation is seen as an "ace in the hole" against organizational penalties and the organization is seen as reluctant to publicize its victimization, the risk-reward calculus shifts strongly toward exploitation of office, especially for the "entitled" and ethically challenged executive. Public organizations—and law enforcement organizations especially—should aggressively sanction executives who divert agency resources and aggressively pursue legal action when possible against those who use retirement as an evasive maneuver.

Firm punishment for executive misbehavior sends two important messages throughout the organization. The first message is that abuse will be dealt with. The second, perhaps more important, message is that the rules are not enforced any less harshly against those on top.

Now we have written at several points in this book about measured, non-zero tolerance approaches towards employee discipline. Resource diversion, however, is in general a worthy candidate for automatic, significant penalties and considerable logic attaches to having those holding high office pay an even more substantial and public price. All too often, however, it's the other way around with a punishing approach towards rank-and-file abusers and a gentler take on comparable transgressions in the executive suite. This is neither fair, nor good leadership, and it is not good management.

## Profiling Risk in the Rising Executive

The prevention of resource diversion at executive levels requires early attention to the kind of thinking that enables abuse. Once established, a sense of entitlement and license is likely to be reinforced by successively more elaborate trappings of office and increased personnel and resources as the individual moves up in the organization. Executives should be on guard for rising stars who seem to confuse the power and authority of the office they hold with their unique skills and personal dominance. This kind of thinking supports a role shift from incumbency to ownership, and owners can take what they want.

Top management thus should stay alert for rising executives who are territorial and possessive with respect to their office, their staff and the resources at their disposal. An executive who constantly refers to "my staff," "my office" or "my car" may not be a resource diversion threat. It still doesn't hurt, however, to point out that he or she is a temporary steward of those "my" things which, like the organization, exist to serve the public, not the comfort or egos of officers and commanders.

Making a dent in the entitlement mindset may also require taking a close look at the accoutrements of office, starting with the offices themselves. Locating top staff in a bullpen of cubicles, as some agencies do, downplays status distinctions and elevates the importance of communication. Assigning a standard-issue cruiser to everyone from the officer in the field to the commissioner down at headquarters also sends an anti-entitlement message.

A greater level of monetary rewards for high-achieving top executives may also, paradoxically, help dampen the entitlement syndrome in public agencies. Where executive salaries are fixed and relatively low, bigger offices, larger staffs, flashy cars and liberal expense accounts often serve as surrogate rewards for outstanding accomplishment. Not only are these rewards susceptible to abuse, but also they reinforce the entitlement mindset that can lead to abuse.

\* \* \*

The following case dramatically highlights key aspects of executive resource diversion. It is the case of Bernie Kerik, who had rocketed to high public positions in the City of New York, becoming Correction Commissioner — yes, Anthony Serra was a subordinate — and then Police Commissioner where, alongside his boss Mayor Rudy Giuliani, he achieved national recognition on and after 9/11. The case is given extended treatment because it offers so much to think about while reinforcing lessons from the cases we've just discussed.

## From Police Commissioner to Inmate # 84888-054

The case of Bernard Kerik, NYPD Commissioner on 9/11, reads like a classic tragedy, where the protagonist rises from the bottom of the heap to the very pinnacle only to be undone by traits that both fueled the rise and set the stage for a mighty fall.

Bernard Kerik had a unique rise to the top of the NYPD. A street cop—on patrol and then undercover—Kerik had never held NYPD rank above detective third grade, and had spent a total of eight years "on the job," when New York Mayor Rudolph Giuliani appointed him the 40th Commissioner of the NYPD in 2000.

All of Kerik's managerial experience had been outside the NYPD. Prior to joining the NYPD at the age of 31, Kerik worked in law enforcement and private security both in the U.S. and abroad. In his last job before becoming a New York City police officer, Kerik worked in New Jersey for the Passaic County Sheriff's Office, where he served for a short time as warden in the country jail.

From day one in 1986, Kerik committed full-throttle to the NYPD, quickly making a name for himself as an aggressive patrol officer and effective undercover narcotics cop. Kerik's narcotics work earned him a detective's shield by 1990, the same year he met Rudolf Giuliani.[27] Giuliani was the "law and order" U.S. Attorney who had narrowly lost New York City's 1989 mayoral race. Kerik and Giuliani first crossed paths at a fundraising event that Kerik was helping organize on behalf of the family of a slain NYPD officer. The two met again at similar events and, as 1993 approached, Giuliani made clear he was running again and asked for the help of his law enforcement supporters, which included an enthusiastic Kerik.[28]

By the time 1993 rolled around, Kerik had put together Giuliani's personal security detail and was moonlighting weekends as the candidate's driver. At the same time, the tireless Kerik had an intense day-job with the New York Drug Enforcement Task Force, where state and local police partnered with the DEA to fight drug trafficking in producing countries, transit point nations and distribution networks throughout the United States. The Task Force produced high profile arrests and major drug seizures, earning commendations for its member officers, including Kerik, who was already decorated for his patrol and undercover work in the NYPD.

After Rudy Giuliani became Mayor in 1994, he plucked Kerik up and out of the rank and file of the NYPD. Kerik was assigned to head up investigations in the New York City Department of Correction, the largest jail system in the U.S., and one of the most problem-prone. Giuliani's first Correction Commissioner was on the job only a year when the Mayor grew impatient with the pace of change and the department's continuing penchant for ending up in the tabloid crosshairs.

So in January 1995 Mayor Giuliani installed a new regime at the Department of Correction and named Bernard Kerik, less than a year removed from front-line detective work, as the First Deputy Commissioner, the department's number two post. Kerik performed well, despite his minimal administrative experience. With zero acculturation to "how things were done" in New York jails, an action orientation from his front-line policing, and an appreciation for NYPD performance gains being achieved by goal-focused, data-driven management, Kerik made a difference. The jails were cleaner, assaults were cut in half, and the Department of Correction ran more smoothly.

As 1997 drew to a close, Correction Commissioner Michael Jacobson decided to accept a professorship at John Jay College of Criminal Justice of the City University of New York. And Kerik, the proven Giuliani loyalist, low-profile team player and tough administrator, was poised for the top spot. Mayor Giuliani made Kerik the Commissioner of Correction on December 23, 1997.

In 2000, NYPD Commissioner Howard Safir was thinking retirement and, in August, announced that he was stepping down. So Rudy Giuliani, known for demanding, but also reciprocating, his subordinates' loyalty, offered Third Grade Detective Bernie Kerik the ultimate post, NYPD Commissioner. Kerik eagerly accepted. Giuliani, who had been re-elected in 1997, was term-limited and would be out as mayor on January 1st, 2002. Bernard Kerik, tightly hitched to Giuliani's star, saw himself departing then as well. The lame-duck Mayor and short-term Police Commissioner seemed ready to ride quietly off into the sunset.

Then came the horror of 9/11. Giuliani and Kerik were thrust onto a national stage before a traumatized citizenry ready for heroes. Giuliani became "America's Mayor," with Kerik his ever-present top cop. Kerik's autobiography, *The Lost Son: A Life in Pursuit of Justice,* published in November 2001 with a hastily added "Ground Zero" afterword, jumped onto the best-seller list.

The Giuliani-Kerik partnership, forged by mutual loyalty and energized amidst a national crisis, continued in the private sector. Kerik became a key player in Giuliani Partners, consulting and taking on law enforcement projects around the globe. Then Giuliani, his sights set on a 2008 presidential run, started playing politics on the national stage. In 2004, Giuliani encouraged the Bush administration, on the cusp of a second term and ready to make major personnel changes, to consider Kerik for a major post.[29] When Tom Ridge, the Department of Homeland Security's first Secretary, announced his resignation shortly after the 2004 November election, Bernie Kerik was the Bush administration's choice to succeed him.

Homeland Security was an amalgam of grafted-together agencies that needed, but resisted, greater integration. Homeland Security also was searching for greater policy coherence in the face of the evolving challenges of global terrorism. Kerik's central role on 9/11, his reputation as a tough administrator and Rudy Giuliani's patronage had vaulted him to the top of the President's list. So, when President Bush told Kerik he wanted someone to take over and "break some china," Kerik answered the call.[30]

That's when the world learned about "the other Bernie Kerik."

The issue that quickly sunk Kerik's nomination concerned his children's nanny. "Nanny-gate" scandals derailed several nominees to top cabinet posts over the years, most notably President Clinton's first *two* picks for Attorney General. Now, eleven years down the road, "nanny" landmines were exploding around Kerik. Kerik had failed to pay employer taxes for which he was responsible. In addition, the nanny had used someone else's social security number, suggesting she may have been unable to qualify for documentation on her own. Given Homeland Security's responsibility for immigration enforcement, the nanny issue alone was enough for Kerik to withdraw his name from consideration. This small leak in Kerik's image, however, became a torrent as more serious issues emerged.

It turns out that Bernie Kerik, during his time at Corrections, solidified his friendship with one Larry Ray, the best man at Kerik's 1998 wedding who chipped in around $10,000 for the reception. Ray said Kerik, then making $150,000 as Corrections Commissioner, claimed to be cash-strapped. Kerik ended the friendship in 2000 when Ray was indicted, along with mob associated co-defendants, for stock fraud and conspiracy. The case dragged on for years, with Ray unsuccessfully trying to get the charges dismissed on the grounds that he was an FBI informant who had been promised immunity.

Kerik established other associations during his time at Corrections that ended up paying off. Kerik struck up a relationship with the principals of Interstate Industrial, a New Jersey contractor interested in maintaining and expanding its work with New York City, as well as generating more work with New Jersey governments. Soon Lawrence Ray was working for Interstate—after Kerik put in a good word—and Kerik's brother ended up working at a Staten Island transfer station managed by Interstate. Beyond being a solid gold reference for landing a job at Interstate, Kerik was also contacting New York City regulators in ways that facilitated Interstate's dealings. Kerik was walking an ethically dubious line.

When benefits began flowing to Kerik via Interstate, the line was crossed. In 1999 and 2000 Kerik received $255,000 in renovations to his Bronx apartment paid ultimately by Interstate, during a time when Kerik was putting in a good word for Interstate with other New York officials. The renovations, along with a separate loan from another party that Kerik had failed to disclose, led to state charges that were pled down to misdemeanors, with Kerik paying a hefty fine.[31] However, Kerik's failure to pay taxes on the $255,000 later became a basis for federal charges that resulted in a plea deal and a four year prison sentence. The federal charges included making false statements on loan applications, to federal investigators and to White House officials checking his background relative to the Homeland Security post.[32]

The headline-grabbing state and federal charges overshadowed other actions by Kerik that led to ethics charges and lurid tabloid exposes connected, in one way or another, to his book.

Key parts of *The Lost Son* deal with Kerik's mother, an alcoholic living life so hard in Ohio that she neglected her son. By the age of four, Kerik had already spent time in foster care and with relatives of his mother's acquaintances when his father, who had remarried and moved to New Jersey, gained legal custody. Kerik's mother continued her downward spiral, ending up beaten to death in a seedy flat in 1964. Nearly four decades later, Kerik's ethical problem was that NYPD detectives had been dispatched to places like Newark, Ohio to work his mother's "cold case," an investigation with zero relevance for New York City taxpayers but considerable value as a central theme in Kerik's book. Kerik ended up paying a $2500 fine, levied by the New York City Board of Ethics during the administration of Giuliani's successor, Michael Bloomberg.

Then there was Kerik's affair with his book's publisher, Judith Regan. The affair got going in 2001 as the Police Commissioner was finishing up his autobiography. Trysts allegedly took place in downtown Manhattan apartments made available to city officials on 24/7 call in the aftermath of 9/11. This saga was front-page tabloid fodder in 2005, and again in 2007, after Regan lost her position and alleged in a court filing that executives of Rupert Murdoch's News Corporation, which owned both Regan's publishing house and Fox News, had pressured her to withhold details about the affair that might damage Giuliani's presidential aspirations.[33]

Kerik battled the charges against him at just about every turn—in the courts, in the media, before conviction and after, prior to his sentencing and beyond. Kerik was jailed for contempt as his federal trail loomed when the judge determined Kerik had leaked sealed information to a person marshaling an internet campaign proclaiming Kerik's innocence and impugning the prosecutors.[34] Even after Kerik began serving his four year sentence in a federal correctional facility in May 2010, his lawyers appealed the sentence as excessive, an argument rejected by an appeals court in 2011.

## When Loyalty Trumps All

Kerik was fearless; a black-belt in martial arts who emerged unscathed from policing's most dangerous assignment, undercover narcotics. Kerik's attitude approached invincibility. "One cop who's known him for years describes Kerik's attitude this way: 'I get shot at, but I don't get hit. I save wounded cops. I don't get wounded.'"[35]

Kerik's career and life path certainly reinforced that notion, at least as Kerik portrays it. When he stumbles, even severely, he rights himself, learns, and goes on, apparently little worse for the wear. The examples pepper his autobiography.

He dropped out of high school and drifted about as a teenager, but martial arts provided structure as did entering the military, where he earned a diploma and got his first law enforcement experience as an MP.

When words failed after Kerik's teenage brother was arrested, a frustrated Kerik unleashed a karate kick that broke his brother's ribs.[36] Years later and redeemed, Kerik's younger brother went to work for him at the Passaic County jail.[37]

Stationed in Korea, Kerik fathered a girl with a Korean woman.[38] She later ended up in the U.S. married to another serviceman so Kerik established contact relative to their daughter; the husband deemed this harassment to a point where federal authorities threatened to arrest Kerik if he didn't desist. [39] He did, but committed himself to being the best parent he could be for his children that followed.

As a Fort Bragg MP making a car stop, Kerik broke a soldier's middle finger (which made the gesture that led to the stop in the first place). This action got Kerik busted from corporal to PFC, but the demotion avoided a threatened court martial guaranteed to be a law enforcement career killer.[40]

In Saudi Arabia, where Kerik worked security at a hospital that served Saudi royalty, he was interrogated by secret police. Responding to what he saw as a veiled threat against his wife, Kerik clamped a headlock on the offending officer, declaring he was ready to "snap your f---ing head off" if that line of questioning continued.[41] The one-way ticket out of the country this earned Kerik had no effect on his career progression.

Undercover narcotics investigation was Kerik's work world before he launched his fast-track managerial career at Corrections. Undercover cops live a lie; suspects are enmeshed in a dangerous high-risk, high-reward enterprise. Everyone is walking the edge and things go south in a hurry. Lose trust—a cop's cover gets blown, drug bosses believe an underling is skimming profits—and you can die. As Kerik and his partners learned, going with your gut—which sometime meant not waiting around for bureaucratic approvals—might be the difference between standing in the middle of a field of fire or ducking for cover just in time. Bernie Kerik always seemed to escape from the tight corners and land squarely on his feet.

If Kerik's life experiences conditioned him to feel pretty invincible, his relationship with Rudy Giuliani, once solidified, added a bulletproof vest.

Giuliani prized loyalty, his actions often underscoring how critical a trait this was. For former U.S. Marshal Howard Safir, who had worked with Giuliani in the U.S. Department of Justice during the 1980s, becoming Mayor Giuliani's first Fire Commissioner was no problem.[42] For William Bratton, whose turnaround of the NYPD repeated his success at other police agencies, making the cover of Time magazine standing in front of an NYPD cruiser was a bad career move—a hogging of Giuliani's law and order spotlight. Giuliani was soon calling for an ethics review of Bratton's book contract,[43] publicly declaring his right to name Bratton's senior commanders[44] and remarking that Bratton had expressed interest in lucrative private sector employment.[45] When Bratton, not surprisingly, resigned, Safir was moved over from the Fire Department to run the NYPD.[46]

While lessons like this probably helped Kerik more finely calibrate his obeisance to the Mayor, he had been all-in with Giuliani from day one. Kerik praised Giuliani while introducing him at 1990s police fundraisers, volunteered early for Giuliani's second mayoral quest and, as the campaign really got rolling, became a weekend fixture behind the wheel of Giuliani's car and as a security presence during the candidate's appearances. Kerik was getting an extended job suitability interview, without a particular job in mind, with the man poised to run the City of New York. Kerik aced his loyalty and reliability review, so Giuliani plucked Kerik from the NYPD ranks to fill a sensitive investigative post in Corrections. When Kerik smartly bought into, and enthusiastically implemented, Giuliani's performance management philosophy, his advancement potential under Giuliani became unlimited.

The loyal Kerik, however, had little practical socialization to ethical issues of public management. His rapid rise to top-tier executive had been fueled by mayoral connections. His workplace worldview had developed in edgy jobs such as private security and undercover narcotics. "Look, I'm not the norm," he would later say in contrasting himself to executive candidate with more typical credentials, "I was booming doors, chasing the Cali cartel, getting into gunfights, and doing all kinds of crazy stuff." [47]

It was not so much that Kerik lacked a college degree, though this was later raised when he became Police Commissioner despite a bachelor's degree being required for captain's rank and above. Kerik's critical lack was management seasoning, and the nuanced judgment of right and wrong that comes with such experience. As he has said, "I didn't focus enough on ethical issues." [48]

Finding out that Kerik hadn't been cut from standard executive cloth wasn't exactly a challenge. Kerik's autobiography identifies pause-worthy issues that a diligent background investigation could also have unearthed, such as personal bankruptcy and a service demotion. But Kerik had already passed the ultimate test, Giuliani's. So Kerik kept swashbuckling along, perhaps oblivious to his transgressions, or else feeling immune from the ramifications. Renovations got done, referrals were made. A book contract got signed, police investigators went to Ohio, and no daggers were drawn at City Hall. After 9/11, heroic status ensued. Rudy Giuliani became "America's Mayor," Bernie Kerik, his top cop.

Kerik's already robust self-image inflated further, fueling a sense of righteousness and, ultimately, victimization that endured through all the revelations, trials and even sentencing. As the federal prosecutors wrote in their sentencing memorandum: "The defendant's egotism and hubris were the tragic flaws that led him to commit the considerable number of crimes to which he ultimately pleaded guilty,"[49]

The judge in Kerik's federal trial presented his views thusly, "Mr. Kerik, if left to his own devices, will obstruct justice ... My fear is that he has a toxic combination of self-minded focus and arrogance, and I fear that combination leads him to believe that his ends justify his means." [50]

When the trial ended and many respectable folks wrote the court urging a lighter sentence because of Kerik's contributions and accomplishments, one name was conspicuously absent—Rudy Giuliani.[51]

When loyalty counts for too much, bad things can happen. A sense of immunity and license can easily take hold in loyalist administrators, especially in those who lack a strong grounding in organizational or professional ethics. So, monitoring for fraud and abuse should never skip over units led by known loyalists or the executive's "favorites," despite subtle or not-so-subtle pressures to look away. Indeed, scrutiny ought to be dialed up, not down, as those who go astray in such roles may not know what it is they do, or may not care.

\* \* \*

Let's complete our resource diversion cases by looking at time and leave abuse, which may well be the most common way in which law enforcement officers, from the officer on the beat to the commanders at headquarters, take an extra measure of compensation from their organizations.

## The Iron Men and Women of Labor, Law Enforcement Style

It was March 2003 when Cleveland *Plain Dealer* reporters began a series of articles on police overtime in Parma, an Ohio city of 90,000 just south of Cleveland. The report made much of individual overtime champions: "One patrolman, with an annual base salary of about $55,000, has claimed so many overtime and off duty hours that he has managed to earn an average of $124,000 in each of the last four years."[52]

The newspaper report focused on a program that generated a general scramble by Parma's uniformed personnel to cash in on overtime opportunities. The all-overtime "Police on Patrol Arresting Speeders" program, founded in 1991, deployed patrol officers to target traffic violators. The assumption was that the traffic fines would more than make up for the officer's time-and-a-half rate of pay because the program would utilize lower paid officers with only a few years on the job. Soon, however, sergeants, lieutenants and captains were eager to be traffic cops for a day. For years, program costs soared beyond any break-even point. However, it took until 2001 for police administrators and the Parma city government to react; and then they had little choice but to end a program so far in the red that it was dragging down the city budget. Still, officers were chagrined. Officers virtually stopped writing traffic tickets, and ramped back other enforcement efforts by about half.[53]

The deeper the reporters looked, the more problems they found. Officers were working mind-boggling hours, the equivalent, for one officer, of "11.3 hours a day, seven days a week, 52 weeks a year for three consecutive years"— a workload that included the officer's off duty security work for the local school system.[54] Further examination showed officers being paid by both the Parma Police Department and by their off-duty employers—for the same hours. Other officers were shown to have double-billed for overtime hours. Those commanders and officers who spoke for the record cited honest mistakes or routine, predictable clerical errors for the anomalies the reporters uncovered.[55]

The reporters were not deterred and kept digging. They next revealed patterns of sick leave and overtime usage suggesting that Parma officers were "changing water into wine."[56] This miracle occurs when two or more officers tag-team a department's sick leave, overtime and minimum staffing rules. It works like this. In week one, Officer A gets sick on Officer B's day off, which brings their unit below minimum staffing levels. Officer B, who has made plain his willingness to fill in, gets called in at time-and-a-half. The next week Officer B gets sick on A's day off, and A comes in at time-and-a-half.

While ensuing investigations confirmed the pattern the reporters had found, they did not uncover evidence that two or more specific officers had conspired to generate overtime for themselves. Nonetheless, the *Plain Dealer*'s investigative reporters produced gross figures—a 33% increase in sick leave and a minimum staffing overtime increase of 38% during the same three year time period—showing a collective conversion of straight time into overtime by Parma officers.[57]

The *Plain Dealer*'s investigation also identified incentives for police personnel to treat the sick leave and overtime systems as linked opportunities to enhance pay. Sick days were "on the clock" in terms of counting hours worked in a week. So a Monday–Friday officer could be out sick on Monday at full pay and then work his fifth day of the week on Saturday at time-and-a-half. Some officers managed to be both out sick and working overtime hours on the same day.[58]

The Parma police department was in and out of the media spotlight for two years, often because key executives were leaving their posts, and not always with their heads held high. The Parma public safety director, who had publicly bemoaned his limited leverage over police overtime and work slowdowns, resigned within a week of the first *Plain Dealer* story. The mayor was out within the year. The new mayor dryly noted that there were "labor and union issues of who is going to be in control" of the department.[59] The police chief, who had proclaimed the *Plain Dealer* exposé a "wake up call,"[60] retired by the end of 2003 and soon became a poster child for the Parma Police Department's troubles. The official investigation of overtime abuse turned up irregularities in the chief's off-duty employment, where records had been falsified to understate his income. The chief was indicted, and pled guilty to filing an inaccurate tax return early in 2005, while two officers faced related charges.[61]

As the wheels of justice ground slowly against Parma police personnel, the *Plain Dealer* and other media outlets turned their attention to the Cleveland Police Department. Though Cleveland was not Parma, dubious overtime patterns were just as easy to find. Cleveland officers trolled for overtime opportunities in their department's time and leave system as enthusiastically as their counterparts in Parma. Cleveland's cops handled more felonies than Parma officers, which meant more time in court. And court provided fertile ground for accumulating overtime, especially for officers aggressively working the system. There was double-time to be harvested from weekends and evenings spent in court, and some assignments at court automatically produced four hours pay regardless of the time actually put in.[62] The enterprising reporters duly noted the "iron men and women" working prodigious hours for the Cleveland Police Department. The report also showed that superiors in positions to rein in overtime abuse, including the internal affairs chief, had themselves accumulated major overtime in the form of "comp time," with some cashing out a year's salary or more after their last day at work.[63]

A key *Plain Dealer* piece was entitled "Police See Overtime as a Perk of the Badge."[64] Cleveland's prior Police Chief expressed his frustration at reining in overtime abuse, noting, "Years of effort haven't achieved the desired result."[65] The new Chief was moved to action after the *Plain Dealer*'s revelations, telling the department "we have become mired in a culture of entitlement" that "must come to an end."[66] The Chief's Executive Assistant, at least, seemed to have taken the message to heart. Having built up a formidable 2003 overtime account before the first *Plain Dealer* story about the Cleveland Police Department appeared in late October, he put in for not a single hour of overtime for the rest of the year.[67]

## The Negation of Management by Systems Abuse

Overtime scandals don't exactly shatter law enforcement agencies. The media coverage starts off with a bang but tends to be short-lived or sporadic thereafter. The system's vulnerabilities can be patched; agency executives issue edicts and pledge reforms. Disciplinary actions move forward against employees who have abused time and leave. Criminal prosecutions are supported against the worst offenders. Cleveland did all of these things, projecting a contrite and reformist agency image, as well as a commitment to fairly applying the law, even to its own. And the department made inroads into the problem, cutting overtime by 39% in a year.[68] Still, the intrepid *Plain Dealer* reporters found in late 2004 that overtime was still being squandered on the four-hour minimum court appearances.[69]

The aftermath of time and leave abuse may be relatively manageable. This doesn't mean that law enforcement executives and supervisors shouldn't be working hard to see that such situations don't arise in the first place. Law enforcement executives are responsible for the integrity of the resource control systems in their agencies. Managers ought to look at emergent systems abuses as if they were disease vectors. If the contagion is not isolated, it spreads to other officers who adopt similar practices and begin probing for weaknesses that can be exploited in other systems.

Management should never enable or ignore employee probes for systems' vulnerabilities, nor become complacent about its control systems. As this book, I hope, has amply demonstrated, no system is without weaknesses, and quite a few have gaping holes through which wrong-minded employees can step in order to loot the organization.

Allowing systems abuse to spread is a recipe for alienating officers from the agency. Those abusing the system get to set the tone and it is not pleasant. Officers beating the system are expressing contempt for management by their actions. For them, managers are the fools who can't keep track of who is working where for how long. And compliant officers also lose respect for managers that ignore widespread abuse, especially if they suspect that the oblivious bosses are trying not to jeopardize their own sweet comp time deals. These jaundiced views are deadly for morale and agency cohesion.

Rank-and-file alienation from management was a major factor in Parma. When the *Plain Dealer* series finally forced the Chief to address the issue, which he did with some indignation, he was as complicit as those he was critiquing. This further angered officers who were already outraged that "their" overtime was being taken away. A dramatic work slowdown ensued. This was seen as a direct slap in the face to the city and the department. And so it was, though the officers attributed the slowdown to, among other things, a post-9/11 enforcement amnesty for the traumatized citizenry.

Neither the mayor, nor the public safety director nor the police chief looked to be much in charge of anything. These officials were caught between an outraged citizenry—who soon defeated a tax surcharge ballot measure to bailout the police department—and a disdainful, out of control rank-and-file. All the officials were gone in a year, having left a legacy of non-management and failed leadership. Even the new mayor conceded that things were in the balance relative to wresting control of the police department back from its members.[70]

It is doubtful that any aspiring police supervisor, commander or chief wants to leave a similar legacy. But it can happen, subtly and progressively, if important control systems are neglected, and violations of those systems are ignored.

## Organization as Territory

When we looked at the Department of Correction case, we emphasized how important it was to disabuse executives of the notion that the resources they managed—programs, employees, equipment—were "theirs." This sense of territory is by no means exclusive to the individual executive, and in fact may be a more critical issue for an organization when it is collectively felt.

When the Parma police, or for that matter the Cleveland police, pushed the envelope on overtime, they may not have been strictly within their rights but, in a real sense, they were awfully close. The time and leave system in most police agencies is a complex terrain— overtime in Cleveland ranged from time-and-a-half to double time-and-a-half depending on the day of the week, the time of day, holiday versus non-holiday and hours already worked in a week. Certain activities performed on overtime earned a minimum number of hours regardless of how much time officers put in, which made officers very eager for that particular work and very efficient when they got it. These complex arrangements had been negotiated in collective bargaining, with the officers, through their union, winning the various overtime rates and minimums.

In these cases, wide swaths of the time and leave systems already lay within the territory of the rank-and-file. Officers did not have to reach very far beyond what they already had coming to them in order to add on a few more overtime hours, cluster their extra hours into time slots with the highest payoffs, or load senior officers into overtime programs budgeted for lower salaried employees. Such territorial expansions occur in part because the rank-and-file already is positioned on the border, thinking how opportunities lying just beyond the boundary, a "water for wine" conversion perhaps, should rightfully be theirs. This attitude often means that even the first cross-border incursion that daring employees make to grab an extra measure of resources is not viewed as wrong-doing. And if it goes unchallenged, other employees are soon likely to follow, most guiltlessly.

The longer managers remain unaware or unconcerned about time and leave abuse that extends employee control over their workdays and pay checks, a form of adverse possession takes place. The border has been moved unilaterally by the constructive action of the employees and the longer they have possession the more they see their tenancy as righteous.

This is not metaphor. Exactly this scenario transpired in Parma. Officers and superiors over the years converted the "all overtime" traffic program into a cash cow through their manipulations over who worked when, and where, doing how much. The public safety director, among others, offered little resistance as the rank-and-file effectively laid claim to how the program was staffed. When fiscal stress in Parma eliminated the program, officers reacted as if the city and agency management had trampled upon their rights of possession. So they counterattacked, dialing back their enforcement efforts by half, making incursions into other areas of management control. No wonder the outgoing public safety director sounded defeated, and the incoming mayor sounded unsure, about their ability to control enough police department territory to actually be in charge.

To help prevent what happened in Parma, senior law enforcement agency managers would do well to see one of their prime responsibilities as border patrol. An alert management is more likely to catch stealth incursions early on, as well as repel formal contract demands that lay claim to territory best ruled by management in the overall interests of the organization.

## Scanning for Systems Anomaly and Abuse

Management ought to scan regularly for system weaknesses. Those involved in system development, and redevelopment, must carefully consider how clients will use and misuse a system, whether it's for pensions, overtime or equipment requisitions. In the ideal systems management world, developers would torture test a system, perhaps even calling in a certified fraud analyst to try to compromise it, in order to spot vulnerabilities prior to rollout. In the less than ideal world, a member of the supervisory staff, or the system itself, would scan continuously for anomalies that indicate something is not working right.

These system scans are not very different from a COMPSTAT-type scan that identifies crime hotspots. Arrests that cluster late in shifts, squads whose overtime costs spike high above similar units, individuals who regularly stand out as champions of weekend overtime for tasks transacted easily during the week— the system, or someone monitoring it, ought to highlight such occurrences.

Identifying anomalies is not a finding of guilt. There may well be legitimate reasons for clusters of excessive overtime. Just as a crime cluster may signal change in perpetrator tastes rather than the failure of police deployments, overtime clusters may be due to situations that management has failed to take into account rather than abuses of the system by employees.

## The Bottom Line on Resource Diversion

We have seen in this chapter that resource diversions have effects inside and outside the police organization. The legitimacy of the police suffers whenever news breaks about pension scams, phony and inflated overtime schemes, or resources siphoned off by the brass. Trust in the police diminishes among the public, legislators and the media—all of whose support is crucial to effective law enforcement. Agency resources devoted to battling the abuse of ill-conceived and poorly managed systems are resources no longer available to fight crime or to better reward cops who do their jobs with integrity.

Resource diversion also impacts the morale, beliefs and behavior of employees in general. When an officer known for working the angles and slacking off wins the disability lottery, other officers get the message that scamming pays. When raids on the overtime system are endemic, respect for the organization and its management plummets. When a boss expropriates substantial organizational resources, employees turn cynical, with dashes of bitterness, fear, envy or disgust thrown in. These subversive and morale-destroying attitudes are the long lasting legacy of resource diversion.

Resource diversion is best understood and addressed as a violation of the organization. A given act of resource diversion may be a crime but that is not necessary for substantial harm to be done to the organization. Managers can and should guard against resource diversion by:

- Educating themselves about control systems governing operations they direct;
- Subjecting those control systems to regular, critical review;
- Addressing fairly and firmly control system violations whenever they arise; and
- Keeping employees mission-focused, purposeful, and integrity-conscious.

Chief executives, for their part, need to watch out for, and be ready to act firmly in response to:

- High ranking officers who fail to separate their personas from their positions, or what belongs to the organization from what belongs to them;
- Allegations about ranking officers misusing resources or personnel they control;
- Claims and behaviors by employee groups that imply entitlement to resources distributed at management's discretion;
- Anomalous behaviors or clusters of behaviors turned up by scans of control system records.

Doing these things will not eliminate resource diversions, which get their start in overlooked flaws in control systems, surreptitious employee behaviors and the emergent megalomania of fast-track but flawed executives. But taking these steps will give law enforcement managers and executives a head start in recognizing resource diversions as they emerge, so that action can be taken to protect the organization before they fully take hold.

# Endnotes

1. John Kenneth Galbraith, *The Great Crash, 1929* (Boston: Houghton Mifflin, 1955): 153.

2. West Virginia Code §61-3-20 (1989); Also, State v. Brown, No. 20472, Supreme Court of Appeals of West Virginia, 188 W. Va. 12; 422 S.E.2d 489; 1992.

3. Brian Donovan and Stephanie Saul, "Cops on Disability," *New York Newsday*, June 26—July 3, 1994. http://www.pulitzer.org/year/1995/investigative-reporting/works/index.html (Accessed March 30, 2005). Elements of this case are drawn from this Pulitzer Prize winning series of investigative reports concerning abuse of the disability pension system, and also from the author's discussions in 2004 and 2005 with police personnel and police retirees.

4. Donovan and Saul, "Cops on Disability—Lucrative Disability" http://www.pulitzer.org/year/1995/investigative-reporting/works/iv14.html (Accessed March 21, 2005).

5. Donovan and Saul, "Cops on Disability—The Road to Reform" http://www.pulitzer.org/year/1995/investigative-reporting/works/iv3.html (Accessed March 21, 2005).

6. Donovan and Saul, "Cops on Disability—Lucrative Disability."

7. Donovan and Saul, "Cops on Disability—Lucrative Disability: Lifeguard Case Study" http://www.pulitzer.org/year/1995/investigative-reporting/works/iv14.html (Accessed March 21, 2005).

8. Ibid.

9. Donovan and Saul, "Cops on Disability—Robust Retirements" http://www.pulitzer.org/year/1995/investigative-reporting/works/iv5.html (Accessed March 21, 2005).

10. Donovan and Saul, "Cops on Disability—Too Painful to Testify but Not to Play Golf" http://www.pulitzer.org/year/1995/investigative-reporting/works/iv7.html (Accessed March 21, 2005).

11. Donovan and Saul, "Cops on Disability—Lucrative Disability" (Accessed March 21, 2005).

12. Errol A. Cockfield Jr. and Emi Endo, "Six-Figure Force: Cops Rising Salaries Are a Focus of County Budget Debates." *Newsday*, February 28, 2003.

13. Donovan and Saul, "Cops on Disability—Lucrative Disability" (Accessed March 21, 2005).

14. "Rikers Island Chief Stripped of His Command after Accusations He Abused His Post." *7online.com* http://abclocal.go.com/wabc/news/investigators/wabc_investigators_102202serra.html (Accessed March 29, 2005).

15. Office of the District Attorney, Bronx County, New York, "Grand Jury Charges High Ranking Correction Department Official with Grand Larceny and Other Offenses," Press Release, February 13, 2003.

16. Office of the District Attorney, Bronx County, New York, "Former High Ranking Official of The New York City Department of Correction Convicted of Grand Larceny and Conflict of Interest," Press Release, March 8, 2005.

17. Ibid.

18. Dan Janison, "Ex-Jail Official Faces Year in Prison," *New York Newsday*, March 9, 2005.

19. Matt Apuzzo, "Ex-Gov. Rowland Gets Year in Prison," *The Philadelphia Inquirer*, March 19, 2005.

20. United States Attorney, Southern District of New York, "Former DEA Associate Special Agent in Charge Pleads Guilty to Embezzlement, Misuse of DEA Resources," Press Release, May 10, 2004.

21. "Rikers Island Chief Stripped of His Command," 7 Online.com.

22. Ibid.

23. Ibid.

24. Ken Belson, "Can a Cool-Headed Star Witness Take the Heat From the Ebbers Defense Team?" *New York Times*, Feb 14, 2005; Brooke A. Masters and Ben White, "Adelphia Founder, Son Convicted of Fraud; Another Son Acquitted of Conspiracy in Partial Verdict," *The Washington Post,* July 9, 2004; Carrie Johnson, "Lay Feels Betrayed by Enron 'Whiz Kid,'" *The Washington Post,* January 16, 2004.

25. Renae Merle, "Boeing CEO Resigns Over Affair with Subordinate, "*The Washington Post,* March 8, 2005.

26. Francesca Di Meglio, "Enron's Andrew Fastow: The Mistakes I Made," Businessweek.com, March 22, 2012.

27. Bernard Kerik, *The Lost Son: A Life in Pursuit of Justice* (New York, Regan Books—Harper Collins, 2001), 234–236

28. Ibid., 236.

29. Mike Allen, Jim VandeHie, "Homeland Security Nominee Kerik Pulls Out," *Washington Post*, December 11, 2004, A1.

30. Craig Horowitz, "Tears of a Cop," New York Magazine, May 21, 2005 http://nymag.com/nymetro/news/people/features/11618/ (Accessed March 4, 2012).

31. Russ Buettner, "Kerik to Cop a Plea," *New York Daily News*, June 30, 2006 http://www.nydailynews.com/news/bernard-kerik-plea-article-1.340839 (Accessed March 30, 2012).

32. United States Attorney, Southern District of New York, "Former New York City Police Commissioner Bernard Kerik Pleads Guilty to Eight Felonies in White Plains Federal Court," November 5, 2009 http://www.justice.gov/usao/nys/pressreleases/November09/kerik bernardpleapr.pdf (Accessed March 6, 2012).

33. Ross Buettner, "Ex-Publisher's Suit Plays a Giuliani-Kerik Angle," *New York Times*, November 14, 2007 http://www.nytimes.com/2007/11/14/business/14regan.html?_r=1& ref=judithregan (Accessed March 9, 2012).

34. Jim Fitzgerald, "Bernie Kerik Jailed After Judge Revokes Bail in Corruption Trial," *The Huffington Post*, October 20, 2009. http://www.huffingtonpost.com/2009/10/20/bernie-kerik-jailed-after_n_327397.html (Accessed March 9, 2012).

35. Craig Horowitz, "Tears of a Cop," *New York Magazine*, May 21, 2005 http://nymag.com/nymetro/news/people/features/11618/ (Accessed March 9, 2012).

36. Kerik, *The Lost Son*, 111.

37. Kerik, *The Lost Son*, 125.

38. Kerik, *The Lost Son*, 62.

39. Kerik, *The Lost Son*, 66.

40. Kerik, The Lost Son, 70.

41. Kerik, The Lost Son, 119.

42. Steven Lee Myers, "Reporter's Notebook: New Team Cleans up Clean-up Plans," *New York Times*, December 31, 1993. http://www.nytimes.com/1993/12/31/nyregion/reporter-s-notebook-new-team-cleans-up-cleanup-plans.html (Accessed March 30, 2012).

43. Clifford Krauss, "Giuliani Expects Bratton Deal for Book to Pass City Review," *New York Times*, March 14, 1996 http://www.nytimes.com/1996/03/14/nyregion/giuliani-expects-bratton-deal-for-book-to-pass-city-review.html?src=pm (Accessed March 31, 2012).

44. David Kocieniewski, "Giuliani Says Police Moves Are Up to Him," *New York Times*, March 6, 1996 http://www.nytimes.com/1996/03/09/nyregion/giuliani-says-police-moves-are-up-to-him.html?src=pm (Accessed March 31, 2012).

45. David Firestone, "City Hall Memo; A Helpful Giuliani Is Drawing Bratton a Map to the Door," *New York Times*, March 26, 1996 http://www.nytimes.com/1996/03/26/nyregion/city-hall-memo-a-helpful-giuliani-is-drawing-bratton-a-map-to-the-door.html (Accessed March 31, 2012).

46. David Firestone, "No Spotlight Needed: Howard Safir," *New York Times*, March 29, 1996. http://www.nytimes.com/1996/03/29/nyregion/man-new-police-commissioner-healm-no-spotlight-needed-howard-safir.html?src=pm (Accessed March 28, 2012).

47. Horowitz, "Tears of a Cop."

48. Ibid.

49. Sam Dolnick, "U.S. Asks Kerik's Judge to Send a Stern Message," *New York Times*, February 8, 2010, A24.

50. Fitzgerald, "Bernie Kerik Jailed After Judge Revokes Bail in Corruption Trial."

51. Jim Fitzgerald, "Bernie Kerik Sentenced to Four Years in Prison," Associated Press, February 18, 2010 http://www.huffingtonpost.com/2010/02/18/bernie-keriks-jail-senten_0_n_467097.html (Accessed March 31, 2012).

52. Timothy Heider and Joseph L. Wagner, "Parma Police Chase After Extra Money," *The Plain Dealer* (Cleveland), March 9, 2003.

53. Ibid.

54. "Parma's Iron Men Working Overtime," *The Plain Dealer* (Cleveland), March 9, 2003.

55. Heider and Wagner, "Police Chase after Extra Money."

56. Joseph L. Wagner and Timothy Heider, "Sick Leave Proves a Healthy Proposition," *The Plain Dealer* (Cleveland), March 10, 2003.

57. Ibid.

58. Ibid.

59. David Tardini, "Cool Cleveland Interview: Parma Mayor Dean DePiero," *Cool-Cleveland.com* http://www.coolcleveland.com/index.php/Main/CoolClevelandInterview-MayorOfParmaDeanDiPiero (Accessed March 5, 2005).

60. Joseph L. Wagner and Timothy Heider, "Parma Reform May Rankle Unions," *The Plain Dealer* (Cleveland), March 23, 2003.

61. Joseph L. Wagner and Timothy Heider, "Parma Officers Indicted In Tax Probe; Former Chief Pleads Guilty To Evasion," *The Plain Dealer* (Cleveland), March 10, 2003.

62. Mark Gillispie and Scott Hiaasen, "Court Overtime Breaks Police Budget," *The Plain Dealer* (Cleveland), November 2, 2003.

63. Ibid.

64. Mark Gillispie, "Police See Overtime as a Perk of the Badge," *The Plain Dealer* (Cleveland), March 14, 2004.

65. Ibid.

66. Ibid.

67. Ibid.

68. Mark Gillispie and Scott Hiaasen, "Campbell Takes Control of Police Overtime Probe," *The Plain Dealer* (Cleveland), November 14, 2004.

69. Ibid.

70. Tardini, "Cool Cleveland Interview: Parma Mayor Dean DePiero."

# Epilogue

# Managing Imperfection

The reader might by now be more than taken aback by the litany of law enforcement mistakes and debacles featured in this book. And if the reader happens to be a law enforcement officer aspiring to higher rank, he or she might well be rethinking those plans. For who would want to manage and lead law enforcement organizations that this book portrays as veritable minefields where, if that simmering problem over there doesn't explode, the one over here likely will?

The citizen-reader should not despair, and neither should future law enforcement leaders now in the ranks. The diagnostic categories used in this book were developed for a general analysis of organizations. This book could just as easily have been written about corporations, or non-profit firms, or public sector agencies in general. I have been developing cases in those areas for years. There are more than enough cases of corporate, non-profit and public sector failures to populate each of this book's diagnostic categories more densely than I have for law enforcement agencies.

This book, I hope, will point the way towards making our law enforcement organizations run better by illuminating the nature of the mistakes agencies make. Mistakes are learning tools, for individuals to be sure, but also for organizations. Unlike an individual, whose mistakes usually generate direct feedback and clear signals about needed behavior changes, organizational mistakes generate diffuse feedback in every direction, both within and beyond the organization. Signals regarding corrective action can easily, and even deliberately, be missed. This book's purpose has been to make the reader more attuned to danger signals, quicker to recognize exactly what is wrong, and more ready to mount an appropriate response.

The "normal accident" framework is appropriate for an initial scan when things go awry in a law enforcement setting. If flaws are revealed whose remediation will substantially or completely solve the problem, as happened with Minnesota's lethal police vehicles, much good comes from a straightforward analysis.

The "structural failure" framework can reveal problems that may call for major organizational surgery, such as was performed on the Immigration and Naturalization Service (INS) in the wake of 9/11 when it was split in two with its enforcement arm ending up in the Department of Homeland Security.

"Oversight failure" analysis brings quality control problems into sharp focus and, if conducted early enough (which also means regularly enough), most problems arising from inadequate oversight can be cured by organizational self-therapy that rehabilitates the suspect monitoring systems. When oversight mechanisms are misused or neglected, however, even an organization like the NYPD can find itself in a very painful relationship with legislative committees, prosecutors and investigative commissions aggressively exposing how things have gone wrong.

A "cultural deviation" analysis is as necessary as it is unpalatable, not unlike a test for cancer. Such an analysis may discover renegade units eating away at the organization and cutting out the rot frequently requires a very public and embarrassing operation. But in the final analysis, organizations like the LAPD or the New Orleans Police Department are better off uncovering and fixing their own deviant cultures before investigative reporters, prosecutors or the U.S. Department of Justice come in to do the job.

Many executives—indeed, most employees—are incapable of making an "institutionalization" diagnosis for their organizations. They are too close to recognize the disease, and may well themselves be part of the problem. And when this happens, what should be second opinions—those of legislators and the media and chief executives—end up defining the problem and setting the agenda for reform. Agencies that would prefer to avoid the beating taken by the FBI Lab or the New Jersey State Police should, without prompting, conduct periodic, serious self-exams. And top-level executive, legislative and judicial policy-makers ought to be ready to remove the leadership of any criminal justice agency gripped by institutionalization since, as we saw in the Luzerne County courts, the condition delegitimizes government in general.

Scanning for "resource diversion" ought to be continual and, in a healthy agency, should be conducted by oversight units that cast a skeptical eye on both the organization's control systems and how employees interface with those systems. The scan should not skip anyone, not the tough commissioner who is the mayor's favorite and not groups of rank-and-file officers armed with union contracts and retaliatory instincts. Despite their power—indeed, because of their power—these actors, when caught picking the taxpayer's pocket, instantly become high-profile co-stars, alongside their agencies, on *Eyewitness News* hidden videos, on the front page of the local paper or, like Bernie Kerik, on a brightly lit national stage.

# When Organizational Failures
# Have Multiple Causes

With few exceptions, such as the defective police vehicles in Minnesota, the cases we have looked at in this book have exhibited symptoms from several diagnostic categories. As noted at the start of this book, each case was categorized based on the author's assessment of the primary dysfunction besetting the agency. This allowed us to explore each failure category, which was the principal aim of this book. As a practical matter, however, if an organization can identify and target the primary dysfunction, substantial improvement is likely even if secondary causes remain to be addressed.

But this doesn't mean managers shouldn't run multiple tests on the problems that beset their operations. The overtime abuse in the two Ohio police agencies was facilitated by rank-and file cultures frequently at odds with the efficiency goals of their organizations. As we saw very clearly in Parma, foreclosing overtime opportunities to stop the resource bleeding seemed only to crystallize concerted employee action that severely diminished enforcement efforts. With the resource diversion problem substantially resolved, a cultural deviation issue moved to the top of the list.

The Chief who remodeled his home with labor and equipment borrowed from the New York City Department of Correction was diverting resources, and that's how prosecutors approached the case. However, the fact that employees blew the whistle to a TV outlet that had little problem making incriminating tapes raised the issue of oversight failure in the agency. One problem was solved, but another potential problem still warranted review.

Oversight failure was also a residual issue after federal oversight and internal reforms were prescribed for the institutionalization that helped perpetuate racial profiling in the New Jersey State Police. The Attorney General's Office in New Jersey, if not complicit in allowing profiling to continue—which it denied—was woeful in its oversight of a police agency under its jurisdiction. In fact, the Attorney General did become an object of intense official scrutiny.

How does a law enforcement agency decide what to address when the problematic situation exhibits multiple symptoms that qualify for more than one diagnostic category?

Sometimes one symptom can drown out all others. In the JonBenet Ramsey case, the Boulder Police Department was hampered by both resource inadequacy and hierarchical/inter-agency friction. But the friction was fueling struggles that made it hard to look clearly at resource issues. The police chief and the district attorney should have firmly addressed the rapidly escalating struggles early on but did not—an abdication of leadership that hampered an already difficult investigation and ultimately caused the Governor of Colorado to step in.

Sometimes, when multiple symptoms suggest the presence of two or more types of failure, the highest treatment priority should be given to actions that quickly make significant progress against major elements of the problem. The FBI Lab, like its parent agency, struggled with institutionalization, a chronic condition requiring long-term, holistic rehabilitation. Yet there was also a lack of qualified oversight of the Lab that could have been addressed more quickly and cleanly by a commitment to accreditation review. While the FBI Lab held off accreditation until 1998, it would have made a difference at least a decade earlier.

When the FBI Lab was certified, critics noted that more work was needed to excise the Lab's "prosecutorial bias,"[1] an institutionalized mindset harder to eradicate. Indeed, the FBI has been prominent among our cases, thanks to institutionalization which creates fault lines throughout the agency. Like the San Andreas, any one fault can slip at any time. For this reason, if you study law enforcement organization and management as I do, the FBI is always worth watching. As good a job as it does day to day and year to year, the earthquakes are inevitable.

In general, vulnerabilities to failure arising from normal accidents, oversight failure and resource diversions are more easily targeted and quickly addressed than vulnerabilities arising from structural failure, cultural deviation and institutionalization.

* * *

We are now going to look at one last organizational case that underscores how deep-rooted, multi-faceted organizational problems can persist, defying remediation and putting the lives of public safety officers at risk.

## The Needless Sacrifices of 9/11

The events of 9/11 killed more public safety officers than any event in U.S. history. Thirty-seven Port Authority police officers died,[2] as did twenty-three NYPD officers[3] and 343 New York City Fire Department (FDNY) personnel.[4] They died as heroes, but some of these heroes died needlessly due to failed equipment and ill-considered organizational structures that left them too long in buildings on the verge of collapse.[5]

The death toll for firefighters was by far the highest, and their deaths were due partially to the inability of their radios to connect them to the command post.[6] The FDNY's radios were not well suited for the distances and terrain of the World Trade Center. The towers were over a quarter mile high, the Trade

Center complex stood on sixteen acres, and the Center's millions of tons of steel and concrete were a formidable impediment to effective transmissions to and from handheld radios.

The police radio system operated much more effectively. The NYPD, whose officers went on vertical patrols in housing projects and other high-rise buildings and worked widely separated from each other on the street, had a radio system whose boosted signals were better suited for the conditions at the World Trade Center.

The FDNY radio system had been upgraded in the wake of the 1993 World Trade Center bombing, when radio communications had broken down between firefighters, and between the Fire Department and other first responders, notably the NYPD. A repeater system that boosted the range of FDNY radios had been installed in the World Trade Center after the 1993 bombing. New radios were ordered. The city had also purchased another set of radios that would allow FDNY and NYPD commanders to communicate with each other and with the city's Office of Emergency Management during catastrophes.[7]

Despite these efforts, 9/11 looked much like 1993. Most firefighters had the same old radios; the new ones had been taken out of service almost immediately after their introduction because a transmission failure nearly killed a firefighter.[8] Some firefighters, scrambling to the World Trade Center after the end of their shift, had no radios. Other personnel were tuned to un-boosted channels. The repeater system, which needed to be turned on in an emergency, apparently had not been activated in one of the Twin Towers.[9] All of this might have been less of a problem if firefighters and their chiefs were privy to more accurate intelligence coming over the police airwaves, but the radios carried by police officers and firefighters were not inter-operable and the special radios designed to keep Fire Chiefs and Police Commanders on the same page in an emergency had been gathering dust for years.

The NYPD and FDNY on-scene commanders were also operating at a physical distance. Fire command posts were established in the lobby of each tower, and on the street just to the west of the complex.[10] Coordination between the several fire command posts was also hampered by radio difficulties and, at one point, a runner was sent with updates from one post to another.[11] While FDNY commanders were working on the west side of the World Trade Center complex, as well as inside, NYPD commanders were blocks away, at the northeast corner of the complex, directing emergency service units and other personnel.[12] This physical separation of police and fire command structures only compounded the communications problems.

Because the police radio system was more reliable, police commanders more effectively translated intelligence about the state of the two towers into orders designed to move officers out of harm's way. Police commanders radioed their personnel to evacuate just after the first tower collapsed at 9:59AM.[13] Not only was that message transmitted successfully, but almost immediately thereafter that message was reinforced because officers could directly monitor transmissions from police helicopters which were reporting that the remaining tower was buckling. That was twenty minutes before the tower fell, and most police officers were making a beeline towards the ground floor as unaware firefighters kept trudging upwards.

FDNY commanders were completely unaware of what the police helicopter pilot had reported. Some Port Authority personnel and police officers that were evacuating urged firefighters to join them. But firefighters, most of whom heard no orders to evacuate from their chiefs on their radios, stayed in the building. Though FDNY commanders had given orders to clear out after the first tower collapsed, firefighters with non-working radios had heard nothing. Other firefighters were switching channels trying to make sense of the flood of transmission traffic and, for some reason, though an evacuation had been ordered, apparently no commander transmitted a "Mayday" to cut through the babble.[14]

When the first tower fell, most firefighters in the remaining tower did not even realize what had occurred. Some continued searching for any remaining civilians on floors that had been radioed in as fully evacuated by Port Authority and NYPD officers. When the second tower collapsed, firefighters were still gathered in staging areas, or were paused on floors where they had taken a breather. They died having no idea that the building had been teetering above them, that some of the jobs they were doing had already been done, and with little sense of their impending doom.

## Saving Tomorrow's Heroes

Multiple organizational failure modes hampered the police and fire response at the scene of the atrocious attack on the World Trade Center.

The radios that the fire fighters were carrying worked perfectly fine for 99% of what they did, which was to fight fires in relatively small areas with tight teams whose members were never very far from each other. The glitch ready to express itself in high-rise buildings was always lurking in the radio system but did not capture serious management attention until the 1993 World Trade Center bombing. This is the kind of technological wake-up call generated by a normal accident. Steps were taken to boost fire department radio signals so that they would be more reliable. The events that transpired on 9/11 revealed further shortcoming in the system. Firefighters now have their new radios, which can switch to police channels and access common channels for better coordination in emergency situations.

Structural failure is implicated in the minimal amount of communication that NYPD and FDNY commanders had with each other on 9/11. There were separate NYPD and FDNY command posts, some distance apart, with virtually no cross-communication. This lack of communication was not just a function of poor radios; the police and fire departments in New York City historically had little inclination towards a unified command for anything. Though the city's Office of Emergency Management made plans for a joint and coordinated police-fire response to various contingencies, in practice the police and fire departments did their own thing, even in situations where both were involved.[15]

Cultural division also played a role in the uncoordinated responses of 9/11. The division was based on function, to be sure—police officers fought crime and firefighters fought blazes. But beyond that, the Police and Fire departments had for years circled each other warily. The NYPD has emergency service responsibility that, in most jurisdictions, belongs exclusively to the Fire Department. As a practical matter, NYPD Emergency Services and FDNY Rescue duties overlap, and both may show up to handle the same emergency. When the FDNY took over New York City's Emergency Medical Services, one of the first things it did was eliminate the police band from the medics' radios.[16] In April 2005, the City of New York designated the NYPD as the lead agency at hazardous materials disaster sites, which the FDNY not only opposed vigorously through the policy development phase but which Fire officials continued to criticize publicly after the policy had been finalized.[17]

The World Trade Center bombing of 1993 did as much to exacerbate police/fire hostility as it did to enhance their coordination in emergencies. Rooftop rescues from the World Trade Center by police helicopters in 1993—grandstanding as far as firefighters were concerned, set off a turf war in which the FDNY wrested a "lead agency" designation for aerial rescues.[18] In practice this meant little, since the helicopters still belonged to the police, no one had much taste for joint training, and emergencies provided perfect excuses not to wait for anybody else before taking off. So the police helicopters carried only cops on 9/11, just as they had in 1993. The new hi-tech radios for commander-to-commander coordination between the NYPD and FDNY gathered dust for years before 9/11 because the protocols for their use hadn't been figured out. In a real way, each agency was ready to work with the other, as long as it could be the boss.

The interagency hostility also expressed itself in bad blood between officers in both departments. Cops and firefighters were dispatched to the same incidents—a car wreck, a medical emergency—and friction was sometimes intense.[19] Each force cast a suspicious eye on the other's pay package. The respective union leaders made contract demands that, at minimum, demanded police-firefighter pay parity and, at maximum, demanded that any disparity favoring their workers continue. Firefighters groused when police got an edge. And police, for their part, felt that even parity was unfair since, as far as they were concerned, firefighters sat around the firehouse most of the time doing nothing.

The uncoordinated approach of the two departments on 9/11 had as much to do with structural failure and a cultural divide as with the unprecedented circumstances being confronted. It is instructive that, even though NYPD and FDNY hand-held radios have been inter-operable since shortly after 9/11, the new system "had never been used at an actual emergency" as of May 2005,[20] and Fire Department EMS units were not brought into the interoperable system until July 1, 2008.[21] As with most problems in socio-technical systems, the technical is much easier to fix than the social/structural/cultural.

These problems must be solved. If it requires imposing more coordinated plans of action on the two departments, as has been done in New York, so be it. So be it also if radical surgery is performed to shake up an institutionalized culture. New York's Mayor Michael Bloomberg did this after 9/11 by replacing the fire commissioner (who had previously headed the firefighters' union) with someone whose entire administrative career had been spent outside the department. Not incidentally, Bloomberg's police commissioner had most recent served as U.S. Customs Commissioner, where by necessity he had to work with other agencies—INS, FBI, DEA—in combating cross-border crime.

The tragic events of 9/11 have helped policy makers overcome some of the reluctance to dismantle defective structures and challenge entrenched dysfunctional cultures in law enforcement.

But still today, in all too many instances of organizational dysfunction, executives who should act back off: the structure seems immovable, the incumbents appear too militant, and the culture is known to be intractable. Law enforcement executives retreat behind a poisonous fallacy: if everything has been OK so far, it will probably stay OK for the foreseeable future. Inaction and self-delusion are serious and sometimes lethal mistakes, as we have seen in this book and as 9/11 so clearly demonstrates.

Scores of firefighters and law enforcement officers who died in the collapse of the World Trade Center had taken classes or earned degrees at John Jay College of Criminal Justice, where I have taught for thirty years. One fire fighter who died on 9/11 was an adjunct faculty member in my department. Not one of the 403 fallen heroes deserved to die because their organizations failed them, but some certainly did. My hope is that this book will make law enforcement and public safety managers more aware of, and proactive about, dysfunctions that lurk within their organizations. Rooting out potential failure points is not just some management exercise; it is the right thing to do so that the good men and women who put their lives on the line for our public safety do not fall victim to the mistakes of their organizations.

# Coda: From Organizational to Policy Dysfunction

Some of the cases analyzed in this book had much to do with public policies that limited or prohibited the agencies involved from taking actions that might have headed off trouble.

The 9/11 related cases—"Welcome Wagon at the INS" and "The First 9/11"—are typical. One way we made sense of what went wrong was to consider the "subordination of law enforcement" where law enforcement units had to knuckle under to other organizations having less interest in aggressively pursuing potential or already committed terrorist crimes. Border enforcement at airports prior to 9/11 took too much of a back seat to FAA and airline preferences that passengers be moved along quickly. In the investigation of the USS Cole bombing in Yemen led by John O'Neill, the State Department's preferences regarding smooth diplomatic relations with the Yemeni government prevailed over the FBI's desires to move fast and hard before the trail grew cold.

The failure potential in these cases went up significantly because policies and policy interpretations favored a less aggressive enforcement approach that softened the up the country for 9/11's heinous crimes. These limiting policy positions were, and are, supra-organizational—agencies may jockey for position within the parameters the policies set forth, but there is only so far they can go.

Similarly, in "Winning the Disability Lottery," public policy was a culprit in encouraging police officers to jump at the chance for a disability pension mid-career or earlier, because the deal was far better than if they retired in due course. We saw that, when legislatures were considering liberalized police disability policies, municipal officials warned that the result would be a rush for the exit by officers who would otherwise have served their full careers. Those mayors and city managers turned out to be right.

Indeed the consequences of short-sighted public pension policies in general are now coming home to roost. Pension costs eat up an ever larger hunk of state and local budgets, pushing some jurisdictions to and beyond the brink of bankruptcy.[22] And, in bankruptcy, some jurisdictions have legally reneged on pension commitments to police and firefighters, including those already retired.[23] The policy boomerang is on the way back and public employees are at ground zero.

This book has been about the dynamics of organization, rather than public policy. However, students who have not yet studied criminal justice policy would be well-advised to do so as a follow-up to the lessons in this book.

As an entrée to that next step in your education, or as a refresher for your existing awareness of policy, we will end with a 2012 case whose legal outcome will be up in the air for some time after this book is published—the killing of Trayvon Martin. What is not up in the air, as far as police professionals and many public policy researchers are concerned, is the degree to which the job of the police is made harder by ever more liberalized policies regarding the sale, ownership and use of firearms.

## *Walking with Your Hood up*

Starting from the house in the gated-community where he and his father were weekend guests, seventeen-year-old Trayvon Martin took a walk to the local 7-Eleven early on the evening of February 26, 2012. At the 7-Eleven Martin bought Skittles and iced tea. He ambled back towards the residence, entering the gated community either through the main gate or through a commonly used shortcut.[24] Trayvon Martin was wearing a hooded sweatshirt, and he had the hood up: It was raining.

Enter George Zimmerman. A member of neighborhood watch for the gated community, Zimmerman was driving in his car when he spotted Trayvon Martin. Zimmerman, first in his car and then on foot, started tracking Martin. Zimmerman called 911 to tell police he was following an individual "up to no good" or "on drugs or something."[25] Zimmerman's initial wrong assumption was eerily similar to the one police made that led to Amadou Diallo's death and the similarity didn't end there: Zimmerman, early in the 911 call, went on to describe Martin's "hand in his waistband" and next said Martin was coming towards him with "something in his hands." [26]

The police dispatcher took that in, as well as Zimmerman's remarks about "these assholes, they always get away" and "these f---ing punks"[27] and told Zimmerman that "we don't need you" on Martin's tail, having already advised him that officers were on the way.[28] Zimmerman, according to the probable cause affidavit filed by investigators for the State Attorney, still followed Martin.[29] Zimmerman, towards the end of the 911 call, reported that Martin was out of his sight.[30] Though exactly who then moved to where is not at all clear, Zimmerman and Martin were soon in an encounter.

Zimmerman was armed. Martin was not.

Witnesses, for the most part, only heard the encounter—sounds of struggle, fear and anger, screams for help and then a single gunshot. One witness told CNN he saw some of the struggle but darkness made it difficult to determine who was doing what to whom.[31] The encounter ended with Martin putting a nine millimeter bullet into Trayvon Martin at close range.

When police arrived, Trayvon Martin was face down and unresponsive.[32] Standing near Martin was George Zimmerman, his gun holstered inside his waistband.[33] Zimmerman was disarmed by an officer, who noted Zimmerman had a bloody nose and blood on the back of his head.[34] Paramedics arrived, pronouncing Martin dead at 7:30PM.[35]

Zimmerman was taken to Sanford Police headquarters for questioning. He was released five hours later, since he claimed to be acting in self-defense, which stopped police in their tracks. Florida has a robust "Stand Your Ground Law." That law says that anyone "not engaged in an unlawful activity ... who is attacked in any ... place where he or she has a right to be" and reasonably believes they face serious harm cannot be arrested, detained, charged, prosecuted or sued civilly for causing "death or great bodily harm" to the attacker.[6]

Trayvon Martin soon became a cause célèbre'—nationwide. His distraught parents, helped by civil rights leaders, began a media offensive. The media, once alerted, ran with the story. Trayvon Martin was young, black, unarmed and belonged where he was. Zimmerman was Hispanic white, armed and his misreads had set the incident in motion. Mounting pressure forced a focus on whether the deadly encounter resulted from provocation on George Zimmerman's part, one of the few circumstances under which the immunities of Florida's "Stand Your Ground Law" do not apply.

In a busy few weeks, the Sanford Police Chief temporarily stepped down amid critiques of Zimmerman's quick release and the department's perfunctory investigation.[37] The prosecutor for Seminole County, where Sanford is located, also stepped aside.[38] A special prosecutor was then appointed from outside Seminole County.[39] Her preference was for a direct investigation by prosecutorial staff, as opposed to a slower track grand jury inquiry.[40]

On April 11, 2012, six weeks after Trayvon Martin was killed, George Zimmerman was arrested and charged with second-degree murder.[41] The judicial proceedings, including any trial, threatened to eclipse, as a media event, the murder trial of Casey Anthony in nearby Orlando that Time Magazine just a year earlier had nominated as the "social media trial of the century."[42]

## When Public Policy Is a Problem for Policing

Protesters directed significant outrage at the Sanford Police Department over its inaction following the death of Trayvon Martin. The police chief, who soon took leave to help calm the storm, contended that the hands of the police were tied. Taking leave was a responsible act, and the chief's contention was pretty much on the money.

In Florida, the legislature had for years been expanding citizens' rights to carry concealed weapons, capping off those efforts in 2005 with a first-in-the-nation "Stand Your Ground" statute so broad that opponents, including New York's Mayor Mike Bloomberg, have called it the "license to murder" law.[43] However, thanks to the muscular gun lobby and the endorsement of "stand your ground" by the well-financed American Legislative Exchange Council (ALEC) that pushes conservative-agenda "model legislation" from state to state, similar laws have been passed in at least sixteen additional states since 2005.[44]

And "stand your ground" is just one facet of an across-the-board gun de-control push that makes the job of the police harder and more dangerous, stymies prosecutors and accelerates an arms race among both criminals and the law-abiding, who may just end up, fearful and minimally trained, on neighborhood watch carrying a weapon. But, much as the liberalization of pension policies proceeded apace until they collapsed the finances of government jurisdictions, it appears that "guns anywhere, anytime" policies will also proceed apace—despite the Trayvon Martins, Virginia Techs and urban Uzi shootouts that kill innocents—until some as yet unknown critical mass is reached that restores sensible gun controls as a realistic policy option.

That may not be soon.

In Florida, Stand Your Ground proponents are seemingly undaunted by the Trayvon Martin case. The state legislator who introduced Florida's Stand Your Ground law was anticipating that a successful prosecution of George Zimmerman would actually prove the law's worth, validating the exception from immunity for individuals who provoked and/or pursued the victims.[45] And, presumably, if George Zimmerman is acquitted, that too will show that the law is good.

In Virginia, on February 28, two days after Trayvon Martin was killed, the governor signed into law a bill removing the one-gun-a-month limitation on gun purchases.[46] In so doing, Virginia reverted back to the "all-you-can-buy" approach to gun sales that had been in place until 1993, when other states, especially to the north, pleaded for limits to reduce "straw purchasers" buying dozens of guns at a time and heading up to Philadelphia, New York or Boston to sell the Virginia guns on city streets to local felons.

So the gospel of zero gun control is resisted by many local governments, nowhere more strongly than in the large cities of Northeast. New York handgun owners, for instance, face strict licensing, carry restrictions and a limit on the number of guns that an individual can purchase.[47] Philadelphia has fewer firearms restrictions but about as many as state law allows. The city does require prompt reporting of lost guns to help identify "straw purchasers" who tend to "lose" a lot of guns to their criminal customers.[48] But even that did not sit well with Pennsylvania's pro-gun legislators, who introduced bills in 2012 that would further eat away at local gun regulation.[49] As the furor over Trayvon Martin was peaking, Philadelphia's Mayor Michael Nutter was on his way to Harrisburg, the state capitol, along with several other mayors, to try to head off that legislation.[50]

Law enforcement officials and prosecutors were, for the most part, even more vehemently opposed to "stand your ground" and guns aplenty laws. Former Miami Police Chief John Timoney called 'stand your ground' a "recipe for disaster," a stance he and other Florida police officials had taken prior to the law's 2005 enactment.[51] They correctly envisioned "road rage" killings and drug rival shootouts where the survivor walked after claiming self-defense.[52]

Prosecutors also don't like stand your ground laws. As former South Florida US Attorney Kendall Coffey noted, "It becomes … very difficult … to get any kind of homicide conviction beyond a reasonable doubt … In Florida, since the stand your ground law was enacted … generally people don't even get prosecuted. When they have attempted to prosecute these claims of self-defense, there have almost always been acquittals."[53]

It is hard not to conclude that stand your ground "ties the hands … of prosecutors and police," who "should be rising up against that law," given the burdens it imposes on them.[54] In the end, Sanford's Police Department did not fail in the Trayvon Martin case nearly as much as Florida's gun policies failed law enforcement, criminal justice, Trayvon Martin and others struck down— all victims of pro-gun policies gone wild.

As I noted at the start of this section, I hope you continue on to, or revisit, the study of how public policy impacts the operations of the criminal justice system generally, and law enforcement organizations in particular. You should have learned enough in this book to diagnose and fix many of the problems that arise from within law enforcement organizations. But learning about the public policies that handicap or enable law enforcement organizations is also critical, particularly if you aspire to the highest ranks of law enforcement. At that level you will be as much a player in the public policy arena as you will be a leader of your organization.

Even if a law enforcement career is not your aspiration, knowing more about the public policies that affect you, and how to influence them, is a critical competency. Laws emerge daily from the legislative labyrinths that affect your health, your safety and even your ability to participate in the shaping of the law itself.

"Stand your ground?" That's not the only "model law" pushed state-to-state across the country by the American Legislative Exchange Council (ALEC). "Voter ID" laws are another pre-fabricated product ALEC had pushed into state legislative hoppers across the country. "Voter ID" laws disproportionately disenfranchise poor, minority and urban voters less likely to have, or get, the strictly regulated forms of photo identification these laws require.

Another "Voter ID" target? Look in the mirror.

Many voter ID laws erect barriers against students voting in their "college town." Want to vote? Go back home on Election Day, or get yourself an absentee ballot. Also—getting back to guns—gun advocates are pushing to end prohibitions against carrying concealed firearms on college campuses,[55] never mind the college shootings that keep occurring and the potential for more with armed individuals at the Friday night frat party.

So whether or not you end up in criminal justice, public policy matters to *you*. And you, along with others, can make a difference. The mobilization over the Trayvon Martin killing proved this, and not just in Florida.

On April 17, 2012, ALEC announced that it was disbanding its Public Safety and Elections Task Force—the very body that had worked to spread "stand your ground" and "voter ID" laws across the country.[56]

Hope you enjoyed, and got a lot out of, this book.

# Endnotes

1. National Association of Criminal Defense Lawyers, "Statement of Larry S. Pozner, President, on FBI Laboratory Accreditation," News Release, Washington, DC, September 22, 1998.

2. The Port Authority Police Department Memorial (Online) http://www.panynj.gov/AboutthePortAuthority/PortAuthorityPolice/InMemoriam/ (Accessed May 1, 2005).

3. NYPD Memorial of the September 11th Attack on the World Trade Center (Online), http://www.nyc.gov/html/nypd/html/memorial.html (Accessed May 1, 2005).

4. FDNY Memorial (Online), http://www.nyc.gov/html/fdny/html/memorial/index.shtml (Accessed May 1, 2005).

5. Jim Dwyer and Kevin Flynn, *102 Minutes: The Untold Story of the Fight to Survive Inside the Twin Towers* (New York: Times Books, 2005) In general, this book chillingly illustrates that entrenched organizational dysfunctions can have fatal consequences.

6. National Commission on Terrorist Acts upon the United States, *The 9/11 Commission Report* (New York: WW Norton, 2004): 297–99.

7. Dwyer and Flynn, *102 Minutes*, 60.

8. Ibid., 55.

9. *The 9/11 Commission Report*, 297.

10. Ibid., 301.

11. Dwyer and Flynn, *102 Minutes*, 204.

12. *The 9/11 Commission Report*, 302.

13. Dwyer and Flynn, *102 Minutes*, 215.

14. Ibid., 218.

15. Ibid., 59.

16. Ibid., 9.

17. Michelle O'Donnell, "Fire Chief Who Assailed Mayor's Policy Is Set to Testify," *New York Times*, May 9, 2005.

18. Dwyer and Flynn, *102 Minutes*, 133–34.

19. Ibid., 57.

20. Michelle O'Donnell, "City Hall Limits Testimony on Emergency Protocols," *New York Times*, April 28, 2005.

21. Salvatore Cassano (FDNY Chief of Department), "Testimony Before the Federal Communications Commission," Brooklyn, New York, July 30, 2008, 4 http://transition.fcc.gov/realaudio/presentations/2008/073008/cassano.pdf (Accessed April 1, 2012).

22. Roger Lowenstein, "The Next Crisis: Public Pension Funds," *The New York Times Magazine*, June 25, 2010, MM9.

23. Charles Osgood, "Slashing One City's Pensions in Rhode Island," *The Osgood File*, March 13, 2012 http://www.westwood-backup.com/pg/jsp/osgood/transcript.jsp?pid=33849 (Accessed April 17, 2012).

24. Haeyoun Park, "A Deadly Encounter," *The New York Times*, April 2, 2012.

25. Transcript of 911 Call, provided as link in, Adam Weinstein, "The Trayvon Martin Killing, Explained," *Mother Jones*, March 18, 2012 http://motherjones.com/politics/2012/03/what-happened-trayvon-martin-explained (Accessed on April 15, 2012).

26. Ibid.

27. State of Florida v. George Zimmerman, 1712FO4573, Circuit Court of the 18th Judicial Circuit (Seminole County), Affidavit of Probable Cause http://media.miamiherald.com/smedia/2012/04/12/18/16/JdX5J.So.56.pdf (Accessed April 16, 2012).

28. Transcript of 911 Call.

29. Affidavit of Probable Cause.

30. Transcript of 911 Call.

31. Vivian Kuo, "Witness Details Trayvon Martin Killing," *CNN.com*, March 29, 2012 http://articles.cnn.com/2012-03-29/justice/justice_florida-teen-shooting_1_witness-voices-window?_s=PM:JUSTICE (Accessed April 16, 2012).

32. Sanford Police Department Incident Report, http://www.scribd.com/doc/86948628/Trayvon-Martin-Police-Report (Accessed April 16, 2012).

33. Ibid.

34. Ibid.

35. Ibid.

36. Florida Statutes, Chapter 776, Justifiable Use of Force, http://www.flsenate.gov/Laws/Statutes/2011/Chapter0776/All (Accessed April 16, 2012).

37. ———, "Gov. Rick Scott Appoints Special Prosecutor for Trayvon Martin Case," *Tampa Bay Times*, March 23, 2012 http://www.tampabay.com/news/politics/gubernatorial/gov-rick-scott-appoints-special-prosecutor-for-trayvon-martin-case/1221406 (Accessed April 16, 2012).

38. Ibid.

39. Ibid.

40. Rene Stutzman, "Special prosecutor: I May Need No Grand Jury in Trayvon Martin Case," *Orlando Sentinel,* March 28, 2012 http://articles.orlandosentinel.com/2012-03-28/news/os-trayvon-martin-prosecutor-corey-20120328_1_grand-jury-special-prosecutor-civil-rights-leaders# (Accessed April 16, 2012).

41. Lizette Alvarez and Michael Cooper, "Prosecutor Files Charge of 2nd-Degree Murder in Shooting of Martin," *New York Times,* April 12, 2012, A1.

42. John Cloud, "How the Casey Anthony Murder Case Became the Social-Media Trial of the Century," *Time Magazine,* June 16, 2011 http://www.time.com/time/nation/article/0,8599,2077969,00.html (Accessed April 16, 2012).

43. ———, "NYC Mayor, Civil Rights Groups Target Gun Laws," Reuters, April 11, 2012 http://news.yahoo.com/nyc-mayor-civil-rights-groups-target-gun-laws-205340796.html (Accessed April 17, 2012).

44. John Nichols, "How ALEC Took Florida's 'License to Kill Law National," *The Nation,* March 21, 2012 http://www.thenation.com/blog/166978/how-alec-took-floridas-license-kill-law-national (Accessed April 16, 2012).

45. Marc Caputo, "Stand Your Ground May Yet Survive," *The Miami Herald,* April 15, 2012 http://www.miamiherald.com/2012/04/15/2750993_p2/stand-your-ground-may-yet-survive.html (Accessed April 15, 2012).

46. Laura Vozzella, "McDonnell Signs Bill Lifting One-Handgun-per-Month Limit," *Virginia Politics,* February 28, 2012 http://www.washingtonpost.com/blogs/virginia-politics/post/mcdonnell-signs-bill-lifting-one-handgun-per-month-limit/2012/02/28/gIQAtT0kgR_blog.html (Accessed April 17, 2012).

47. Alisa Chang, "City's Tough Handgun Laws Could Be Challenged by Supreme Court Ruling on Chicago," *WNYC News,* June 28, 2010 http://www.wnyc.org/articles/wnyc-news/2010/jun/28/citys-tough-handgun-laws-could-be-challenged-by-supreme-court-ruling-on-chicago/ (Accessed April 17, 2012).

48. Anna Pan, State Bill Would Allow Citizens to Sue Cities Over Gun Laws," *The Daily Pennsylvanian,* February 27, 2012 http://thedp.com/index.php/article/2012/02/state_bill_could_allow_citizens_to_sue_city_over_gun_laws (Accessed April 17, 2012).

49. Ibid.

50. Dana DiFilippo, "Mayors Blast Bill Targeting Local Gun Control Laws," *Philadelphia Daily News,* March 27, 2012 http://www.philly.com/philly/news/breaking/Mayors-blast-bill-targeting-local-gun-control-laws.html (Accessed March 31, 2012).

51. ———, "Embarrassed by Bad Laws," *The New York Times,* April 17, 2012, A20.

52. Ibid.

53. Interview with Kendall Coffey, *News Nation with Tamryn Hall, MSNBC,* March 20, 2012 http://video.msnbc.msn.com/newsnation/46798588/#46798588 (Accessed April 17, 2012).

54. Zachary Roth, "Bill Keller: Martin Protesters Used Case 'to Score Political Points'," MSNBC, April 12, 2012. http://mojoe.msnbc.msn.com/_news/2012/04/12/11162368-bill-keller-martin-protesters-used-case-to-score-political-points (Accessed April 16, 2012).

55. National Conference of State Legislatures, "Guns on Campus: Overview," http://www.ncsl.org/issues-research/educ/guns-on-campus-overview.aspx (Accessed April 17, 2012).

56. Press Release, American Legislative Exchange Council, April 17, 2011 http://www.alec.org/2012/04/alec-sharpens-focus-on-jobs-free-markets-and-growth-announces-the-end-of-the-task-force-that-dealt-with-non-economic-issues/ (Accessed April 17, 2012).

# BIBLIOGRAPHY

*American Experience: Eleanor Roosevelt.* dir. Sue Williams, prod. Kathryn Dietz and Sue Williams, WGBH-Boston/Public Broadcasting System, 1999.

Anderson, John and Hilary Hevenor. *Burning Down the House: MOVE and the Tragedy of Philadelphia.* New York: W.W. Norton, 1990.

Ancchiarico, Frank and James B. Jacobs. *The Pursuit of Absolute Integrity: How Corruption Control Makes Government Ineffective.* Chicago: University of Chicago Press, 1996.

Assefa, Hizkias and Paul Wahrhaftig. *The MOVE Crisis in Philadelphia: Extremist Groups and Conflict Resolution.* Pittsburgh: University of Pittsburgh Press, 1990.

Bowser, Charles W. *Let the Bunker Burn: The Final Battle with MOVE.* Philadelphia: Camino Press, 1989.

Bratton, William. *Turnaround: How America's Top Cop Reversed the Crime Epidemic.* New York: Random House, 1998.

Burrough, Bryan. *Public Enemies: America's Greatest Crime Wave and the Birth of the FBI 1933–34.* New York: Penguin, 2004.

Cannon, Lou. *Official Negligence: How Rodney King and the Riots Changed Los Angeles and the LAPD.* Boulder, CO.: Westview, 1999.

Cartwright, William. *Mexico: Facing The Challenges Of Human Rights And Crime.* Ardsley, NY: Transnational Publishers, 2000.

Charles, Michael T. "Accidental Shooting: An Analysis." *Journal of Contingencies and Crisis Management* 8, no. 3 (September 2000): 157.

Chiles, James. *Inviting Disaster: Lessons from the Edge of Technology.* New York: Harper Business, 2002.

City of Philadelphia, *Report of the Philadelphia Special Investigation Commission.* Philadelphia, 1986.

Columbia Accident Investigation Board, *Report of the Columbia Accident Investigation Board.* U.S. Government Printing Office: Washington, D.C., 2003.

Commission on the Intelligence Capabilities of the United States Regarding Weapons of Mass Destruction, *Report of the Commission on the Intelligence Capabilities of the United States Regarding Weapons of Mass Destruction.* Washington, D.C.: 2005.

Coyle, Pamela. "Cajun Stew Brewing." *ABA Journal* (September 2000).

Crank, John P. *Understanding Police Culture.* Cincinnati: Anderson, 1999.

Daniloff, Nicholas. "Chernobyl and Its Political Fallout: A Reassessment." *Demokratizatsiya* 12, no.1 (Winter 2004).

Daniloff, Nicholas. "Media Developments In The Soviet Union." Harold W. Anderson Lecture. Washington, D.C.: World Press Freedom Committee/ Center for Strategic and International Studies, November 30, 1987.

Donovan, Brian and Stephanie Saul. "Cops on Disability." *New York Newsday,* June/July 1994.

Dorner, Dietrich. *The Logic of Failure: Recognizing and Avoiding Errors in Complex Situations.* New York: Perseus Books, 1996.

Dwyer, Jim and Kevin Flynn. *102 Minutes: The Untold Story of the Fight to Survive Inside the Twin Towers.* New York: Times Books, 2005.

Evans, Rob and David Hencke. "Wallis Simpson, The Nazi Minister, The Telltale Monk and An FBI Plot." *The Guardian,* June 29, 2002.

Federal Bureau of Investigation. "History of the FBI, Postwar America: 1945–1960's." Federal Bureau of Investigation, http://www.fbi.gov/libref/historic/history/postwar.htm.

Federal Bureau of Investigation. *Crime in the United States, 2003.* Washington, D.C.: 2003.

Federal Emergency Management Administration, United States Fire Administration. *The World Trade Center Bombing: Report and Analysis .* Washington, D.C.: 1993.

Fox, Robert. "The Blue Plague Of American Policing." *Law Enforcement News,* May 15/30, 2003.

Frankel, Jay. "Exploring Ferenczi's Concept of Identification with the Aggressor: Its Role in Trauma, Everyday Life, and the Therapeutic Relationship." *Psychoanalytic Dialogues* 12 (2002): 101–39.

Galbraith, John Kenneth. *The Great Crash, 1929.* Boston: Houghton Mifflin, 1955.

Gladwell, Malcolm. *Blink: the Power of Thinking without Thinking.* New York: Back Bay Books, 2005.

Harris, Thomas. *The Silence of the Lambs.* New York: St. Martin's Press, 1988.

Harry, Margot. *Attention, MOVE! This is America*. Chicago: Banner Press, 1987.

Inter-branch Commission on Juvenile Justice. *Report of the Inter-branch Commission on Juvenile Justice*. Philadelphia: 2010.

Kelly, John F. and Phillip K. Wearne. *Tainting Evidence: Inside the Scandals at the FBI Crime Lab*. New York: The Free Press, 1998.

Kerik, Bernard. *The Lost Son: A Life in Pursuit of Justice*. New York: Regan Books—Harper Collins, 2001.

Kessler, Ronald. *The Bureau: The Secret History of the FBI*. New York: St. Martin's Press, 2002.

Kidd, Don. "High Speed Pursuits—Intent to Harm Standard." *CJI Legal Briefs* 6, no. 3 (Fall 2001): 7–10.

Knapp Commission. *Knapp Commission Report on Police Corruption*. New York: Braziller, 1972.

Lasley, James R. and Michael K. Hooper. "On Racism and the LAPD: Was the Christopher Commission Wrong?" *Social Science Quarterly 79*, no. 2 (June 1998): 378–89.

Law Enforcement News. "The LEN Interview: Renae Griggs." *Law Enforcement News*, January 2004.

Maas, Peter. *Serpico*. New York: Viking Press, 1973.

McAlary, Mike. *Buddy Boys: When Good Cops Turn Bad*. New York: Putnam & Sons, 1987.

McAlary, Mike. *Good Cop, Bad Cop*. New York: Pocket Books, 1994.

McLean, Bethany and Peter Elkind. *Smartest Guys in the Room: The Amazing Rise and Scandalous Fall of Enron*. New York: Portfolio, 2003.

Medvedev, Gregori. *The Truth about Chernobyl*. New York: Basic Books, 1991.

Merola, Mario. *Big City D.A.* New York: Random House, 1988.

Mintzberg, Henry. "The Five Basic Parts of the Organization." In *Classics of Organization Theory*, ed. Jay Shafritz and J. Steven Ott, New York: Harcourt, 2001. 222–33.

Mintzberg, Henry. *The Structure of Organizations*. Upper Saddle River, NJ: Prentice-Hall, 1979.

National Commission on Terrorist Attacks Upon the United States, *The 9/11 Commission Report: Final Report of the National Commission on Terrorist Attacks Upon the United States*. New York: W.W. Norton, 2003.

National Highway Traffic Safety Administration. "Vehicle Advisory for Law Enforcement Agencies." Washington, D.C.: April 1, 1999.

National Law Enforcement and Corrections Technology Center, "High-Speed Pursuit: New Technologies Around the Corner." Washington, D.C.: National Institute of Justice, October 1996.

New York City Department of Investigation, "A Report to Mayor Michael R. Bloomberg and Commissioner Nicholas Scoppetta: The Department of Investigation's Examination of the Circumstances Surrounding the Assault of a Firefighter and Subsequent Cover-up at the New York City Fire Department Engine Company 151/Ladder Company 76 on Staten Island." New York, 2004.

Newcombe, Tod. "An Interview with Philly's Top Cop John F. Timoney." *Government Technology,* April 2000.

Pennsylvania State Police, "Police Pursuit Reporting System." Harrisburg, PA, 2005.

Perrow, Charles. *Normal Accidents: Living with High Risk Technologies,* 2nd ed. Princeton: Princeton University Press, 1999.

Perrow, Charles. *Normal Accidents: Living with High Risk Technologies.* New York: Basic Books, 1984.

Pinkley, Alphonso. *Lest We Forget—White Hate Crimes: Howard Beach and Other Racial Atrocities.* Chicago: Third World Press, 1994.

Quinn, Jim. "MOVE v. the City of Philadelphia." *The Nation* 242, March 29, 1986.

Reavis, Dick J. *The Ashes of Waco: An Investigation.* Syracuse, NY: Syracuse University Press, 1998.

Reske, Henry J. "FBI Head Rebuts Report." *ABA Journal 79,* (Mar 1993): 29.

Rowan Jr., Carl T. "Badge of Dishonor: D.C. Confidential." *The New Republic* 218, January 19, 1998, 20–23.

Rowan Jr., Carl T. "The Death of a Police Department." *LEEA Advocate,* Spring 1996, 30–34.

Schiller, Lawrence. *Perfect Murder, Perfect Town: JonBenet and the City of Boulder.* New York: Harper Collins, 1999.

Schrecker, Ellen W. *The Age of McCarthyism: A Brief History with Documents.* Boston: Bedford, 1994.

Shapiro, Walter. "Lessons of Los Angeles." *Time* 139, May 18, 1992, 38.

Stewart, James B. *Disney War.* New York: Simon and Schuster, 2005.

Theoharis, Athan G. "The FBI and The Politics of Surveillance, 1908–1985." *Criminal Justice Review 15,* no. 2 (1990): 221–30.

United States Department of Justice, Civil Rights Division. *Investigation of the New Orleans Police Department.* Washington, D.C.: 2011.

U.S. Department of Education, Institute of Education Sciences, "The Nation's Report Card: Trial Urban District Assessment 2003." Washington, D.C.: 2004.

U.S. Department of Justice, "Report Regarding Internal Investigation of Shootings at Ruby Ridge, Idaho During the Arrest of Randy Weaver." Court TV Online, http://www.courttv.com/archive/legaldocs/government/rubyridge.html.

U.S. Department of Justice, Office of Inspector General, *The Immigration and Naturalization Service's Contact with Two September 11 Terrorists.* Washington, D.C., 2002.

U.S. Department of Labor, Bureau of Labor Statistics. *Career Guide to Industries, State and Local Government.* Washington, D.C., 2004.

U.S. House of Representatives, Committee on Government Reform. *The Tragedy of Waco: New Evidence Examined.* 106th Cong., 2nd Sess., 2000, H. Rep. 106-1037.

U.S. Nuclear Regulatory Commission, "Fact Sheet on the Accident at Three Mile Island." (Washington, D. C.: March 2004)

U.S. Senate Select Committee To Study Governmental Operations with Respect to Intelligence Operations, Church Committee, "Final Report—Book II, Intelligence Activities and the Rights of Americans." 94th Cong., 2nd Sess., 1976, S. Rep. 94-755.

Vaughan, Diane. *The Challenger Launch Decision: Risky Technology, Culture and Deviance at NASA.* Chicago: University of Chicago Press, 1997.

Wagner-Pacifici, Robin. *Discourse and Destruction: The City of Philadelphia versus MOVE.* Chicago: University of Chicago Press, 1994.

Walker, Samuel. *The New World of Police Accountability.* Thousand Oaks, CA: Sage, 2005.

Webb, Gregg G. "New Insights into J. Edgar Hoover's Role." *Studies in Intelligence* 48, no. 1 (2004).

Weisburd, David, Rosann Greenspan and Edwin E. Hamilton. "Police Attitudes Toward Abuse Of Authority: Findings From A National Study." Washington, D.C.: National Institute of Justice, 2000.

Weiss, Murray. *The Man Who Warned America.* New York: Harper Collins, 2003.

Wilms, Wellford W. "From the Age of Dragnet to the Age of the Internet: Tracking Changes Within the Los Angeles Police Department." *In California Policy Options*, ed. Daniel J. B. Mitchell (UCLA School of Public Policy and Education, 2004): 157–72.

Wilson, James Q. *Bureaucracy: What Government Agencies Do and Why They Do It.* New York: Basic Books, 1989.

Wise, David. *Spy: The Inside Story of How the FBI's Robert Hanssen Betrayed America.* New York: Random House, 2002.

Wright, Lawrence. *The Looming Tower: Al Qaeda and the Road to 9/11.* New York: Vintage Books, 2006.

# INDEX